CUET-UG

[COMMON UNIVERSITY ENTRANCE TEST]

SECTION II : DOMAIN SPECIFIC

History Simplified !

KEY INSIGHTS

CHAPTER-WISE TIME CAPSULES

1200+ QUESTIONS FROM THE ARCHIVES

DIVERSE TYPE QUESTIONS

10 FULL-LENGTH MOCK TEST PAPERS

GOLDMINE FOR BOARD EXAMS

Foreword

The National Curriculum Framework (NCF) 2005 emphasizes connecting school education with real-life experiences, moving beyond rote learning and rigid subject boundaries. It promotes a child-centered approach, as outlined in the National Policy on Education (1986), by fostering critical thinking, creativity, and interdisciplinary learning. The success of this initiative depends on teachers and school principals, who must encourage reflection, discussion, and imaginative activities among students.

This CUET-UG preparation book, CUET-UG History Simplified! developed with insights from Anuradha Mondal, a student, aims to reduce curricular burden by incorporating interactive discussions, hands-on experiences, and group activities. Flexibility in daily schedules is emphasized while ensuring effective learning and preparation. This is an absolute goldmine for high school board examination too, as it has been prepared carefully for those students who want to ace both their board exams and CUET-UG. Considering the current examination patterns, MCQ questions, and critical thinking-based questions, this would be your only go-to revision book for board examination and blueprint for CUET-UG. This acknowledges the contributions of educators, institutions, and the National Monitoring Committee in shaping the content. As part of its commitment to continuous improvement, we welcome comments and suggestions for future refinements.

Preface

History is more than just dates and events rather it's the story of humanity, a tale of victories, struggles, and turning points that have shaped our world. Yet, when it comes to preparing for exams like CUET-UG, this fascinating subject often feels like a maze of timelines and details. This book, CUET-UG History Simplified!, is designed to be your ultimate compass to navigate this maze and guide you to success in the Exam.

We know the challenges you face, Too much information, too little time. Complex concepts that refuse to stick or A fear of missing out on exam-critical questions. To address these, we have crafted a resource that transforms your preparation into a journey through history, one that's clear, structured, and even enjoyable. We have added Bite-sized summaries for instant understanding, a Treasure Chest of Practice Questions, Diverse Question Types with Answers which can decode any format, Mock Test Papers which simulate real exam challenges and deciphered PYQs with solutions to sharpen strategy through past trends.

Think of yourself as a time traveler exploring the landmarks of history. If you have ever felt trapped in timelines, let this book guide you out and onward. It also doubles as your revision partner for board exams, crafted with precision to meet both CUET-UG and Board expectations. History is not just a subject rather it's a legacy waiting for you to conquer.

Gear up, explorer. Your success story awaits!

Sincerely,
Anuradha Mondal

THE AUTHOR'S JOURNEY

I am Anuradha Mondal, a passionate history enthusiast and the author of this book. Scoring a perfect 200 in CUET History was a proud moment, but the journey to that point was far from easy.

I wasn't the kind of student who always topped exams. Throughout school, I faced constant comparisons and doubts. No matter how hard I worked, my efforts were often overlooked or questioned. Comments like "She's boasting" or "Someone else must have done better" were common, yet they only strengthened my determination.

History, to me, was never just a subject. I saw it as a powerful and living story, a narrative of humanity filled with struggles, decisions, and triumphs. When I began to connect deeply with it, visualizing events and simplifying complex topics, everything began to change. I shifted my focus from blind repetition to meaningful learning.

This book is more than a study guide. It is a reflection of my journey and is built for students who have ever felt underestimated. Inside, you will find mock tests and strategies shaped by real experience, created to help you prepare for CUET and board exams effectively.

Success is not defined by where you begin, but by how strongly you believe in your journey. Let us not just study History. Let us experience it, connect with it, and use it to write our own stories of victory.

Contents

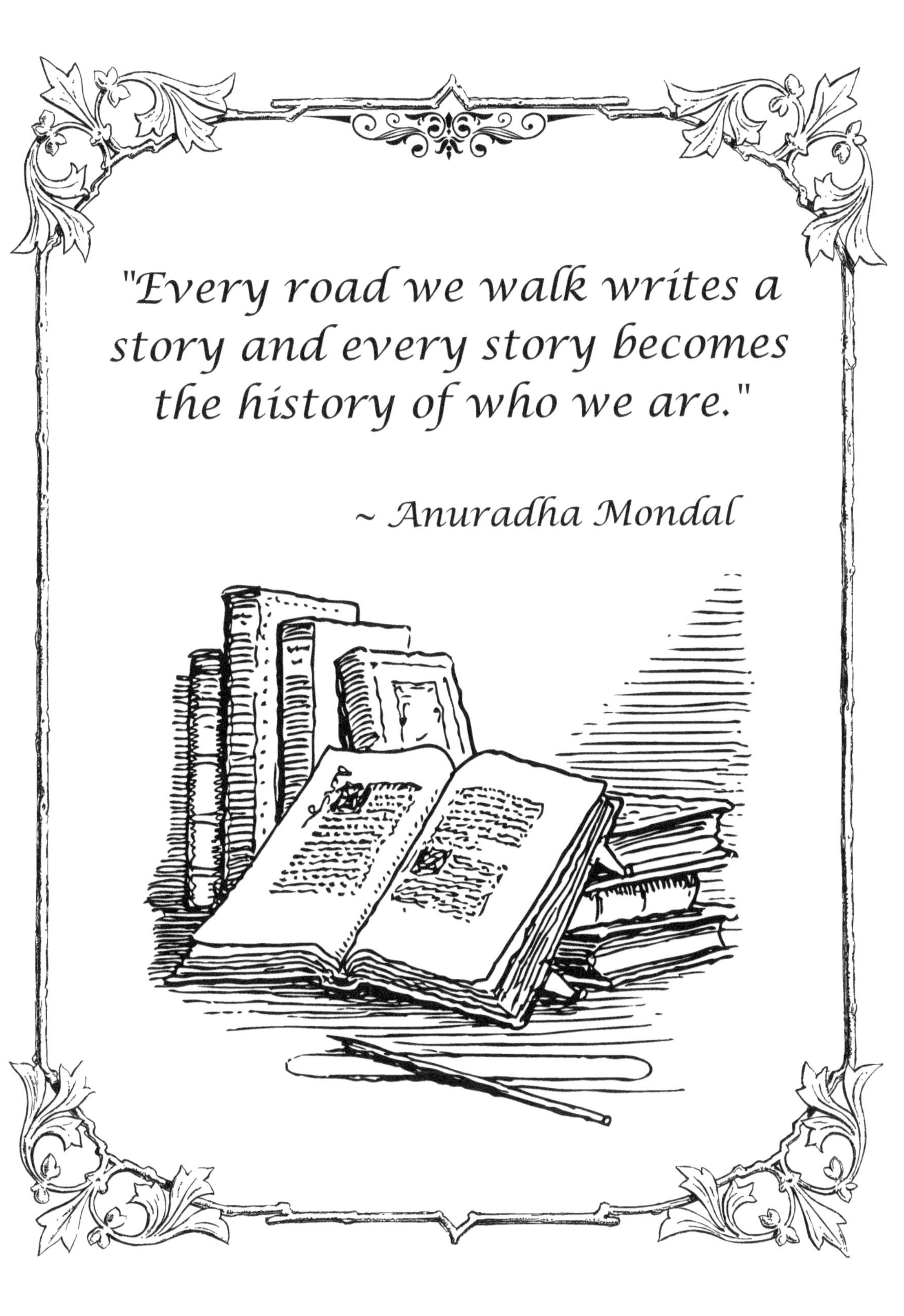

"Every road we walk writes a story and every story becomes the history of who we are."

~ Anuradha Mondal

Syllabus

(AS PER THE LATEST NTA CUET–UG SYLLABUS)

Unit I: The Story of the First Cities - Harappan Archaeology

Broad overview: Early urban centers.
Story of discovery: Harappan civilization.
Excerpt: Archaeological report on a major site.
Discussion: How it has been utilized by archaeologists/historians.

Unit II: Political and Economic History – How Inscriptions Tell a Story
Broad overview: Political and economic history from the Mauryan to the Gupta period.
Story of discovery: Inscriptions and the decipherment of the script. Shifts in the understanding of political and economic history.
Excerpt: Ashokan inscription and Gupta period land grant.
Discussion: Interpretation of inscriptions by historians.

Unit III: Social Histories Using the Mahabharata
Broad overview: Issues in social history, including caste, class, kinship, and gender.
Story of discovery: Transmission and publications of the Mahabharata.
Excerpt: From the Mahabharata, illustrating how it has been used by historians.

Unit IV: A History of Buddhism - Sanchi Stupa
Broad overview:
(a) A brief review of religious histories of Vedic religion, Jainism, Vaishnavism, and Shaivism.
(b) Focus on Buddhism.
Story of discovery: Sanchi Stupa.
Excerpt: Reproduction of sculptures from Sanchi.
Discussion: Ways in which sculpture has been interpreted by historians, and other sources for reconstructing the history of Buddhism.

Unit V: Medieval Society Through Travellers' Accounts
Broad overview: Outline of social and cultural life as they appear in travelers' accounts.
Story of their writings: A discussion of where they traveled, why they traveled, what they wrote, and for whom they wrote.
Excerpts: From Alberuni, Ibn Battuta, Bernier.
Discussion: What these travel accounts can tell us and how they have been interpreted by historians.

Unit VI: Religious Histories - The Bhakti-Sufi Tradition
Broad overview:
(a) Outline of religious developments during this period.
(b) Ideas and practices of the Bhakti-Sufi saints.
Story of transmission: How Bhakti-Sufi compositions have been preserved.
Excerpt: Extracts from selected Bhakti-Sufi works.
Discussion: Ways in which these have been interpreted by historians.

Unit VII: New Architecture - Hampi
Broad overview:
(a) Outline of new buildings during the Vijayanagara period—temples, forts, irrigation facilities.
(b) Relationship between architecture and the political system.
Story of discovery: Account of how Hampi was found.
Excerpt: Visuals of buildings at Hampi.
Discussion: Ways in which historians have analyzed and interpreted these structures.

Unit VIII: Agrarian Relations - The Ain-i-Akbari
Broad overview:
(a) Structure of agrarian relations in the 16th and 17th centuries.
(b) Patterns of change over the period.
Story of discovery: Account of the compilation and translation of Ain-i-Akbari.
Excerpt: From the Ain-i-Akbari.
Discussion: Ways in which historians have used the text to reconstruct history.

Unit IX: The Mughal Court - Reconstructing Histories Through Chronicles
Broad overview:
(a) Outline of political history c. 15th-17th centuries.
(b) Discussion of the Mughal court and politics.
Story of discovery: Account of the production of court chronicles, and their subsequent translation and transmission.
Excerpts: From the Akbarnama and Padshahnama.
Discussion: Ways in which historians have used the texts to reconstruct political histories.

Unit X: Colonialism and Rural Society: Evidence from Official Reports
Broad overview:
(a) Life of zamindars, peasants, and artisans in the late18th century.
(b) East India Company, revenue settlements, and surveys.
(c) Changes over the nineteenth century.
Story of official records: An account of why official investigations into rural societies were undertaken andthe
types of records and reports produced.
Excerpts: From Firminger's Fifth Report, Accounts of FrancisBuchanan-Hamilton, and DeccanRiots Report.
Discussion: What do the official records tell and do not tell, and how they have been used by historians?

Unit XI: Representations of 1857
Broad Overview:
(a) The events of 1857-58.
(b) How these events were recorded and narrated.
Focus: Lucknow.
Excerpts: Pictures of 1857. Extractsfrom contemporaryaccounts.
Discussion: How the pictures of 1857 shaped British opinion of what had happened.

Unit XII: Colonialism and Indian Towns: Town Plans and Municipal Reports
Broad Overview: The growth of Mumbai, Chennai, hill stations, and cantonmentsin the 18th and 19th centuries.
Excerpts: Photographs and paintings. Plans of cities. Extract from town plan reports. Focus on Kolkata town
planning.
Discussion: How the above sources can be used to reconstruct the history of towns? What these sourcesdo
not reveal.

Unit XIII: Mahatma Gandhi Through Contemporary Eyes
Broad Overview:
(a) The nationalist movement 1918-48,
(b) The nature of Gandhian politics and leadership.
Focus: Mahatma Gandhi in 1931.
Excerpts: Reports from English and Indian languagenewspapers and other contemporary writings.
Discussion: How newspapers can be a source of history.

Unit XIV: Partition through Oral Sources
Broad Overview:
(a) The history of the 1940s:
(b) Nationalism, Communalism, and Partition.
Focus: Punjab and Bengal.
Excerpts: Oral testimonies of those who experienced partition.
Discussion: Ways in which these have been analyzed toreconstruct the history of the event.

Unit XV: The Making of the Constitution
Broad Overview:
(a) Independence and the new nation-state.
(b) The making of the Constitution.
Focus: The Constitutional Assembly debates.
Excerpts: From the debates.
Discussion: What do such debates reveal and how they canbe analyzed?

How To Use This Book ?

This is not just another CUET-UG History book rather it is your personal battle plan for scoring a perfect 200/200. Think of it as a weapon carefully designed for precision, where every page, every section, and every mock test serves a purpose to help you achieve your goal. If you are serious about dominating this exam, then you need to know exactly how to extract the maximum benefit from this book.

A book is only as powerful as how well it is used. Some students merely skim through pages, while toppers extract every single ounce of value from it. The question is: Which one do you want to be?

If your answer is 200/200, then here's exactly how you will use this book to its fullest potential.

STEP 1: MASTERING CONCISE KEY NOTES

Every chapter in this book begins with a Concise Time Capsule. These are not just simple summaries: they are your cheat codes for fast revision. Each capsule is designed to compress an entire chapter into its most essential facts, events, concepts, and dates all in one place.

The smartest way to use them is to treat them like your daily warm-up routine. Every morning, before starting your study session, pick one or two capsules and revise them like flashcards. Close your book and see if you can recall every single key point. If not, read it again and again until it sticks.

These capsules serve as your final go to resource before the exam. In the last 24 hours before CUET-UG, this is what you will be skimming through not long textbook chapters. They are meant to give you the illusion of a full syllabus revision in just a few hours.

Tip: If you ever feel overwhelmed by the syllabus, just read through the Time Capsules. They will immediately bring you back on track without wasting hours on lengthy books.

STEP 2: SOLVING QUESTIONS FROM ARCHIVES

If you think CUET-UG asks random questions, you are mistaken. Exams follow patterns. Every year, certain topics keep appearing over and over again in slightly different ways. Smart students spot these patterns. Average students ignore them.

This book has an entire "Questions from Archives" section for each chapter. These questions are not just for practice rather they are your secret weapon. The way to use them is simple:

- After finishing a chapter, immediately attempt its archive questions.
- If you get any question wrong, don't just move on but find out why.
- Write down the concept behind it in a separate practice notebook.
- Keep track of which type of questions CUET-UG repeats the most and which ones rarely appear.

By doing this, you will begin to recognize question trends, and when you sit for the actual exam, you will already know what's coming.

Tip: If a question has been asked in CUET-UG more than twice, it will likely appear again in some form. Focus more on these.

STEP 3: DEALING WITH HIGH YIELD TOPICS

You don't need to know everything to score 200/200. You just need to know the right things. CUET-UG does not treat all topics equally. Some are highly important, while others are barely touched upon.

This book has categorized questions into:

Red Zone Topics (Most Important) – These questions have appeared in CUET-UG at least 3+ times. They should be your top priority.
Yellow Zone Topics (Moderate Importance) – These questions appear occasionally. Revise them after Red Zone topics.
Green Zone Topics (Least Important) – These type of questions are rarely asked. Revise them after Yellow Zone topics.

Tip: But remember, if you aim for a perfect score of 200, it's not just about categorizing questions into zones rather it's about mastering all of them.

BONUS STEP 4: DOUBLE YOUR IMPACT – BOARD EXAMS MASTERY

Why settle for just CUET-UG, when the same preparation can make you a top scorer in your Boards too? This book mirrors the latest Board examination trends with MCQs, source based questions, picture-based questions and critical analysis, all designed to strengthen your conceptual core and exam readiness.
Treat this as your final revision pad for Boards. Each chapter has been designed to serve dual purposes: to ace MCQs with speed and tackle Board-style questions with depth.

You are not just preparing for a test: you are shaping a legacy just like the great revolutions and reforms you study in history.

FINAL WORDS: FOLLOW THIS PLAN & 200/200 IS YOURS

This book is not meant for casual reading but it is your blueprint for success. If you follow this plan to the letter, you will walk into CUET-UG with unshakable confidence, and when you walk out, you will have the perfect score in your hands.

Use the book strategically.
Train like you fight.
Trust the system. Execute smartly.

Now, go own CUET-UG and your Board Exams. Your perfect score is waiting!

Chapter 1 : Bricks, Beads and Bones

CONCISE KEY NOTES

Introduction to Harappan Civilization
- Also known as Indus Valley Civilization (IVC).
- Named after Harappa, the first discovered site.
- Time Span: 6000 BCE – 1300 BCE
  - Early Harappan (6000 BCE – 2600 BCE): Formative phase.
  - Mature Harappan (2600 BCE – 1900 BCE): Urban peak.
  - Late Harappan (1900 BCE – 1300 BCE): Decline phase.

Material Culture & Artefacts
- BP stands for Before Present
- BCE stands for Before Common Era
- CE stands for the Common Era.
- The present year is 2015 according to this dating system.
- c. stands for the Latin word circa and means "approximate."
- Archaeologists use the term "culture" for a group of objects, distinctive in style, that are usually found together within a specific geographical area and period of time.
- Seals:
  - Most distinctive artifacts of Harappan or Indus Valley Civilisation – Harappan Seal.
  - Made of steatite (soft stone).
  - Contain animal motifs & undeciphered script.
- Pottery:
  - Distinctive red & black designs.
  - Used for storage, cooking, and rituals.
- Beads & Ornaments:
  - Made of carnelian, faience, lapis lazuli, shell.
- Weights & Measures:
  - Standardized binary & decimal system.
- Bricks:
  - Baked & sun-dried, standard ratio (4:2:1).
- . These objects were found from areas as far apart as Afghanistan, Jammu, Balochistan (Pakistan) and Gujarat.

Economy & Subsistence Strategies
- Agriculture:
  - The Harappans ate a wide range of plant and animal products including fish.
  - Archeo-botanists : specialists in ancient plant remains.
  - Crops: Wheat, barley, lentils, chickpea, sesame, millets (Gujarat), rare rice.
  - Ploughing evidence:
    - Ploughed field at Kalibangan (furrows at right angles, suggests two crops were grown together).
    - Terracotta plough models Cholistan and Banawali (Haryana).
  - Irrigation:
    - Canals at Shortughai (Afghanistan).
    - Dholavira reservoirs for water storage.

- Domesticated Animals:
  - According to archaeo-zoologist/zoo-archeologist, Cattle, sheep, goat, buffalo, pig.
  - Wild animals: Boar, deer, gharial (hunting evidence).
  - Bones of fish & fowl found.
- Saddle Querns:
  - Processing of food required grinding equipment as well as vessels for mixing, blending and cooking.
  - These were made of stone, metal and terracotta.
  - FROM ERNEST MACKAY, Further Excavations at Mohenjodaro, 1937.

Urban Planning & City Layout

- The most unique feature of the Harappan civilisation was the development of urban centres.
- Citadel & Lower Town:
  - Citadel: Raised area, walled, housed elite.
  - Lower Town: Larger, walled, common people's houses.
- Buildings & Houses:
  - Multi-roomed houses with courtyards, private wells, bathing areas.
- The most distinctive features of Harappan cities was the carefully planned drainage system.
- Drainage System:
  - Covered brick drains, soak pits, street drains, house connection.
  - Grid-pattern streets (right-angled intersections).

The Citadel: Special Public Structures

- Warehouse: Large structure: lower parts of bricks, upper parts possibly wooden.
- Great Bath:
  - Large rectangular tank in a courtyard with corridors on all sides.
  - Two flights of steps (north & south) led to the tank.
  - Made watertight using gypsum mortar.
  - Nearby building had 8 bathrooms with drains, possibly for ritual bathing.

Lower Town : Domestic Architecture

- Lower Town at Mohenjodaro provides examples of residential buildings.
- Homes ensure privacy with no ground level windows and indirect entrances.
- Each house had brick paved bathrooms connected to street drains.
- Some houses had staircases to upper floors and rooftops.
- Many had wells, some were accessible to public use.
- Around 700 wells existed in Mohenjodaro.

Social Differences: Evidence from Burials

- Burials mostly in simple pits: some lined with bricks.
- Some graves contained pottery & ornaments (e.g., shell rings, jasper beads, micro-beads).
- Copper mirrors were found in some graves, but few valuables were buried

Social Status & Luxury Goods

- Utilitarian Objects: Made from common materials like stone/clay (e.g., querns, pottery, needles).
- Luxury Objects: Rare, made from costly materials & advanced techniques.
  - Faience Pots: Made from ground sand & fired.

- ○ Gold Jewellery: Found in hoards, not burials.
  - ○ Spindle Whorls (Faience): Daily-use object but made from rare material.

Craft Production & Specialized Settlements
- Chanhudaro: Major craft hub for bead-making, shell-cutting, metalworking, seal-making.
- Materials for beads: Carnelian, jasper, quartz, steatite, gold, bronze, shell, terracotta.
- Techniques: Molding (steatite paste), grinding, polishing, drilling (special drills at Chanhudaro, Lothal, Dholavira).
- Nageshwar & Balakot: Specialized shell craft production.
- Lothal: Bead-making & craft center.

Procurement of Raw Materials
- Local: Clay, riverine resources.
- Regional:
  - ○ Copper: Khetri region (Rajasthan also known as Ganeshwar Jodhpura Culture by archaeologist).
  - ○ Gold: South India.
  - ○ Carnelian: Bharuch (Gujarat).
  - ○ Steatite: South Rajasthan, North Gujarat.
- International Trade:
  - ○ Oman: Copper (nickel traces match Harappan artefacts).
  - ○ Afghanistan (Shortughai): Lapis lazuli.
  - ○ Mesopotamia: Possible trade of Harappan jars & goods.

Trade and Contacts
- Harappans traded with Meluhha (Indus region), Oman, Bahrain (Dilmun), and Mesopotamia.
- Key traded goods: carnelian, lapis lazuli, copper, gold, wood.
- Mesopotamian texts call Meluhha a land of seafarers; communication was likely by sea.
- Seals from Mesopotamia depict humped bulls, showing Indus influence.
- Dilmun seals in Bahrain carried Harappan motifs; their weights followed the Harappan standard.
- Ships and boats are depicted on Harappan seals, indicating maritime trade.

Seals, Script, and Weights
- Seals and Sealings: Used for long-distance trade; clay seals ensured goods weren't tampered with.
- Harappan Script:
  - ○ Undeciphered; not alphabetical (375-400 signs).
  - ○ Written right to left.
  - ○ Found on seals, copper tools, jars, tablets, jewellery, bone rods, signboards.
  - ○ Suggests widespread literacy.
- Weights:
  - ○ Made of chert; cubical and unmarked.
  - ○ Smaller units in binary system (1, 2, 4, 8, 16, etc.), higher units in decimal system (160, 200, etc.).
  - ○ Likely used for measuring jewellery and beads.
  - ○ Metal scale-pans found.

Harappan Excavation & Archaeologists
- First Site Discovered: Harappa (by Daya Ram Sahni, 1921).
- Excavations:
  - Mohenjodaro – Rakhaldas Banerji (1922).
  - John Marshall: First to recognize Harappan Civilization as advanced.
  - Alexander Cunningham: First Director General of Archaeological Survey Of India, noted bricks used for railway construction (1875).

Miscellaneous Facts
- Mohenjodaro was better preserved than Harappa (Harappa's bricks were stolen for railway construction).
- Lothal (Gujarat) – Important port city, dockyard, bead factory.
- Dholavira (Gujarat) – Water reservoirs, stone construction.
- Chanhudaro – Specialized in bead making, bangle making.
- Kalibangan – Fire altars & ploughed field evidence.

Governance and Society
- Standardization: Uniformity in pottery, seals, weights, and bricks (same ratio across regions).
- Political Structure Theories:
  - No rulers, society was egalitarian.
  - Multiple rulers for different cities (Mohenjodaro, Harappa, etc.).
  - A single centralized state due to uniformity in artefacts and settlement planning.

Decline of the Civilization (~1800 BCE)
- Mature Harappan sites abandoned: shift to Gujarat, Haryana, Western UP.
- Decline in weights, seals, writing, long-distance trade, and craft specialization.
- Material culture transformed: Rural lifestyle replaced urban settlements.
- Possible Reasons for Decline:
  - Environmental factors: Climate change, deforestation, excessive floods, river shifts, overuse of land.
  - Political factors: Collapse of central authority.
  - Economic decline: Disintegration of trade networks.

Theories of Harappan End (Massacre Controversy)
- Deadman Lane, Mohenjodaro (1931): 3–8 metre width : Skeletons found; assumed massacre.
- R.E.M. Wheeler (1947): Linked Harappan collapse to Aryan invasion (Rigveda's Indra = "fort-destroyer"), His Book Ancient India 1947 written by him along with My Archeological Mission to India and Pakistan (1976)
- George Dales (1964): Debunked massacre theory—skeletons were from different periods: no evidence of war.
- S.N Roy : Noted the story of Indian Archeology

Early Discoveries and Confusion
- Ancient artefacts often found by locals due to floods, soil erosion, or ploughing.
- Alexander Cunningham (First Director-General of ASI, mid-19th century) focused on Early Historic period (6th century BCE-4th century CE) and used Chinese Buddhist pilgrims' accounts for investigations.

- Harappan artefacts were found but not recognized as ancient; Cunningham received a Harappan seal but misclassified it.

Discovery of Harappan Civilization
- Daya Ram Sahni (early 20th century) excavated Harappa and found seals older than Early Historic levels.
- Rakhal Das Banerji discovered similar seals at Mohenjodaro, leading to the identification of a single archaeological culture.
- John Marshall (Director-General, ASI, 1924) announced the discovery of the Indus Valley Civilization, making India's history 3000 years older.
- Similar seals were found in Mesopotamian excavations, confirming the civilization's antiquity and contemporaneity with Mesopotamia.
- Marshall excavated horizontally, causing loss of stratigraphic context.

Advanced Excavation Techniques
- R.E.M. Wheeler (Director-General, ASI, 1944) introduced stratigraphic excavation, preserving site layers. He was an ex-army brigadier who brought military precision practice of archaeology.
- Post-Partition (1947), most major sites went to Pakistan, prompting Indian archaeologists to find sites within India.
- New discoveries: Kalibangan, Lothal, Rakhigarhi, Dholavira, with ongoing research in Punjab, Haryana, and Kutch.

Modern Archaeological Methods
- Stratigraphy: Identifying occupation layers based on artefacts, texture, and colour.
- Artefact Classification: Based on material (stone, metal, clay, etc.) and function (tools, ornaments, ritual use).
- Scientific Techniques: Surface exploration, DNA analysis (archaeogenetics), and detailed material analysis.
- Growing international collaborations in Harappan archaeology since the 1980s.

Problems in Understanding the Past
- Material Survival: Organic materials like wood, cloth, and leather decompose; stone, clay, and metal survive.
- Interpreting Religious Practices:
    - Terracotta figurines = Mother Goddesses
    - Priest King = Rare Stone Statuary of men seated with one hand on the knee.
    - Seals with animals = Nature worship
    - "Proto-Shiva" seal = Early Hindu deity
    - Fire altars and Great Bath = Ritual sites
    - Conical stones = Lingas
- Interpretations rely on later traditions and comparative studies
- Shamans : Shamans are men and women who claim magical and healing powers, as well as an ability to communicate with the other world.

Important Figures

Fig 1.1 A Harappan Seal

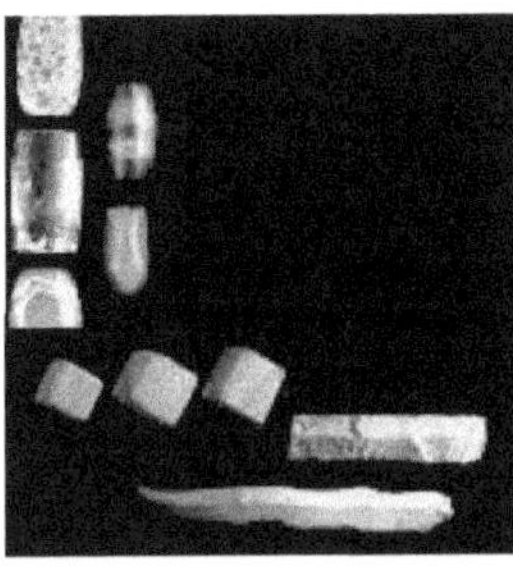

Fig. 1.2 Beads, weights, blades

Fig. 1.3 A terracotta bull

Fig. 1.5 Reservoir at Dholavira

Fig. 1.8 Saddle quern

Fig. 1.11 A copper mirror

Fig. 1.12 A faience pot

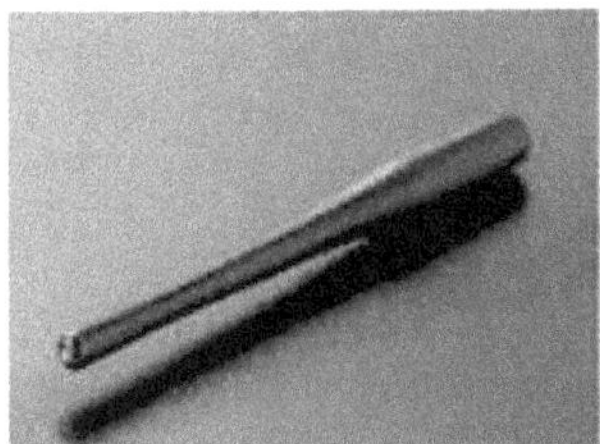

Fig. 1.13 A tool and beads

Fig. 1.14 Pottery

Fig. 1.15 A terracotta figurine

Fig. 1.17 A Harappan jar found in Oman

Fig. 1.18 This is a
cylinder seal from the
Indus Region

Fig. 1.19 The round "Persian Gulf"
seal found in Bahrain sometimes
carries Harappan motifs.

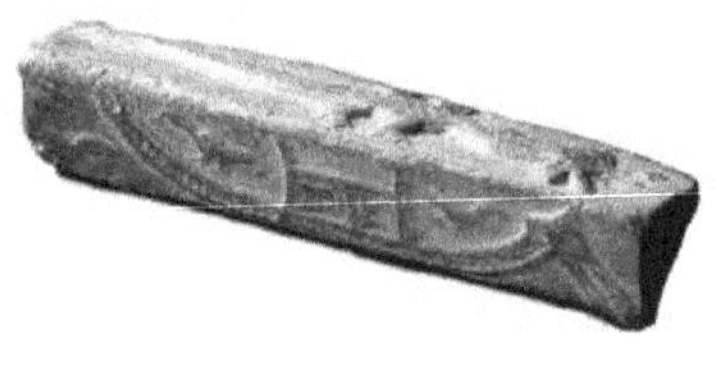

Fig. 1.20 Seal depicting
a boat

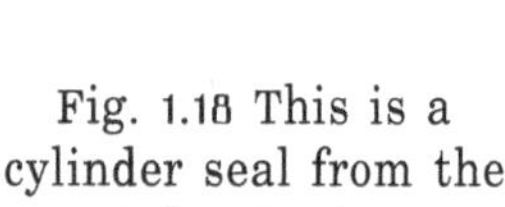

Fig. 1.18 This is a
cylinder seal from the
Indus Region

Fig. 1.22 A sealing from Ropar

Fig. 1.23 A "priest-king"

Fig. 1.24 Cunningham's sketch
of the firstknown seal from
Harappa

Fig. 1.26 Was this a mother
goddess?

Fig. 1.27 A "proto-Shiva" seal

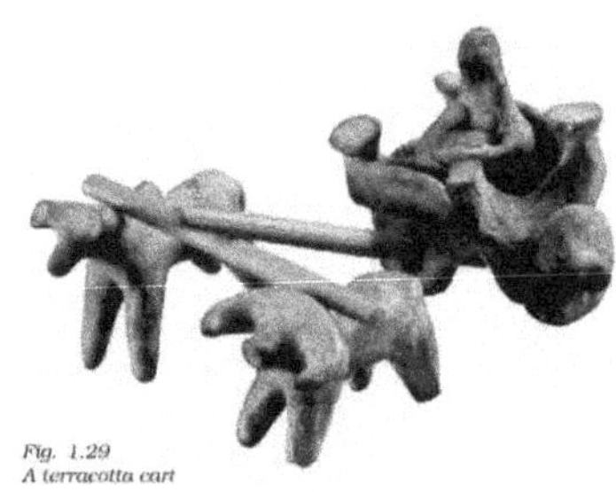

Fig. 1.29 A terracotta cart

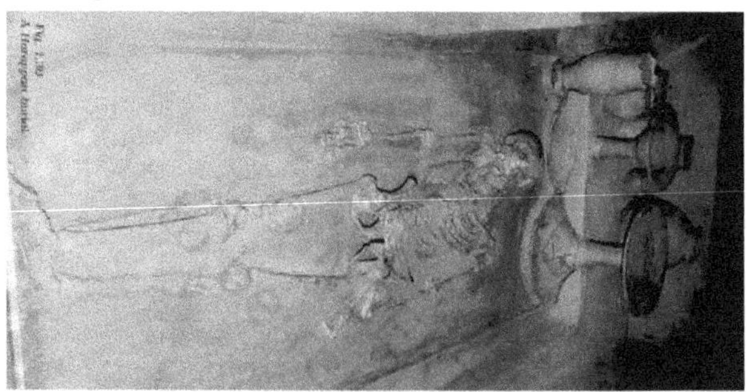

Fig. 1.30 A Harappan burial

Chapter 1 : Mapwork

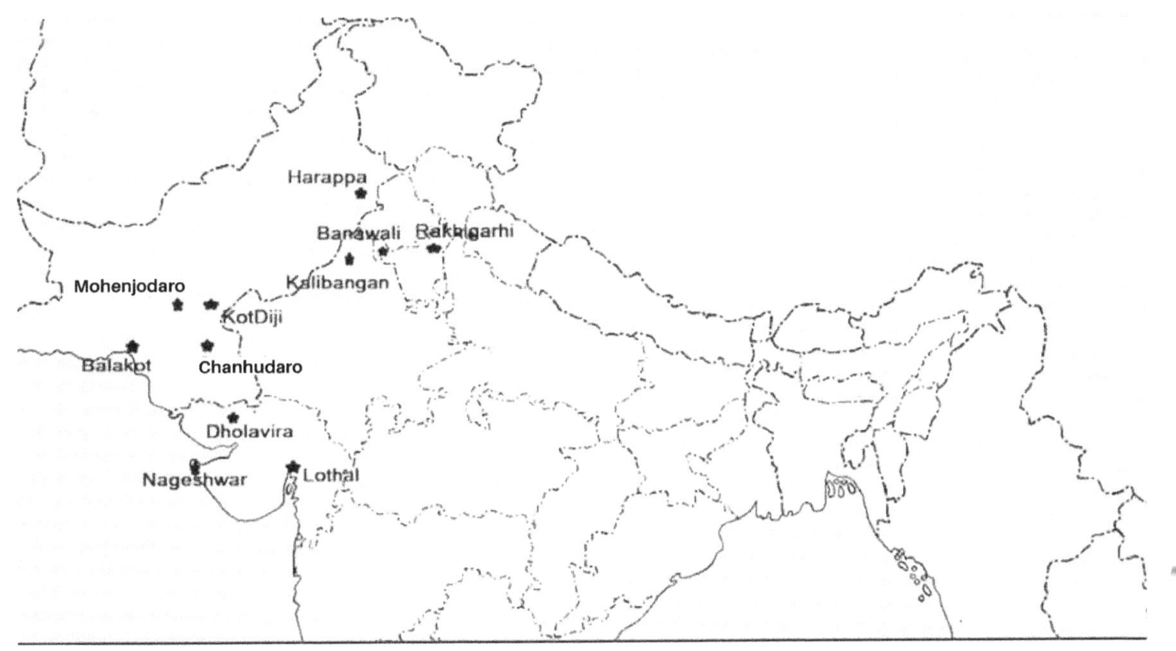

SOME IMPORTANT CITIES IN INDUS VALLEY CIVILISATION

- Harappa
- Mohenjodaro
- Rakhigarhi
- Banawali
- Kalibangan
- Kot Diji
- Chanhudaro
- Dholavira
- Lothal
- Nageshwar
- Balakot

Chapter 1 : Bricks, Beads and Bones

QUESTIONS FROM ARCHIVES

Question 1 :
Harappan civilisation is also known as -
a) Vedic Civilisation
b) Indus Valley Civilisation
c) Aryan Civilisation
d) None of the above

Question 2 :
The most distinctive artefact of Harappan Civilisation—
a) Tools
b) ornaments
c) Seal
d) weapons

Question 3 :
Harappan seal is made of stone named —
a) carnelian
b) quartz
c) gold
d) steatite

Question 4 :
Harappan civilisation is dated between :
a) 2600-1900 BCE
b) 2600-1800 BCE
c) 2600-1700 BCE
d) 2600- 1600 BCE

Question 5 :
Harappan culture includes -
a) Seals & beads
b) weights
c) baked bricks
d) All of the above

Question 6 :
How many total Harappan sites are there in Sind ?
a) 52
b) 65
c) 29
d) 106

Question 7 :
 Specialists in ancient plant remains
a) archaeo-botanists
b) archaeo- zoologists
c) all of the above
d) none of these

Question 8 :
Millets are found from sites in -
a) Gujarat
b) Haryana
c) Rajasthan
d) Punjab

Question 9 :
Grains found at Harappan sites -
a) wheat
b) Barley
c) Chickpea
d) All of these

Question 10 :
Specialists in ancient animal remains -
a) archaeo-zoologists
b) Zoo-archaeologists
c) archaeo-botanists
d) Both a and b

Question 11 :
Which of the following statement(s) is are correct about the subsistence strategies of Harappa ?

i) The Harappans ate wide range of plant and animal products, including fish
ii) Archaeologists have been able to reconstruct dietary practices from finds of charred grains and seeds.
iii) studied by archaeo-zoologists specialist in ancient plant remains.
iv)Animal bones were found at Harappan sites include cattle , sheep , goat buffalo and pig , these animals were domesticated.

a) Only (i) is correct
b) (i) and (ii) are correct
c) (i), (ii) , (iv) are correct
d) All of these

Question 12 :
Terracotta models of the plough have been found at sites in :
a) Cholistan
b) Banawali
c) both (a) and (b)
d) none of these

Question 13 :
Evidence of ploughed field found at –
a) shortughai
b) Dholavira
c) Lothal
d) Kalibangan

Question 14 :
Assertion – The field had two sets of furrows at right angles
Reason – suggests that two different crops were grown together

a) Both A and R are true and R is the correct explanation of A.
b) Both A and R are true but R is not the correct explanation of A
c) A is true but R is false.
d) R is true but A is false

Question 15 :
Traces of canals have been found at –
a) Lothal
b) Dholavira
c) Shortughai
d) Kalibangan

Question 16 :
Shortughai is in –
a) India
b) Iran
c) Pakistan
d) Afghanistan .

Question 17 :
Water reservoirs are found from which Harappan sites –
a) Kalibangan (Rajasthan)
b) Shortughai (Afghanistan)
c) Banawali (Haryana)
d) Dholavira (Gujarat)

Question 18 :
Harappan sites are located in which type of lands –
a) Arid lands
b) Semi arid lands
c) Fertile lands
d) None of these

Question 19 :
The most unique feature of the Harappan Civilisation–
a) development of urban centres
b) carefully planned drainage system
c) carefully planned architecture
d) None of these

Question 20 :
Which one of the following is the most well known site of Harappan Civilisation–
a) Lothal
b) Harappa
c) Mohenjodaro
d) Chanhudaro

Question 21 :
Who is known as the father of Indian Archaeology ?
a) R.E.M.Wheeler
b) James Princep
c) Ernest Mackay
d) Alexander Cunningham

Question 22 :
The most distinctive features of Harappan cities was
a) development of urban centres
b) carefully planned drainage system
c) carefully planned architecture
d) None of these

Question 23 :
Lower town at Mohenjodaro is the example of –
a) Citadel
b) Residential buildings
c) Great Bath
d) Courtyard

Question 24 :
According to the scholars the estimation of the total number of wells in Mohenjodaro was about –
a) 900
b) 700
c) 1200
d) 800

Question 25 :
The 'Great Bath' was found from which part of the indus Valley Civilisation ?
a) Lothal
b) Harappa
c) Mohenjodaro
d) Rangpur

Question 26 :
Name the Director General of Archaeological Survey Of India (ASI) who announced the discovery of new civilisation of Indus Valley to the world –

a) Alexander Cunningham
b) John Marshall
c) James Prinsep
d) Colin Mackenzie

Question 27 :
Assertion- In Mohenjodaro the settlement is divided into two sections .
Reason- one is located higher than the lower town because of the raised platform on which it was built

a) Both A and R are true and R is the correct explanation of A.
b) Both A and R are true but R is not the correct explanation of A.
c) A is true but R is false.
d) R is true but A is false.

Question 28 :
Mohenjodaro is also known as –
a) Mound of deads
b) Mound of muds
c) Mound of sands
d) None of these

Question 29 :
Assertion- Harappan probably had a belief of afterlife
Reason - at burials in Harappan sites the dead were generally laid in pits with ornaments , pottery , etc
a) Both A and R are true and R is the correct explanation of A.
b) Both A and R are true but R is not the correct explanation of A.
c) A is true but R is false.
d) R is true but A is false.

Question 30 :
Assertion – the archaeologists try to find out the social and economic differences among the Harappans.
Reason – studying Burials and artefacts were evidence to establish the social differences in Harappan society.

a) Both A and R are true and R is the correct explanation of A.
b) Both A and R are true but R is not the correct explanation of A.
c) A is true but R is false.
d) R is true but A is false.

Question 31 :
Consider the statements about the 'Great bath' and choose the correct option

i) the great bath was located at Citadel.
ii) the great bath was a large rectangular tank in a Courtyard surrounded by a corridor on all four sides.
iii) there were two flights of steps on the North and south .
iv) the great bath was meant for some kind of a special ritual bath.

a) Only (i) is correct
b) (i) and (ii) are correct
c) (iii) and (iv) are correct
d) All of
the above are correct

Question 32 :
Assertion- there are two types of artefacts - "utilitarian" and "luxuries" .
Reason- "utilitarian" artefacts were made from costly, non local materials with complicated technologies.
a) Both A and R are true and R is the correct explanation of A.
b) Both A and R are true but R is not the correct explanation of A.
c) A is true but R is false.
d) R is true but A is false.

Question 33 :
A tiny settlement exclusively devoted to craft production, including bead making , shell cutting, metal-working , seal and weight making .
a) Chanhudaro
b) Lothal
c) Mohenjodaro
d) Rakhigarhi

Question 34 :
Which of the following statement(s) is are correct.
I) The variety of materials used to make beads is remarkable.
II) stones used includes –carnelian , jasper , crystal, quartz and steatite
III) metals like copper, bronze , gold ,shell, faience , terracotta.
IV) the shapes were numerous– disc shaped , cylindrical, spherical, barrel – shaped , segmented.

a) Only (i) is correct
b) (i) and (ii) are correct
c) (iii) and (iv) are correct
d) (i), (ii), (iii), (iv) are correct

Question 35 :
Which of these was a luxury object ?
a) Sickle
b) saddle quern
c) Pots of faience
d) All the above

Qestion 36 :
Which of the following Harappan civilisation sites are presently outside India ?
a) Kalibangan
b) Dholavira
c) Shortughai
d) Chanhudaro

Question 37 :
Which one of the following settlements are near the coast –
a) Nageshwar and Balakot
b) Chanhudaro
c) lothal
d) Rangpur

Question 38 :
The best source of lapis– lazuli , a blue stone that was apparently very highly valued was found in –
a) Bharuch in Gujarat
b) Kalibangan in Rajasthan
c) Khetri in Rajasthan
d) Shortughai in Afghanistan

Question 39 :
Match The Following :

Column A	Column B
I) Nageshwar and Balakot	a) Gold
II) Khetri region of Rajasthan	b) shells
III) south India	c) Carnelian
IV) Bharuch in Gujarat	d) Copper

a) I – C, II – A, III – D, IV – B
b) I – B, II – D, III – A, IV – C
c) I – A, II – C, III – B, IV – D
d) I – D, II – B, III – C, IV – A

Question 40 :
Which among the following is a very soft stone ?
a) Jasper
b) diamond
c) carnelian
d) Steatite

Question 41 :
Which of the following site is known as centre of 'Ganeshwar – Jodhpura culture' by archaeologists ?
a) Mohenjodaro
b) Khetri
c) Nageshwar
d) Rangpur

Question 42 :
How was inter- country communication done during Harappan Civilisation –
a) waterways
b) Railways
c) Roadways
d) Air ways

Question 43 :
Mesopotamian texts datable to the third millennium BCE refer to copper coming from a region called Magan . Magan was probably the ancient name of –
a) Harappa
b) Oman
c) Russia
d) Qatar

Question 44 :
Mesopotamian texts mention contact with regions named Dilmun , Dilmun is probably the island of –
(a) Bali
b) Bahrain
c) Sumerian
d) Persian Gulf

Question 45 :
According to the Mesopotamian texts Meluhha is referred to which region ?
a) Sumerian region
b) Harappan Region
c) Babylonian region
d) Akkadian region

Question 46 :
Mesopotamian texts refer to Meluhha as a land of –
a) seafarers
b) landfarers
c) islandfarers
d) farers

Question 47 :
In Harappan civilisation, exchanges were regulated by a precise system of weights which were usually made of stone called ______.
a.Chert
b.None of these
c.Carnelian
d.Steatite

Question 48 :
Identify The Following :

a) Priest – King
b) Rudra
c) Terracotta figurine
d) mother goddess

Question 49 :
Which one of the following is are considered as a possible reason for the end of Harappan Civilisation—
a) Flood
b) Deforestation
c) Climatic change
d) All of these

Question 50 :
___ is a narrow alley, varying from 3 to 6 feet in width.
a.Elfreth's Alley
b.Deadman Lane
c.Printer's Alley
d.Artillery Passage

Question 51 :
'My archaeological mission to India and Pakistan' written by –

a) John Marshall
b) George Dales
c) Alexander Cunningham
d) R.E.M.Wheeler

Question 52 :
Identify This Picture.

a) Cow
b) Oxen
c) Bull
d) Buffalo

Question 53 :
Study of layers is called
a) Pedology
b) Hydrology
c) stratigraphy
d) none of these

Question 54 :
' The story of Indian Archaeology' is written by –
a) John Marshall
b) Rakhal Das Banerji
c) S.N.Roy
d) Daya Ram Sahni

Question 55 :
Name the director General of ASI in 1944 , an ex –army brigadier who brought military precision to the practice of archaeology.
a) R.E.M.Wheeler
b) John Marshall
c) S.N.Roy
d) None of these

Question 56 :
Identify This Picture.

a) Priest – King
b) Rudra
c) Terracotta figurine
d) mother goddess

Question 57 :
"My Archaeological Mission to India and Pakistan" was written by R.E.M Wheeler in
___
a.1874
b.1976
c.1970
d.1876

Question 58 :
___ is the name used for god Shiva in puranic traditions.
a.Pashupati
b.Mahadev
c.Rudra
d. None of these

Question 59 :
Identify this Picture.

a) Proto–shiva
b) Rudra
c) Shamans
d) mother goddess

Question 60 :
One horn animal depicted on seals which was regarded as mythical composite creatures
a) bull
b) horse
c) unicorn
d) none of these

Question 61 :
___ are men and women who claim magical and healing powers, as an ability to communicate with other worlds
a.Lingas
b.Gamesmen
c.Shamans
d.None of the above

Chapter 2 : Kings, Farmers and Towns

CONCISE KEY NOTES

Chapter Overview

- "The period from c. 600 BCE to 600 CE saw the rise of large states, extensive trade networks, urban centers, and economic transformations."
- "The Mauryan and Gupta Empires were two of the most powerful political entities of the time."
- "Agriculture remained the backbone of the economy, with new irrigation techniques increasing productivity."
- "Trade flourished, both internally and externally, with connections to Rome, China, and Southeast Asia."
- "This chapter explores the political, economic, and social developments of the period."
- James Princep officer in the Mint of the East India Company, deciphered Brahmi and kharosthi scripts.
- Epigraphy – study of inscription.
- Inscriptions are writings engraved on hard surface such a stone metal or pottery the earliest inscriptions were in prakrit.

The Rise Of Mahajanapadas (c. 600 BCE – 400 BCE)

- "Sixteen Mahajanapadas emerged in northern and central India, with powerful states like Magadha dominating the period."
- "Most Mahajanapadas were ruled by kings, but some like Vajji had an oligarchic government (Gana-Sanghas)."
- "Magadha became the most powerful due to its fertile land, iron resources, and strong military, including war elephants."
- "The capital shifted from Rajagaha (Rajgir) to Pataliputra (Patna) in 4th century BCE."

The Mauryan Empire (c. 321 BCE – 185 BCE)

Chandragupta Maurya (c. 321 BCE – 297 BCE)

- "Founded the first pan-Indian empire, extending from Afghanistan Baluchistan to Kalinga (orissa) ."
- "Greek ambassador Megasthenes, who visited his court, wrote the Indica, which provides valuable insights."
- Arthshastra composed by Kautilya or Chanakya minister of Chandragupta.

Ashoka and Dhamma (c. 268 BCE – 232 BCE)

- Ashoka is the first ruler to inscribe his messages on stone and pillars across the empire.
- "His edicts, written in Prakrit, were inscribed in Brahmi script; some in the northwest used Greek and Aramaic."
- "The Kalinga War (c. 261 BCE) led to mass slaughter, after which Ashoka embraced Dhamma and non-violence."
- "Dhamma Mahamattas were appointed to spread his message of tolerance and social ethics."

Administration of the Mauryan Empire
- "Five major political centers: Pataliputra, Taxila, Ujjayini, Tosali, and Suvarnagiri."
- "The empire had a strong revenue system, with taxes on agriculture and trade."
- "Megasthenes mentions a well-organized military with six subcommittees managing different arms."
- 1st- Navy
- 2nd- manage transport provinces
- 3rd- responsible for foot Soldier
- 4th- horses
- 5th- chariots
- 6th- elephants
- second subcommittee- arranging Bullock carts to carry equipments ,procuring food for soldiers and fodders for animals ,recruiting servants and artisans to look after the soldiers.

Chiefs and Kings in the South:
- New kingdoms emerge in Deccan such as cholas, cheras and pandyas in Tamiakaml the name of (ancient Tamil country)
- A chief is a powerful man whose position may or may not be hereditary.
- His functions include performing special rituals leadership in warfare and arbitrating disputes.
- Satavahanas- who ruled over parts of Western and Central India (2nd century BCE - 2nd century CE).
- Shakas -A people of Central Asian Origin who established kingdoms in the Northwest and western parts of the subcontinent.

Post Mauryan Kingdoms And Economic Changes
- The Kushanas (c. 100 BCE - 300 CE)
1. "The Kushanas ruled a vast empire stretching from Central Asia to northern India."
2. Colossal Statues Of kushana rulers have been found installed in a Shrine at mat near Mathura also similar statues found in Shrine from Afghanistan.
3. Many Kushana rulers also adopted the title Deva Putra or son of god inspired by Chinese rulers who called themselves sons Of Heaven.
4. "They issued the largest number of gold coins, facilitating long-distance trade."
- The Gupta Empire (c. 320 CE - 550 CE)
- "Founded by Chandragupta I, the Guptas established a powerful empire centered in Pataliputra."
- "Samudragupta's conquests are described in the Prayag Prashasti (Allahabad Pillar Inscription) composed in Sanskrit by Harishena the court poet of Samudragupta
- "Trade flourished, with Roman gold coins found in India."

Changing Countryside
The Sudarshana Lake:
- Artificial reservoir from the Maurya period.
- Restored by Shaka ruler Rudradaman (2nd century CE) without taxes after storm damage.
- Repaired again by a Gupta ruler (5th century CE).

Popular Perceptions of Kings
- Jatakas & Panchatantra reveal public views on rulers.

- Jatakas written in Pali (~1st millennium CE).
- Gandatindu Jataka: A wicked king overtaxes people; they curse him and flee to forests.

Increasing Production:
- Plough agriculture spread in Ganga & Kaveri valleys (6th century BCE).
- Iron-tipped ploughshares improved farming in rainy areas.
- Paddy transplantation boosted yield but was labor-intensive.

Paddy Transplantation:
- Used in water-rich areas.
- Saplings grown first, then transplanted into waterlogged fields.
- Ensures higher survival & yield.
- "Agriculture was the primary occupation, with peasants growing .
- Small peasants & large landholders mentioned in early Tamil literature (Sangam texts).
- Large landowners - Vellalar.
- Ploughmen - Uzhavar.
- Slaves - Adimai.
- Gahapati - Head of household, controlled women, children, and workers living under the same roof.
- Harshacharita - Biography of Harshavardhana (Kannauj dynasty), written by Banabhatta.
- Prabhavati Gupta - Daughter of Chandragupta II, married to Vakataka ruler of Deccan.

Land Grants And New Rural Elites
Life in a Village:
- Harshacharita (7th century CE) by Banabhatta - Biography of Harshavardhana.
- Rural life near Vindhya forests, farming rice, millet, barley.
- Trade in honey, wax, logs, flowers.

Land Grants & Elites:
- Land grants (mainly copper plates) to Brahmanas & religious institutions.
- Prabhavati Gupta (daughter of Chandragupta II) married into Vakataka dynasty; owned land.
- Land grants:
  - Expanded agriculture (some historians).
  - Weakened royal power (others).

Agrahara:
- Land grant to Brahmanas.
- Exempted from taxes.
- Right to collect dues from locals.

Trade, Coins and Urbanisation
History of Pataliputra
- Originally Pataligrama.
- 5th century BCE - Magadhan rulers shifted capital from Rajagaha, renamed it Pataliputra.
- 4th century BCE - Mauryan Empire's capital, among largest cities in Asia.
- Later declined, noted by Chinese pilgrim Xuan Zang.

New Cities
- Towns emerged (6th century BCE), capitals of mahajanapadas.
- Located along trade routes:
    - Pataliputra – River routes.
    - Ujjaini – Land routes.
    - Puhar, Mamallapuram – Coastal, sea routes.
    - Mathura – Commercial & cultural hub.

Urban Populations
- Kings, elites, and craftsmen lived in cities.
- Artefacts found:
    - Northern Black Polished Ware (fine pottery for elites).
    - Gold, silver, copper, bronze, ivory, glass, shell, terracotta items.
- Inscriptions found in cities mentioned:
    - Donor's name & occupation.
    - Occupations in towns – Weavers, scribes, carpenters, potters, goldsmiths, blacksmiths, officials, religious teachers, merchants, and kings.
- Guilds (Shrenis):
    - Organizations of craft producers & merchants.
    - Managed raw materials, regulated production & marketed goods.
    - Used iron tools to meet urban elite demands.

Trade Networks (6th Century BCE Onwards):
- Overland & overseas trade connected India with Central Asia, China, the Mediterranean, and Africa.
- Merchants, seafarers & peddlers played a key role.
- Goods traded: Salt, grain, cloth, metals, finished products, stone, timber, medicinal plants, textiles, and horses.
- Indian goods reached the Roman Empire & Mediterranean.

Archaeological Evidence:
- Bead-making industry found in Kodumanal (Tamil Nadu).
- Local traders likely supplied stones mentioned in the *Periplus* to coastal ports.

Coins & Kings:
- Coinage facilitated exchanges: punch-marked silver & copper coins (6th century BCE) were common.
- Numismatists use coins to reconstruct trade networks.
- Indo-Greeks issued the first coins with ruler names & images (2nd century BCE).
- Kushanas issued large gold coin hoards (1st century CE).

Inscriptions And Administration
Coins and Trade:
- Roman and Parthian coins have been found in North India and Central Asia, indicating active trade.
- Archaeological sites in South India also contain Roman coins, showing trade beyond political boundaries.
- Tribal republics like the Yaudheyas (Punjab and Haryana, 1st century CE) issued copper coins.

- Gupta rulers issued spectacular gold coins, aiding long-distance transactions.
- The collapse of the Western Roman Empire led to a decline in long-distance trade, affecting prosperity.

Deciphering Inscriptions
- Brahmi script, used in most Ashokan inscriptions, is the ancestor of modern Indian scripts.
- European scholars, with Indian pandits, deciphered Brahmi by comparing it with Bengali and Devanagari.
- James Prinsep successfully deciphered Ashokan Brahmi in 1838.
- Kharosthi script was used in inscriptions in the northwest and was read using Indo-Greek coin evidence.
- Prinsep identified Prakrit as the language of Kharosthi inscriptions.

Historical Evidence from Inscriptions
- Asokan inscriptions use titles like Devanampiya ("beloved of the gods") and Piyadassi ("pleasant to behold").
- Epigraphists confirm that different inscriptions were issued by the same ruler.

Limitations of Inscriptions
- Technical issues: faint engravings, missing letters, and damage affect interpretation.
- Scholars debate and reinterpret inscriptions due to uncertain meanings of words.
- Not all inscriptions have been found, and many have been lost over time.
- Inscriptions focus on grand events and often reflect the ruler's perspective rather than daily life.

TIMELINE OF MAJOR EVENTS
- c. 600–500 BCE: Emergence of Mahajanapadas, early urbanization, and punch-marked coins.
- c. 321 BCE: Chandragupta Maurya establishes the Mauryan Empire.
- c. 272 BCE – 231 BCE: Reign of Ashoka, Kalinga War, and spread of Dhamma.
- c. 200 BCE – 100 CE: Indo-Greek and Kushana rule in north India, Roman trade flourishes.
- c. 320 CE: Beginning of Gupta rule, economic prosperity.
- c. 606 CE – 647 CE: Harshavardhana rules Kanauj, Xuan Zang visits India.
- c. 712 CE: Arab conquest of Sind.

Important Figures

Fig. 2.1
An inscription, Sanchi (Madhya Pradesh), c. second century BCE

Fig. 2.3
The lion capital

Fig. 2.6
The gift of an image
This is part of an image from Mathura. On the pedestal is a Prakrit inscription, mentioning that a woman named Nagapiya, the wife of a goldsmith (*sovanika*) named Dharmaka, installed this image in a shrine.

Fig. 2.4
A Kushana coin
Obverse: King Kanishka
Reverse: A deity

Fig. 2.5
Sandstone sculpture of a Kushana king

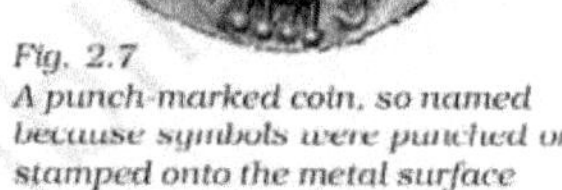

Fig. 2.7
A punch-marked coin, so named because symbols were punched or stamped onto the metal surface

Fig. 2.8
A Yaudheya coin

Fig. 2.9
A Gupta coin

Fig. 2.10
An Asokan inscription

Important Figures

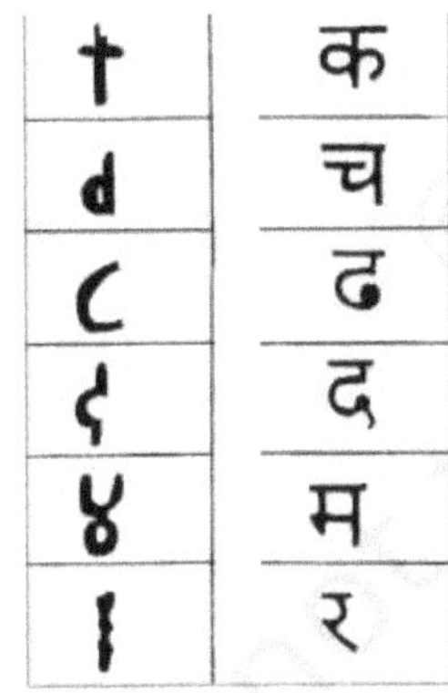

Fig. 2.11
Asokan Brahmi with Devanagari equivalents

Fig. 2.12
A coin of the Indo-Greek king Menander

Fig. 2.13
A copperplate inscription from Karnataka, c. sixth century CE

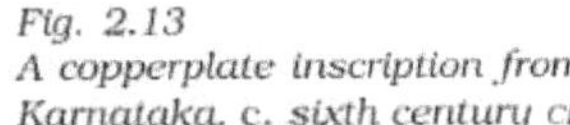

Chapter 2 : Mapwork

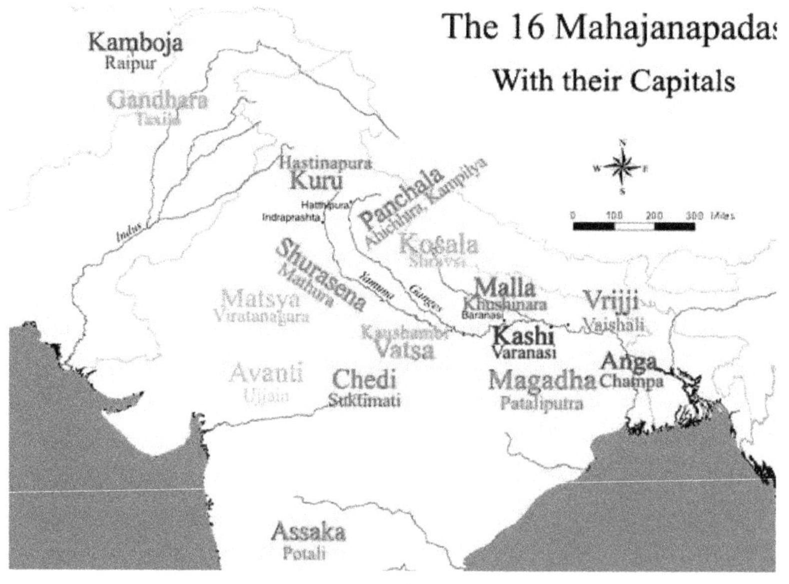

Chapter 2 : Kings, Farmers and Towns

QUESTIONS FROM ARCHIVES

Question 1 :
Epigraphy is the study of –
a) inscriptions
b) sculptures
c) Manuscripts
d) None of these

Question 2 :
Name the officer in the mint of East India Company , who deciphered Brahmi and Kharosthi script
a) S.N.Roy
b) Daya Ram Sahni
c) James Prinsep
d) R.E.M.Wheeler

Question 3 :
Name the two scripts that was used in the earliest inscriptions and coins
a) Tamil and Telugu
b) Hindi and Sanskrit
c) Brahmi and Kharosthi
d) English and Bengali

Question 4 :
King Ashoka is referred as 'piyadassi 'in few inscriptions . What is the meaning of the word 'Piyadassi' ?
a) pleasant to behold
b) beloved nature
c) beloved of gods
d) beloved of kings

Question 5 :
The earliest inscriptions were in –
a) Pali
b) Prakrit
c) sanskrit
d) Tamil

Question 6 :
writings engraved on hard surfaces such as stone, metal or pottery is known as
a.Manuscripts
b.Sculptures
c.Inscriptions
d.Calligraphy

Question 7 :
Elaborate stone structures kept on the burial in central and south ?

a.Northern black polished ware
b.Pillars
c.Boulders
d.Megaliths

Question 8 :
Palaeography is a style of –

a) painting
b) calligraphy
c) photography
d) writing

Question 9 :
___refers to a form of government where power is exercised by a group of men.
a.Monarchy
b.Autocracy
c.Oligarchy
d.Plutocracy

Question 10 :
Which Mahajanapada was the most powerful from 6th to 4th century BCE?
a.Panchala
b.Vajji
c.Kuru
d.Magadh

Question 11 :
Which of the following statement(s) is are correct –

i) The sixth century BCE is often regarded as a major turning point in early Indian history
ii) It is an era associated with early states , cities , growing use of iron, development of coinage , witnessed growth of diverse system of thought including Buddhism and Jainism.

a) Statement I is correct
b)Statement II is correct
c) Both are correct
d) None are correct

Question 12 :
How many mahajanapadas were there ?
a) 16
b) 17
c) 18
d) 19

Question 13 :
Which one is not a Mahajanpad ?
a.Avanti
b.Panchala
c.Koashala
d.Awadh

Question 14 :
Dharmasutras are __ texts composed by Brahmanas.
a.Hindi
b.Tamil
c.Sanskrit
d.Telugu

Question 15 :
Who won the famous battle of Kalinga ?
a) Ajatasattu
b) Mahapadma Nanda
c) Ashoka
d) Bimbisara

Question 16 :
What was the capital of Magadh ?
a. Rajagaha
b.Taxila
c. Sanchi
d. Ujjayini

Question 17 :
Later in the fourth century BCE, the capital of Magadha was shifted to
a. Rajagaha
b.Taxila
c. Sanchi
d. Pataliputra

Question 18 :
 Magadha was considered as the most powerful Mahajanapada from sixth to fourth century BCE. Historians put forward different kinds of explanations for the growth of Magadha.

Which of the following statements is incorrect regarding the growth of Magadha?

(a) Magadha was a region where agriculture was especially productive.
(b) Iron mines were accessible and provided resources for tools and weapons.
(c) Magadha's proximity to the sea makes it a business hub. Many foreign traders used to come here for trading purposes.
(d) Elephants, an important component of the army, were found in forests in the region.

Question 19 :
Who was the founder of Mauryan Empire ?
a) Bimbisara
b) Samudragupta
c) Ajatasattu
d) Chandragupta Maurya

Question 20 :
Name the Greek ambassador in the court of Chandragupta Maurya-

a) Deimachus
b) Megasthenes
c)Dionysius
d)None of these

Question 21 :
Which one of the following is the author of Arthashastra?
(a) Kalhana.
(b) Kalidasa.
(c) Kautilya.
(d) Banabhatta

Question 22 :
Special officers who were appointed for spreading the message of Dhamma were known as ?
a.Dhamma Mahamatta
b.Dhamma Guru
c.None of these
d.Dhamma Matta

Question 23 :
Name the languages in which the Ashokan inscriptions were written.
(a) Pali, Prakrit, and Greek
(b) Pali, Sanskrit, and Aramaic
(c) Prakrit, Aramaic, and Greek
(d) Pali, Sanskrit, and Greek

Question 24 :
Name the book written by the greek ambassador Megasthenes in the court of Chandragupta Maurya ?
a) Arthashastra
b) Indica
c) prayaga prashasti
d) None of these

Question 25 :
Consider the following statement(s) about the Mauryan Empire :

There were five major political centres in the empire
ii) Megasthenes wrote about the Mauryan Empire in his book Indica
iii) Megasthenes mentions a committee with six subcommittee for coordinating military activity.
iv) Ashoka tried to hold his empire together by propagating dhamma.
a) (i) and (ii) are correct
b) (iii) and (iv) are correct
c) All are correct
d) None are correct

Question 26 :
______ a people of Central Asian Origin for established kingdoms in the North Western and western parts of the subcontinent.

a) Kushanas
b) Mauryas
c) Satvahanas
d) Shakas

Question 27 :
_____ an epic written in Tamil .

a) Silappadikaram
b) Indica
c) Arthashastra
d) None of these

Question 28 :
The cholas cheras and pandyas (the ancient name of the Tamil country which include parts of present day—
a) Telengana , Andhra Pradesh, Karnataka
b) Andhra Pradesh and Chhatisgarh
c) Andhra Pradesh , Kerala in addition to Tamil Nadu
d) None of these

Question 29 :
Kushana rulers adopted the title called —
a) Devaraj
b) Devaputra
c) Devsena
d) Devtulya

Question 30 :
Prayaga Prashasti is also known as–
a) Ashok Chakra
b) Allahabad Pillar
c) Qutub Minar
d) Taj Mahal

Question 31 :
The Prayaga Prashasti was composed in
(a) Sanskrit.
(b) Pali.
(c) Prakrit.
(d) Brahmi.

Question 32 :
The Prayaga Prashasti (also known as the Allahabad Pillar Inscription) was composed in Sanskrit by Harishena. Harishena was the court poet of which of the following kings?
(a) King Samudragupta
(b) King Ashoka
(c) King Chandra Gupta Maurya
(d) King Kanishka

Question 33 :
According to the rock inscription Sudarshan lake, an artificial reservoir was repaired by

(a) king Kanishka
(b) king Rudradaman
(c) ruler Harshavardhana
(d) Chandragupta II

Question 34 :
The Jatakas were written in—
a) Pali
b) Prakrit
c) Tamil
d) Sanskrit

Question 35 :
The story which describes the plight of the subjects of a wicked king ; these included elderly women and men ,cultivators , herders, village boys and even animals.

a) Panchatantra
b) Gandatindu Jataka
c) Jataka
d) Manusmriti

Question 36 :
Which among the following statement(s) is are correct about the strategies for increasing production .
I. The iron tipped ploughshare used to turn alluvial soil in areas which had high rainfall.
II. Introduction of transplantation .
III. Use of Irrigation, through wells and tanks and also canals.
IV. The latter , powerful men including kings , such activities are often recorded in the inscriptions.
a) I and II are correct
b) III and IV are correct
c) None are correct
d) All above are correct

Question 37 :
Which one of the following statements is incorrect regarding the word 'Gahapati'?
(a) They are the owner, master or head of a household.
(b) They are the owner of the resources – land, animals and other things – that belonged to the household.
(c) They are the officials of the king.
(d) They belonged to the urban elite, including wealthy merchants

Question 38 :
Tamil Sangam literature mentions slaves as
(a) Pannai
(b) Adimai
(c) Uzhavar
(d) Vellalar

Question 39 :
Tamil Sangam literature mentions large landowners as
(a) Pannai
(b) Adimai
(c) Uzhavar
(d) Vellalar

Question 40 :
Harshacharita is the biography of which ruler ?
a) Ashoka
b) samudragupta
c) Harshavardhana
d) chandragupta

Question 41 :
Harshacharita was composed by whom ?
a) Ashoka
b) Chanakya
c) Banabhatta
d) Samudragupta

Question 42 :
Harshavardhana was the ruler of ?
a) Kanauj
b) Pataliputra
c) Rajgaha
d) Deccan

Question 43 :
Prabhavati Gupta was the daughter of which ruler ?
a) Chandragupta
b) Chandragupta II
c) Samudragupta
d) Harshavardhana

Question 44 :
Who was the first ruler to inscribe his messages to his subjects and officials on stone surfaces – natural rocks as well as polished pillars ?
a) Samudragupta
b) Chandragupta
c) Ashoka
d) Chandragupta II

Question 45 :
_____ was the owner , master or head of a household.
a) Pannai
b) Mahamatta
c) adimai
d) Gahapati

Question 46 :
An ________ was a land granted to a brahman who was usually exempted from paying land revenue and other dues to the king .
a) Agrahara
b) Dakshina
c) Namaskaram
d) none of these

Question 47 :
When did the chinese pilgrim Xuan Zang visited Pataliputra ?
a) 7th century
b) 6th century
c) 5th century
d) 9th century

Question 48 :
Suvarnagiri was important for tapping the gold mines of Karnataka, what does the literally meaning of Suvarnagiri ?
a) Golden Temple
b) Golden Mountain
c) Golden Statue
d) Golden palace

Question 49 :
Match the following :

Column A   Column B

i) Pataliputra   a) land routes
ii) Ujjayini   b) riverine routes
iii) Puhar   c) bustling centres
iv) Mathura   d) near coast sea routes

a) i-b , ii-c , iii-d, iv-a
b) i-b , ii-d , iii-c , iv-a
c) i-b , ii-a , iii-d , iv-c
d) i-c , ii-a , iii-d , iv-b

Question 50 :
What were the guilds of the merchants and craftsmen called ?
a) shrenis
b) adimai
c) vellalar
d) murid

Question 51 :
Periplus in Greek means ?
a) Bead making
b) shell cutting
c) ships
d) sailing around

Question 52 :
" Erythraean" was the Greek name for which sea ?
a) red sea
b) Mediterranean sea
c) Arabian sea
d) Caribbean sea

Question 53 :
The first gold coin was issued in the first century CE by:
(a) Mauryas
(b) Mughals
(c) Kushanas
(d) Rajputs

Question 54 :
The spectacular gold coins which facilitated long distance transactions were issued by
(a) Kushanas
(b) The Mauryan rulers
(c) The Saka rulers
(d) The Gupta rulers

Question 55 :
Study of coins is known as ?
a.Gemology
b.Petrology
c.Numismatics
d. Epigraphy

Question 56 :
Yaudheyas belong to which state ?
a.Haryana
b. Gujarat
c. Punjab
d. Both A and C

Question 57 :
James Princep was able to decipher Ashokan Brahmi in
a. 1818
b. 1828
c. 1838
d. 1848

Question 58 :
Which of these archaeological sources are used to reconstruct the ancient Indian history ?
a. Vedas
b. Inscriptions
c. Coins
d. Both B and C

Question 59 :
Ashoka is mentioned by which titles in his inscriptions?
(a) Ashoka, Piyadassi
(b) Devanampiya, Piyadassi
(c) Dhamma, Piyadassi
(d) Chakravarti, Dhamma

Question 60 :
Which of the following problems were faced by archaeologists while deciphering the inscriptions ?
a) Faint letters
b) damaged letters
c)exact meaning of the words
d) All of the above

Question 61 :
Which one of the following statements is incorrect regarding the duties of chiefs and chiefdom)
i) his functions include performing special rituals leadership in warfare and arbitrating disputes
ii) a chief is a powerful man whose position are hereditary.
iii) generally there are regular Armies and officials in chiefdoms
iv) he receives gifts from his subordinate and often distributes this amongst his supporters.
a) i & ii
b) only ii
c) ii & iii
d) none of theses

Question 62 :

a) sandstone sculpture of Kushana king
b)sandstone sculpture of Gupta king
c)sandstone sculpture of Maurya king
d)sandstone sculpture of shaka king

Question 63:
Identify The picture.

From where did this sculpture found?
a. Gujarat
b. Mathura
c. varanasi
d. Pataliputra

Chapter 3 : Kinship, Caste, And Class

CONCISE KEY NOTES

Chapter Overview
- "Kinship, caste, and class were key social structures in early Indian society."
- "These structures evolved through Brahmanical traditions, historical texts, and societal practices."
- "Kinship defined family roles, caste determined social hierarchy, and class influenced access to resources."
- "The Manusmriti, Mahabharata, Buddhist texts, and inscriptions provide crucial insights."
- "This chapter explores the interconnections of social structures and their impact on early societies."

V.S. Sukthankar's Critical Edition of the Mahabharata:
- Project Start: 1919, led by V.S. Sukthankar, a Sanskrit scholar.
- Objective: To create a Critical Edition of the Mahabharata by comparing multiple Sanskrit manuscripts from different regions.
- Methodology:
- Collected manuscripts written in various scripts from across India (Kashmir to Tamil Nadu).
- Compared verses and identified those common across most versions.
- Variations were documented in footnotes and appendices.
- Completion: Took 47 years; final edition ran over 13,000 pages.

Family And Kinship Structures:
The Concept of Patriliny:
- "Patriliny (tracing descent through the male line) was dominant in early societies."
- "The Mahabharata reinforces the idea that land and throne should pass through male heirs."
- "Women had no claims to inheritance and were married off into other families."
- "Rigvedic mantras emphasize the importance of 'producing fine sons'."
- Kula: Family.
- Jnati: Kin group.
- Vamsha: Lineage.
- Matriliny: Inheritance through the female line (less common).

Marriage Rules and Practices:
- "Endogamy (marrying within the caste or group) and exogamy (marrying outside the group) were strictly regulated."
- "Eight forms of marriage were described in the Manusmriti, with arranged marriages being the most respected."
- "Polygyny (multiple wives) was common among rulers, while polyandry (a woman having multiple husbands) was rare but existed in texts like the Mahabharata."
- Gotra: A system of classifying people (especially Brahmanas) based on their lineage from a Vedic seer (rishi).
- Each gotra was named after a Vedic sage, and all members of the same gotra were considered his descendants.

Key Rules About Gotra:

1. Women were expected to give up their father's gotra and adopt their husband's gotra after marriage.
2. Marriage within the same gotra was prohibited (exogamy).

Evidence from the Satavahana Dynasty:

- Satavahana rulers' inscriptions (2nd century BCE – 2nd century CE) provide insights into marriage and gotra practices.
- Some queens retained their father's gotra instead of adopting their husband's gotra.
- Example:
  - Names of Satavahana rulers found in inscriptions:
    - *Gotami-puta Siri-Satakani* ("Son of Gotami")
    - *Vasithi-puta Siri-Pulumayi* ("Son of Vasithi")
  - These names suggest that mothers' gotras were used in naming kings.
- Brahmanical texts prescribed strict gotra rules, but historical evidence shows flexibility in practice.
- Satavahanas followed matronymic naming practices, indicating an alternative tradition to strict patrilineal norms.

Varna And Jati: Social Hierarchy

Varna System:

- "The Dharmashastras defined four varnas based on occupation and birth."
  - Brahmanas: Priests and scholars, responsible for religious learning.
  - Kshatriyas: Warriors and rulers, responsible for protection and governance.
  - Vaishyas: Traders, agriculturists, and craftsmen.
  - Shudras: Laborers, denied education and rituals.

Ekalavya (Mahabharata Story & Caste Norms):

- Ekalavya, a Nishada (forest-dweller), wanted to learn archery from Drona.
- Drona, bound by caste norms, refused to teach him.
- Ekalavya made a clay idol of Drona and trained himself, becoming highly skilled.
- When Drona saw his talent, he demanded his right thumb as guru dakshina, ensuring Ekalavya wouldn't surpass Arjuna.
- Ekalavya cut off his thumb, symbolizing caste oppression.

Non Kshatriya Kings:

Brahmanical View on Kingship

- According to the Dharmashastras, only Kshatriyas could be kings.
- However, historical evidence shows that several ruling dynasties were not of Kshatriya origin.

1. Mauryas (c. 4th–2nd century BCE)
   - Origins debated:
     - Buddhist texts (e.g., Ashokavadana) claim they were Kshatriyas.
     - Brahmanical texts call them of "low origin" (possibly from a non-Kshatriya or Shudra background).
   - Chandragupta Maurya became a powerful emperor despite caste debates.

2. Shungas & Kanvas (2nd–1st century BCE)
- These dynasties succeeded the Mauryas and were Brahmanas.
- Contradiction: Brahmanas were not traditionally supposed to be kings, yet they ruled.

3. Satavahanas (c. 2nd century BCE – 3rd century CE):
- Claimed to be Brahmanas, yet ruled as kings.
- King Gotami-puta Siri-Satakani:
- Called himself "Eka-Bamhana" (a unique Brahmana).

Jati and Social Mobility
- "Jatis (sub-castes) emerged based on professions and were more fluid than varnas."
- "The Mandasor inscription describes a guild of silk weavers who migrated for better opportunities."
- "Shrenis (guilds) provided professional identity, sometimes allowing upward mobility."

Women And Property Rights
Stridhana: Limited Wealth for Women:
- "Women could not inherit family property but could retain stridhana (gifts received at marriage)."
- "The Manusmriti warned women against managing wealth independently."
- "Some royal women, like Prabhavati Gupta, wielded power, but these were exceptions."

Hidimba and Ghatotkacha:
- Hidimba (Rakshasi) sent by her brother Hidimb to capture the Pandavas but fell in love with Bhima.
- Bhima killed Hidimb, and Yudhishthira allowed Bhima to marry Hidimba under the condition that he would return after some time.
- Their son Ghatotkacha, a powerful warrior, later helped the Pandavas in the Kurukshetra war.

Social Conflict And Untouchability : The Chandalas and Social Margins
- "Chandalas (untouchables) performed menial and 'polluting' tasks like disposing of corpses."
- "They lived outside villages and had severe restrictions on movement."
- "The Manusmriti prescribed degrading rules for their existence."Untouchability (Accounts by Chinese Travelers)
- Fa Xian (5th century CE) Observed that "untouchables" had to sound a clapper in the streets to warn others of their presence.
- This shows the rigid enforcement of caste-based discrimination.
- Xuan Zang (7th century CE)
- Noted that executioners and scavengers were forced to live outside cities.
- Indicates social exclusion of certain groups in urban centers.

Matanga Jataka (Story of a Chandala Bodhisattva):
- Matanga (Bodhisattva) was born in a Chandala (outcaste) family near Banaras.
- A wealthy merchant's daughter, Dittha Mangalika, insulted him, calling him inauspicious.
- His son, Mandavya Kumara, became a respected Brahmana and provided food to Brahmanas.
- When Matanga begged for alms, Mandavya rejected him as an unworthy outcaste.
- Matanga rose into the air and disappeared, proving spiritual superiority over caste barriers.

Challenges to Caste Hierarchy
- "Buddhism rejected caste distinctions and emphasized ethical conduct over birth."
- "Tamil Sangam literature praised generosity over birth-based status."
- "Inscriptional evidence shows cases of upward mobility through trade and military service."
- Mrichchhakatika written by Shudraka(c. Fourth century CE).

Kingship And Social Order:
Brahmanical Justification for Kingship:
- "The Mahabharata presents kings as divine rulers maintaining dharma."
- "The Satavahana rulers claimed Brahmanical legitimacy despite having non-Kshatriya origins."
- "The Shakas and Kushanas were labeled as 'mlechchhas' (outsiders) but assimilated into the system."

Land Grants and Power Structures
- "Kings granted land to Brahmanas, reinforcing religious and political authority."
- "The copperplate inscriptions of the Gupta period record such land donations."

Historians and the Mahabharata
- Language & Composition:
  - Written in simple Sanskrit, making it widely accessible.
  - Contains narrative (stories) and didactic (moral teachings) sections.
- Authorship & Dating:
  - Likely started by charioteer-bards (Sutas) who celebrated Kshatriya warriors.
  - Brahmanas later compiled and expanded it (c. 5th century BCE – 4th century CE).
  - Krishna-Vishnu connection added between 200 BCE – 200 CE.
  - Didactic portions (like Manusmriti) included by 200-400 CE.
- Archaeological Evidence:
  - B.B. Lal's excavation at Hastinapura (1951-52) found mud-brick houses, supporting a possible historical basis for the epic.
  - Unclear if the battle truly happened, as no direct evidence exists.
- Dynamic Text:
  - Evolved over centuries, with regional variations and retellings.
  - Inspired literature, sculpture, and performing arts across India.

Important Figures

Fig. 3.1
A terracotta sculpture
depicting a scene from
the Mahabharata
(West Bengal),
c. seventeenth century

Fig. 3.3
A Satavahana ruler and his wife
This is one of the rare sculptural
depictions of a ruler from the wall
of a cave donated to Buddhist
monks. This sculpture dates to
c. second century BCE.

Fig. 3.5
Silver coin depicting a Shaka ruler,
c. fourth century CE

Fig. 3.4
A battle scene
This is amongst the earliest sculptural depictions of a
scene from the *Mahabharata*, a terracotta sculpture from
the walls of a temple in Ahichchhatra (Uttar Pradesh),
c. fifth century CE.

Fig. 3.6
Depiction of a mendicant seeking
alms, stone sculpture (Gandhara)
c. third century, CE

Important Figures

Fig. 3.9
Lord Ganesha the scribe
According to tradition, Vyasa
dictated the text to the deity.
This illustration is from a Persian
translation of the *Mahabharata*,
c. 1740-50.

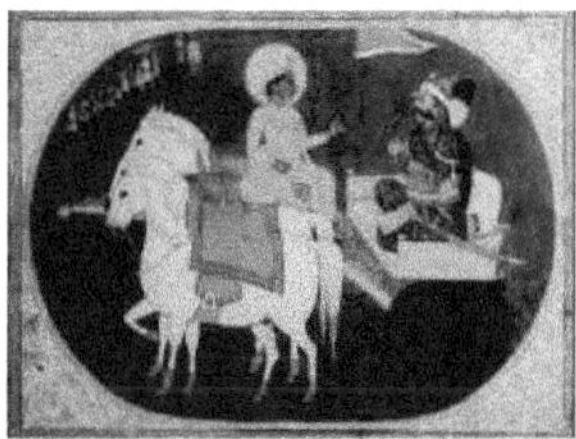

Fig. 3.8
Krishna advises Arjuna on the battlefield
This painting dates to the
eighteenth century. Perhaps the
most important didactic section of
the *Mahabharata* is the *Bhagavad Gita*, which contains the advice
offered by Lord Krishna to Arjuna.
This scene is frequently depicted
in painting and sculpture.

Fig. 3.7
A chief and his follower, stone sculpture, Amaravati (Andhra Pradesh), c. second century CE

Chapter 3 : Kinship, Caste and Class

QUESTIONS FROM ARCHIVES

Question 1 :
Which historical source provides the most comprehensive depiction of early Indian social categories and kinship structures?
a) Arthashastra
b) Ramayana
c) Mahabharata
d) Rigveda

Question 2 :
Who led the project to prepare the Critical Edition of the Mahabharata in 1919?
a) R.C. Majumdar
b) D.D. Kosambi
c) V.S. Sukthankar
d) Romila Thapar

Question 3 :
According to the Dharmashastras, which of the following was the only occupation assigned to Shudras?
a) Agriculture
b) Trade and commerce
c) Servitude
d) Warfare

Question 4 :
Which Brahmanical term refers to the lineage traced through the father?
a) Gotra
b) Matriliny
c) Patriliny
d) Jati

Question 5 :
The Manusmriti prescribes how many forms of marriage, out of which the first four were considered "good"?
a) Six
b) Eight
c) Ten
d) Twelve

Question 6 :
Assertion (A): The Satavahana rulers identified themselves through matronymics (mother's lineage).
Reason (R): The Brahmanical texts strictly enforced patriliny, but regional variations existed.
  a) Both A and R are true, and R is the correct explanation of A
b) Both A and R are true, but R is not the correct explanation of A
c) A is true, but R is false
d) A is false, but R is true

Question 7 :
Assertion (A): The Mahabharata contains both narrative and didactic sections.
Reason (R): The didactic sections were likely added later to emphasize social norms.
a) Both A and R are true, and R is the correct explanation of A
b) Both A and R are true, but R is not the correct explanation of A
c) A is true, but R is false
d) A is false, but R is true

Question 8 :
The term _________ was used in Sanskrit texts to refer to the larger network of kinfolk.
a) Vamsha
b) Gotra
c) Kula
d) Jnati

Question 9 :
The Buddhist text Majjhima Nikaya highlights a conversation between King Avantiputta and Kachchana, where social distinctions were questioned based on _________.
a) Occupation
b) Birth
c) Wealth
d) Religion

Question 10 :
B.B. Lal excavated the site of _________ in 1951–52, believed to be the capital of the Kuru kingdom.
a) Indraprastha
b) Mathura
c) Hastinapura
d) Kaushambi

Question 11 :
Which of the following texts is considered the most important Dharmashastra, compiled between c. 200 BCE and 200 CE?
a) Arthashastra
b) Manusmriti
c) Brihadaranyaka Upanishad
d) Mahabharata

Question 12 :
According to the Mahabharata, which ruling family was involved in a feud over land and power?
a) Mauryas
b) Satavahanas
c) Kauravas and Pandavas
d) Shakas and Pallavas

Question 13 :
What does the Purusha Sukta of the Rigveda claim about the origin of the varna system?
a) It was created by the Mauryan kings
b) It was a result of economic differences
c) It originated from different parts of the cosmic being Purusha
d) It was formed due to migration patterns

Question 14 :
Which of the following Satavahana rulers is known for claiming the title "Eka Bamhana" (Unique Brahmana)?
a) Siri-Satakani
b) Rudradaman
c) Siri-Pulumayi
d) Siri-Yana-Satakani

Question 15 :
Assertion (A): The Mahabharata was composed over nearly a thousand years.
Reason (R): The text evolved through oral traditions before being written down by Brahmanas.
a) Both A and R are true, and R is the correct explanation of A
b) Both A and R are true, but R is not the correct explanation of A
c) A is true, but R is false
d) A is false but R is true

Question 16 :
Assertion (A): The Dharmashastras emphasized the importance of kanyadana (gift of a daughter in marriage).
Reason (R): The practice of kanyadana reinforced the patriarchal control over marriage alliances.
a) Both A and R are true, and R is the correct explanation of A
b) Both A and R are true, but R is not the correct explanation of A
c) A is true, but R is false
d) A is false, but R is true

Question 17 :
The Mahabharata describes a marriage system called _________, where one woman marries multiple husbands.
a) Polygyny
b) Polyandry
c) Exogamy
d) Endogamy

Question 18 :
The excavation at Hastinapura by B.B. Lal found evidence of houses made of _________ in the second phase (c. 12th-7th century BCE).
a) Stone
b) Mud and mud-bricks
c) Wood
d) Granite

Question 19 :
Which term was used in Sanskrit texts to designate families?
a) Vamsha
b) Kula
c) Jnati
d) Gotra

Question 20 :
The Mahabharata was considered an itihasa, which means:
a) A fictional tale
b) A divine revelation
c) A historical account
d) A war strategy

Question 21 :
Which ruling dynasty's women retained their father's gotra name instead of adopting their husband's gotra?
a) Mauryas
b) Guptas
c) Satavahanas
d) Kushanas

Question 22 :
In the Mahabharata, why did Drona refuse to teach archery to Ekalavya?
a) Ekalavya was not a Kshatriya
b) Ekalavya belonged to a rival kingdom
c) Drona had already promised Arjuna that he would be the best archer
d) Ekalavya was blind

Question 23 :
Assertion (A): The Mahabharata was initially composed by charioteer-bards (sutas).
Reason (R): The text was later taken over by Brahmanas and written down systematically.
a) Both A and R are true, and R is the correct explanation of A
b) Both A and R are true, but R is not the correct explanation of A
c) A is true, but R is false
d) A is false, but R is true

Question 24:
B.B. Lal's excavations at Hastinapura revealed houses with walls made of _________ during the second phase of settlement.
a) Reed and bamboo
b) Mud and mud-bricks
c) Stone
d) Copper

Question 25 :
In the Mahabharata, who is depicted as the eldest of the Pandava brothers?
a) Arjuna
b) Bhima
c) Yudhishthira
d) Nakula

Question 26 :
The term 'gotra' was primarily associated with which group in early Indian texts?
a) Kshatriyas
b) Vaishyas
c) Brahmanas
d) Shudras

Question 27 :
Which of the following practices was discouraged by Brahmanical texts to maintain the purity of the varna system?
a) Endogamy
b) Exogamy
c) Polygyny
d) Polyandry

Question 28 :
The Mahabharata is classified under which genre of ancient Indian literature?
a) Itihasa
b) Purana
c) Veda
d) Upanishad

Question 29 :
Assertion (A): The Satavahana rulers often used matronymics in their names.
Reason (R): This practice indicated a matrilineal system prevalent in their society.

a) Both A and R are true, and R is the correct explanation of A
b) Both A and R are true, but R is not the correct explanation of A
c) A is true, but R is false
d) A is false, but R is true

Question 30 :
In the context of early Indian society, _________
refers to the practice of marrying outside one's
own gotra.
a) Endogamy
b) Exogamy
c) Polygamy
d) Monogamy

Question 31 :
The Mahabharata was traditionally attributed to
the sage _________.
a) Valmiki
b) Vyasa
c) Vashistha
d) Viswamitra

Question 32 :
Which ruler is known to have rebuilt the
Sudarshana Lake, as mentioned in inscriptions?
a) Ashoka
b) Chandragupta Maurya
c) Rudradaman
d) Harsha

Question 33:
Which of the following statements about the
Critical Edition of the Mahabharata is correct?
a) It was started in 1947 after India's
independence
b) It removed all regional variations in the text
c) It was led by V.S. Sukthankar and took 47
years to complete
d) It compiled only oral versions of the
Mahabharata

Question 34 :
According to the Manusmriti, who was responsible
for performing sacrifices and receiving gifts?
a) Kshatriyas
b) Brahmanas
c) Vaishyas
d) Shudras

Question 35 :
Which term refers to occupational guilds in early
Indian society?
a) Vamsha
b) Shreni
c) Gotra
d) Jati

Question 36 :
Which of the following statements about the
Mahabharata is true?
a) It was written in one sitting by Valmiki
b) It was composed over 1,000 years and had
multiple contributors
c) It only contains war narratives with no
social discussions
d) It was first written in Pali and later
translated into Sanskrit

Question 37 :
Which type of marriage was considered ideal
in Brahmanical texts?
a) Marriage within the same gotra
b) Gandharva marriage based on mutual
attraction
c) Kanyadana, where the bride is given as a
gift to a groom
d) Polyandry, where one woman has multiple
husbands

Question 38 :
Which of the following factors contributed to
social differences in early Indian societies?
a) Unequal distribution of wealth
b) Extension of agriculture into forested areas
c) Emergence of craft specialists as distinct
social groups
d) All of the above

Question 39 :
Why did the Mahabharata contain multiple
versions and regional variations?
a) It was orally transmitted for centuries
before being written
b) Different rulers modified it to suit their
rule
c) It was influenced by Buddhist and Jain
texts
d) It was originally written in Tamil and
later translated

Question 40 :
Which type of marriage involved a woman
choosing her partner voluntarily, often
without the involvement of family elders?
a) Rakshasa marriage
b) Gandharva marriage
c) Arsha marriage
d) Brahma marriage

Question 41 :
Assertion (A): The Mahabharata was composed over a long period and reflects multiple social ideas.
Reason (R): The text contains both narrative and didactic sections that were added over centuries.
a) Both A and R are true, and R is the correct explanation of A
b) Both A and R are true, but R is not the correct explanation of A
c) A is true, but R is false
d) A is false, but R is true

Question 42 :
Assertion (A): The Dharmashastras described Shudras as being restricted to the occupation of servitude.
Reason (R): Early Buddhist texts provide evidence that some Shudras accumulated wealth and gained social status.
a) Both A and R are true, and R is the correct explanation of A
b) Both A and R are true, but R is not the correct explanation of A
c) A is true, but R is false
d) A is false, but R is true

Question 43 :
The Manusmriti prescribed that chandalas should live _________ from villages and cities.
a) In palaces
b) In isolated settlements outside the village
c) In monasteries
d) Among the Brahmanas

Question 44 :
According to the Mahabharata, Ekalavya was a ________ by birth but mastered archery despite being denied formal training.
a) Brahmana
b) Nishada
c) Vaishya
d) Kshatriya

Question 45 :
What were the duties mentioned in Manusmriti concerning Chandalas?

They had to live outside the village.
2. They use discarded utensils.
3. They had to dispose of the bodies of those who had no relatives.
a) 1 and 2 only
b) 2 and 3 only
c) 1 and 3 only
d) 1,2 and 3

Question 46 :

Identify The Following Picture,
a) Gajapati Ruler and his wife
b) Sakshahana Ruler and his wife
c) Satvahana Ruler and his wife
d) Sakatam Ruler and his wife

Question 47 :
Who observed that untouchables had to sound a clapper so that others could avoid seeing them?
a) Xuan Zang
b) Fa Xian
c) Megasthenes
d) Kalidasa

Question 48 :
In the Puranaruru excerpt, how is the patron described by the bard?
a) As a wealthy king who never helps the poor
b) As someone who pretends to be poor to avoid giving
c) As a generous man who helps bards despite not being very rich
d) As a blacksmith known for making spears

Chapter 4 : Thinkers, Beliefs, And Buildings

CONCISE KEY NOTES

Chapter Overview
- This chapter explores the philosophical traditions and religious movements that shaped early Indian society.
- It examines the role of Buddhism, Jainism, and Brahmanical traditions in shaping beliefs, practices, and architecture.
- It also looks at the construction and preservation of stupas and temples, highlighting their significance."
- Sanchi's Great Stupa is a major case study in this chapter.

A Glimpse Of Sanchi
- The most wonderful ancient buildings in the state of Bhopal are Sanchi Kanakhera.
- Taj-ul Iqbal Tarikh Bhopal (A History of Bhopal), translated by H.D. Barstow, 1876.
- European Interest: 19th-century Europeans fascinated by Sanchi Stupa.
- French Request: Sought Shahjehan Begum's permission to take the eastern gateway to France.
- Preservation: French & English settled for plaster-cast replicas; original remained in Bhopal.
- Begum's Role: Shahjehan & Sultan Jehan Begum funded site preservation.
- John Marshall: Dedicated volumes on Sanchi to Sultan Jehan Begum; she funded their publication.
- Survival: Escaped damage from contractors, builders, and artifact hunters.
- Significance: Key Buddhist center; transformed early Buddhist studies.
- Archaeological Value: Preserved by the Archaeological Survey of India.

The Background: A Time of Intellectual Ferment
- The mid-first millennium BCE saw the emergence of new thinkers like Zarathustra in Iran, kong zi in China, Socrates , plato and Aristotle in Greece and Buddha, Mahavira, and Upanishadic philosophers.
- It was also a period of social and economic change in the Ganga valley, leading to philosophical debates.
- Thinkers tried to answer fundamental questions about life, rebirth, and the ultimate reality.

Sacrificial Tradition and Its Critique:
- The Rigveda (c. 1500–1000 BCE) describes sacrifices to deities like Agni, Indra, and Soma for health and prosperity.
- Later, elaborate sacrifices like the rajasuya and ashvamedha were performed by kings.
- Thinkers like Buddha and Mahavira questioned the necessity of sacrifices and emphasized personal effort and morality.
- Kutagarashala – literally a hut with a pointed roof where travelling medicants Halted.

Buddhist Teaching and Texts
Life and Teachings of the Buddha
- Siddhartha Gautama, later known as the Buddha, was born into the Sakya clan and renounced royal life

- He sought enlightenment through meditation and taught the Four Noble Truths and the Eightfold Path.
- Buddhism rejected caste distinctions and emphasized ethical conduct over birth-based status."
- Buddha's message spread across the subcontinent and beyond through Central Asia to China , Korea and Japan , Sri Lanka, Myanmar, Thailand and Indonesia.

The Sutta Pitaka and Vinaya Pitaka:
- Buddha's teachings were compiled orally and later written down in Pali in texts like the Tipitaka.
- Tipitaka- literally three baskets to hold different types of texts.
- The Vinaya Pitaka contains rules for monks and nuns, while the Sutta Pitaka records Buddha's teachings, and Abhidhamma Pitaka dealt with Philosophical matters.
- When Buddhism spread to East Asia pilgrims Fa Xian and Xuan Zang travelled all the way from China to India in search of texts .

Followers of Buddha:
- Sangha - an organisation of monks who too become teachers of Dhamma.
- These monks live simply processing only the essential requisites for survival such as a bowl to receive food once a day, and lived on alms known as Bhikkhus.
- It was Ananda Buddha's dearest discipl who persuaded him to allow women into the Sangha Buddha's Foster mother Maha Pajapati Gotami was the first woman to be obtained as bhikkhuni.

Jainism and Its Principles: Mahavira and His Teachings
- Vardhamana who came to be known as Mahavira in the sixth century BCE.
- Mahavira, the 24th Tirthankara, preached non-violence (ahimsa) and asceticism."
- Most important idea in Jainism entire world is animated.
- Jain philosophy emphasized the eternal nature of the soul and the role of karma.
- Monks and nuns followed 5 strict vows of -non-violence, truth, celibacy, and non-possessiveness.

Stupas and Buddhist Architecture: The Great Stupa
- Stupas were built to house Buddha's relics and became sacred sites.
- Chaitya originated from the word Chita meaning funeral Pyre.
- The Sanchi stupa, commissioned by Ashoka, remains a major Buddhist monument.
- It has a large hemispherical dome, a harmika, a chhatri, and intricately carved gateways.
- To stupas describe places associated with Buddha's life- born - Lumbini, enlightenment- Bodh Gaya , First sermon- Sarnath , nibbana - Kusinagara
- By second century number of stupas at Bharhut, Sanchi and Sarnath had been built .
- Later elaborately carved with niches and sculptures- Amaravati , Shah- ji - ki - Dheri Peshawar (Pakistan) .

How Were Stupas Built?
- Inscriptions found on railings and pillars at stupas record donations from kings, merchants, artisans, and monks.
- The Satavahanas and local guilds financed the construction of Sanchi's gateways.

Amaravati
- 1796: Local raja found Amaravati Stupa ruins, reused stones.
- Colin Mackenzie: British official visited, documented sculptures (unpublished).

- 1854: Walter Elliot (Guntur commissioner) collected Amaravati sculptures, took them to Madras ("Elliot marbles").
- Amaravati Stupa: One of the largest Buddhist stupas.
- 1850s: Slabs from Amaravati sent to Calcutta, Madras, London.
- British Officials: Used sculptures in gardens; removals continued.
- H.H. Cole (Archaeologist): " it seems to me a suicidal and indefensible policy to allow the country to be looted of original works of ancient art " Opposed removal, favored plaster-cast replicas.

Why Sanchi survived Amaravati not ?

- Amaravati's Downfall: Discovered before scholars realized preservation's importance.
- Sanchi (1818): Three gateways standing, fourth fallen but intact; mound in good condition.

Preservation Factors: Sanchi remained intact, while Amaravati was reduced to a mound.

Symbolism in Buddhist Art

- Wandering storytellers carrying Scrolls - Charanachitras.
- Early Buddhist art used symbols like the wheel (dharma chakra), Bodhi tree, and empty throne instead of depicting Buddha.
- Jataka tales were illustrated on stupas, showing Buddha's previous lives.

Rise Of Temple Architecture: The Emergence of Hindu Temples

- The first temples appeared around the 3rd century CE, housing images of gods like Vishnu and Shiva.
- Early temples had a garbhagriha (sanctum), while later ones had towering shikharas.

Kailashnatha Temple: A Marvel of Rock-Cut Architecture

- Ellora's Kailashnatha Temple was carved from a single rock, demonstrating advanced engineering.

Timeline Of Major Events

- c. 1500-1000 BCE: Early Vedic traditions emerge.
- c. 600 BCE: Buddha and Mahavira spread their teachings.
- c. 300 BCE: Ashoka's patronage leads to the expansion of Buddhism.
- c. 200 BCE: The first stupas are constructed.
- c. 100 CE: Mahayana Buddhism develops.
- c. 300 CE: Earliest Hindu temples built.
- c. 600 CE: Kailashnatha Temple at Ellora is carved from rock.
- 1814- founding of the Indian Museum Calcutta.

Important Figures

Fig. 4.1
A sculpture from Sanchi

Fig. 4.2
Shahjehan Begum

Fig. 4.5
An image of a tirthankara from
Mathura, c. third century CE

Fig. 4.3
The Great Stupa at Sanchi

Fig. 4.6
A page from a fourteenth-century
Jaina manuscript

Fig. 4.7
A sculpture (c. 200 CE) from
Amaravati (Andhra Pradesh),
depicting the departure of the
Buddha from his palace

Fig. 4.8
A woman water-carrier, Mathura,
c. third century CE

Fig. 4.9
A votive inscription from Sanchi
Hundreds of similar inscriptions
have also been found at Bharhut
and Amaravati.

Important Figures

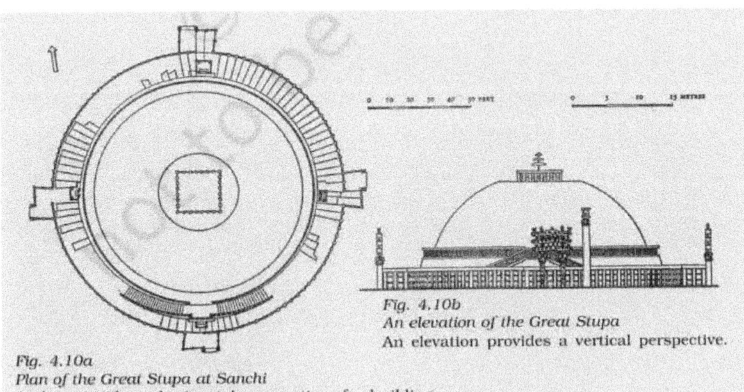

Fig. 4.10a
Plan of the Great Stupa at Sanchi
A plan provides a horizontal perspective of a building.

Fig. 4.10b
An elevation of the Great Stupa
An elevation provides a vertical perspective.

Fig. 4.11
The eastern gateway, Sanchi
Notice the vibrant sculpture.

Fig. 4.12
A section of the gateway

Fig. 4.13
A part of the northern gateway

Fig. 4.14 (far right)
Worshipping the Bodhi tree

Fig. 4.15 (middle right)
Worshipping the stupa

Fig. 4.16 (below)
Setting in motion the wheel of dharma

Important Figures

Fig. 4.17
The woman at the gate

Fig. 4.18
An elephant at Sanchi

Fig. 4.19
Gajalakshmi

Fig. 4.20
A painting from Ajanta
Note the seated figure and those
serving him.

Fig. 4.21
A serpent at Sanchi

Fig. 4.22
An image of the Buddha from
Mathura, c. first century CE

Fig. 4.24
An image of Durga, Mahabalipuram
(Tamil Nadu), c. sixth century CE

Fig. 4.23
The Varaha or boar avatar of
Vishnu rescuing the earth goddess,
Aihole (Karnataka) c. sixth
century CE

Important Figures

Fig. 4.25
A temple in Deogarh
(Uttar Pradesh), c. fifth century CE

Fig. 4.26
Vishnu reclining on the serpent
Sheshnag, sculpture from Deogarh
(Uttar Pradesh), c. fifth century CE

Fig. 4.27
Entrance to a cave at Barabar
(Bihar), c. third century BCE

Fig. 4.28
Kailashnatha Temple, Ellora
(Maharashtra). This entire structure
is carved out of a single piece of
rock.

Fig. 4.29
A Bodhisatta from Gandhara
Note the clothes and the hairstyle.

Fig. 4.30
A rock-cut sculptural panel at
Mahabalipuram

Chapter 4 : Mapwork

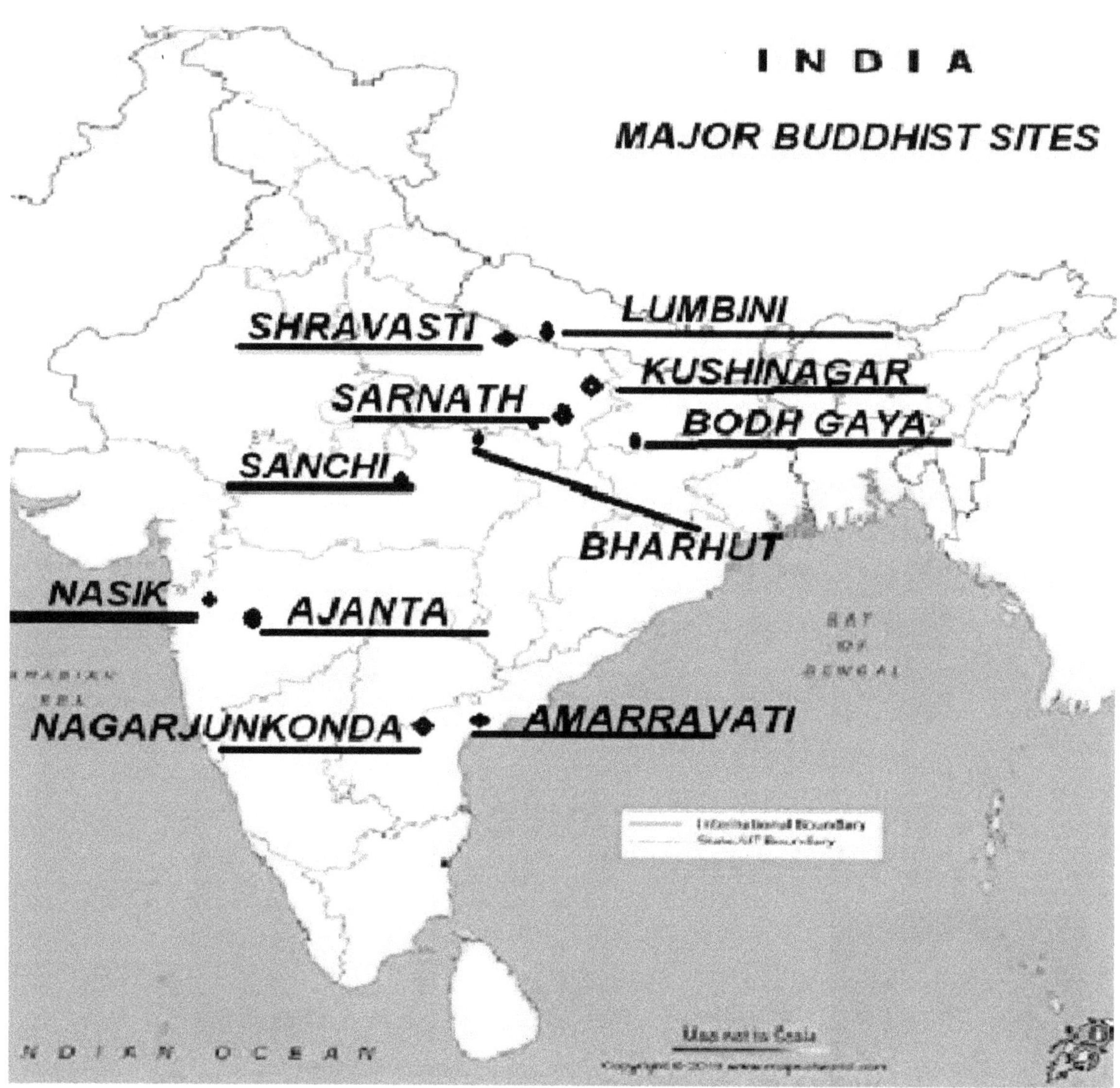

Chapter 4 : Thinkers, Beliefs, And Buildings

QUESTIONS FROM ARCHIVES

Question 1 :
Where is Sanchi located ?
a.Gwalior
b.Bhopal
c.Bhubaneshwar
d.Aurangabad

Question 2 :
"Taj–ul–Iqbal Tarikh Bhopal " (A History of
Bhopal) was translated by _______
a) H.D.Barstow
b) Alexander Cunningham
c) John Marshall
d) Shahjehan Begum.

Question 3 :
Match the following :

Column A	Column B
i) Zarathustra	a) Greece
ii) Plato & Aristotle	b) India
iii) Kong zi	c) Iran
iv) Gautama Buddha	d) China

a) i–a, ii–b, iii–c, iv–d
b) i–c, ii–d, iii–b , iv–a
c) i–c, ii–d, iii– a , iv–b
d) i–c , ii–a , iii–d , iv–b

Question 4 :
 A hut with a pointed roof is known as _?
a.Kutagrashala
b.Velyvan
c.Amravatika
d.Jetavan

Question 5 :
Which pitaka included rules and regulations
for those who joined the sangha or monastic
order?
a.Sutta Pitaka
b.Abhidhamma Pitaka
c.Vinaya Pitaka
d.Tipitaka

Question 6 :
 Buddha's teachings are found mainly in which
pitaka?
a.Tipitaka
b.Sutta Pitaka
c.Vinaya Pitaka
d.Abhidhamma Pitaka

Question 7 :
Zarathustra belongs to which country ?
a.India
b.China
c.Greece
d.Iran

Question 8 :
 Which pitaka deals with philosophical matters?
a.Vinaya Pitaka
b.Sutta Pitaka
c.Dipavamsa
d.Abhidhamma Pitaka

Question 9 :
Mahavira was formerly known as __________
a.Vardhaman
b.None of these
c.Ajatasattu
d.Siddharth

Question 10 :
The RigVeda consist of hymns in praise of
variety of dieties especially -----
a. Agni,Indra,Soma
b. Agni,Soma,Pavan
c. Agni,Brahma,Shiva
d. Shiva,Vishnu,Brahma

Question 11 :
Agni is the god of ----
a. Water
b. Air
c. Earth
d. Fire

Question 12 :
Which are the following statement(s) is/are correct about the idea in Jainism:
i) the most important idea in Jainism is that the entire world is animated.
ii) Asceticism and penance are required to free oneself from the cycle of Karma.
iii) non- injury to living beings, specially to humans ,animals ,plants, and insects is Central to Jaina philosophy.
iv) the principal of ahimsa is emphasized with Buddhism.
a. i & ii are correct
b. ii & iv are correct
c. i, ii, iii are correct
d. i, iii, iv are correct

Question 13 :
Assertion - Jaina monks and nuns took five vows.
Reason - Abstain from killing, stealing, and lying ,observe celibacy, abstain from possessing property.
a) Both A and R are true and R is the correct explanation of A.
b) Both A and R are true but R is not the correct explanation of A.
c) A is true but R is false.
d) R is true but A is false.

Question 14 :
What is Hagiography?
a.A biography of rulers
b. A Biography of authors
c. A Biography of gods
d.A biography of saints and spiritual leaders

Question 15 :
Gautam Buddha's father was the chief of ___________ clan.
a.Sakya
b.Shakha
c.Satavahana
d. Brahmana

Question 16 :
Where did Buddha born ?
a.Lumbini
b.Bodh Gaya
c.Kushinagar
d.Sarnath

Question 17 :
Who was the first woman to be ordained as Bhikkuni ?
a.Mahamaya
b. Ananda
c. Yashoda
d.Mahapajapati Gotami

Question 18 :
" Be lamps unto yourself as all of you must workout your own liberation" -This line is said by whom ?
a. Vardhamana
b.Buddha
c. Mahavira
d.Mahapajapati gotami

Question 19 :
Where did Buddha give his 1st sermon ?
a.Lumbini
b.Bodh Gaya
c.Kushinagar
d.Sarnath

Question 20 :
Where did Buddha attained enlightenment ?
a.Lumbini
b.Bodh Gaya
c.Kushinagar
d.Sarnath

Question 21 :
Fa Xian and Xuan Zang came from which country ?
a. Sri Lanka
b. China
c. Indonesia
d. Japan

Question 22 :
Relics of the Buddha such as his body remains or objects used by him were buried here these were known as—
a. Museum
b.Stupa
c. Harmika
d. Yashti

Question 23 :
Ashokavandana is a _______ text ?
a.Hindu
b.Ajivika
c.Buddhist
d.Jaina

Question 24 :
Shah-ji-ki-Dheri is located in?
a.Bharhut
b.Peshawar
c. Bhopal
d.Amravati

Question 25 :
A balcony-like structure that represents the abode of the god is called __?
a.Harmika
b.Yashti
c. Chhatri
d.Anda

Question 26 :
 Where are Elliot marbles situated ?
a.Guntur
b.Bharut
c.Amaravati
d.Madras

Question 27 :
Who wrote the line "It seems to me a suicidal and indefensible policy to allow the country to be looted of original works of ancient art." ?
a.Colin Mackenzie
b.H.H. Cole
c.Walter Elliot
d.None of these

Question 28 :
In 1854 who was hired as the Commissioner of Guntur (Andhra Pradesh) ?
a.Colin Mackenzie
b.H.H. Cole
c.Walter Elliot
d.None of these

Question 29 :
Assertion - Amravati was discovered before Scholars understood the value of the finds and realize how critical it was to preserve things where they had been found instead of removing them from the site.
Reason - Sanchi was discovered in 1818, there were number of factors help to keep Sanchi as it was and so it stands .
a) Both A and R are true and R is the correct explanation of A.
b) Both A and R are true but R is not the correct explanation of A.
c) A is true but R is false.
d) R is true but A is false.

Question 30 :
Sanchi was discovered in-
a. 1818
b. 1819
c. 1820
d. 1870

Question 31 :
 Which of the following options is the most probable explanation for the incorporation of the 'Shailabhanjika' Motif in Sanchi Stupa?
a.Religious Idol
b.Auspicious Symbol
c.Strength and Wisdom
d.Mahaparinibbana

Question 32 :
Wandering storytellers carrying Scrolls of the cloth or paper with pictures on them and pointing to the pictures as they tell the story were known as-
a. Charanachitras
b. Monks
c .Nuns
d. None of these

Question 33 :
From which country Buddhism spread to East Asia ?
a. Japan
b. Tibet
c. China
d. India

Chapter 5 : Trough The Eyes Of Travellers

CONCISE KEY NOTES

Chapter Overview
- This chapter explores accounts of foreign travellers who visited the Indian subcontinent between the 10th and 17th centuries.
- These travellers included Al-Biruni (11th century, from Uzbekistan), Ibn Battuta (14th century, from Morocco), and FranÇois Bernier (17th century, from France).
- Their writings give valuable insights into social, cultural, economic, and political life.
- They observed local customs and practices that were often overlooked by indigenous writers.

Al-Biruni And The Kitab-Ul-Hind (11th Century):
- Born in 973 CE in Khwarizm (modern Uzbekistan), Al-Biruni was a scholar well-versed in Arabic, Persian, Syriac, and Sanskrit.
- He came to India during Mahmud of Ghazni's invasion in 1017.
- Fascinated by Indian culture, he learned Sanskrit and translated many Hindu texts into Arabic.

The Kitab-ul-Hind: A Systematic Study of India
- Written in Arabic, it covered religion, astronomy, festivals, alchemy, social customs, and laws in 80 chapters.
- Metrology - science of measurement.
- Al-Biruni used a structured approach: asking a question, describing Hindu traditions, and then comparing them with other cultures.
- He admired India's intellectual achievements but criticized its rigid caste system.
- The term "Hindu" was derived from an old Persian word used sixth fifth century BCE, to refer to the region east of the river Sindhu (indus)
- Arabs in Persian called the region Al Hind and the people Hindi.
- Later Turks referred to the people east of the Indus as Hindu and their land as Hindustan and their language as Hindavi.

Overcoming Barriers To Understanding:
- Al-Biruni's Challenge: He recognized obstacles in understanding Indian society.
- Language Barrier: Sanskrit was vastly different from Arabic and Persian, making translation difficult.
- Religious Differences: The contrast in beliefs and practices created another barrier.
- Cultural Insularity: The local population's self-absorption hindered his understanding.
- His Approach: He relied heavily on Brahmanical texts, including the Vedas, Puranas, Bhagavad Gita, Patanjali's works, and Manusmriti, to study Indian society.

Al-Biruni's description on caste system:
- Al-Biruni compared Indian caste divisions with Persian social classes.
- He criticized the idea of pollution in the caste system, arguing that all things strive for purity.
- He noted that while Islam preached equality, Indian society was hierarchical.

Ibn Battuta And The Rihla (14th Century)

- Born in 1304 in Tangier, Morocco, Ibn Battuta was a judge and scholar who traveled extensively.
- He visited India in 1333 and was appointed qazi (judge) by Muhammad bin Tughlaq.
- He documented his experiences in Rihlā, a detailed travelogue."
- Chinese port town – Zaytun (now known as Quanzhou)
- Ibn battuta's account is often compared with Marco Polo who visited China and also India from his home iin Venice in the late 13th century.
- According to Ibn Battuta – 40 days to travel from Multan to Delhi .
- 50 days from Sindh to Delhi.
- Distance from Daulatabad to Delhi covered in 40 days, Gwalior to Delhi took 10 days.

Observations on Indian Society:
- Ibn Battuta arrived in Delhi in the 14th century.
- Ibn Battuta described Indian cities as wealthy and densely populated, with thriving markets.
- He found the postal system highly efficient, with foot-posts (dawa) and horse-posts (uluq).
- The foot post has three stations per mile also the foot post is Quicker than the horsposed and used to transport the fruits of Khurasan which are much desired in India.
- He noted that Delhi was well-fortified, with high walls and strong gates.
- Daulatabad market price for male and female singers which is known as tarababad.

Unique Descriptions: The Coconut and the Paan
- He compared coconuts to human heads and described how betel leaves were chewed with areca nut.
- His descriptions helped foreign readers visualize Indian flora and customs.

Ibn Battuta on Indian Trade and Agriculture
- He observed that Indian textiles, especially muslin, were highly valued worldwide.
- He noted that Indian farmers cultivated two crops annually due to fertile soil.
- Indian bazaars were centers of social and cultural life, featuring music, dance, and public performances.
- The travelogue of Abdur Razzaq written in 1440s.
- Calicut – Present day Kozhikode in Kerala.

Francois Bernier And His Critical Account (17th Century):
- A French doctor, philosopher, and historian, Bernier lived in India from 1656 to 1668.
- He was a physician to Dara Shukoh and later worked under Danishmand Khan.
- "Unlike Ibn Battuta, he criticized Indian society, comparing it negatively with Europe."
- Berniers works were published in France in 1670 –71.
- Translated into English Dutch German and Italian within next five years.
- 1725- account reprinted eight times in French.
- 1684- reprinted Three times in English.

Bernier on Mughal Landownership:
- He wrongly believed that all land in Mughal India was owned by the emperor.
- He argued that lack of private property led to economic stagnation and peasant oppression.
- His views influenced European ideas of 'oriental despotism'.
- Concept of the Asiatic mode of production – Karl Marx (19th century)

Depiction of Indian Cities:
- Bernier described Mughal cities as 'camp towns' that depended on imperial presence.
- However, historical records show that towns had strong economic foundations.
- Merchants in western India these group called Mahajans and their chief Sheth .
- In urban centres such a Ahmedabad Mahajans were collectively represented by the Chief of the merchant community who called Nagar Sheth.

Bernier on the Indian Caste System
- He saw Indian society as rigid, with a stark divide between the rich and the poor.
- He claimed there was no middle class, though historical evidence contradicts this.

Role Of Women, Slavery and Social Life
- Women participated in agriculture, trade, and court politics.
- Royal women influenced diplomacy and administration.
- Bernier noted the practice of sati but ignored women's broader social roles.
- Ibn Battuta noted that slaves were traded and gifted regularly.
- Some slaves served as musicians and palace guards.
- Female slaves were sometimes spies for the Sultan.

Other Travellers who visited the subcontinent

- Portuguese arrived in India in about 1500
- Jesuit Roberto Nobili
- Duarte barbosa who wrote a detailed account of trade and Society in South India.
- Famous French Jeweller Jean Baptiste Tavernier who travelled India at least six times.
- Italian doctor Manucci never return to Europe and settle down in India.
- Palsaery A Dutch Traveller visited subcontinent early decades of 17th century.
- Afanasii Nikitn 15th century Russia.

Important Figures

A boat carrying passengers, a terracotta sculpture from a temple in Bengal (c. seventeenth-eighteenth centuries)

A seventeenth - century painting depicting Bernier in European clothes

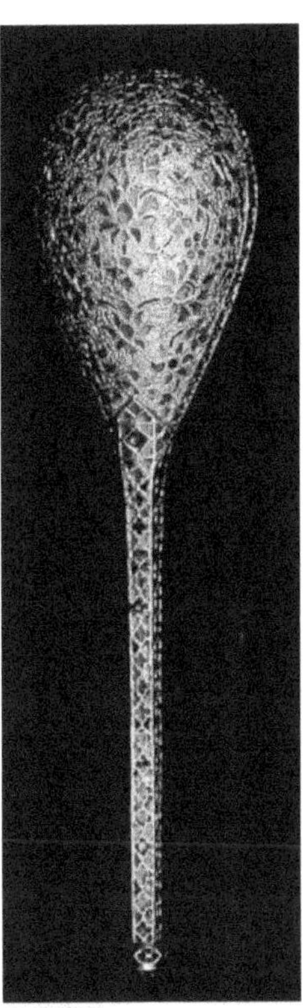

Fig. 5.12
A gold spoon studded with emeralds and rubies, an example of the dexterity of Mughal artisans

Chapter 5 : Through the Eyes Of Travellers

QUESTIONS FROM ARCHIVES

Question 1 :
Al-Biruni came from ___________.
a) France
b) Morocco
c) Portugal
d) Uzbekistan

Question 2 :
Who among the following was a Moroccan traveller
a) Al-Biruni
b) Francois Bernier
c) Abdur Razzaq
d) Ibn Battuta

Question 3 :
Al-Biruni studied the works of which of these
Greek Philosophers ?
a) Archimedes
b) Euclid
c) Plato
d) None of these

Question 4 :
Metrology is the science of -----
a) measurement
b) alchemy
c) astronomy
d) calculating distance

Question 5 : Who belongs to Uzbekistan?
a.Ibn Batuta
b.Abdur Razzaq
c.Francois Bernier
d.Al- Biruni

Question 6 :
Abdur Razzaq Samarqandi belongs to which place ?
a.Morocco
b.Uzbekistan
c.Kabul
d.Herat

Question 7 :
Who took Al- Biruni to Ghazni ?
a.Sultan Mahmud
b.Akbar
c.Ahmed Shah Abdali
d.Nadir Shah

Question 8 :
The book 'Kitab-ul-Hind' was written by----a.
Ibn-Battuta
b. Bernier
c. Al-Biruni
d. Tavernier

Question 9 :
Where did Al-Biruni develop an interest in
India ?
 a. China
 b. Uzbekistan
 c. Punjab
 d. Ghazni

Question 10 :
Who gave the most important description of
Vijayanagara in the fifteenth century ?

a. Marco Polo
b. Al-Biruni
c. Abdur Razzaq
d. Francois Bernier

Question 11 :
Who among the following translated several
sanskrit works including Patanjali's work on
grammar into Arabic ?

a. Marco Polo
b. Al-Biruni
c. Ibn Battuta
d. Mahmud Balkhi

Question 12 :
Consider the following statement and choose the
incorrect among them :

i) Al-Biruni's Kitab-ul-Hind , written in Arabic
ii) It's a voluminous text divided into 100
chapters.
iii) It consists subjects such as
religion,philosophy, festivals,astronomy,
alchemy, social life , laws and metrology .
a. (I) is incorrect
b. (II) is incorrect
c. (III) is incorrect
d. None of these

Question 13 :
Al-Biruni was born in 973 in __________ present day Uzbekistan
a. Kabul
b.Ghazni
c. Khwarizm
d. Syria

Question 14 :
How many chapters is " Kitab-ul-Hind " divided into ?
a. Eighteen
b. Eighty
c. Eight
d. Eighty eight

Question 15 :
Ibn Battuta's book of travels Is called-
a. Kitab-ul-Hind
b. Travels in the Mughal Empire
c. Rihla
d.None of these

Question 16 :
Which among the following is a Moroccan traveller ?
a. Ibn Battuta
b. Duarte Barbosa
c. Manucci
d. Francois Bernier

Question 17 : Ibn Battuta born in --
a. Khwarizm
b.Tangier
c. Istanbul
d. Sultan

Question 18 :
Islamic religious law is known as -----
a. Ulama
b. Sharia
c. Both a and b
d.None of these

Question 19 :
Ibn Battuta set off for India In the year ----
a. 1332-1333
b. 1442-1443
c. 1732-1733
d. 1221-1222

Question 20 :
After how many years did Ibn Batuta return home ?
a.27
b.32
c.30
d.25

Question 21 :
When Ibn Battuta reached sindh in 1333 who was the sultan of Delhi ?
a. Jahangir
b. Razia Sultana
c. Sultan Mahmud
d. Muhammad Bin Tughlaq

Question 22 :
Which one of the following statements is appropriate about Ibn Battuta?
i) He was appointed as Qazi during Muhammad Bin Tughlaq's empire .
ii) He wrote the book Travels in the Mughal empire.
iii) He translated Patanjali's work.
iv) He was a historian, philosopher and doctor

Question 23 :
Who among the following travellers account is often compared with that of Marco Polo ?
a. Jean Baptiste Tavernier
b. Manucci
c. Al-Biruni
d. Ibn Battuta

Question 24 :
According to Ibn Battuta how many days it took to travel from Sind to Delhi ?
a. 40
b. 50
c. 30
d. 60

Question 25 :
Which of the following travellers wrote detailed account of trade and society in South India.
a. Roberto Nobili
b. Francois Bernier
c. Manucci
d. Duarte Barbosa

Question 26 :
Who among the following was one of the most famous French jeweller ?
a. Roberto Nobili
b. Jean Baptiste Tavernier
c. Manucci
d. Duarte Barbosa

Question 27 :
Who was the eldest son of emperor Shah Jahan ?
a. Dara shukoh
b. Shah Shuja
c. Murad Baksh
d. Aurangzeb

Question 28 :
To which of these countries did Francois Bernier belong to ?
a. Britain
b.England
c. Italy
d. France

Question 29 :
To which king did Francois Bernier dedicate his major writings ?
a. Louis XIV
b. Louis XVI
c. Louis XIII
d. Louis XII

Question 30 :
Which of the following was not one of the barriers as discussed by Al-Biruni ?
a. Language
b. Difference in religious beliefs and practices
c. Slavery
d. The self absorption & consequent insularity of the local population.

Question 31 :
Who wrote the description about the paan and the coconut ?
a. Al-Biruni
b. Ibn-Battuta
c. Francois Bernier
d. Manucci

Question 32 :
Tarababad is __________.
a. Market place for musical instruments
b. Market place for female singers
c. Market place for male singers
d. Market place for male & female singers

Question 33 :
Assertion (A)- Ibn-Battuta found Indian subcontinent full of exciting opportunities.
Reason (R) - Ibn Battuta account's that most cities had crowded streets, bright colourful markets stacked with wide variety of goods .

a. Both Assertion (A) and reason (R) are correct and Reason (R) is the correct explanation of Assertion (A).
b.Both Assertion (A) and reason (R) are correct but Reason (R) is not the correct explanation of Assertion (A).
c. Assertion (A) is correct , Reason (R) is incorrect
d.Assertion (A) is incorrect , Reason (R) is correct

Question 34 :
According to Ibn Battuta's account, the city that rivalled Delhi in size __________
a. Gwalior
b. Tarababad
c. Daulatabad
d. Multan

Question 35 :
The travelogue of Abdur Razzaq was written in -
a. 1440s
b. 1450s
c. 1470s
d. 1480s

Question 36 :
From whose account we get to know about the efficient postal system ?
a. Al-Biruni
b. Francois Bernier
c. Ibn-Battuta
d. None of these

Question 37 :
The horse post is also known as -
a. Uluq
b. Dawa
c. Pahi-kashta
d. None of these

Question 38 :
Who among the following travellers wrote the book " Travels in the mughal empire " ?
a. Manucci
b. Pelsaert
c.Ibn-Battuta
d. Bernier

Question 39 :
The concept of the Asiatic mode of production in the 19th century was given by
a. Karl Marx
b. Montesquieu
c. Manucci
d. AbulFazl

Question 40 :
According to Bernier the negative effects of the crown ownership of land was :
1. Absence of ownership of land to the farmers.
2. poor agricultural production.
3. Land holders could not pass on their land to their children.
4. Large amount of investments.
Which among the following statement(s) are correct
a. 1 & 2
b. 1,2,3
c. 1 & 3
d. 1 & 4

Question 41 :
Which one of the following travellers described Mughal cities as " camp towns "
a. Karl Marx
b. Ibn-Battuta
c. Al-Biruni
d. Bernier

Question 42 :
 Who were nagarsheth ?
a. Head of the merchant community
b. Head of village community
c. Head of village panchayat
d. None of the above

Question 43 :
Who among the following travellers have mentioned " A strange nation " when he saw the populated port of Calicut (present-day Kozhikode) in Kerala ?
a. Al-Biruni
b. Ibn-Battuta
c. Francois Bernier
d. Abdur Razzaq

Question 44 :
who among the following travellers given the description of sati ?
a. Al-Biruni
b. Ibn-Battuta
c. Francois Bernier
d. Abdur Razzaq

Question 45 :
who among the following travellers given the   description of female slaves ?
a. Al-Biruni
b. Ibn-Battuta
c. Francois Bernier
d. Abdur Razzaq

Question 46 :
Kozhikode is the name of which medieval town/city ?
a. Varanasi
b. Delhi
c. Calicut
d. Hampi

Chapter 6 : Bhakti-Sufi Traditions

CONCISE KEY NOTES

Religious Landscape & Sources:
- Oral compositions by poet-saints were later compiled by disciples.
- Hagiographies (saints' biographies) provide insights but are not always historically accurate.

"Great" & "Little" Traditions:
- Coined by sociologist Robert Redfield.
- Great Tradition: Practices from dominant social categories (priests, rulers).
- Little Tradition: Local customs different from the mainstream.
- Interaction led to mutual adaptation of both traditions.

Mosaic of Religious Beliefs & Practices:
- Increasing worship of Vishnu, Shiva, and the Goddess in multiple forms.

Integration of Cults
- Puranic traditions spread Brahmanical ideas to women & Shudras.
- Brahmanas also adapted local beliefs, leading to fusion.
- Example: Jagannatha in Puri – a tribal deity merged with Vishnu worship.
- Goddess worship also absorbed local deities into Puranic identities (e.g., Lakshmi, Parvati).

Difference & Conflict:
- Tantric Practices: Inclusive of caste & gender, influenced Shaivism & Buddhism.
- Vedic vs. Puranic traditions: Vedic deities (Agni, Indra) declined, while Vishnu, Shiva, and Goddess worship expanded.
- Bhakti traditions emerged in contrast to orthodox Vedic rituals, emphasizing devotion over rituals.

Early traditions of Bhakti Two categories:
- Saguna Bhakti (with form/attributes) - worship of deities like Vishnu, Shiva.
- Nirguna Bhakti (formless) - abstract devotion, often anti–idolatry.

Alvars & Nayanars
- Alvars: Devotees of Vishnu.
- Nayanars: Devotees of Shiva.
- Sang devotional hymns, identified sacred shrines, leading to temple constructions.

Attitudes Towards Caste:
- Alvars & Nayanars challenged caste hierarchy.
- Bhakti saints hailed from diverse backgrounds, including lower castes.
- Nalayira Divyaprabandham (Alvar compositions) was called the "Tamil Veda", equating it with the Sanskrit Vedas.
- Twelve Alvars composition were compiled in an Anthology known as Nalayira Divyaprabandham (Four thousand sacred composition)
- Poems of Appar Sambandar Sundarar formed The Tevaram.

Women in Bhakti:
- Andal: Alvar who saw herself as Vishnu's beloved.
- Karaikkal Ammaiyar: Nayanar who followed asceticism, rejecting traditional beauty norms.
- Tondaradippodi = Alvar who was the chaturvedin (bramhana)
- Marperu = Lord Shiva who resides in Thanjavur, Tamil Nadu.

Relations with the State:
- Bhakti poets opposed Buddhism & Jainism (competition for royal patronage).
- Chola rulers (9th-13th century) built grand Shiva & Vishnu temples (e.g., Chidambaram, Thanjavur, Gangaikondacholapuram).
- Royal support led to Bhakti hymns becoming part of temple rituals.
- Chola Ruler (Parankata-I) consecrated metal images of Appar Sambandar Sundarar in Shiva Temples which were carried in processions during the festival of the saints.

Basavanna & Virashaiva Tradition (12th century, Karnataka):
- Led by Basavanna, minister in Kalachuri court.
- Followers: Virashaivas (Lingayats), worshippers of Shiva as Linga.
- Rejected caste system, rebirth theory, and followed burial over cremation.
- Encouraged widow remarriage & post-puberty marriages.
- Virashaiva tradition is derived from Vachanas sayings composed in Kannadiga from women and men who joined the movement.

Islamic Rule & Religious Policies:
- In 711, Arab General Muhammad Qasir conquered Sindh which became part of Caliph's domain.
- Arab and Turks established Delhi Sultanate (13th century) → Followed by regional Sultanates & Mughal Empire.
- Muslim rulers guided by Shari'a (Islamic law).
- Zimmi Status: Non-Muslims (Jews, Christians, Hindus) protected under Muslim rule but paid Jizya tax.
- Mughals, esp. Akbar & Aurangzeb, gave land & tax exemptions to non-Muslim religious institutions.
- Ulama = Scholars of Islamic Studies.

Shari'a (Islamic Law):
- Based on Qur'an & Hadis (Prophet's words & deeds).
- Expanded using Qiyas (analogy) & Ijma (community consensus).

Popular Practice of Islam:
- Core beliefs: Five Pillars of Islam
    a. Shahada (Faith in one God, Allah, & Prophet Muhammad).
    b. Salat (5 daily prayers).
    c. Zakat (Charity).
    d. Sawm (Fasting in Ramzan).
    e. Hajj (Pilgrimage to Mecca).
- Islam blended with local traditions (e.g., Khojahs used local languages & devotional poetry like ginans).
- Malabar Coast Muslims adopted matriliny & local customs.

Mosque Architecture:
- Universal features: Orientation towards Mecca, Mihrab (prayer niche), Minbar (pulpit).
- Local adaptations: Different materials & styles (e.g., Kerala mosques with shikhara-like roofs).

Evolution of Religious Identities:
- Terms Hindu & Muslim were not common initially.
- People were identified by regions (e.g., Turks = Turushka, Persians = Parashika).
- Mlechchha: Term for foreign migrants, not necessarily a religious identity.

Sufism (Islamic Mysticism):
- Sufis rejected materialism & emphasized love & devotion to God.
- Khanqahs (hospices) established by Shaikhs/Pirs for disciples (murids).
- Silsilas (spiritual lineages) connected masters to Prophet Muhammad.

Khanqahs & Activities:
- Khanqah: Sufi lodge with a mosque, courtyard, and boundary wall.
- Open kitchen (langar) runs on futuh (charity).
- People from all backgrounds (soldiers, merchants, poets, yogis) visited for discipleship, healing, and blessings.
- Famous visitors: Amir Khusrau, Amir Hasan Sijzi, historian Ziyauddin Barani.

Major Chishti Sufi Teachers & Dargahs:

MAJOR TEACHERS OF THE CHISHTI *SILSILA*		
SUFI TEACHERS	YEAR OF DEATH	LOCATION OF *DARGAH*
Shaikh Muinuddin Sijzi	1235	Ajmer (Rajasthan)
Khwaja Qutbuddin Bakhtiyar Kaki	1235	Delhi
Shaikh Fariduddin Ganj-i Shakar	1265	Ajodhan (Pakistan)
Shaikh Nizamuddin Auliya	1325	Delhi
Shaikh Nasiruddin Chiragh-i Dehli	1356	Delhi

Chishti Devotional Practices:
- Ziyarat (Pilgrimage): Visiting Sufi shrines for spiritual grace (barakat).
- Most Revered Shrine: Khwaja Muinuddin Chishti (Ajmer).
- Qawwali & Sama': Mystical music and zikr (divine name chanting) for divine connection.
- Royal Patronage: Akbar visited Ajmer Dargah 14 times, donated a cauldron for pilgrims' meals.

Data Ganj Bakhsh (Lahore):
- Abu'l Hasan al Hujwiri (1039) wrote *Kashful-Mahjub* on Sufism.
- His tomb, *Data Darbar*, became a major pilgrimage site.

Mughal Devotion to Sufis:
- Jahanara's Pilgrimage to Ajmer (1643):
  - Walked barefoot, applied itar (perfume) on the tomb.
  - Considered Ajmer Dargah sacred, followed rituals strictly.

Sufi Poetry & Languages:
- Hindavi & Local Languages: Used for communication.
- Baba Farid's verses: Incorporated in *Guru Granth Sahib*.
- Malik Muhammad Jayasi's *Padmavat*: Used love as an allegory for the soul's journey to the divine.
- Bijapur Sufis: Composed poems in *Dakhani* (Urdu variant), similar to Lingayat vachanas and Marathi abhangs.

Sufis and the State:
- Suhrawardi (Delhi Sultans) and Naqshbandi (Mughals) were state-associated but in different ways from Chishtis.
- Some sufis accepted courtly positions, but many refused state gifts.
- Example: Shaikh Nizamuddin Auliya rejected land and gardens offered by a ruler, as did Shaikh Fariduddin before him.

Bhakti-Sufi Traditions & Dialogue:
- Kabir (14th-15th century): A key poet-saint who rejected religious divisions.
- Hagiographies claim that Kabir was born hindu and raised by a poor muslim family who belongs to the community of Weavers or Julahas according to Vaishnava tradition.
- His verses are found in:
  - *Kabir Bijak* (Varanasi)
  - *Kabir Granthavali* (Rajasthan)
  - *Adi Granth Sahib* (Sikh scripture)
- Used different religious terms for the divine (Allah, Ram, Brahman, Atman).
- Criticized both Hindu polytheism & Muslim ritualism.
- His Guru was Ramananda.

Baba Guru Nanak (1469-1539):
- Born in Punjab in a Hindu merchant family, influenced by sufis & bhaktas.
- Rejected ritualistic practices & emphasized *nirguna bhakti* (formless God).
- Founded Sikhism, establishing community worship (*sangat*) & spiritual successors (*gurus*).
- His hymns, along with others', were compiled in the *Adi Granth Sahib* by Guru Arjan.
- Guru Gobind Singh later formalized Sikh identity with the *Khalsa Panth*.
- 9th Guru was Guru Teg Bahadur.

Shankaradeva and Vaishnavism in Assam:
- 15th-century proponent of Bhagavati Dharma (based on Bhagavad Gita & Bhagavata Purana).
- Emphasized Naam Kirtan (recitation of Lord's names) and Sat Sanga (congregations).
- Established Satra (monasteries) & Naam Ghar (prayer halls).
- Major work: Kirtana-ghosha.

Meerabai (1498-1547 CE) – Bhakti Poetess:
- Rajput princess, married into the Mewar royal family.
- Devoted to Krishna, considered him her husband (Sakhi Bhava).
- Faced opposition from her in-laws but continued her devotion.
- Composed bhajans in Braj, Rajasthani, and Gujarati.
- Major Works: Padavali (collection of bhajans).
- Meerabai's preceptor (guru) is believed to be Ravidas (Raidas), a leather worker.
- Meerabai considered him her spiritual guide and even mentioned him in her bhajans.

Important Figures

A twelfth-century bronze sculpture of Manikkavachakar, a devotee of Shiva who composed beautiful devotional songs in Tamil

Jagannatha (extreme right) with his sister Subhadra (centre) and his brother Balarama (left)

Sculpture of a Buddhist goddess, Marichi (c.tenth century, Bihar), an example of the process of integration of different religious beliefs and practices

A twelfth-century bronze image of Karaikkal Ammaiyar

An image of Shiva as Nataraj

Important Figures

Atiya mosque, Mymensingh district, Bangladesh, built with brick, 1609

The Shah Hamadan mosque in Srinagar, built in 1395, is famed for its Kashmiri wooden architecture, spire, carved eaves, and papier mache decorations.

Fig 8 : The dargah of Shaikh Salim Chishti in Fatehpur Sikri symbolized the bond between the Chishtis and the Mughal state.

Chapter 6 : Mapwork

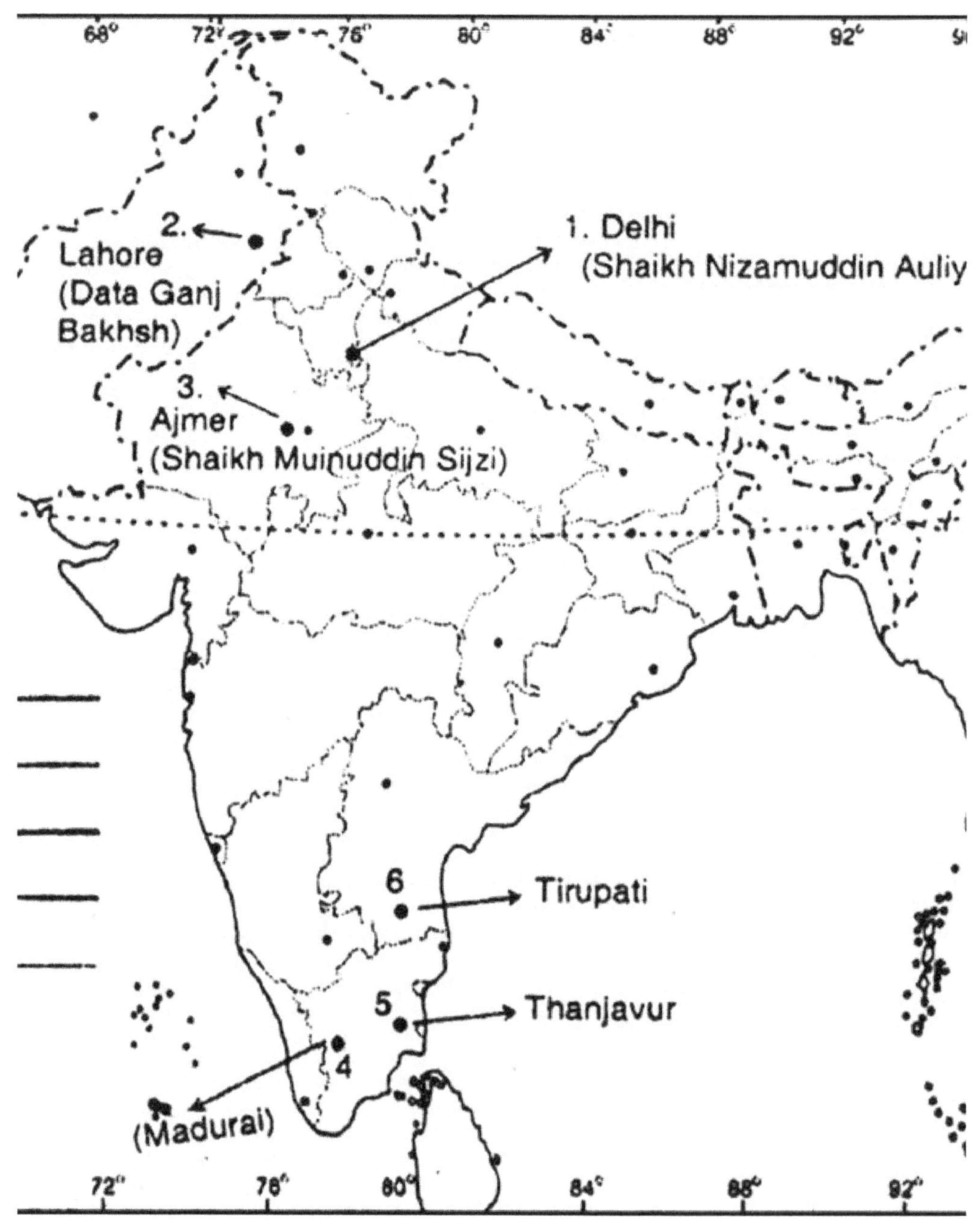

Chapter 6 : Bhakti-Sufi Traditions

QUESTIONS FROM ARCHIVES

Question 1 :
The terms great and little traditions were coined by a sociologist named ________.
a. Karl Marx
b. Montesquieu
c. Robert Redfield
d. Nicolo De Conti

Question 2 :
The principal deities of the Vedic Pantheon --
a. Agni,Indra,Kubera
b. Soma,Indra,Surya
c. Agni,Soma, Varun
d. Agni, Indra, Soma

Question 3 :
Who were Alvars ?
a. Devotees of shiva
b. Devotees of soma
c. Devotees of Vishnu
d. Devotees of Agni

Question 4 :
Identify the correct statement about Tantric practices during eight to eighteenth century :
a. Close association with Buddhism and Jainism.
b. Tantric practices were not open to women and lower cast people.
c. Many ideas of Tantricism were influenced shaivism as well as Buddhism.
d. All of the above

Question 5 :
 Who were Nayanars ?
a. Devotees of vishnu
b. Devotees of Shiva
c. Devotees of Durga
d. None of these

Question 6 :
One of the major anthologies of compositions by the Alvars were __________ which is also described as Tamil veda .

a. Tiruttundar-Puranam
b. Dravida Veda
c. Nalayira Divyaprabandham
d. None of these

Question 7 :
Which of the following statement is correct about the bhakti traditions ?
i) Bhakti traditions are divided into two broad categories Saguna and nirguna .
ii) Nirguna bhakti focused on the worship of specific dieties such as Shiva , Vishnu and their avatars (incarnations) and forms of the Goddess or devi .
iii) Saguna bhakti on the other hand worship of an abstract form of God .
iv) All of the above

Question 8 :
Name the woman Alvar who saw herself as beloved of Vishnu : her verses express her love for the diety .
a. Andal
b. Tondaradippodi
c. Karaikkal Ammaiyar
d. Sundarar

Question 9 :
The poems of Appar , Sambandar and Sundarar are from the ----
a. Nalayira Divyaprabandham
b. Tevaram
c. Vachanas
d. None of these

Question 10 :
Match the following :

Column A	Column B
a. Andal	i) Devotee of Shiva
b.Tondaradippodi	ii) Devotee of vishnu
c. Appar	iii) Alvar Brahmana
d. Karaikkal Ammaiyar	iv) Nayanar Saint

a. a–i, b–ii , c–iii , d–iv
b. a–ii, b–iii , c–iv , d–i
c. a–i, b–iv , c–iii , d–ii
d. a–iv, b–iii , c–i , d–ii

Question 11 :
Who resides as Marperu in Thanjavur , Tamil nadu ?
a. Shiva
b. Vishnu
c. Agni
d. Surya

Question 12 :
Magnificent Shiva temples made by the Chola rulers include --
a. Chidambaram
b. Thanjavur
c. Gangaikondacholapuram
d. All of these

Question 13 :
Chola ruler who had consecrated metal images of Appar,Sambandar,and Sundarar in a Shiva temple ?
a. Parantaka
b. Parantaka I
c. Parantaka II
d. None of these

Question 14 :
Lingayats believe that after death, the devotee will be united with _________ and will not return to this world.
a. Vishnu
b. Krishna
c. Durga
d. Shiva

Question 15 :
Read the given information and identify the personality :
i) He rejected sacrifices,ritual baths,image worship and authorities.
ii) He advocated Nirguna Bhakti
iii) He organized his followers into a community
iv) He proposed a simple way to connect to the Divine through "shabad"

a. Tulsi Das
b. Chaitanya
c. Guru Arjan
d. Guru Nanak

Question 16 :
The religious literature of lingayats is known as
a. Shabad
b. Vachana
c. Agrahara
d.None of these

Question 17 :
Who among the following was the Minister in the court of kalachuri ruler ?
a. Lingayats
b. Parantaka
c. virashaiva
d. Basavanna

Question 18 :
Jangama refers to -
a. Buddhist monk
b. Jain monk
c. wandering monk
d. brahmin monk

Question 19 :
The 12th century witness to the emergence of a new Movement in Karnataka which was led by a bramhana named ?
a. Virshaiva
b. Appar
c. Sundarar
d. Basavanna

Question 20 :
Considered the following statements about the lingayats and identify the   correct option :
a. The lingayats encouraged certain practices disapproved in the Dharmasutras.
b. Such as post marriage and remarriage of the widows
c. Virashaiva tradition is derived from vachanas composed in Kannada by women and men who joined the movement.
d. All of the above

question 21 :
Worship of abstract form of god is known as ----
a. Saguna
b.Nirguna
c.Virashaiva
d. None of these

Question 22 :
22. Study the picture and answer the following :

1. What is the literal meaning of Jagannatha ?
a. Lord of the world
b. Lord of the universe
c. Lord of Puri
d. None of these

2. Lord Jagannatha is a form of which god ?
a. Vishnu
b. Brahma
c. Chaitanya
d. Ganesha

3. Lord Jagannatha is the principal diety of which
state ?
a. Bengal
b. Orissa
c. Mysore
d. None of these

4. Which one is Lord Jagannatha ?
a. Extreme right
b. Centre
c. left
d. All of these

5. This picture is one of the most striking example
of :
a. Nayanar Bhakti movement
b. Saguna Bhakti movement
c. Alvar Bhakti movement
d. Integration of cults

Question 23 :
What is sharia ?
a. Islamic scholars
b. Law governing muslim community
c. Muslim sufi saints
d. Tax that non Muslim has to pay to
the government.

Question 24 :
In 711 an Arab general who conquered
the sind, which became part of the
Caliph's domain ?
a. Muhammad bin Tughlaq
b. Muhammad Qasim
c. Muhammad GhazGhazni
d. None of these

Question 25 :
Ulama refers to –
a. scholars of Islamic studies
b. Law governing muslim community
c. Muslim sufi saints
d. Tax that non Muslim has to pay to
the government.

Question 26 :
Non-Muslim had to pay a religious tax
called ?
a. Sharia
b.Ulama
c. zimmi
d. Jizya

Question 27 :
Considered the following statements
and identify the incorrect one :
a. All those who adopted Islam accepted
the five pillars of Faith.
b. There is one God Allah and prophet
Muhammad is his messenger.
c. Offering prayers four times a day .
d. Fasting during the month of Ramzan
and performing The Pilgrimage to
Mecca.

Question 28 :
Which mosque is often regarded as the "jewel in
the crown" of all the existing mosques of
Kashmir?
a. Atiya mosque
b. Shah hamadan mosque
c. Kerala mosque
d.None of these

Question 29 :
Identify the picture.

a) Sundarar
b) Sambandar
c) Karaikkal Ammaiyar
d) Andal

Question 30 :
_________means a chain which signifies a
continuous link between master and disciple .
a. Wali
b.Hujwiri
c. Silsila
d. Chishti

Question 31 :
Identify the term :
It is a practice where women after marriage
remain in the natal home with the children and
the husbands may come to stay with them.
a. Matrilocal residence
b. Patrilocal residence
c. Dargah
d.All of these

Question 32 :
Who composed the prem-akhyan padmavat ?
a. Amir Khusrau
b. Ratansen
c. Malik Muhammad Jayasi
d. Guru Granth Sahib

Question 33 :
Shaikh Nizamuddin's hospice compromised
several small rooms and a big hall called
a. Qalandars
b. Dargah
c. Jama'at khana
d. Ziyarat

Question 34 : Shaikh Muinuddin Sijzi is
located at -
a. Ajodhan
b. Ajmer
c. Delhi
d. None of these

Question 35 :
  The ninth Guru, whose compositions were
compiled in the Guru Granth Sahib was:
(a) Guru Tegh Bahadur
(b) Baba Guru Nanak
(c) Guru Gobind Singh
(d) Guru Arjan

Question 36 :
"Naam Ghar" refers to:
(a) Prayer Hall
(b) Temples
(c) Religious places
(d) All of the above

Question 37 :
Who composed Kirtana-ghosha?
(a) Shankaradeva
(b) Mirabai
(c) Kabir Das
(d) Raidas

Question 38 :
Tulsidas, a prominent leader of the Bhakti
Movement, belong from :
(a) Gwalior.
(b) Haryana.
(c) Uttar Pradesh.
(d) Bihar.

Question 39 :
Who among the following wrote the biography of Shaikh Muinuddin Chishti which was titled As Munis al Arwah ?
a. Akbar
b. Amir Khusrau
c. Malik Muhammad jayasi
d. Jahanara

Question 40 :
Which of the following statement(s) is/are correct about Mirabai?
(i) Mirabai (c. fifteenth-sixteenth centuries) is perhaps the best-known woman poet within the Sufi tradition.
(ii) She was a Rajput princess from Merta in Marwar who was married against her wishes to a prince of the Sisodia clan of Mewar, Rajasthan.
(iii) According to some traditions, her preceptor was Raidas, a leather worker.
(iv) Her songs continue to be sung by women and men, especially those who are poor and considered "low caste" in Karnataka and Kerala
Identify the incorrect options.
(a) (i) & (ii)
(b) (i) & (iv)
(c) (ii) & (iii)
(d) All of the above.

Question 41 :
What does the Vaishnava tradition attempt to convey about Kabirdas's origins in their hagiographies?
a. He was a Muslim born into a family of recent converts to Islam.
b. He was born a Hindu but raised by a Muslim family of weavers.
c. He was originally an Arabic scholar who became a Hindu saint.
d. He was a Muslim by birth but later converted to Vaishnavism.

Question 42 :
Who is suggested to have initiated Kabirdas into the practice of bhakti according to some accounts?
a. Kabirdas's father
b. A Muslim saint
c. Guru Ramananda
d. A Vaishnava scholar

Question 43 :
observe the picture and answer the following :

Question : Which historical place is this?
(A) Jama Masjid
(B) Humayun's Tomb
(C) Atiya Mosque
(D) Shah Hamadan Mosque

Question : Which material has been used to build it?
(A) White Marble
(B) Limestone
(C) Red Sandstone
(D) Brick

Question : present-day it is located in which country ?
(A) India
(B) Pakistan
(C) Nepal
(D) Bangladesh

Question 44 :
Amongst the most revered Shrine is that of Khwaja Muinuddin, which is popularly known as
a. Abul Hasan al Hujwiri
b. Gharib Nawaz
c. Amir Hassan sijzi
d. Shaikh Nizamuddin

Question 45 :
Match Column A with Column B and choose the correct option

Column A.	Column B
1) Shri Chaitanya.	I) Bengal
2) Muktabai.	II) Rajasthan
3) Ramananda.	III) Maharashtra
4) Meera bai.	IV) Uttar Pradesh
5) Ramanujacharya.	V) Tamil Nadu

A. 1 – I, 2 – III, 3 – IV, 4 – II, 5 – V
B. 1 – III, 2 – I, 3 – V, 4 – IV, 5 – II
C. 1 – II, 2 – IV, 3 – I, 4 – III, 5 – V
D. 1 – V, 2 – II, 3 – III, 4 – I, 5 – IV

Chapter 7 : An Imperial Capital : Vijayanagara

CONCISE KEY NOTES

Introduction to Vijayanagara :
- Vijayanagara means "City of Victory."
- It was both a city and an empire (14th–16th century).
- Empire stretched from the Krishna River (north) to the extreme south.
- City was sacked in 1565 and later abandoned.
- Known as Hampi in local traditions (name from goddess Pampadevi).

Discovery of Hampi :
- 1800: Discovered by Colonel Colin Mackenzie (Engineer, East India Company).
- 1815: Became Surveyor General of India.
- Used local memories of Virupaksha temple priests to study the ruins.
- 1856: Photographs of monuments taken for the first time.
- 1836: Epigraphists started collecting inscriptions.
- Historians used foreign travelers' accounts, Telugu, Kannada, Tamil, Sanskrit literature.

Founders and Political Structure :
- Founded in 1336 by Harihara and Bukka.
- Competed with Deccan Sultans and Gajapatis of Orissa for fertile river valleys.
- Borrowed and developed architectural techniques.
- Locally called Karnataka Samrajyamu.

Kings and Trade :
- Krishnadeva Raya (1509–29): Most famous ruler.
- Wrote Amuktamalyada (Telugu work on statecraft).
- Encouraged trade and foreign merchants:
  - Horses, elephants, gems, sandalwood, pearls imported.
  - Portuguese (1498) became key traders due to superior muskets.
- Markets flourished in spices, textiles, precious stones.

Decline of Vijayanagara :
- Sangama dynasty (till 1485) → Saluva dynasty (till 1503) → Tuluva dynasty→Aravidu
- Krishnadeva Raya's military expansion:
  - Conquered Raichur doab (1512).
  - Defeated Orissa (1514).
  - Defeated Bijapur (1520).
- 1565 Battle of Talikota (Rakshasi-Tangadi): Defeated by combined armies of Bijapur, Ahmadnagar, Golconda.
- City sacked, empire shifted focus eastward (Aravidu dynasty).

Nayakas and Amara-Nayaka System :
- Nayakas = Military chiefs controlling forts, often rebellious.
- Amara-Nayaka System (similar to Delhi Sultanate's Iqta System):
  - Nayakas collected taxes, maintained cavalry, and paid tribute to the king.
  - Many became independent in the 17th century, weakening the empire.

Vijayanagara: City Layout & Fortifications
- Built in Tungabhadra basin, surrounded by granite hills.
- Fortification system:
    - Seven lines of forts (described by Abdur Razzaq).
    - Included agricultural tracts (to prevent starvation during sieges).
    - Fort walls built without mortar, using wedge-shaped stones.

Water Management :
- Kamalapuram tank (15th century): Supplied city and irrigation.
- Hiriya canal (built by Sangama rulers) drew water from Tungabhadra river.
- Krishnadeva Raya's tank: 15,000-20,000 workers, water transported 15 km via pipes (Described by Paes).

Sacred Centre :
- Associated with Virupaksha temple, Pampadevi, Jaina shrines.
- Temples as power centers:
    - Kings ruled on behalf of Virupaksha (signed orders as Shri Virupaksha).
    - Used title "Hindu Suratrana" (Hindu Sultan).
- Rayagopurams (royal gateways) were monumental imperial symbols.
- Vitthala Temple: Dedicated to Vitthala (Vishnu), features chariot shrine.
- Temple bazaars lined with shops, pavilions, chariot streets.

Royal Centre :
- Included palaces, audience halls, temples.
- Mahanavami Dibba (Festival platform):
    - 40 ft high, 11,000 sq ft base.
    - Dussehra/Navaratri festival: Worship of state horse, animal sacrifice, dances, processions.
    - Processions included caparisoned elephants, horses, nayakas' tribute gifts.
- Lotus Mahal: Indo-Islamic style, probable council chamber.
- Elephant Stables: Housed royal elephants, arched Indo-Islamic domes.
- Hazara Rama Temple: Personal royal temple, Ramayana panels on walls.

Economy & Trade :
- Bazaars described by Domingo Paes:
    - Diamonds, rubies, emeralds, pearls, textiles, fruits, grains.
    - Evening fairs selling horses, limes, oranges, jackfruit, mangoes.
- Portuguese traveler Fernao Nuniz:
    - Markets stocked with mutton, pork, venison, birds, rats, cats, lizards.
- Chinese porcelain found, indicating foreign trade.

Foreign Travelers' Accounts:
- Nicolo de Conti (Italy, 15th century).
- Abdur Razzaq (Persia, 15th century).
- Afanasii Nikitin (Russia, 15th century).
- Duarte Barbosa (Portugal, 16th century).
- Domingo Paes (Portugal, 16th century).
- Fernao Nuniz (Portugal, 16th century).

Vijayanagara's Legacy & Conservation :
- Hampi ruins first photographed (1856) by Alexander Greenlaw.
- Inscriptions recorded (1876) by J.F. Fleet.
- 1902: Archaeological Survey of India started conservation.
- 1976: Recognized as a site of national importance.
- 1986: Declared a UNESCO World Heritage Site.
- 1980s onwards: Detailed mapping of ruins.

Chapter 7 : Mapwork

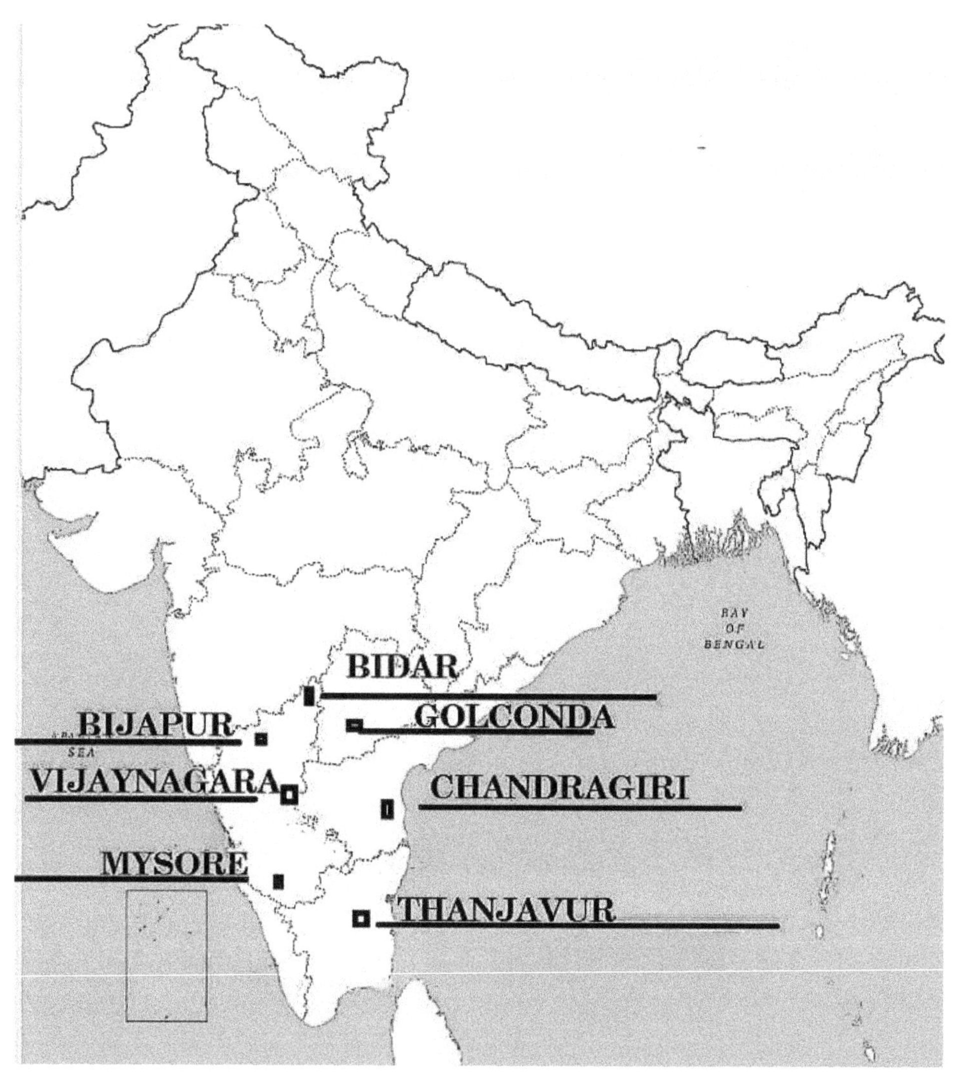

Important Figures

This c.1825 copy of a Thomas Hickey painting, held by the Royal Asiatic Society, shows Mackenzie with his peon Kistnaji and Brahmana assistants: a Jaina pandit and Cauvellery Ventak Letchmiah.

A Mahanavami Dibba

The gopuram or gateway of the Brihadishvara temple at Thanjavur

Carvings on the mahanavami dibba

A photograph of the Lotus Mahal

Important Figures

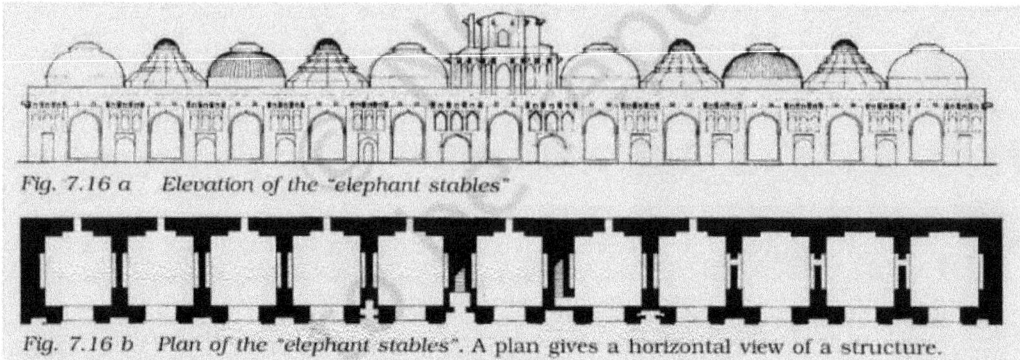

Fig. 7.16 a   *Elevation of the "elephant stables"*

Fig. 7.16 b   *Plan of the "elephant stables". A plan gives a horizontal view of a structure.*

"Elephant stables" located close to the Lotus Mahal

Sculpture from the Hazara Rama temple

An aerial view of the Virupaksha temple

The chariot of the Vitthala temple

Swing pavilion from Gingee

Important Figures

Krishnadeva Raya's statue at Chidambaram
shows his ideal image, but Paes describes him
as medium height, fair, sturdy, and slightly
fat, with smallpox scars.

Chapter 7 : An Imperial Capital : Vijaynagara

QUESTIONS FROM ARCHIVES

Question 1 :
The ruins at hampi were brought to light in 1800 by an engineer and antiquarian named –
a. Alexander Cunningham
b. Alexander greenlaw
c. John Marshall
d. Colin Mackenzie

Question 2 :
When was the Vijayanagara Empire founded ?
a. 1336
b. 1337
c. 1338
d. 1565

Question 3 :
While historians use the term Vijayanagara Empire, contemporaries described it as ?
a. Gajapati rulers
b. Declan sultans
c. Karnataka Samrajyamu
d. None of these

Question 4 :
Brihadishvara temple is located at –
a. Belur
b. Thanjavur
c. Penukonda
d. Nagalapuram

Question 5 :
Chennakeshava temple is located at ?
a. Belur
b. Thanjavur
c. Penukonda
d. Chandragiri

Question 6 :
Local communities of merchants were known as _______________ or horse merchants
a. Sheth
b. Nagarsheth
c. Ashvapati
d. Kudirai Chettis

Question 7 :
Arrange the dynasties of the Vijaynagar kingdom in chronological order: a) Saluva dynasty, b) Sangma Dynasty, C) Tuluva dynasty D) Aravidu Dynasty
a.c,a,b,d
b.a,b,d,c
c.b,a,c,d
d.b,c,a,d

Question 8 :
. The first dynasty that ruled over Vijaynagar Empire was
a.Aravidu Dynasty
b.Tuluva Dynasty
c.Saluva Dynasty
d.Sangam Dynasty

Question 9 :
In Vijayanagar, Deccan Sultans were termed as __________
a.Gajapati
b.Ashvapati
c.Narapati
d.Rayas

Question 10 :
Where is Kamalapuram Tank located?
a.Vijayanagara
b.Mysore
c.Bijapur
d.Golconda

Question 11 :
Who composed Amuktamalyada?
a.Harihara
b.Bukka
c.Saluvas
d.Krishnadeva Raya

Question 12 :
The combined armies of which states routed the Army of rama raya in 1565 ?
a. Golkonda, Ahmednagar, Vijayanagara
b. Bijapur, Ahmednagar, Bidar
c. Bijapur, Ahmednagar, Golconda
d. None of these

Question 13 :
Which famous ruler found a Suburban Township of nagalapuram near Vijayanagara after his mother's death ?
a. Saluva Narasimha Raya
b. Krishna deva Raya
c. Harihara
d. Bukka

Question 14 :
Which word was used for the Greeks and other people who entered the subcontinent from the north west?
a.Yavana
b.Chettis
c.Amara
d.Rayas

Question 15 :
Who among the following was regarded as the
"establisher of the yavana kingdom" ?Who among
the following was regarded as the "establisher of
the yavana kingdom" ?
a. Samudragupta
b. Harihara
c. Krishna Deva Raya
d. Rama Raya

Question 16 :
Krishnadeva raya belongs to which dynasty ?
a. Sangama
b. Saluva
c. Tuluva
d. Aravidu

Question 17 :
Amuktamalyada was composed in which language
?
a. Telugu
b. Tamil
c. Malayalam
d. kannada

Question 18 :
The military chiefs were called --
a. Rayas
b. Nayakas
c. Amara Nayakas
d. Ministers

Question 19 :
Kamalapuram tank was built in ?
a. Fifteenth century
b. Sixteenth century
c. Seventeenth century
d. None of these

Question 20 :
Local goddess of Vijayanagara was ?
a. Vishnu
b. Parvati
c. Laxmi
d. Pampadevi

Question 21 :
The word Amara is believed to be derived from
the sanskrit word _____________.
a. Sultan
b.Nayaka
c. Samara
d. None of these

Question 22 :
Which of the following statements is correct
about the Amara-nayaka system ?
a. The Amara- Nayakas were chiefs .
b. This system were derived from the
mansabdari system .
c. Kings had no control over the Amara-
Nayakas.
d. The amara-nayakas were military
commanders who were given territories to
govern by the raya .

Question 23 :
In which year Hampi declared as World
Heritage site by UNESCO ?In which year Hampi
declared as World Heritage site by UNESCO ?
a. 1858
b. 1878
c. 1988
d. 1987

Question 24 :
Who among the following wrote : " in our study
of this monuments of Vijayanagara we have to
imagine a whole series of vanished wooden
elements- columns ,brackets, beams, ceilings
overhanging eaves, and Towers - decorated with
plaster and painted perhaps brightly"
a. John M. Fritz
b.George Michell
c. M.S.Nagaraja Rao
d. All of the above

Question 25 :
In which year Hampi was recognised as a site
of national importance ?
a. 1978
b. 1858
c. 1988
d. None of these

Question 26 :
Vitthala temple is dedicated to -
a. Lord Shiva
b. Lord vishnu
c. Lord surya
d. Lord Ganesha

Question 27 :
Virupaksha is also recognised as a form of
a. Shiva
b. Karthikeya
c. Vishnu
d. Krishna

Question 28 :
The Hazara Rama temple was used by
a. The servants of the king
b. The king and his ministers
c. The king and his family
d. The king and the soldiers

Question 29 :
The Lotus Mahal is used for which purpose
a. A place where ceremony took place
b. A place where King met his advisors
c. A place where Queen resides
d. A place where Gods were worshipped

Question 30 :
Who captured the 1st detailed photograph of
archaeological remains at Hampi?
a.Alexander Greenlaw
b.Collin Mackenzie
c.John Marshall
d.None of these

Question 31 :
Name the ambassador of Persia who was sent to
Calicut?
a.Abdur Razzaq
b.None of these
c.Barbosa
d.Collin Mackenzie

Question 32 :
Which two rivers served as source of water for
the Vijayanagara Kingdom ?
a. Krishna, Godavari
b. Krishna, Tungabhadra
c. Tungabhadra, Kaveri
d. Mahanadi, Kaveri

Question 33 :
The Hiriya canal was built by kings of which
dynasty ?
a.Sangama
b.Saluva
c.Tuluva
d.Aravidu

Question 34 :
Which Traveller called the "mahanavami Dibba"
as the house of victory ?
a. Domingo Paes
b. Afanasii Nikitin
c. Duarte Barbosa
d. Fernao Nuniz

Chapter 8 : Peasants, Zamindars and the State

CONCISE KEY NOTES

Chapter Overview
- This chapter discusses the agrarian society of the Mughal Empire (16th-17th centuries).
- 85% of India's population lived in villages, engaged in agriculture, trade, and tax collection.
- The Mughal state, peasants, and zamindars were the key players in rural society.
- Main sources: Ain-i-Akbari by Abu'l Fazl, regional revenue records, and East India Company documents.

Peasants and Agricultural Production : Village and Agricultural Structure
- "During the sixteenth and seventeenth centuries about 85 per cent of the population of India lived in its villages."
- "Both peasants and landed elites were involved in agricultural production and claimed rights to a share of the produce."
- The village was the basic unit of agricultural production.

Sources of Agrarian History
- Peasants did not write about themselves, so historians rely on:
  - Mughal court records (Ain-i-Akbari, Persian chronicles).
  - Regional revenue records (Gujarat, Maharashtra, Rajasthan, Bengal).
  - East India Company reports (17th-18th century).
- "The Ain meticulously recorded the arrangements made by the state to ensure cultivation, enable revenue collection, and regulate zamindars."

Types of Peasants
- "The term which Indo-Persian sources most frequently used for a peasant was raiyat or muzarian."
- Two categories of peasants:
  - Khud-kashta - Resident cultivators who worked on their own land in their village.
  - Pahi-kashta - Migrant cultivators working on land in other villages.

Land Ownership
- "Cultivation was based on the principle of individual ownership. Peasant lands were bought and sold like any other property."
- Landholding sizes:
  - Gujarat: 6 acres = Affluent peasant.
  - Bengal: 5 acres = Average holding; 10 acres = Rich farmer.

Irrigation and Agricultural Technology : Water Management
- "Monsoons remained the backbone of Indian agriculture, as they are even today."
- Artificial irrigation systems were built:
  - Persian wheels (Fig. 8.2) used in Lahore, Dipalpur.
  - Bucket irrigation in Agra, Chandwar, Bayana.
- "In northern India, the state undertook digging of new canals (nahr, nala) and also repaired old ones like the Shahnahr in Punjab during Shah Jahan's reign."

The Village Community : Caste and Rural Society
- "The cultivators were a highly heterogeneous group, divided by caste and economic status."
- Lower caste agricultural laborers (majur) faced discrimination.
- Some intermediate castes (Ahirs, Gujars, Malis, Sadgops, Kaivartas) rose in status due to cattle rearing and horticulture.

Panchayats and Headmen
- Village Panchayat: Governing body of elders and influential villagers.
- Headman (Muqaddam or Mandal):
  - Supervised village affairs and tax collection.
  - Could be dismissed by elders or zamindars.
- Panchayats ensured caste norms were upheld:
  - "One of the duties of the village headman was to oversee the conduct of the members of the village community, chiefly to prevent any offence against their caste."
  - Had the power to levy fines and expel members from the community.
  -

Women in Agrarian society
- Shared Agrarian Work: Men ploughed; women sowed, weeded, threshed, winnowed.
- No Gendered Division: Household was core unit; both genders worked together.
- Cultural Taboos: Menstruating women barred from ploughs, potter's wheels, betel groves.
- Artisan Roles: Women spun yarn, kneaded clay, embroidered, worked in homes/markets.
- High Female Mortality: Led to bride-price, accepted remarriage.
- Patriarchal Control: Men led households; women faced strict rules and punishments.
- Petitions: Women sought justice via panchayats; often unnamed in records.
- Property Rights: Women inherited, sold land; female zamindars existed (e.g., Rajshahi).

Role of Zamindars
- Zamindars were powerful landlords who controlled land, collected revenue, and maintained armed forces.
- "They derived power from large personal landholdings (milkiyat), military resources, and hereditary status."
- A parallel army! Zamindars collectively controlled 384,558 cavalry, 4,277,057 infantry, 1,863 elephants, and 4,260 cannons.

Mughal Land Revenue System : Tax Collection
- Jama: Assessed revenue.
- Hasil: Actual revenue collected.
- "The Mughal state sought to maximize revenue, but actual collection depended on local conditions."

Land Classification under Akbar
- Polaj: Annually cultivated land.
- Parauti: Left fallow for recovery.
- Chachar: Left fallow for 3-4 years.
- Banjar: Left uncultivated for 5+ years.

Revenue Collection Methods
- Kankut: Estimate-based.
- Batai: Crop-sharing.
- Lang batai: Heap division.

• Pargana was an administrative
subdivision of a Mughal province.

• Peshkash was a form of tribute
collected by the Mughal state.Ain-i-Akbari as a Source

• Amin was an official responsible
for ensuring that imperial
regulations were carried out in
the provinces.

Flow of Silver :

• Mughal Empire (like Ming, Safavid, Ottoman) was politically stable in 16th–17th
centuries.
• Stability boosted overland trade from China to the Mediterranean.
• New World discoveries expanded Asia-Europe trade.
• India's overseas trade grew in volume and diversity.
• Huge inflow of silver bullion into Asia to pay for Indian goods.
• India, lacking silver mines, benefited greatly from this inflow.
• Led to stable silver currency (rupya) and cash-based economy.
• Boosted coin minting, trade, and tax collection under the Mughals.
• Giovanni Careri (Italian traveller, c.1690) described global flow of silver into India.

"The Ain-i-Akbari was the culmination of a large historical, administrative project by
Abu'l Fazl."

Five Books (Daftars):
Manzil-abadi: Imperial household.
Sipah-abadi: Military and administration.
Mulk-abadi: Revenue system (most important for agrarian history).
"The Ain remains an extraordinary document, despite minor data inconsistencies."

Mughal Empire Timeline:
• 1526: Babur defeats Ibrahim Lodi at Panipat - Mughal Empire begins.
• 1530-40: Humayun's first reign.
• 1540-55: Humayun exiled after defeat by Sher Shah.
• 1555-56: Humayun regains power.
• 1556-1605: Akbar's reign.
•1605-27: Jahangir's reign.
•1628-58: Shah Jahan's reign.
•1658-1707: Aurangzeb's reign.
•1739: Nadir Shah invades and sacks Delhi.
• 1761: Ahmad Shah Abdali defeats Marathas (3rd Battle of Panipat).

Important Figures

A silver rupya issued by Akbar (obverse and reverse)

A silver rupiya issued by Aurangazeb

Chapter 8 : Peasants Zamindars and the States

QUESTIONS FROM ARCHIVES

Question 1 :
During the sixteenth and seventeenth centuries how much percent of the population of India lived in its villages ?
a. 65 percent
b. 75 percent
c. 55 percent
d. 85 percent

Question 2 :
Name the basic unit of agriculture society?
a.Village
b.State
c.Town
d.City

Question 3 :
Who wrote Ain-i-Akbari ?
a.Ibn Battuta
b. Al-Biruni
c.Abul Fazal
d. Harshavardhan

Question 4 :
Abul fazl was the court historian of which mughal emperor ?
a. Akbar
b. Babur
c.Humayun
d.Nasiruddin

Question 5 :
The term which Indo-Persian sources of the Mughal period most frequently used to denote a peasant was__?
a.Muzarian
b.Raiyat
c.Gulam
d.Both A and B

Question 6 :
Name the peasants who plough up the fields, mark the limits of each field, for identification and demarcation, with borders of earth, brick and thorn?
a.Khud Kashta
b.Ahoms
c.Pahi Kashta
d. Asamis

Question 7 :
During the 17th century several new crops from different parts of the world reach the Indian subcontinent one of them was ________which was introduced to India via Africa and Spain .
a. Cotton
b. Sugarcane
c. Rice
d. Maize

Question 8 :
Name the term used for perfect crop?
a.Do Fasla
b.Polaj
c.Jins-i-Kamil
d.None of these

Question 9 :
Which crop was an important Jins-i-Kamil of Central India?
a.Sugarcane
b.All of these
c.Maize
d.Wheat

Question 10 :
Tobacco was banned by which ruler?
a.Aurangzeb
b.Sher Shah Suri
c.Akbar
d.Jahangir

Question 11 :
From where did the vegetables like chillies, tomatoes come to India ?
a.New World
b.Middle world
c.Old World
d.Continental World

Question 12 :
In which region did Tobacco arrive first in India?
a.Punjab
b.Deccan
c.Chotanagpur
d.Malabar

Question 13 :
How many Daftars of Ain are there ?
a.5
b.8
c.9
d.7

Question 14 :
Akbar's "auspicious sayings" were included in_
a.1st book of Ain
b. 4th book of Ain
c. 5th book of Ain
d. both b and c

Question 15 :
Identify which of the following statements is correct about Ain-i-Akbari?
a.Mulk-Abadi gives information about the fiscal aspect of the state.
b.Manzil-Abadi is related to the royal household
c.Sipah-Abadi is related to civil and military administration.
d. All of the above

Question 16 :
Which of the following communities was menial?
a.Jangil
b.Mandal
c.Halalkhoran
d.Majur

Question 17 :
Who composed the poem Chandimangala?
a.Kalaketu
b.None of these
c.Mukundaram Chankrabarti
d.Zafar Mian

Question 18 :
Find out from the following pairs which one is not correctly matched
a. Makka : Maize
b. Muqaddam : peasants
c. Rabi : spring
d. Kharif : Autumn

Question 19 :
The _______ who cultivated land around Vrindavan (Uttar Pradesh)
a. Rajputs
b. Ahirs
c. Gauravas
d. Gujjars

Question 20 :
In the eastern region which intermediate pastoral and fishing castes acquired the status of Peasants ?
a. Ahirs , Gujjars
b. Gujjars , Malis
c. Rajputs , Jats
d. Sadgops , Kaivartas

Question 21 :
The Panchayat was headed by a head man known as
a. Mandal
b. Muqaddam
c. Both a and b
d. None of these

Question 22:
Ahom kings belong to ______
a. Madhya Pradesh
b. Andhra Pradesh
c. Orissa
d. Assam

Question 23 :
What is jins-i-kamil during the mughal empire ?
a. Half crops
b. Perfect crops
c. Kharif crops
d. Ravi crops

Question 24 :
Consider the following statements and identify the correct option
Statement 1 – one important function of the panchayat was to ensure that caste boundaries among the various communities inhabiting the village were upheld.
Statement 2 – Panchayat also had the authority to Levy fines and inflict more serious forms of punishment like expulsion from the community.

a. Statement 1 is correct
b. Statement 2 is correct
c. Both are correct
d. None of these

Question 25 :
which documents and village surveys made in the early years of British rule have revealed the existence of substantial numbers of artisans sometimes as high as 25 percent of the total household in the villages ?
a. Marathi
b.Bengali
c. Both
d. None of these

Question 26 :
Assertion- zamindar in Bengal reremunerated blacksmiths , carpenters, even goldsmiths for their work by paying them "a small daily allowance and diet money".
Reason- this later came to be described as the jajmani system.

a. Both assertion and Reason are true and Reason is the correct explanation of assertion
b. Both Assertion and Reason are true but Reason is not the correct explanation of assertion.
c. Assertion is correct reason is wrong
d. Reason is correct assertion is wrong

Question 27 :
Which of the following statement(s) is /are correct about the women in agrarian society.Which of the following statement(s) is /are correct about the women in agrarian society.
i) women and men had to work shoulder to shoulder in the fields, while men tilled and ploughed , women sowed, weeded, threshed, winnowed the harvest.
ii) menstruating women were not allowed to touch plough or the Potters wheel in western India, or enter the groves where betel-leaves (paan) were grown in bengal.
iii) peasant and artisan women work only in the fields.
iv) women were considered an important resource in agrarian society also because they were child bearers in a society dependent on labour.

a. Statement i and ii are correct
b. Statement ii and iii are correct
c. Statement i , ii, iv are correct
d. All the statements are correct

Question 28 :
Forest dwellers were known as _______ in the contemporary texts.
a. Jangli
b. Mowgli
c. Santhals
d. Paharias

Question 29 :
An administrative subdivision of a Mughal province is called ?
a. Pargana
b. Village
c. City
d. Town

Question 30 :
what do you understand by the term Khud-Kashta ?
a. Revenue collectors
b. Head of jati panchayat
c. Peasants who were resident of the village
d. Non resident peasants

Question 31 :
Which among the following state produced 50 varieties of rice alone according to the Ain During Mughal province ?
a. Punjab
b. Agra
c.Delhi
d. Bengal

Question 32 :
During the Mughal provinces Bengal was famous for its_
____
a. Cotton
b. Rice
c. Jute
d. Sugar

Question 33 :
The mandal or muqaddam was chosen through the consensus of ----
a. By Voting
b. By the village elders
c. By the ruler
d. By the panchayat

Question 34 :
__________ was a form of tribute collected by the Mughal State.
a. Tax
b. Peshkash
c. Revenue
d. None of these

Question 35 :
In the panchayat each cast had :
a. Sabha Panchayat
b. Jati panchayat
c. Both A and B
d. None of these

Question 36 :
In the 18th century , women zamindars were known in
a. Bengal
b. Gujrat
c. Rajasthan
d. Punjab

Question 37 :
Lohanis tribes belong from which state ?
a. Gujrat
b. Punjab
c. Afghanistan
d. Sind

Question 38 :
What do you understand about Milkiyat ?
a.Large amount of money given to Zamindars
b.A small piece of land of Zamindar
c.Huge land of Zamindars
d. All of these

Question 39 :Chachar is a land that has lain fallow for
a. 2 to 3 years
b. 3 to 4 years
c. 1 to 2 years
d. None of these

Question 40 :
Consider the statement and answer the following :
Statement 1 - the Mughal Empire was among the large territorial empires in Asia that had managed to consolidate power and resources during the 16th and 17th centuries.
statement 2 - this Empires wear Ming (China) Safavid (Iran) and Ottoman (Turkey) .
a. Statement 1 is correct
b. Statement 2 is correct
c. Both are correct
d. None are correct

Question 41 :
Testimony of which Traveller provides a graphic account about the way silver travel across the globe to reach India ?
a. Ibn-Battuta
b. Marco Polo
c. Jean Baptiste Tavernier
d. Giovanni Careri

Question 42 :
____ coins are more prevalent during the Mughal empire.
a. Gold
b. Copper
c. Bronze
d. Silver

Question 43 :
The Ain is made up of five books what is the first book called
a. Manzil-Abadi
b. Mulk-Abadi
c. Sipah- Abadi
d. None of these

Question 44 :
In the third battle of Panipat, the Marathas were defeated by
a. Bahadur Shah
b. Nadir Shah
c. Sher Shah
d. Ahmad Shah Abdali

Question 45 :
Consider the following statements:
1. The Ain has been translated for use by a number of scholars.
2. Henry Bloachman was associated with the Asiatic Society of Bengal.
3. Henry Bloachman has given the standard translation of volume 1.
4. The other two volumes were translated by H.S.Jarrett .
Which of the following is/are correct ?
a.1 only
b.2 only
c.All of the above
d.None of the above

Question 46 :
The Ain is made up of five books what is the second book called
a. Manzil-Abadi
b. Mulk-Abadi
c. Sipah- Abadi
d. None of these

Question 47 :
The Ain is made up of five books what is the third book called
a. Manzil-Abadi
b. Mulk-Abadi
c. Sipah- Abadi
d. None of these

Question 48 :
Identify which of the following statement is correct about the Ain-i-i Akbari ?
a. Sipah-Abadi is related to military and civil administration
b. Mulk - Abadi deals with the fiscal side of the empire
c. Manzil-Abadi concerns the Imperial household and its maintenance
d. All of the above

Question 49 :
The bengali poem- chandimangala compose by Mukundaram chakrabarti , who was the hero of the poem ?
a. Kalaketu
b. Zafar Mian
c. Sulaimani
d. None of these

Question 50 :

Which of the following ruler issued this coin ?
a. Akbar
b.Aurangzeb
c. Jahangir
d. None of these

Chapter 9 : Kings and Chronicles – The Mughal Courts

CONCISE KEY NOTES

The Mughals and Their Empire
- The term *Mughal* comes from Mongol, but the rulers never used it. They called themselves Timurids, as they were descendants of Timur from the paternal side.
- *"Babur, the first Mughal ruler, was related to Genghis Khan from his mother's side. He spoke Turkish and referred derisively to the Mongols as barbaric hordes."*
- The empire was established through conquests and alliances with local chieftains.
- *"His successor, Nasiruddin Humayun (1530-40, 1555-56) expanded the frontiers of the empire but lost it to the Afghan leader Sher Shah Sur, who drove him into exile."*
- Akbar (1556-1605) expanded and consolidated the empire into the largest and strongest kingdom of its time.
- The power of the dynasty diminished after Aurangzeb's death (1707).
- The last Mughal emperor, Bahadur Shah Zafar II, was overthrown by the British in 1857.

The Production of Chronicles
- Mughal emperors commissioned chronicles to document their reigns.
- *"Chronicles are an indispensable source for any scholar wishing to write a history of the Mughals."*
- They were written to convey the ideology of kingship and glorify the emperor.
- In Persian Mahabharata is known as – Razmnama (book of wars)
- Kitabkhana – where collection of manuscripts were kept and new manuscripts were produced.
- Akbar's favourite calligraphy – Nastaliq a fluid style with long horizontal strokes
- Key Mughal chronicles:
  - *Akbar Nama* (by Abu'l Fazl)
  - *Badshah Nama* (by Abdul Hamid Lahori)
  - *Alamgir Nama* (by Muhammad Kazim)
- Chronicles had dual purposes:
  - *"At one level, they were a repository of factual information about the institutions of the Mughal state."*
  - *"At the same time, these texts were intended as conveyors of meanings that the Mughal rulers sought to impose on their domain."*

The Painted Image
- Paintings played a crucial role in conveying Mughal ideology.
- *"Chronicles narrating the events of a Mughal emperor's reign contained, alongside the written text, images that described an event in visual form."*
- Abu'l Fazl regarded painting as a "magical art" that brought objects to life.
- *"Even inanimate objects look as if they have life."*
- Paintings illustrated key events, court life, wars, and diplomacy.
- The Muslim orthodox scholars (ulama) opposed paintings, citing Islamic prohibitions on depicting living beings.

The Akbar Nama and Badshah Nama
- The Akbar Nama was written by Abu'l Fazl over 13 years (1589-1602).
- It had three volumes:
  - First Volume: History of mankind from Adam to Akbar's 30th year.
  - Second Volume: Akbar's reign until 1601.
  - Third Volume (Ain-i Akbari): A detailed account of Akbar's administration.

- *"In the Ain-i Akbari, the Mughal Empire is presented as having a diverse population consisting of Hindus, Jainas, Buddhists, and Muslims and a composite culture."*
- The Badshah Nama, written by Abdul Hamid Lahori, was an official history of Shah Jahan.
- Gifting manuscripts was a diplomatic custom:
    - *"The Nawab of Awadh gifted the illustrated Badshah Nama to King George III in 1799."*

The Ideal Kingdom
- Mughal rulers claimed divine legitimacy (farr-i izadi).
- *"Abu'l Fazl placed Mughal kingship as the highest station in the hierarchy of objects receiving light emanating from God."*
- Akbar promoted sulh-i kul (universal peace), ensuring religious harmony.
- Akbar abolished pilgrimage tax in 1563 and jizya tax in 1564
- *"The emperor stood above all religious and ethnic groups, mediated among them, and ensured that justice and peace prevailed."*

Capitals and Courts
- Fatehpur Sikri was built in the 1570s, near Ajmer, as a mark of devotion to Shaikh Salim Chishti.
- Shah Jahan shifted the capital to Delhi (Shahjahanabad) in 1648.
- *"In the Mughal court, status was determined by spatial proximity to the king."*
- Kornish - form of ceremonial salutation in which courtier places palm of his right hand against his head and bent his head .
- chahar taslim - mode of salutation which begins with placing the back of the right hand on the ground, and raising it gently till the person stands erect, when he puts the palm of his hand upon the crown of his head. It is done four (chahar) times. Taslim literally means submission.
- The Jharoka Darshan (public audience) strengthened imperial authority.
- Shab-i barat is the full moon night on the 14 Shaban, the eighth month of the hijri calendar, and is celebrated with prayers and fireworks in the subcontinent. It is the night when the destinies of the Muslims for the coming year are said to be determined and sins forgiven.

Titles and gifts
 • Mughal emperors adopted grand titles at coronation or after victories to inspire awe: these.
announced by ushers (naqib).
 • Titles were crucial in Mughal polity, marking a person's rank and merit.
 Example: "Asaf Khan" (from minister Asaf of King Solomon).
 Example: "Mirza Raja" was given to Jai Singh and Jaswant Singh by Aurangzeb.
Royal gifts included:
• Khilat (robe of honour worn by emperor),
•Sarapa (tunic, turban, sash),
• Jewelled ornaments, like the rare padma murassa (jeweled lotus).
• Courtiers offered gifts to the emperor — nazr (small) or peshkash (large).
• Gifts in diplomacy symbolized honour and respect.

Imperial household
- The harem was a private palace space for royal women.
- Jahanara Begum controlled Chandni Chowk market and was highly influential.
- Nur Jahan (Jahangir's wife) was one of the most powerful Mughal women.
- Humayun Nama by Gulbadan Begum, Babur's daughter and Akbar's aunt, offers a rare glimpse into the Mughal domestic world.

The imperial officials
• Nobility (officers) was a key pillar, recruited from diverse ethnic and religious groups to prevent any dominant faction.
• Nobles described as a guldasta (bouquet) loyal to the emperor.
• Turani and Iranian nobles served since Humayun; Rajputs and Indian Muslims (Shaikhzadas) joined from 1580.
• Raja Bharmal Kachhwaha of Amber (Rajput) joined first; Akbar married his daughter.
• Raja Todar Mal, a Khatri, was Akbar's finance minister.
• Under Jahangir, Iranians gained power (esp. via Nur Jahan).
• Aurangzeb appointed Rajputs and Marathas in large numbers.

All officials held mansabs with two ranks:
• Zat (status & salary), Sawar (number of horsemen).
• 1,000 zat+ ranked as umara (nobles).
•Nobles led campaigns, managed provinces, and maintained cavalry with branded horses (dagh).
• Other top officials: Diwan-i-Ala (finance), Sadr-us-Sudur (grants/qazis).
• Court nobles (Tainat-i-Rakab) guarded emperor, attended daily.

Titles and Territorial Claims
• Mughal emperors assumed grand titles (e.g., Shahenshah, Jahangir, Shah Jahan) to assert dominance.

Safavids and Qandahar
• Control of Kabul and Qandahar was crucial for Mughal security.
• Qandahar, once held by Humayun and Akbar, was claimed by the Safavids.
• In 1622, the Safavids captured Qandahar after defeating the Mughal garrison.

The Ottomans: Pilgrimage and Trade
• Mughals maintained ties with Ottomans to ensure safe passage for pilgrims to Mecca and Medina.
• Mughal emperors sent goods to Red Sea ports (Aden, Mokha); proceeds were donated in Hijaz.
• Aurangzeb redirected funds to India after learning of fund misuse, calling India "as much a house of God as Mecca."

Jesuits at the Mughal Court
• Jesuits gave Europe early insights into the Mughal Empire.
• Akbar invited Jesuits; first mission came to Fatehpur Sikri in 1580.
• Jesuits engaged in religious debates, taught royal children, and joined Akbar on campaigns.
• Their writings confirmed details from Persian chronicles about court life and governance.

Important Figures

The mausoleum of Timur in Samarkand, 1404

An eighteenth–century depiction of Humayun's wife Nadira crossing the desert of Rajasthan

This nastaliq folio by Muhammad Husayn of Kashmir, Akbar's court calligrapher known as "zarrin qalam" (golden pen), features his signature on the lower fourth of the page.

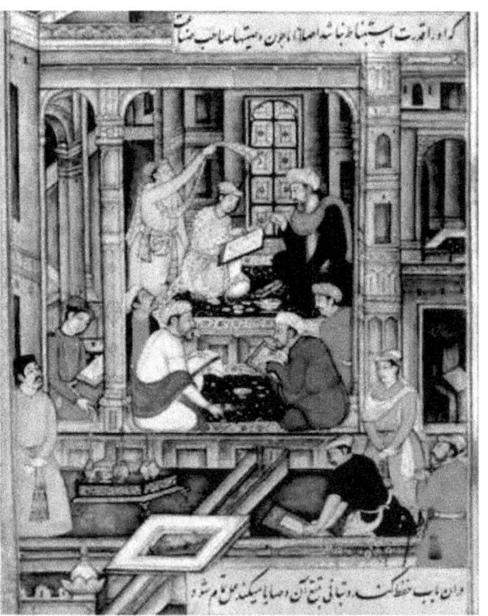

A Mughal kitabkhana

Important Figures

Jahangir shooting the figure of poverty, painting by the artist Abu'l Hasan

The Buland Darwaza, Fatehpur Sikri

Dara Shukoh's wedding

Jahangir's dream

Important Figures

Religious debates in the court Padre Rudolf Acquaviva was the leader of the first Jesuit mission. His name is written on top of the painting.

Blue tiles from a shrine in Multan, brought by migrant artisans from Iran

Chapter 9 : Kings And Chronicles

QUESTIONS FROM ARCHIVES

Question 1 :
The Mughal rulers referred to themselves as _______ rather than Mughals.
(a) Chaghtai Turks
(b) Timurids
(c) Mongols
(d) Rajputs

Question 2 :
Which Mughal emperor is credited with making Persian the leading language of the Mughal court?
(a) Babur
(b) Humayun
(c) Akbar
(d) Jahangir

Question 3 :
Assertion (A): The Mughal court followed strict protocols for diplomatic envoys.
Reason (R): Ambassadors were allowed to freely move around the court without following any customs.
(a) Both A and R are true, and R is the correct explanation of A.
(b) Both A and R are true, but R is not the correct explanation of A.
(c) A is true, but R is false.
(d) A is false, but R is true.

Question 4 :
The Akbar Nama was written by _______.
(a) Abdul Hamid Lahori
(b) Abu'l Fazl
(c) Gulbadan Begum
(d) Badauni

Question 5 :
Which Mughal emperor introduced the policy of sulh-i kul (absolute peace)?
(a) Babur
(b) Akbar
(c) Aurangzeb
(d) Jahangir

Question 6 :
The Mughal emperor who transferred his capital to Lahore for 13 years was _______.
(a) Babur
(b) Akbar
(c) Jahangir
(d) Shah Jahan

Question 7 :
The _______ was the official chronicler of Shah Jahan's reign and wrote the Badshah Nama.
(a) Abu'l Fazl
(b) Abdul Hamid Lahori
(c) Badauni
(d) Mirza Raja Jai Singh

Question 8 :
The Ain-i Akbari was the third volume of the _______.
(a) Akbar Nama
(b) Badshah Nama
(c) Humayun Nama
(d) Alamgir Nama

Question 9 :
The Mughal court ceremony of sijda involved _______.
(a) Complete prostration before the emperor
(b) Saluting the emperor by raising hands
(c) Kissing the emperor's robe
(d) Bowing slightly with folded hands

Question 10 :
The Mughal emperor who was deeply influenced by the philosophy of light and incorporated it into his kingship was _______.
(a) Babur
(b) Akbar
(c) Jahangir
(d) Aurangzeb

Question 11 :
The imperial Mughal library, where manuscripts were created and stored, was called the _______.
(a) Diwan-i khas
(b) Kitabkhana
(c) Shahi Mahal
(d) Darbar

Question 12 :
Assertion (A): The Mughal nobility was composed of diverse ethnic and religious groups.
Reason (R): The Mughal emperors ensured that no single group dominated the administration.
(a) Both A and R are true, and R is the correct explanation of A.
(b) Both A and R are true, but R is not the correct explanation of A.
(c) A is true, but R is false.
(d) A is false, but R is true.

Question 13 :
The Safavid rulers of Iran frequently disputed Mughal control over _______.
(a) Lahore
(b) Kabul
(c) Qandahar
(d) Kashmir

Question 14 :
The term used to describe the Mughal emperor as the axis of the universe was ______.
(a) Sulh-i kul
(b) Farr-i izadi
(c) Axis mundi
(d) Ain-i Ak

Question 15 :
The Mughal emperor who re-imposed the jizya tax on non-Muslims was ______.
(a) Akbar
(b) Jahangir
(c) Aurangzeb
(d) Shah Jahan

Question 16 :
Assertion (A): The Mughal emperors adopted European artistic techniques in their paintings.
Reason (R): European paintings brought by Jesuit missionaries influenced Mughal miniature art.
(a) Both A and R are true, and R is the correct explanation of A.
(b) Both A and R are true, but R is not the correct explanation of A.
(c) A is true, but R is false.
(d) A is false, but R is true.

Question 17 :
The Mughal emperor who built Shahjahanabad as a new capital was ______.
(a) Akbar
(b) Jahangir
(c) Shah Jahan
(d) Aurangzeb

Question 18 :
The elite group of Mughal courtiers and officers who held high ranks were called ______.
(a) Umara
(b) Faujdar
(c) Subadar
(d) Mir Bakshi

Question 19 :
The Persian term used for the Mughal finance minister was ______.
(a) Mir Bakshi
(b) Diwan-i Ala
(c) Sadr-us Sudur
(d) Mansabdar

Question 20 :
The official records of events maintained at the Mughal court were called ______.
(a) Akhbarat
(b) Farman
(c) Ain-i Akbari
(d) Zat

Question 21 :
Assertion (A): The Mughal empire included a diverse population of Hindus, Muslims, Jainas, and Parsis.
Reason (R): The policy of Sulh-i Kul promoted religious tolerance and ensured stability in the empire.
(a) Both A and R are true, and R is the correct explanation of A.
(b) Both A and R are true, but R is not the correct explanation of A.
(c) A is true, but R is false.
(d) A is false, but R is true.

Question 22 :
Assertion (A): The Mughal court used the motif of a lion and a lamb sitting together as a symbol of justice.
Reason (R): This motif represented the harmonious coexistence of the strong and the weak under Mughal rule.
(a) Both A and R are true, and R is the correct explanation of A.
(b) Both A and R are true, but R is not the correct explanation of A.
(c) A is true, but R is false.
(d) A is false, but R is true.

Question 23 :
The Mughal emperor who issued the order to abolish jizya and pilgrimage taxes in his empire was ______.
(a) Babur
(b) Akbar
(c) Jahangir
(d) Aurangzeb

Question 24 :
The Mughal emperor who was given the title 'Alamgir' (Conqueror of the World) was ______.
(a) Akbar
(b) Jahangir
(c) Shah Jahan
(d) Aurangzeb

Question 25 :
The Persian term used for land grants given to religious scholars and institutions under the Mughals was ______.
(a) Madad-i Maash
(b) Iqta
(c) Zamindari
(d) Jagir

Question 26 :
The Mughal emperor who transferred his court to Lahore for strategic reasons was _______.
(a) Babur
(b) Akbar
(c) Shah Jahan
(d) Aurangzeb

Question 27 :
The system of ranking Mughal officials by their zat (personal rank) and sawar (cavalry rank) was known as the _______.
(a) Iqta system
(b) Mansabdari system
(c) Jagirdari system
(d) Zamindari system

Question 28 :
The Mughal emperor who commissioned the Badshah Nama to record his reign was _______.The Mughal emperor who commissioned the Badshah Nama to record his reign was _______.
(a) Akbar
(b) Jahangir
(c) Shah Jahan
(d) Aurangzeb

Question 29 :
The architectural symbol used to represent the emperor's divine authority in paintings was _______.
(a) The lion and the lamb
(b) The canopy
(c) The halo
(d) The globe

Question 30 :
The Persian term used to refer to a petition presented by a nobleman to the emperor for an applicant's recruitment was _______.
(a) Farman
(b) Akhbarat
(c) Tajwiz
(d) Zat

Question 31 :The Mughal emperor who is credited with abolishing the practice of sijda (complete prostration) at court was _______.
(a) Babur
(b) Akbar
(c) Jahangir
(d) Shah Jahan

Question 32 :
The festival celebrated in the Mughal court that marked the Iranian New Year was _______.
(a) Jashn-i Wazn
(b) Nauroz
(c) Shab-i Barat
(d) Jharoka Darshan

Question 33 :
The emperor who introduced the Jharoka Darshan to strengthen the connection between the ruler and the public was _______.
(a) Babur
(b) Humayun
(c) Akbar
(d) Aurangzeb

Question 34 :
The term "Sulh-i Kul" refers to the Mughal policy of _______.
(a) Military conquest
(b) Religious tolerance
(c) Strict Islamic governance
(d) Trade expansion

Question 35 :
The title given to the finance minister of the Mughal empire was _______.
(a) Mir Bakshi
(b) Subadar
(c) Diwan-i Ala
(d) Mansabdar

Question 36 :
The chronicler who accompanied Emperor Humayun and later worked in Akbar's court was _______.
(a) Badauni
(b) Abu'l Fazl
(c) Abdul Hamid Lahori
(d) Gulbadan Begum

Question 37 :
The Mughal capital city that was built by Akbar but later abandoned due to water scarcity was _______.
(a) Lahore
(b) Shahjahanabad
(c) Fatehpur Sikri
(d) Agra

Question 38 :
The Mughal emperor who was forced into exile by Sher Shah Suri but later regained his throne was _______.
(a) Babur
(b) Humayun
(c) Akbar
(d) Jahangir

Question 39 :
The Akbar Nama and the Badshah Nama were written in which language?
(a) Arabic
(b) Turkish
(c) Persian
(d) Sanskrit

Question 40 :
The institution responsible for the production and preservation of Mughal manuscripts was called ______.
(a) Diwan-i Khas
(b) Kitabkhana
(c) Madad-i Maash
(d) Ain-i Akbari

Question 41 :
The official calligraphic style preferred by Akbar's court for manuscript writing was ______.
(a) Kufic
(b) Nastaliq
(c) Shikasta
(d) Devnagari

Question 42 :
The Mughal emperor who translated Sanskrit texts like the Mahabharata into Persian was ______.
(a) Babur
(b) Akbar
(c) Jahangir
(d) Shah Jahan

Question 43 :
The Persian translation of the Mahabharata was called ______.
(a) Akbar Nama
(b) Ain-i Akbari
(c) Razmnama
(d) Babur Nama

Question 44 :
The art of miniature painting flourished under which Mughal emperor?
(a) Babur
(b) Akbar
(c) Aurangzeb
(d) Bahadur Shah Zafar

Question 45 :
The ceremony in which nobles and officials performed kornish involved ______.
(a) Bowing with hands folded
(b) Prostrating fully on the ground
(c) Raising the right hand to the forehead in salute
(d) Placing the emperor's foot on their head

Question 46 :
Which famous Safavid painter was invited to work in the Mughal court?
(a) Mir Sayyid Ali
(b) Abu'l Hasan
(c) Mansur
(d) Bihzad

Question 47 :
The Persian term taswir, as used in Mughal chronicles, refers to ______.
(a) Calligraphy
(b) Architecture
(c) Painting
(d) Music

Question 48 :
The production of paintings in Mughal manuscripts caused tension with which group?
(a) Hindu Rajputs
(b) European traders
(c) Orthodox Muslim scholars (ulama)
(d) Portuguese missionaries

Question 49 :
The Mughal emperor who built the Red Fort and Jama Masjid in Delhi was ______.
(a) Babur
(b) Akbar
(c) Shah Jahan
(d) Aurangzeb

Question 50 :
The term farr-i izadi refers to ______.
(a) The Mughal taxation system
(b) The Persian concept of Divine Light in kingship
(c) The Mughal military rank system
(d) The official history written by Mughal emperors

Question 51 :
The Mughal emperor depicted in paintings as wearing a halo was ______.
(a) Babur
(b) Akbar
(c) Jahangir
(d) Aurangzeb

Question 52 :
The Mughal title Shahenshah means ______.
(a) Emperor of the World
(b) King of the Kings
(c) Conqueror of Hindustan
(d) Defender of Islam

Questiom 53 :
The Buland Darwaza was built by Akbar after his victory in ______.
(a) Bengal
(b) Gujarat
(c) Punjab
(d) Kabul

Chapter 10 : Colonialism And The Countryside

CONCISE KEY NOTES

Chapter Overview :
- "This chapter explores how colonial rule transformed the countryside, affecting zamindars, peasants, and tribal communities."
- "It covers British land revenue systems such as the Permanent Settlement, the impact on different social groups, and resistance movements."
- "The chapter also discusses the sources used to study colonial rural history, such as official reports, revenue records, and travel accounts."

Land Revenue Systems And Zamindari Crisis :
- The Permanent settlement introduced by governor general of Bengal Charles Cornwallis in 1793.
- "Zamindars were made revenue collectors responsible for fixed payments to the Company."
- "The expectation was that they would improve agriculture and be loyal to the British."
- "However, many zamindars defaulted on payments due to high revenue demands.
- Lathyal- one who holds the lathi or stick functioned as a strong man of the Zamindar.

Auction of Estates and Fictitious Sales :
- "In 1797, the estates of the Raja of Burdwan were auctioned due to unpaid revenue."
- "However, zamindars used legal loopholes to retain control through agents who repurchased the lands."
- "Over 75% of zamindaris changed hands after the Permanent Settlement."
- Taluqdar refers one who holds the Taluq or a collection came to refer to a territorial unit.
- Ryot is the way the term raiyat used to designate peasants.
- Sunset law- if payment did not come in by sunset of the specific date the zamindari was fiable to be auctioned
- when the permanent settlement was imposed Tejchand was the Raja of Burdwan
- Mehtab Chand helped the British during the Santhal rebellion and the 1857 revolt.

The Rise of Jotedars (Rich Peasants) :
- "Jotedars acquired large tracts of land, often more than zamindars."
- "They controlled local trade, moneylending, and sharecropping arrangements."
- "Unlike absentee zamindars, they lived in villages and directly influenced rural affairs."
- Jotedars where most powerful in North Bengal .

The Fifth Report :
- Published in: 1813
- Purpose: To document the administration and activities of the East India Company in India.
- Content: 1002 pages, including 800+ pages of appendices (zamindar petitions, revenue reports, judicial administration notes).
- Focus Areas: Bengal and Madras (now Tamil Nadu).
- Produced by: A Select Committee of the British Parliament.
- Debates & Scrutiny: British political groups debated Company misrule and corruption.
Impact: Basis for intense parliamentary discussions on the Company's role.

Why Was It Published?

- British groups opposed the Company's monopoly over Indian trade.
- Traders & manufacturers wanted open access to Indian markets.
- Reports of Company misrule and corruption were widely publicized.
- British Parliament wanted to regulate and control Company rule.

Criticism & Limitations :

- Exaggerated decline of zamindars' power.
- Overestimated zamindari land loss.
- Recent research suggests zamindars found ways to retain control.
- Benami term used in Hindi and several other Indian languages for transaction made in the name of a fictitious or relatively insignificant person where does the real beneficiary remains unamed.

Tribal Communities And Land Alienation: The Paharias Of Rajmahal Hills

- "Practiced shifting cultivation, hunting, and gathering."
- "Regularly raided settled villages, compelling zamindars to pay tribute for peace."
- "The British saw them as 'wild' and encouraged settled agriculture to 'civilize' them."

Francis Buchanan (Buchanan-Hamilton) :

- Physician (Bengal Medical Service, 1794-1815).
- Surgeon to Lord Wellesley.
- Founded Calcutta Alipore Zoo & managed Botanical Gardens.
- Surveyed British territories in India.
- Returned to England (1815), later adopted Hamilton surname.
- Policy of Pacification – proposed in the 1780s by Augustus Cleveland the collector of Bhagalpur.

The Santhals: From Settlers to Rebels :

- Encouraged by the British to clear forests and settle as peasants in Damin-i-Koh (1832).
- "Population rose from 3,000 in 1838 to 82,000 in 1851."
- Soon faced oppression from moneylenders (dikus) and zamindars."
- "Rebelled in 1855-56, leading to the creation of the Santhal Pargana."
- Carving out 5,500 square miles from the districts of Bhagalpur and Birbhum.
- Sidhu Manjhi – leader of the Santhal rebellion.

Agrarian Crisis In Western India: The Deccan Riots (1875) :
The Cotton Boom and Peasant Indebtedness :

- In 1857 the Cotton supply Association was founded in Britain and in 1859 the Manchester cotton company was formed objective was to encourage cotton production in every part of the world.
- During the American Civil War (1861-65), British textile mills turned to India for cotton.
- Deccan peasants took loans to grow cotton, hoping for high profits.
- However, after 1865, American cotton supply resumed, and Indian prices crashed.
- Moneylenders refused further loans and demanded repayment.
- Sahukar – someone who acted as both a money lender and a trader.

Peasant Revolt Against Moneylenders :

- On 12 May 1875, peasants in Supa attacked moneylenders, burned account books (bahi khatas), and looted grain.

Complaints of Ryots Against Moneylenders :
- Unfair Harvest Deals – Took harvest but didn't credit accounts.
- No Receipts – Payments made, but no proof given.
- Fake Debts – Added extra amounts to loan records.
- Loss of Land & Property – Seized for unpaid loans.
- Forced New Loans – Old interest added as new debt every 3 years.
- Tricked into Signing – Ryots signed without understanding.
- Low Crop Prices – Forced to sell produce cheaply.

Limitation Law (1859) :
Purpose: Limited the validity of loan bonds to three years to prevent excessive interest accumulation.
Moneylenders' Tactic: Forced ryots to sign new bonds every three years, resetting debt terms and bypassing the law.

Deccan Riots Commission (1878) :
- "Investigated the causes of the uprising but blamed moneylenders, not British revenue policies."
- "Revealed how peasants were trapped in debt cycles and forced to sign unfair loan agreements."

Important Timelines :

- 1765: East India Company gets Diwani of Bengal
- 1773: Regulating Act passed
- 1793: Permanent Settlement in Bengal
- 1800s: Santhals settle in Rajmahal hills
- 1818: First revenue settlement in Bombay Deccan
- 1820s: Agricultural prices fall
- 1840s-50s: Agrarian expansion in Bombay Deccan
- 1855-56: Santhal rebellion
- 1861: Cotton boom begins
- 1875: Deccan ryot rebellion

Chapter 10 : Colonialism And The Countryside

QUESTIONS FROM ARCHIVES

Question 1 :
Assertion (A): The Permanent Settlement introduced in Bengal in 1793 ensured a fixed revenue demand for zamindars.
Reason (R): The British wanted to create a class of loyal landlords who would have both political stability and economic security.
(a) Both A and R are true, and R is the correct explanation of A.
(b) Both A and R are true, but R is not the correct explanation of A.
(c) A is true, but R is false.
(d) A is false, but R is true.

Question 2 :
Assertion (A): The Santhals initially accepted British rule and settled in the Damin-i-Koh region.
Reason (R): The British assured them permanent land ownership and protection from exploitation.
(a) Both A and R are true, and R is the correct explanation of A.
(b) Both A and R are true, but R is not the correct explanation of A.
(c) A is true, but R is false.
(d) A is false, but R is true.

Question 3 :
Assertion (A): The Paharias resisted British efforts to bring them under settled agriculture.
Reason (R): The British associated forests with wildness and wanted to "civilize" the forest dwellers.
(a) Both A and R are true, and R is the correct explanation of A.
(b) Both A and R are true, but R is not the correct explanation of A.
(c) A is true, but R is false.
(d) A is false, but R is true.

Question 4 :

The Raja of Burdwan avoided losing his zamindari by using ___________ purchases at auctions.
(a) Benami
(b) Legal
(c) Foreign
(d) Permanent

Question 5 :
The Deccan Riots of 1875 were primarily caused by the ___________ exploitation of peasants.
(a) British administrators'
(b) Zamindars'
(c) Moneylenders'
(d) Paharias'

Question 6 :
The ___________ was a report submitted to the British Parliament in 1813, highlighting the mismanagement of the East India Company.
(a) Fourth Report
(b) Seventh Report
(c) Fifth Report
(d) Deccan Report

Question 7 :
Under the Permanent Settlement, zamindars were expected to pay revenue ___________.
(a) According to the annual harvest
(b) Permanently fixed, irrespective of production
(c) Based on the trade earnings
(d) Only when the government demanded

Question 8 :
The Santhal Revolt (1855-56) led to the creation of ___________, a separate administrative region for the Santhals.
(a) Rajmahal Pargana
(b) Deccan Pargana
(c) Santhal Pargana
(d) Burdwan Pargana

Question 9 :
What was the main reason for the failure of the Permanent Settlement in Bengal?
(a) The British overestimated the financial capabilities of zamindars
(b) Ryots refused to pay rent to zamindars
(c) The system created instability in the villages
(d) The British continuously changed revenue rates

Question 10 :
The Limitation Law of 1859 was passed to:
(a) Fix permanent revenue rates for peasants
(b) Limit the number of villages a zamindar could own
(c) Restrict the accumulation of interest on moneylenders' loans
(d) Prohibit the zamindars from collecting rent

(A): The jotedars in Bengal were more powerful than the zamindars in rural areas.
Reason (R): Unlike zamindars, jotedars lived in villages, had control over land, and resisted the zamindars' attempts to increase rent.
(a) Both A and R are true, and R is the correct explanation of A.
(b) Both A and R are true, but R is not the correct explanation of A.
(c) A is true, but R is false.
(d) A is false, but R is true.

Question 12 :
Assertion (A): The Paharias of Rajmahal hills were known for their resistance to settled agriculture.
Reason (R): The British policy of pacification involved providing allowances to Paharia chiefs, which led to their complete acceptance of British rule.
(a) Both A and R are true, and R is the correct explanation of A.
(b) Both A and R are true, but R is not the correct explanation of A.
(c) A is true, but R is false.
(d) A is false, but R is true.

Question 13 :
Assertion (A): The Santhals were initially encouraged by the British to settle in the Damin-i-Koh region.
Reason (R): The British wanted to transform the Santhals into settled agriculturists to generate more land revenue.
(a) Both A and R are true, and R is the correct explanation of A.
(b) Both A and R are true, but R is not the correct explanation of A.
(c) A is true, but R is false.
(d) A is false, but R is true.

Question 14 :
Assertion (A): The Deccan Riots of 1875 were directed primarily against the British administration.
Reason (R): The British had introduced harsh land revenue policies that directly caused the riots.
(a) Both A and R are true, and R is the correct explanation of A.
(b) Both A and R are true, but R is not the correct explanation of A.
(c) A is false, but R is true.
(d) A is true, but R is false.

Question 15 :
The ___________ was a law passed in 1859 that limited the validity of loan bonds to three years.
(a) Deccan Agricultural Law
(b) Limitation Law
(c) Land Revenue Law
(d) Ryotwari Settlement

Question 16 :
The Deccan Riots of 1875 were mainly caused by the oppressive practices of ___________.
(a) British officials
(b) Moneylenders (sahukars)
(c) Zamindars
(d) Peasant leaders

Question 17 :
The ___________ was a report presented in 1878 to investigate the causes of the Deccan Riots.
(a) Fifth Report
(b) Santhal Report
(c) Deccan Riots Commission Report
(d) Paharia Report

Question 18 :
The expansion of ___________ cultivation in the Bombay Deccan during the American Civil War led to increased indebtedness of peasants.
(a) Indigo
(b) Rice
(c) Cotton
(d) Wheat

Question 19 :
The British introduced the Ryotwari Settlement in the Bombay Deccan because they believed ___________.
(a) Zamindars were inefficient in collecting revenue
(b) Directly settling revenue with ryots would prevent them from becoming landless
(c) It would permanently fix revenue rates
(d) The system would allow moneylenders to control the land

Question 20 :
The Santhal Rebellion (1855-56) was caused by ___________.
(a) Exploitation by zamindars, moneylenders, and British officials
(b) Conflict between Santhals and the Paharias
(c) A severe famine in the region
(d) High taxation imposed by the Santhal chiefs

Question 21 :
The ___________ was introduced in Bengal in 1793 to ensure a fixed revenue demand from zamindars.
(a) Ryotwari Settlement
(b) Mahalwari Settlement
(c) Permanent Settlement
(d) Zamindari Abolition Act

Question 22 :
Under the Permanent Settlement, zamindars were required to pay revenue ___________.
(a) Based on annual agricultural production
(b) In a permanently fixed amount regardless of production
(c) Only during periods of surplus harvest
(d) After consulting village heads

Question 23 :
The ___________ were a class of rich peasants in Bengal who controlled local trade, lent money to poorer peasants, and resisted zamindari demands.
(a) Paharias
(b) Santhals
(c) Jotedars
(d) Ryots

Question 24 :
The British introduced the ___________ law, which stated that if revenue was not paid by sunset of the due date, the zamindari would be auctioned.
(a) Limitation Law
(b) Sunset Law
(c) Permanent Law
(d) Rent Law

Question 25 :
The Santhals were given land to settle in the ___________ region by the British in the early 19th century.
(a) Jangal Mahals
(b) Damin-i-Koh
(c) Rajmahal Hills
(d) Burdwan Pargana

Question 26 :
In 1797, an auction was held in Burdwan where the estates of the Raja were sold because he had:
(a) Rebelled against British rule
(b) Failed to pay the fixed revenue
(c) Given land to the Paharias
(d) Refused to cultivate cash crops

Question 27 :
The Fifth Report submitted to the British Parliament in 1813 primarily discussed:
(a) The role of zamindars in the Deccan Riots
(b) The problems of permanent settlement in Bengal
(c) The causes of the Santhal rebellion
(d) The trade policies of the East India Company

Question 28 :
The Santhals were brought to the Rajmahal hills by the British to:
(a) Serve as military recruits
(b) Expand settled agriculture
(c) Collect forest produce
(d) Act as zamindars under British rule

Question 29 :
The Paharias primarily resisted British rule by:
(a) Adopting Western agricultural techniques
(b) Filing petitions in colonial courts
(c) Raiding settled villages and attacking outsiders
(d) Joining the British military forces

Question 30 :
The British encouraged the clearing of forests in India because they:
(a) Wanted to protect the Paharias' way of life
(b) Aimed to increase land revenue from agriculture
(c) Wanted to expand hunting reserves
(d) Needed more land for British settlement

Question 31 :
The Deccan Riots of 1875 were mainly caused by:
(a) High revenue demands and debt traps of moneylenders
(b) Conflict between zamindars and British officials
(c) Peasants refusing to grow British crops
(d) The rise of industrialization in India

Question 32 :
The term "benami purchase" in the context of zamindari auctions refers to:
(a) Buying property in the name of a fictitious person
(b) Paying revenue directly to the British government
(c) Using legal documents to avoid taxation
(d) Buying land from the British at discounted rates

Question 33 :
The Ryotwari system was introduced in:
(a) Bengal
(b) North India
(c) The Bombay Deccan
(d) Punjab

Question 34 :
What was a key reason for the failure of many zamindars to pay revenue under the Permanent Settlement?
(a) The revenue demand was set too high
(b) Peasants refused to work for zamindars
(c) The British reduced the prices of cash crops
(d) The zamindars invested heavily in industry

Question 35 :
The Limitation Law of 1859 was introduced to:
(a) Stop zamindars from collecting rent
(b) Control the excessive charging of interest by moneylenders
(c) Fix the price of agricultural goods
(d) Restrict the amount of land owned by peasants

Question 36 :
The ____________ was a rebellion led by the Santhals in 1855-56 against the exploitation by moneylenders, zamindars, and British officials.
(a) Paharia Revolt
(b) Deccan Riots
(c) Santhal Rebellion
(d) Indigo Revolt

Question 37 :
The ____________ system in the Bombay Deccan directly settled revenue with individual ryots rather than zamindars.
(a) Mahalwari
(b) Ryotwari
(c) Permanent
(d) Zamindari

Question 38 :
Who was the leader of the santhal revolt ?
(a) Birsa Munda
(b) Gonoo
(c) Shah mal
(d) Sidhu Manjhi

Question 39 :
During the American Civil War (1861-65), the demand for ____________ from India increased, leading to a short-term economic boom in the Deccan.
(a) Indigo
(b) Jute
(c) Cotton
(d) Opium

Question 40 :
The ____________ was a report presented to the British Parliament in 1813, highlighting the mismanagement and corruption of the East India Company.
(a) Deccan Riots Report
(b) Fifth Report
(c) Santhal Inquiry Report
(d) Bengal Revenue Report

Question 41 :
The Permanent Settlement was introduced by:
(a) Lord Wellesley
(b) Lord Cornwallis
(c) Warren Hastings
(d) Robert Clive

Question 42 :
Under the Ryotwari system, revenue was collected directly from:
(a) Zamindars
(b) Village headmen
(c) Ryots (peasants)
(d) Moneylenders

Question 43 :
The Deccan Riots Commission was established in:
(a) 1857
(b) 1861
(c) 1875
(d) 1882

Question 44 :
The main reason why zamindars defaulted on revenue payments under the Permanent Settlement was:
(a) High initial revenue demands
(b) Resistance from peasants
(c) Opposition from British officials
(d) Decrease in agricultural land

Question 45 :
The Santhal Pargana was created after the:
(a) Deccan Riots
(b) Santhal Rebellion
(c) Paharia Uprising
(d) Indigo Revolt

Question 46 :
The British pacification policy towards the Paharias included:
(a) Granting them land rights
(b) Imposing high taxes
(c) Offering allowances to their chiefs
(d)Banning shifting cultivation

Question 47 :

The jotedars in Bengal were known for:
(a) Supporting the zamindars
(b) Controlling local trade and land
(c) Collecting rent for the British
(d) Introducing new agricultural methods

Question 48 :
Which group was responsible for providing loans to peasants in colonial India?
(a) British officials
(b) Zamindars
(c) Moneylenders (sahukars)
(d) Village panchayats

Question 49 :
The cotton boom in the Deccan was caused by:
(a) The American Civil War
(b) The Industrial Revolution in India
(c) A decline in rice cultivation
(d) British policies promoting textiles

Question 50 :
The ______________ was an important source of information about the impact of British rule on rural Bengal in the 18th century.
(a) Deccan Riots Report
(b) Fifth Report
(c) Santhal Inquiry Report
(d) Indigo Commission Report

Question 51 :
The British encouraged the settlement of Santhals in Damin-i-Koh primarily to:
(a) Establish them as zamindars
(b) Expand settled agriculture and increase land revenue
(c) Use them as soldiers in the British army
(d) Convert them into traders

Question 52 :
The Raja of Burdwan attempted to avoid revenue payment by:
(a) Shifting his zamindari to his mother's name
(b) Seeking financial aid from the British government
(c) Raising rent from peasants unfairly
(d) Organizing an armed rebellion against the British

Question 53 :
Under the Permanent Settlement, if a zamindar failed to pay the revenue on time:
(a) He was given a grace period to clear dues
(b) His estate was auctioned to recover the arrears
(c) He could negotiate with the British for lower payments
(d) The revenue was adjusted based on agricultural productivity

Question 54 :
The main reason why the Paharias withdrew deeper into the Rajmahal Hills was:
(a) The intrusion of Santhal settlers into their lands
(b) British policies promoting nomadic lifestyles
(c) Their preference for living away from agriculture
(d) Their decision to become traders

Question 55 :
Match the following groups with their geographical regions:
A. Paharias	1. Rajmahal Hills
B. Santhals	2. Damin-i-Koh
C. Ryots.	3. Bengal and Deccan
D. Jotedars	4. North Bengal
(a) A-1, B-2, C-3, D-4
(b) A-2, B-1, C-4, D-3
(c) A-3, B-4, C-2, D-1
(d) A-4, B-3, C-1, D-2

Question 56 :
The Deccan Riots of 1875 were targeted at:
(a) British soldiers
(b) Moneylenders who exploited peasants
(c) Zamindars who increased rent
(d) Ryots who refused to cultivate cash crops

Question 57 :
The British passed the Limitation Law in 1859 to:
(a) Limit the revenue demands on zamindars
(b) Restrict peasants from borrowing money
(c) Control the accumulation of interest on debts
(d) Reduce the number of villages under zamindari control

Question 58 :
What was the primary occupation of the Paharias before British intervention?
(a) Settled agriculture
(b) Trade and business
(c) Shifting cultivation and forest produce gathering
(d) Working as zamindari officials

Question 59 :
The Fifth Report exaggerated the collapse of zamindari power because:
(a) The British wanted to justify their control over rural Bengal
(b) Zamindars completely lost their estates and had no influence
(c) It was written based on direct testimonies of zamindars
(d) The British were afraid of peasant uprisings

Question 60 :
Match the following British officials with their policies or reports:
A. Lord Cornwallis	1. Introduced Permanent Settlement
B. Augustus Cleveland	2. Policy of pacification for the Paharias
C. Francis Buchanan	3. Conducted surveys on rural economy
D. Charles Cornwallis	4. Governor-General during American War of Independence

(a) A-1, B-2, C-3, D-4
(b) A-3, B-1, C-4, D-2
(c) A-2, B-4, C-1, D-3
(d) A-4, B-3, C-2, D-1

Question 81 :
Read the passage and answer the following:

"The Santhals, however, soon found that the land they had brought under cultivation was slipping away from their hands. The state was levying heavy taxes on the land that the Santhals had cleared, moneylenders (dikus) were charging them high rates of interest and taking over the land when debts remained unpaid, and zamindars were asserting control over the Damin area. By the 1850s, the Santhals felt that the time had come to rebel against zamindars, moneylenders and the colonial state, in order to create an ideal world for themselves where they would rule. It was after the Santhal Revolt (1855-56) that the Santhal Pargana was created, carving out 5,500 square miles from the districts of Bhagalpur and Birbhum."

1.Why did the Santhals lose the land they had cultivated?
(a) They willingly abandoned it for better land
(b) Heavy taxes, high-interest loans, and zamindari control
(c) British policy allowed them only temporary settlement
(d) They sold their lands to British and officers for profit

2.The term "dikus" in the passage refers to:
(a) British officers
(b) Santhal landlords
(c) Moneylenders and exploiters
(d) Peasant leaders

3.What was the primary reason for the Santhal Revolt of 1855-56?
(a) To fight against the British military occupation
(b) To overthrow the zamindars and moneylenders
(c) To gain equal rights in British administration
(d) To demand higher wages from European traders

4.What action did the British take after the Santhal Revolt?
(a) They completely banned the Santhals from land ownership
(b) They created the Santhal Pargana region
(c) They abolished zamindari rule across India
(d) They allowed Santhals to become government officers

5.The Santhals initially agreed to settle in Damin-i-Koh because:
(a) The British promised them land ownership and protection
(b) They were forced into the settlement by zamindars
(c) They wanted to serve as British soldiers
(d) They needed a temporary place to live during a famine

Question 82 :
Match the following revenue systems with their characteristics:
A. Permanent Settlement	1. Revenue collected directly from ryots
B. Ryotwari Settlement	2. Revenue collected through zamindars
C. Mahalwari Settlement	3. Revenue fixed permanently
D. Sunset Law	4. Zamindars lost land if revenue was unpaid by sunset
(a) A-3, B-1, C-2, D-4
(b) A-2, B-1, C-4, D-3
(c) A-1, B-2, C-3, D-4
(d) A-4, B-3, C-1, D-2

Question 83 :
Match the following events with their outcomes:
A. Santhal Revolt (1855-56)	1. Creation of the Santhal Pargana
B. Deccan Riots (1875)	2. Establishment of a commission to investigate moneylender practices
C. American Civil War	3. Increased demand for Indian cotton
D. Fifth Report (1813)	4. Criticism of East India Company's land policies
(a) A-1, B-2, C-3, D-4
(b) A-4, B-3, C-2, D-1
(c) A-2, B-1, C-4, D-3
(d) A-3, B-4, C-1, D-2

Chapter 11 : Rebels and Raj

CONCISE KEY NOTES

Introduction :
- In May 1857, sepoys in Meerut revolted, attacking British officers, seizing arms, and destroying buildings.
- Telegraph lines to Delhi were cut as rebels advanced to the Red Fort: Bahadur Shah II was informed of British mistreatment of Hindus and Muslims.
- More locals joined in Delhi, killing Europeans and looting: Delhi came under rebel control with the emperor's support.
- After brief calm on 12-13 May, mutinies spread across the Gangetic valley and west of Delhi.

Pattern of the Uprising and Communication:
- Revolts spread town to town, signaled by gunfire or bugles. Rebels looted arms, burned records, and targeted British allies.
- Proclamations urged Hindu–Muslim unity. Commoners attacked moneylenders and the rich, turning the mutiny into a mass rebellion.
- Similar revolt patterns suggest planning and coordination.
- Letters, emissary travel, and protected officers like Hearsey show organized efforts.
- Panchayats in places like Kanpur reveal collective sepoy decision-making.

Leaders and Followers :
- Leadership was crucial, often drawing from pre-British authority figures.
- Meerut sepoys turned to Mughal emperor Bahadur Shah II, who reluctantly accepted leadership.
- In Kanpur, Nana Sahib was compelled to lead: Rani of Jhansi and Kunwar Singh faced similar pressures in their areas.
- In Awadh, people rallied around Birjis Qadr, the young Nawab's son.
- Leadership also came from religious figures, local chiefs, and prophets.
- A fakir in Meerut, preachers in Lucknow, and leaders like Shah Mal (U.P.) and Gonoo (Singhbhum) mobilized peasants, zamindars, and tribals.

Two Rebels of 1857 : Shah Mal & Maulvi Ahmadullah Shah
- A Jat cultivator from U.P., Shah Mal led a revolt against the British land revenue system that dispossessed villagers.
- He united 84 villages to resist British rule, targeting moneylenders, traders, and landlords. He supported Delhi's sepoys by cutting communication lines and sending supplies.
- He occupied a British bungalow, set up a justice hall, and built an intelligence network.
- Locals felt empowered, but Shah Mal was killed in battle in July 1857.

Maulavi Ahmadullah Shah :

• A preacher from Hyderabad, he rallied people for jehad and rebellion from 1856, gaining fame as "Danka Shah."
  • Despite British attempts to silence him, his popularity grew, especially among Muslims who saw him as prophetic.
  • After imprisonment, he was chosen leader by the 22nd Native Infantry and led them to victory at the Battle of Chinhat.
  • Seen as invincible by followers, he became a symbol of resistance.

Rumours and Prophecies:
  • Rumours and prophecies played a major role in the 1857 rebellion.
  • A key rumour claimed cartridges were greased with cow and pig fat, offending both Hindus and Muslims this spread quickly despite British denials.
  • Another rumour said bone dust was mixed into flour to destroy caste and religion, prompting widespread food refusal.
  • Fears of forced Christian conversion and a prophecy that British rule would end in 1857 (100 years after Plassey) fueled unrest.
  • The mysterious circulation of chapattis was seen as a sign of revolt.

Why People Believed:
  • Rumours reflected fears of losing faith, culture, and power.
  • British reforms—Western education, new laws, land changes, annexations, and social reforms—disrupted traditional life.
  • Many saw these as deliberate attempts to destroy religion and customs.

Awadh in Revolt:
  • In 1851, Lord Dalhousie called Awadh "a cherry that will drop into our mouth," and it was annexed in 1856 after years under British influence via the Subsidiary Alliance.
  • The Nawab lost military power and became dependent on the British Resident.
  • The British sought Awadh for its fertile land (indigo, cotton) and strategic trade location.
  • Annexation marked the final stage of British territorial expansion from Bengal.

"The life was gone out of the body"
  • Dalhousie's annexations, especially Awadh's, caused deep unrest.
  • Nawab Wajid Ali Shah was exiled to Calcutta for misrule, though he was beloved by the people.
  • Lucknow mourned his loss and some followed him to Kanpur; the city felt lifeless, as described by observers and folk songs.
  • His fall devastated livelihoods tied to the court—artists, poets, artisans, and officials were left without support.

Firangi Raj and the end of a World
  • The 1857 British annexation of Awadh dismantled taluqdar power and authority, removing their traditional semi-autonomous status under the Nawab.
  • The Summary Settlement (1856) redistributed land but increased exploitation, while rigid British revenue policies worsened conditions for both landholders and peasants.
  • Widespread discontent grew as traditional social structures collapsed and economic conditions deteriorated across all classes.

- Sepoys, mostly from Awadh villages, were influenced by these grievances and suffered deteriorating relations with British officers marked by racial abuse.
- The rebellion united taluqdars, peasants, and sepoys against British rule, with rural connections serving as a crucial link in the uprising.

What the Rebels Wanted:
- The 1857 rebellion narrative was dominated by British perspectives as victors, who portrayed rebels as barbaric and ungrateful.
- Rebel voices were largely silenced due to widespread illiteracy and British suppression.
- The absence of rebel-written records makes reconstructing their viewpoint difficult, with most information filtered through British sources that offer little insight into their true motives and goals.

The Vision of Unity:
- 1857 rebel proclamations transcended religious divides, with Muslim princes addressing Hindu sentiments and framing the rebellion as a joint Hindu-Muslim struggle against British rule.
- Proclamations emphasized peaceful pre-colonial coexistence, with one in Bahadur Shah's name calling for fighting under both Muhammad and Mahavir's banners.
- British attempts to create Hindu-Muslim divisions, including a Rs 50,000 effort in Bareilly (December 1857), failed to disrupt rebel unity.

Against the Symbols of Oppression:
- Rebels condemned British rule for annexations, broken treaties, and harmful policies that ruined various classes, while fearing forced Christianity.
- The uprising aimed to restore traditional life and protect livelihood, faith, and identity, eventually targeting both British officials and their local allies.
- Actions like burning account books and looting moneylenders revealed desires for justice and equality, while proclamations united diverse social groups against colonial oppression.

The Search for Alternative Power:
- Following British collapse, rebels in Delhi, Lucknow, and Kanpur established alternative governance systems aimed at restoring pre-colonial order, reviving courtly traditions while appointing officials, collecting revenue, and maintaining public order.
- Rebel military efforts featured structured armies with clear command chains, though most couldn't withstand British counterattacks, with Awadh's resistance lasting longest through organized Lucknow court leadership into early 1858.

Repression:
- British suppression of the 1857 rebellion involved martial law with suspended legal procedures and summary executions, while forces from Calcutta and Punjab faced fierce resistance, especially in Delhi.
- The slow reconquest saw widespread participation (three-fourths of Awadh's adult males), with the British using both military force and strategic incentives—rewarding loyalists while punishing rebels with dispossession, death, or exile.

- Historical understanding relies on British sources due to scarce rebel perspectives, with colonial documents, sensationalist newspapers, and visual art (paintings, cartoons) from both sides providing glimpses of the conflict through different lenses.

Celebrating The Saviours:
- British art depicted the 1857 rebellion as emotionally charged propaganda.
- Paintings celebrated imperial heroes and British triumph. Thomas Jones Barker's *Relief of Lucknow* is a key example.
- The painting highlights figures like Henry Lawrence, Colonel Inglis, James Outram, and Colin Campbell.
- Composition and lighting emphasized British victory and suffering. Such art reassured the British public and symbolized restored colonial power.

English Women and the Honour of Britain:
- Reports of violence against English women and children fueled anger and calls for revenge.
- Artworks like *In Memoriam* showed women as victims and British forces as rescuers.
- Some images, like Miss Wheeler's, portrayed women as heroic defenders.
- Rebels were demonized, and the conflict was framed as a religious struggle using symbols like the Bible.

Vengeance and Retribution:
- British outrage after the 1857 revolt led to calls for violent retribution, justified by press and visuals.
- Harsh executions like hanging and blowing from guns were widely publicized; mercy was mocked, especially Canning's leniency.
- The revolt inspired nationalism, hailed as the First War of Independence and a united Indian uprising.
- Leaders like Rani Lakshmi Bai were celebrated as heroic warriors; her valor lives on in the saying "Khoob lari mardani woh to Jhansi wali rani thi.".

Important Figures

Fig. 10.1
Portrait of Bahadur Shah

Fig. 10.3
Rani Lakshmi Bai, a popular image

Fig. 10.4
Nana Sahib

Fig. 10.5
Henry Hardinge, by Francis Grant,
1849

Fig. 10.7
Bengal sepoys in European-style
uniform

Important Figures

Fig. 10.8
A mosque on the Delhi Ridge, photograph by Felice Beato, 1857-58
After 1857, British photographers recorded innumerable images of desolation and ruin.

Fig. 10.9
Secundrah Bagh, Lucknow, photograph by Felice Beato, 1858

Fig. 10.11
"In Memoriam", by Joseph Noel Paton, 1859

Fig. 10.10
"Relief of Lucknow", painted by Thomas Jones Barker, 1859

Fig. 10.12
Miss Wheeler defending herself against sepoys in Kanpur

Fig. 10.14
The caption at the bottom reads "The British Lion's Vengeance on the Bengal Tiger", Punch, 1857.

Fig. 10.17
"The Clemency of Canning"

Chapter 11 : Mapwork

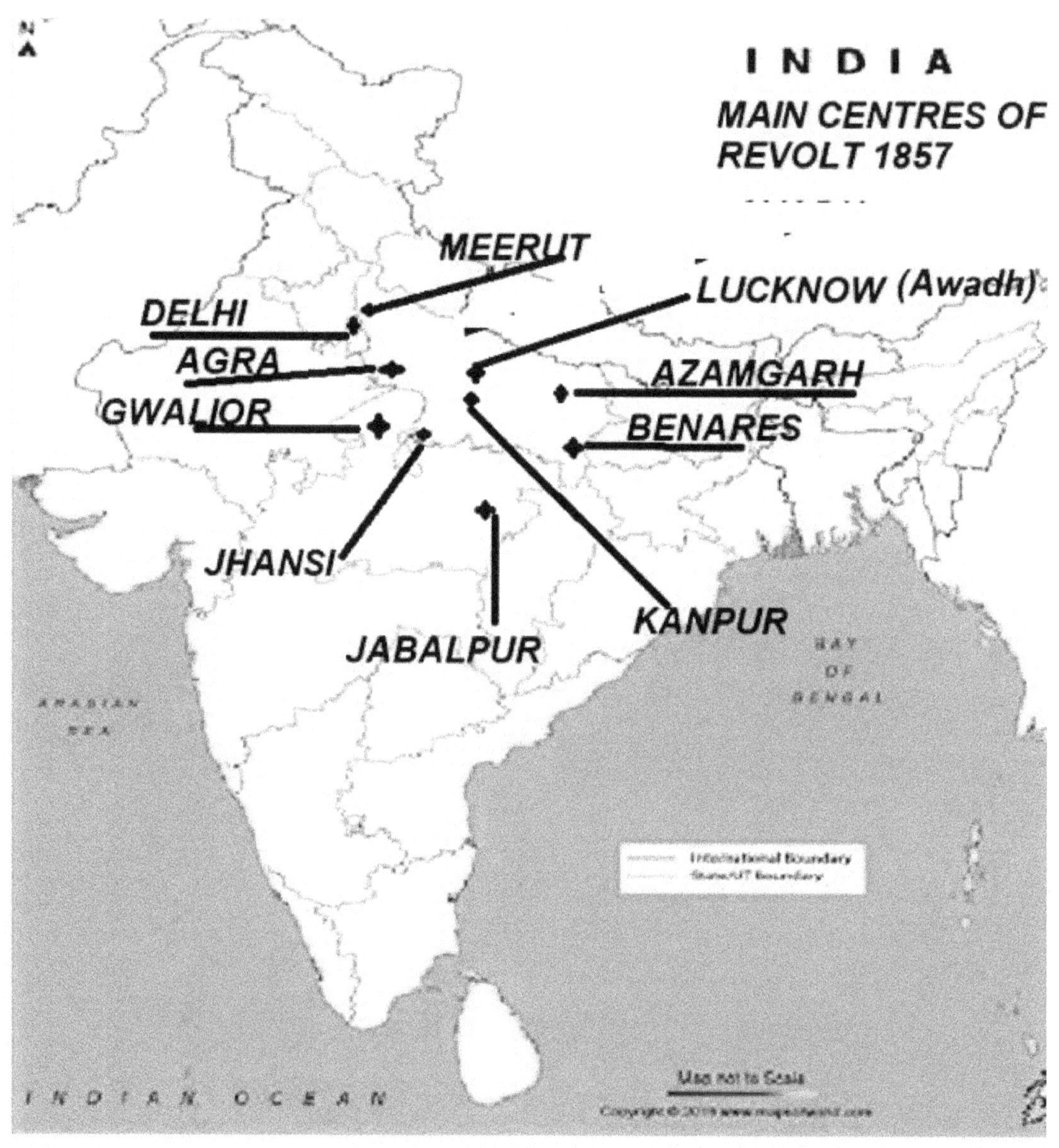

Chapter 11 : Rebels And Raj

QUESTIONS FROM ARCHIVES

Question 1 :
Who was responsible for introducing the Subsidiary Alliance system?
a. Lord Hardinge
b. Lord Wellesley
c. Lord Canning
d. Lord Bentinck

Question 2 :
Who led the rebellion in Kanpur during the uprising of 1857?
a. Nana Sahib
b. Shah Mal
c. Baaji Rao
d. Shivaji

Question 3 :
Who led the revolt in Delhi in 1857?
a. Bhukt Khan
b. Birji Qadr
c. Bahadur Shah
d. Siraj-Ud-Daula

Question 4 :
Who took charge of the rebellion in Jhansi?
a. Rani Lakshmi Bai
b. Birjis Qadr
c. Haz Sahib
d. Nawab Wajid Ali Shah

Question 5 :
When did the soldiers at Meerut cantonment rebel during the revolt of 1857?
a. 13th May 1857
b. 24th May 1857
c. 10th May 1857
d. 20th May 1857

Question 6 :
Which Governor-General aimed to reform Indian society with new policies?
a. Lord Canning
b. Harding
c. Hastings
d. William Bentinck

Question 7 :
What was the immediate reason for the 1857 rebellion?
a. Western Education
b. Widow Remarriage
c. Introduction of greased cartridges
d. Abolition of sati

Question 8 :
Which kingdom did the British refer to as "a cherry that will one day fall into their lap"?
a. Panchal
b. Bihar
c. Awadh
d. Bengal

Question 9 :
Where did the revolt of 1857 first begin?
a. Delhi
b. Meerut
c. Panipat
d. Lucknow

Question 10 :
Who was known by the title "Danka Shah"?
a. Bahadur Shah
b. Birjis Qadar
c. Maulvi Ahmadullah
d. Shah Mal

Question 11 :
Which of the following was not a valid reason for the British annexing Awadh in 1857?
a. Wajid Ali Shah was unpopular.
b. The Subsidiary Alliance System was readily accepted.
c. Mangal Pandey started the rebellion from Awadh.
d. Material benefits were g
iven to taluqdars.

Question 12 :
When was the practice of Sati abolished in India?
a. 1833
b. 1829
c. 1858
d. 1857

Question 13 :
Who initiated the uprising of 1857?
a. Sepoys
b. Money Lenders
c. Mughal Rulers
d. Village Panchayats

Question 14 :
Who led the rebellion of 1857 in Kanpur?
a. Rani Laxmi Bai
b. Nana Sahib
c. Bahadur Shah Zafar
d. Peshwa Baji Rao II

Question 15:
Match the leaders with the places where they led the revolt:

List-I	List-II
(i) Delhi	(a) Nana Sahib
(ii) Kanpur	(b) Bahadur Shah
(iii) Arrah	(c) Kunwar Singh
(iv) Lucknow	(d) Birjis Qadr

Options:
a. (d), (b), (c), (a)
b. (b), (a), (c), (d)
c. (b), (d), (c), (a)
d. (a), (c), (b), (d)

Question 16:
Lord Dalhousie compared the kingdom of Awadh to which fruit?
(a) Pineapple
(b) Apple
(c) Cherry
(d) Strawberry

Question 17 :
When was Awadh officially annexed into the British Empire?
(a) 1856
(b) 1848
(c) 1866
(d) None of the Above

Question 18 :
Which of the following statements regarding the 1857 Revolt is/are accurate?
(i) On May 10, 1857, sepoys in Meerut mutinied, starting with the native infantry and spreading rapidly.
(ii) The local people of Meerut and nearby areas supported the sepoys.
(iii) The sepoys looted weapons, attacked Europeans, and destroyed their properties.
(iv) On May 11, 1857, they reached the Red Fort gates.
(a) Only (iii) and (iv)
(b) (i) and (ii)
(c) All of the above
(d) Only (i)

Question 19 :
What does the term "Bell of Arms" refer to?
(a) A storeroom for storing weapons
(b) Energetic and lively
(c) To thoroughly search, often harshly
(d) Sharp or stinging

Question 20 :
Which term is mismatched in its meaning?
(a) Mutiny: Collective defiance within the military
(b) Revolt: Rebellion against authority
(c) Firangi: A derogatory term for foreigners in Hindi and Urdu
(d) Bell of Arms: A place where food is stored

Question 21 :
Which of the following statements about Nawab Wajid Ali Shah is incorrect?
(i) He was exiled to Calcutta for alleged misgovernance.
(ii) He was an unpopular ruler.
(iii) His departure from Lucknow led to cultural unity in the court.
(iv) Many followed him to Kanpur, mourning his departure.
(a) Only (ii) and (iv)
(b) (i) and (ii)
(c) (iii) and (iv)
(d) Only (i)

Question 22 :
Who led the revolt in Delhi during the 1857 uprising?
(a) Bahadur Shah Zafar
(b) Begum Hazrat Mahal
(c) Kunwar Singh
(d) Rani Lakshmi Bai

Question 23 :
Which of these was not a 19th-century rumor about the British?
(a) New cartridges were greased with animal fat.
(b) Flour sold in markets contained bone dust.
(c) The British planned to convert Indians to Christianity.
(d) They aimed to abolish the caste system.

Question 24 :
Birjis Qadr was the younger son of which Nawab?
(a) Nawab Wajid Ali Shah
(b) Nawab Shaukat Ali
(c) Nawab Siraj-ud-daula
(d) Nawab Mir Ali

Question 25 :
Under which policy were Awadh and Satara annexed?
(a) Issue of Misgovernance
(b) Subsidiary Alliance
(c) Doctrine of Lapse
(d) Mahalwari System

Question 26 :
Why did Nana Sahib join the 1857 revolt?
(a) Refusal of Peshwa Baji Rao II's pension by the British
(b) British annexation of Awadh
(c) British capturing Jhansi under Doctrine of Lapse
(d) Nana Sahib rejected the Subsidiary Alliance

Question 27 :
Which leader from Bihar was prominent during the 1857 revolt?
(a) Begum Hazrat Mahal
(b) Kunwar Singh
(c) Rani Lakshmi Bai
(d) Bahadur Shah Zafar

Question 28 :
Who started the Home Rule Movement in India?
(a) Subhash Chandra Bose
(b) Bal Gangadhar Tilak
(c) V. D. Savarkar
(d) Annie Besant

Question 29 :
Which pair of revolt centers and their leaders is incorrect?
(a) Kanpur - Nana Sahib
(b) Jhansi - Rani Lakshmi Bai
(c) Gonoo - Kol tribals
(d) Awadh - Shah Mal

Question 30 :
Who painted "Relief of Lucknow," commemorating British heroes during the rebellion?
(a) Joseph Patron
(b) Thomas Jones Barker
(c) Henry Lawrence
(d) Francie Grant

Question 31 :
The painting titled "In Memoriam", dedicated to the courage of British women during the Revolt of 1857, was created by which artist?
(a) Thomas Jones Barker
(b) Francie Grant
(c) Joseph Noel Paton
(d) Henry Lawrence

Question 32 :
Which Englishwoman bravely resisted Indian rebels in Kanpur during the uprising?
(a) Miss Wheeler
(b) Miss Olivia
(c) Miss Emma
(d) Miss Julliett
Answer: (a) Miss Wheeler

Question 33 :
Consider the following statements:
Rumors significantly influenced the events of the 1857 revolt.
Nana Saheb was adopted by Peshwa Baji Rao II.
The British struggled to control the rebels during May and June 1857.
Awadh was a key center of the revolt.
Which of these are correct?
(a) 1, 2, 3, 4
(b) 1, 2, 3
(c) 1, 3, 4
(d) 2, 3, 4

Question 34 :
What does the term 'Firangi' mean?
(a) Foreigner
(b) Mirror work
(c) Outcaste
(d) A type of drink

Question 35 :
In which month of 1857 did the British finally recapture Delhi?
(a) August
(b) September
(c) June
(d) July

Question 36 : In which year was Awadh annexed into the British Empire?
(a) 1853
(b) 1855
(c) 1856
(d) 1854

Question 37 :
Shah Mal gathered headmen and farmers to fight against the British in which region?
(a) 24 Parganas
(b) Faizabad
(c) Meerut
(d) Chaurasee Des

Question 38 :
 In which year did Rani Lakshmi Bai of Jhansi pass away?
(a) 1858
(b) 1855
(c) 1858
(d) 1857

Question 39 :
Read the passage and answer the following :

"Kanpur became one of the main centers of the revolt, where Nana Saheb led the rebellion. The British forces, under General Havelock, laid siege to the city, and after fierce fighting, the British forces were able to regain control of Kanpur. The siege and relief of Kanpur was a pivotal moment in the revolt, marked by intense battles and great losses on both sides."

1.Who led the rebellion in Kanpur during the Revolt of 1857?
(a) Shah Mal
(b) Nana Saheb
(c) Rani Lakshmibai
(d) Kunwar Singh

2.Which British general led the forces to lay siege to Kanpur?
(a) General Havelock
(b) General Dalhousie
(c) General Outram
(d) General Nicholson

3.What was the significance of the siege and relief of Kanpur in the Revolt of 1857?
(a) It marked the beginning of the revolt.
(b) It was a pivotal moment with intense battles and heavy losses on both sides.
(c) It marked the end of the revolt in northern India.
(d) It resulted in Nana Saheb signing a peace treaty with the British.

4.Which statement is incorrect regarding Kanpur during the Revolt of 1857?
(a) Nana Saheb was the leader of the rebellion in Kanpur.
(b) General Havelock led the British forces to regain Kanpur.
(c) The British lost control of Kanpur after the siege.
(d) The siege of Kanpur witnessed fierce fighting and significant losses.

5.What was the outcome of the British siege of Kanpur?
(a) The British forces were defeated by Nana Saheb's army.
(b) The British forces regained control of Kanpur after intense fighting.
(c) The revolt expanded further into central India from Kanpur.
(d) General Havelock signed a treaty with the rebels in Kanpur.

Chapter 12 : Colonial Cities

CONCISE KEY NOTES

Chapter Overview :
- This chapter explores the process of urbanisation in colonial India.
- It examines the characteristics of colonial cities and their impact on Indian society.
- Focuses on Madras (Chennai), Calcutta (Kolkata), and Bombay (Mumbai), which became major colonial urban centres.
- These cities were originally fishing and weaving villages but became commercial hubs due to the English East India Company.
- British control reshaped urban spaces, governance, architecture, and social structures.

Urbanisation Before British Rule: Towns And Cities In Pre-Colonial Times
- Towns were different from rural areas:
  - Villages were agrarian, while towns were centres of trade, administration, and power.
  - "Towns dominated over the rural population, thriving on the surplus and taxes derived from agriculture."
- Mughal urban centres:
  - Agra, Delhi, and Lahore were imperial capitals with monumental buildings and dense populations.
  - Mansabdars and jagirdars had houses in these cities as a mark of prestige.
  - Services for the nobility, artisanship, and trade flourished in these centres.
- Southern cities like Madurai and Kanchipuram:
  - Focused around temples and were linked with pilgrimage and trade.
- "Medieval towns were places where everybody was expected to know their position in the social order."
- Kotwal (police officer): Maintained law and order in pre-colonial cities.

18th-Century Changes :
- Decline of Mughal power led to the decline of old cities like Delhi and Agra.
- New regional capitals emerged: Lucknow, Hyderabad, Pune (poona), Nagpur, Baroda (present day Vadodara) , Tanjore(present Thanjavur).
- Jawaharlal Nehru's- Ganga Dhar Nehru
- Qasbah- small town In the countryside, often seat of a local notable
- Ganj- small fixed market .
- Qasbah and ganj dealt with fruit, cloth vegetables ,and milk products for noble families and the army .
- European trading settlements grew:
  - Portuguese in Panaji Goa (1510), Dutch in Masulipatnam (1605), British in Madras (1639), Bombay (1661), Calcutta (1690), French in Pondicherry (1673).
- "By the late 18th century, land-based empires were replaced by sea-based European empires."
- Colonial port cities like Madras, Calcutta, and Bombay grew rapidly.

Colonial Cities: Documentation And Governance & British Record-Keeping
- "Colonial rule was based on the production of enormous amounts of data."
- Mapping was essential for governance, taxation, and military control.

- Regular surveys, headcounts, and censuses were conducted to track urbanisation.
- First all-India census in 1872, followed by decennial censuses from 1881 onward.

Municipal Governance and Taxation :
- "Municipal corporations were set up for essential services like water supply, roads, and sanitation."
- "To avoid conflict, the British allowed elected Indian representatives in municipal governance."
- The survey of India established- 1878

Growth Of Colonial Cities : Impact of British Trade and Railways
- "The introduction of railways in 1853 led to economic shifts."
- Traditional trade centres like Mirzapur, Surat, Dhaka, and Masulipatnam declined.
- Calcutta, Bombay, and Madras became centres of British economic and political power.
- "Railway stations became collection points for raw materials and distribution hubs for British goods."
- New industrial towns emerged:
  - Jamshedpur (steel industry).
  - Kanpur (leather, wool, cotton textiles).

Social Changes In Colonial Cities : Racial Segregation
- "White Towns" (Europeans) and "Black Towns" (Indians) were strictly separated.
- "British lived in bungalows with open lawns, while Indians lived in overcrowded settlements."

Social Mobility and New Middle Class :
- Colonial cities provided new jobs: clerks, teachers, doctors, engineers, lawyers.
- "Educated Indians formed the new middle class, questioning traditional customs and participating in nationalist movements."

Women in Colonial Cities :
- More women entered public life as teachers, factory workers, actresses, and writers.
- "Patriarchal norms were challenged, but conservative backlash remained strong."

The first hill stations :
- Simla (shimla) was founded during the course of Gurkha War (1815-16)
- Anglo - Maratha war of 1818 led British interest in Mount Abu.
- Darjeeling was seized from the ruler of Sikkim in 1835.
- Hill stations were strategic for billeting troops, guarding frontiers, and launching military campaigns.
- The cool climate was advantageous as the British linked hot weather to epidemics like cholera and malaria, prompting measures to protect the army.
- Resembling European climates, hill stations became popular among British rulers, leading to the practice of the Viceroy residing there during summers.
- In 1864, Viceroy John Lawrence moved his Council to Shimla, which also became the Commander-in-Chief's residence.
- Hill stations boosted the colonial economy with tea and coffee plantations, attracting immigrant labor and transforming them from exclusive European enclaves.

Amar Katha (My story) :
- Binodini Dasi (1863 to 1941) was the pioneering figure in Bengali theatre in the late 19th and early 20th century.
- She want closely with the drama taste and directed Girish Chandra Ghosh (1844 to 1912).
- Star Theatre (1883) in Calcutta which become a Centre for famous productions.
- She serialised her autobiography between 1910 and 1913 Amar Katha (my story) .
- A remarkable personality she exemplified the problem women faced in the Recasting their roles in society.

Architecture And Town Planning : Madras: Settlement and Segregation
- "Madras was founded in 1639 as a fortified settlement of the East India Company."
- "Inside Fort St. George lived the British, while outside were caste-based settlements."
- "Dubashes (bilingual brokers) controlled trade between Indians and the British."
- "Chintadripet was the weavers' settlement, and Washermanpet was for dyers."

Calcutta: Town Planning
- In 1756 Sirajudaula the nawab of Bengal attack Calcutta and sacked the small fort which the British traders have the built as their depot for goods
- In 1757 Sirajudaula defeated in the battle of Plassey, the East India Company decided to build a new Fort , one that could not be easily attacked.
- Calcutta had grown from three villages called sutanati Kolkata and Govindapur.
- "Fort William was built with a vast open space which came to be locally known as the Maidan or garer-math after the Battle of Plassey (1757) to secure British control."
- Wellesley's Minute (1803): Called for better sanitation, road planning, and town clearance.
- Lottery Committee (1817): Raised funds for urban planning and road construction.
- Prominent merchants in the City- Dwarkanath Tagore and Rustomjee Cowasjee.
- Busti (Bengali and Hindi) insanitary slums became synonym in British record.

Bombay: Industrial Growth and Architecture
- "Bombay's economy boomed after the American Civil War (1861), leading to rapid urbanisation."
- In 1869 The Swiss Canal was open and this further strength Bombay's links with the world economy
- European architectural styles were used to symbolize British imperial dominance.
- The University hall was made with money donated by Sir cowasjee Jehangir readymoney , a rich Parsi Merchant.
- The university library clock tower with similarly founded by the banker Premchand RoyChand and was named after his mother as rajabai Tower.
- "Victoria Terminus (1888) is the finest example of Indo-Gothic architecture in Bombay."
- "The Gateway of India (1911) was built in the traditional Gujarati style to welcome King George V and queen Mary to India ."
- The Industrialist Jamshedji Tata built the Taj Mahal Hotel in a similar style besides being a symbol of Indian Enterprise this building become a challenge to the racial exclusive clubs and hotels maintained by the British.

Important Figures

Fig. 12.1
South-east view of Fort St George, Madras, by Thomas and William Daniell,
based on a drawing by Daniell published in Oriental Scenery, *1798*
European ships carrying cargo dot the horizon. Country boats can be seen in the foreground.

Fig. 12.2
Shahjahanabad in 1857

Fig. 12.3
A view of the city of Goa from
the river, by J. Greig, 1812

Fig. 12.6
The Borah Bazaar in the Fort area,
Bombay, 1885

Fig. 12.7
The Old Fort Ghat in
Calcutta, engraving by
Thomas and William
Daniell, 1787

Important Figures

Fig. 12.8
The Old Court House and Writers' Building, engraving by Thomas and William Daniell, 1786

Fig. 12.9
The New Buildings at Chourangee (Chowringhee), engraving by Thomas and William Daniell, 1787

Fig. 12.11
Chitpore Bazaar by Charles D'Oyly

Fig. 12.14
Trams on a road in Calcutta

Fig. 12.15
A late-nineteenth-century Kalighat painting

Important Figures

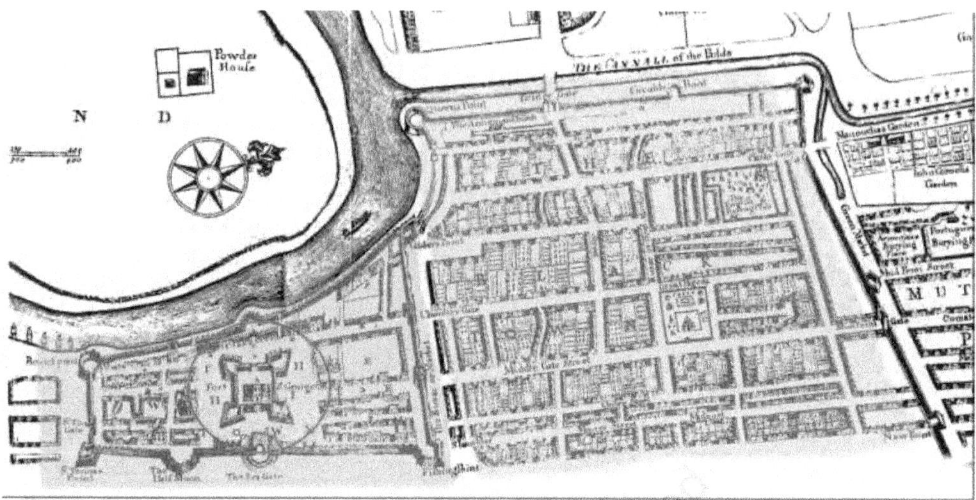

Fig. 12.16
A map of Madras

Fig. 12.17
Part of the Black Town, Madras, by Thomas and William Daniell, based on a drawing by Daniell published in Oriental Scenery, 1798

Fig. 12.18
A garden house on Poonamalee Road

Fig. 12.19
Government House, Calcutta, by Charles D'Oyly, 1848

Important Figures

Fig. 12.24
The Town Hall in Bombay, which now houses the Asiatic Society of Bombay

Fig. 12.25
The Elphinstone Circle
Note the pillars and arches, derived from Graeco-Roman architecture.

Fig. 12.26
Bombay Secretariat, designed by
H. St Clair Wilkins
Drawing from The Builder,
20 November 1875

Fig. 12.27
Victoria Terminus Railway Station, designed by F.W. Stevens

Fig. 12.28
Madras law courts

Important Figures

Fig. 12.29
The Municipal Corporation Building, Bombay, designed by F. W. Stevens in 1888

Fig. 12.30
A Bombay chawl

Chapter 12 : Colonial Cities

QUESTIONS FROM ARCHIVES

Question 1 :
The term "Black Town" in colonial cities referred to:
(a) European residential quarters
(b) Areas near railway stations
(c) Indian settlements often near bazaars and temples
(d) Industrial zones set up by the British

Question 2 :
Madras developed around which fort constructed by the British?
(a) Fort William
(b) Fort St George
(c) Fort Augustus
(d) Fort Calcutta

Question 3 :
Calcutta's Fort William was built after the defeat of which ruler?
(a) Tipu Sultan
(b) Sirajudaula
(c) Mir Qasim
(d) Shuja-ud-Daula

Question 4 :
The Indo-Saracenic architectural style was a combination of:
(a) French and Mughal elements
(b) British Gothic and Italian Renaissance
(c) Hindu and Muslim architectural elements with European forms
(d) Roman and Chinese influences

Question 5 :
The city of Bombay was originally formed by joining:
(a) Three coastal ports
(b) Five urban wards
(c) Seven islands
(d) Ten fishing villages

Question 6 :
Fill in the blank: The _________ was a committee in 1817 responsible for urban improvements in Calcutta, and raised funds through public lotteries.
(a) Bengal Urban Committee
(b) Maidan Planning Commission
(c) Lottery Committee
(d) City Sanitation Board

Question 7 :
Assertion (A): Town planning in colonial India focused more on European areas than Indian settlements.
Reason (R): The British saw Indian areas as symbols of disorder and disease.
(a) Both A and R are true, and R is the correct explanation of A
(b) Both A and R are true, but R is not the correct explanation of A
(c) A is true, but R is false
(d) A is false, but R is true

Question 8 :
The main item exported from Bombay during the American Civil War was:
(a) Jute
(b) Cotton
(c) Opium
(d) Tea

Question 9 :
Fill in the blank: The first all-India census was conducted in ______.
(a) 1857
(b) 1872
(c) 1881
(d) 1901

Question 10 :
The city of Calcutta originally grew from which three villages?
(a) Sutanati, Calcutta, Baranagar
(b) Sutanati, Kolkata, Govindapur
(c) Gobindapur, Chandni Chowk, Kalighat
(d) Fort William, Sutanati, Barrackpore

Question 11 :
Assertion (A): Railway stations in colonial India became important urban centres.
Reason (R): They acted as collection depots for raw materials and distribution centres for imported goods.
(a) Both A and R are true, and R is the correct explanation of A
(b) Both A and R are true, but R is not the correct explanation of A
(c) A is true, but R is false
(d) A is false, but R is true

Question 12 :
The Rajabai Clock Tower in Bombay was funded by:
(a) Cowasjee Jehangir
(b) Dwarkanath Tagore
(c) Premchand Roychand
(d) Jamsetji Tata

Question 13 :
The architectural style used in the Victoria Terminus was:
(a) Neo-Classical
(b) Indo-Saracenic
(c) Neo-Gothic
(d) Romanesque Revival

Question 14 :
Fill in the blank: _______ was the first hill station where the Viceroy officially moved his council during summers.
(a) Darjeeling
(b) Nainital
(c) Mount Abu
(d) Simla

Question 15 :
Who among the following worked as kotwal of Delhi before the Revolt of 1857?
(a) Jawaharlal Nehru
(b) Ganga Dhar Nehru
(c) Motilal Nehru
(d) Dwarkanath Tagore

Question 16 :
Assertion (A): Census figures collected by the British were always accurate.
  Reason (R): The British census operations classified every individual objectively.
(a) Both A and R are true, and R is the correct explanation of A
(b) Both A and R are true, but R is not the correct explanation of A
(c) A is true, but R is false
(d) A is false, and R is false

Question 17 :
The Survey of India was established in:
(a) 1787
(b) 1858
(c) 1878
(d) 1901

Question 18 :
Fill in the blank: The _______ style combined medieval Indian architecture with European elements and was seen in buildings like the Gateway of India.
(a) Indo-Saracenic
(b) Mughal-Gothic
(c) Victorian-Roman
(d) Colonial-Maratha

Question 19 :
Which locality in Madras was originally meant for weavers?
(a) Royapuram
(b) Washermanpet
(c) Mylapore
(d) Chintadripet

Question 20 :
Fill in the blank: The _____________ was a system under which the British collected municipal taxes annually to administer towns.
(a) Lottery Committee
(b) Sanitation Board
(c) Municipal Corporation
(d) Survey Commission

Question 21 :
The earliest colonial hill station established during the Gurkha War was:
(a) Ooty
(b) Simla
(c) Darjeeling
(d) Mussoorie

Question 22 :
Which colonial city was described in the Imperial Gazetteer as having rice fields and a semi-rural atmosphere?
(a) Calcutta
(b) Madras
(c) Bombay
(d) Bangalore

Question 23 :
Fill in the blank: The term "dubash" referred to Indians who acted as intermediaries because they knew English and ___________.
(a) Persian
(b) Arabic
(c) Local languages
(d) Portuguese

Question 24 :
In the 1860s and 70s, the British introduced underground piped water supply and drainage mainly to:
(a) Improve irrigation in villages
(b) Control plague in ports
(c) Sanitize Indian towns due to fear of disease spreading
(d) Increase rainfall harvesting in colonial cities

Question 25 :
Assertion (A): Chawls in Bombay helped foster a strong sense of community.
Reason (R): These were single-room apartments with shared spaces like courtyards and corridors.
(a) Both A and R are true, and R is the correct explanation of A
(b) Both A and R are true, but R is not the correct explanation of A
(c) A is true, but R is false
(d) A is false, and R is false

Question 26 :
The building of Fort William and clearance of the surrounding Maidan in Calcutta was initially done for:
(a) Creating parks for Europeans
(b) Better trade routes
(c) Unobstructed military defence
(d) Constructing temples and ghats

Question 27 :
Fill in the blank: The ________ was built in Gujarati style to welcome King George V and Queen Mary in 1911.
(a) Victoria Memorial
(b) Rajabai Tower
(c) Gateway of India
(d) Bombay High Court

Question 28 :
Who was the Indian woman who pioneered theatre and wrote an autobiography titled Amar Katha?
(a) Pandita Ramabai
(b) Binodini Dasi
(c) Sarojini Naidu
(d) Begum Rokeya

Question 29 :
Fill in the blank: The ___________ was considered a model of ordered urban life in contrast to the densely populated Indian towns.
(a) Black Town
(b) Civil Lines
(c) Busti
(d) Chawls

Question 30 :
Who founded the Star Theatre in Calcutta and later wrote the autobiography Amar Katha?
(a) Sarala Devi
(b) Binodini Dasi
(c) Cornelia Sorabji
(d) Kadambini Ganguly

Question 31 :
Assertion (A): Many Indians began to adopt European architectural styles.
Reason (R): They viewed these styles as symbols of modernity and progress.
(a) Both A and R are true, and R is the correct explanation of A
(b) Both A and R are true, but R is not the correct explanation of A
(c) A is true, but R is false
(d) A is false, and R is false

Question 32 :
Which of the following styles was inspired by medieval churches in northern Europe and used in Bombay's university and High Court buildings?
(a) Indo-Saracenic
(b) Neo-Gothic
(c) Neo-Classical
(d) Mughal Revival

Question 33 :
Fill in the blank: In the town of Madras, ___________ was a settlement of Christian boatmen working for the Company.
(a) Chintadripet
(b) Royapuram
(c) Washermanpet
(d) Triplicane

Question 34 :
Who among the following funded the University Library clock tower in Bombay, later named Rajabai Tower?
(a) Jamsetji Tata
(b) Cowasjee Jehangir
(c) Premchand Roychand
(d) Dinshaw Petit

Question 35 :
What was the main reason behind the demolition of the old Black Town in Madras?
(a) To build a temple complex
(b) To create a green space for British officers
(c) To maintain a clear line of fire around Fort St George
(d) To expand the railway network

Question 36 :
Fill in the blank: The ____________ was a small town in the countryside, often the seat of a local notable and served as a trade centre.
(a) Bustee
(b) Cantonment
(c) Qasbah
(d) Pet

Question 37 :
Fill in the blank: The __________ Committee, formed in 1817, played a key role in planning Calcutta and raising funds through public lotteries.
(a) Health and Sanitation
(b) Improvement
(c) Lottery
(d) Municipal

Question 38 :
The Writers' Building in Calcutta was originally used as:
(a) A railway headquarters
(b) A residential block for Company servants
(c) A printing press
(d) A minting office

Question 39 :
In colonial cities, "White Towns" were typically characterised by:
(a) Thatched huts and narrow lanes
(b) Temples and local markets
(c) Broad streets, bungalows, and European clubs
(d) Fortified Indian palaces

Question 40 :
Fill in the blank: ____________ was the name of the open space left around Fort William in Calcutta for security reasons.
(a) Maidan
(b) Rajpath
(c) Lal Bagh
(d) Parade Ground

Question 41 :
Which city was declared Urbs Prima in Indis during the colonial period?
(a) Calcutta
(b) Madras
(c) Bombay
(d) Delhi

Question 42 :
Fill in the blank: The city of Madras was locally known as ____________ at the time of British settlement.
(a) Tiruchirapalli
(b) Chenapattanam
(c) Chidambaram
(d) Kalahasti

Question 43 :
What was the major factor for the decline of inland commercial towns like Surat and Dhaka in the 18th century?
(a) Famines and droughts
(b) Rise of French colonialism
(c) Shift in trade to British-controlled port cities
(d) Mughal administrative collapse

Question 44 :
Fill in the blank: The _______ was a distinctive colonial housing structure with pitched roof, wide verandas, and servant quarters.
(a) Bungalow
(b) Haveli
(c) Lodge
(d) Hall

Question 45 :
Which of the following was not a function of municipal corporations in colonial cities?
(a) Water supply
(b) Urban policing
(c) Taxation
(d) Public health

Chapter 13 : Mahatma Gandhi And The Nationalist Movement

CONCISE KEY NOTES

Chapter Overview :
- "In January 1915, Mohandas Karamchand Gandhi returned to India from South Africa."
- "Within five years of his arrival, he became the undisputed leader of the Indian nationalist movement."
- "Gandhi's methods of protest included non-violent resistance, civil disobedience, and non-cooperation."
- "His leadership inspired mass participation in India's struggle for independence."
- "This chapter traces the key movements led by Gandhi from the 1920s to 1947."
- The Indian National Congress had expanded across cities, especially after the Swadeshi Movement (1905-07).
- The movement produced prominent leaders like Bal Gangadhar Tilak, Bipin Chandra Pal and Lala Lajpat Rai — known together as "Lal, Bal, Pal", symbolizing all-India unity.
- These leaders supported militant opposition to British rule, while Moderates like Gopal Krishna Gokhale and Mohammad Ali Jinnah advocated a slower, persuasive path.
- Gopal Krishna Gokhale was Gandhi's political mentor: Mohammad Ali Jinnah, like Gandhi, was a London-trained lawyer of Gujarati origin.

Gandhi's Early Political Activities (1915-1919) :
Gandhi's Return to India (1915) :

- "Gandhi had spent two decades in South Africa, leading non-violent campaigns against racial discrimination."
- "On Gokhale's advice, he spent the first year traveling across India to understand the people."
- He made his first public appearance in BHU (Benaras Hindu University) in February 1916
- "He established the Sabarmati Ashram in Ahmedabad in 1916."

Early Struggles in Champaran, Kheda, and Ahmedabad :
- Champaran (1917):
  - "Gandhi's first major struggle in India was in Champaran, Bihar, against indigo planters."
  - "He used non-violent resistance to force an inquiry into the exploitation of peasants."
- Kheda Satyagraha (1918):
  - "Gandhi demanded tax relief for farmers suffering from crop failure."
- Ahmedabad Mill Strike (1918):
  - "He led a hunger strike to support textile workers demanding better wages."

Rowlatt Satyagraha (1919) and Jallianwala Bagh Massacre :
- "In 1919, the British passed the Rowlatt Act, allowing arrest without trial."
- "Gandhi called for a nationwide hartal on 6 April 1919."
- "The protests led to violence in some areas, and the British responded with brutal force."
- Jallianwala Bagh Massacre (13 April 1919):
  - "General Dyer ordered his troops to fire on an unarmed crowd in Amritsar, killing over 1,000 people."
  - "The massacre shocked the nation and strengthened the demand for self-rule."

Non-Cooperation Movement (1920-1922) : The Call for Non-Cooperation
- "In September 1920, the Congress, under Gandhi's leadership, launched the Non-Cooperation Movement."
- "The movement aimed at boycotting British goods, institutions, and titles."

Forms of Protest
- "Students left British schools and colleges."
- "Lawyers gave up their legal practices."

- "Foreign clothes were burnt in public bonfires."
- Fig. 13.3 - Public bonfire of foreign clothes during the Non-Cooperation Movement.

Chauri Chaura Incident and Suspension (1922) :

- "On 5 February 1922, in Chauri Chaura (Uttar Pradesh), protestors set a police station on fire, killing 22 policemen."
- "Gandhi called off the movement, saying it had deviated from non-violence."

Civil Disobedience Movement (1930-1934) : The Salt March (Dandi March, 1930)

- "On 12 March 1930, Gandhi began a 240-mile march from Sabarmati to Dandi with 78 followers."
- "On 6 April 1930, he made salt at Dandi, defying the British salt law."
- Fig. 13.4 - The Salt March (Dandi, 1930).

Spread of the Movement :

- "The Civil Disobedience Movement spread across India."
- "Women participated in large numbers, led by Sarojini Naidu and Kasturba Gandhi."

Gandhi-Irwin Pact (1931) :

- "Gandhi agreed to suspend the movement in exchange for negotiations."
- "He participated in the Second Round Table Conference in London (1931), but it failed."
- Fig. 13.5 - Gandhi at the Round Table Conference.

Quit India Movement (1942-1945) : The Demand for Complete Independence :

- "On 8 August 1942, Gandhi gave the call for Quit India at Bombay's Gowalia Tank Maidan."
- "He declared, 'Do or Die'."
- "The British immediately arrested Gandhi, Nehru, and other leaders."
- "Mass protests erupted across India."
- Fig. 13.6 - Quit India Movement (1942), mass protests.

Brutal British Repression :

- "The British responded with mass arrests, shootings, and aerial bombings."
- "The movement was crushed by 1944, but it prepared the ground for independence."

Partition And Independence (1947) :

Gandhi's Role in Preventing Communal Violence

- "In 1946-47, widespread communal riots broke out between Hindus and Muslims."
- "Gandhi traveled to riot-hit areas, urging peace and unity."
- "He fasted in Delhi in January 1948 to stop Hindu-Muslim violence."

Assassination of Gandhi (30 January 1948) :

- "On 30 January 1948, Nathuram Godse, a Hindu extremist, shot Gandhi in Delhi."
- "His last words were 'Hey Ram'."
- "India lost its greatest leader, but his ideas of non-violence and truth continue to inspire."**

Important Figures

Fig. 11.2
Mahatma Gandhi in Johannesburg,
South Africa, February 1908

Fig. 11.4
Non-cooperation Movement,
July 1922

Fig. 11.6
On the Dandi March,
March 1930

Fig. 11.7
Satyagrahis picking up natural salt at the end
of the Dandi March, 6 April 1930

Fig. 11.10
Mahatma Gandhi and Rajendra
Prasad on their way to a meeting
with the Viceroy, Lord Linlithgow,
13 October 1939

Chapter 13 : Mapwork

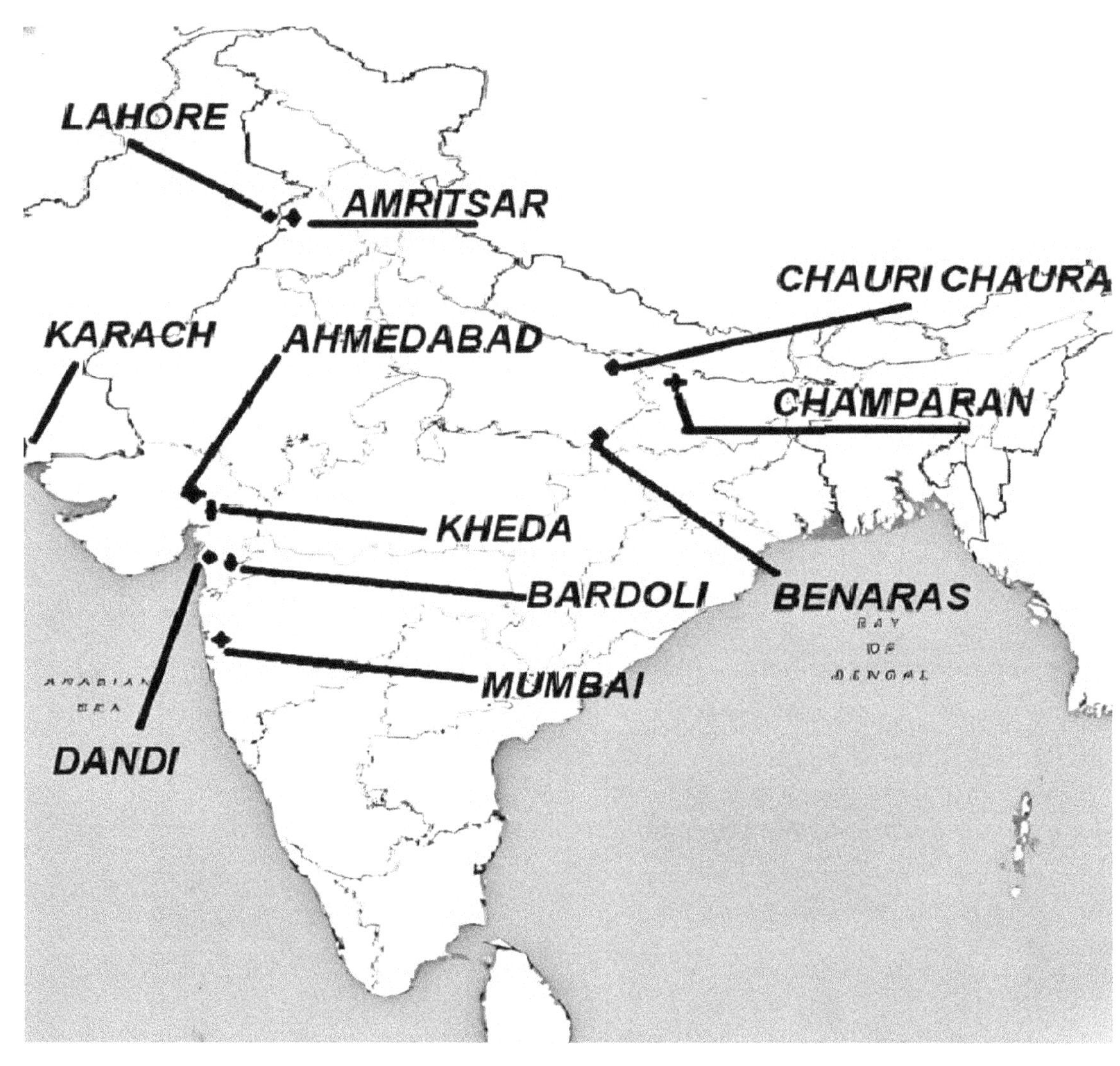

Chapter 13 : Mahatma Gandhi And The National ist Movement

QUESTIONS FROM ARCHIVES

Question 1 :
Who among the following was the Viceroy of India when the Civil Disobedience Movement began?
a) Lord Irwin
b) Lord Linlithgow
c) Lord Willingdon
d) Lord Mountbatten

Question 2 :
The Civil Disobedience Movement was started in response to which of the following?
a) Rowlatt Act
b) Jallianwala Bagh Massacre
c) Simon Commission
d) Salt Laws

Question 3 :
Which of the following was a key feature of the Dandi March?
a) Protest against the Simon Commission
b) Protest against the Jallianwala Bagh Massacre
c) Violation of the Salt Laws
d) Demand for Dominion Status

Question 4 :
Fill in the blank: The Second Round Table Conference was held in _______.
a) 1929
b) 1931
c) 1935
d) 1942

Question 5 :
Which of the following leaders was NOT involved in the Quit India Movement?
a) Mahatma Gandhi
b) Subhas Chandra Bose
c) Jawaharlal Nehru
d) Sardar Patel

Question 6 :
Fill in the blank: The slogan "Do or Die" was given during the _______ Movement.
a) Non-Cooperation
b) Civil Disobedience
c) Quit India
d) Swadeshi

Question 7 :
What was the primary objective of the Gandhi-Irwin Pact?
a) To grant India full independence
b) To end the Civil Disobedience Movement
c) To allow Indians to make their own salt
d) To introduce provincial autonomy

Question 8 :
Who among the following opposed separate electorates for the Depressed Classes at the Round Table Conference?
a) Dr. B.R. Ambedkar
b) Mahatma Gandhi
c) Jawaharlal Nehru
d) Sardar Patel

Question 9 :
Fill in the blank: The Non-Cooperation Movement was launched in the year _______.
a) 1919
b) 1920
c) 1925
d) 1930

question 10 :
What was the major outcome of the Civil Disobedience Movement?
a) Immediate independence for India
b) Introduction of separate electorates
c) Increased participation of women in the freedom struggle
d) Complete abolition of the Salt Laws

Question 11 :
Who among the following was NOT associated with the Non-Cooperation Movement?
a) Mahatma Gandhi
b) Subhas Chandra Bose
c) Jawaharlal Nehru
d) Lord Irwin

question 12 :
The Gandhi-Irwin Pact was signed in which year?
a) 1929
b) 1931
c) 1935
d) 1942

Question 13 :
Which event led to Mahatma Gandhi calling off the Non-Cooperation Movement?
a) Rowlatt Act
b) Jallianwala Bagh Massacre
c) Chauri Chaura Incident
d) Simon Commission Protest

Question 14 :
Fill in the blank: The Rowlatt Act was passed in the year ________.
a) 1917
b) 1919
c) 1922
d) 1925

Question 15 :
The Quit India Movement was launched in response to which of the following?
a) Jallianwala Bagh Massacre
b) Failure of the Cripps Mission
c) Civil Disobedience Movement
d) Simon Commission

Question 16 :
Fill in the blank: The ________ was a significant movement that aimed at uniting Hindus and Muslims during the Non-Cooperation Movement.
a) Civil Disobedience Movement
b) Khilafat Movement
c) Swadeshi Movement
d) Home Rule Movement

Question 17 :
Who among the following was the political mentor of Mahatma Gandhi?
a) Bal Gangadhar Tilak
b) Gopal Krishna Gokhale
c) Lala Lajpat Rai
d) Bipin Chandra Pal

Question 18 :
Fill in the blank: The Jallianwala Bagh Massacre took place in ________.
a) 1918
b) 1919
c) 1920
d) 1922

Question 19 :
Which of the following statements best describes Mahatma Gandhi's view on untouchability?
a) He considered it a social evil that must be eradicated.
b) He supported separate electorates for untouchables.
c) He believed untouchability was a religious practice.
d) He had no strong opinion on the issue.

Question 20 :
Fill in the blank: The British government sent the ________ Commission in 1928 to review the political situation in India.
a) Rowlatt
b) Simon
c) Cabinet Mission
d) Wavell

Question 21 :
Who among the following first referred to Mahatma Gandhi as the "Father of the Nation"?
a) Jawaharlal Nehru
b) Subhas Chandra Bose
c) Sardar Patel
d) B.R. Ambedkar

Question 22 :
The Dandi March started from which place?
a) Ahmedabad
b) Sabarmati Ashram
c) Bombay
d) Bardoli

Question 23 :
Fill in the blank: The ________ was responsible for ordering the Jallianwala Bagh massacre.
a) Lord Linlithgow
b) General Dyer
c) Lord Irwin
d) Sir Stafford Cripps

Question 24 :
What was the main objective of the Khilafat Movement?
a) To protest against the Jallianwala Bagh massacre
b) To demand complete independence from British rule
c) To support the Turkish Caliphate and oppose British policies
d) To promote industrialization in India

Question 25 :
Fill in the blank: Mahatma Gandhi was arrested in March 1922 and sentenced to ________ years of imprisonment.
a) 3
b) 5
c) 6
d) 7

Question 26 :
Which of the following best describes the significance of the Salt March?
a) It was a protest against British taxation policies.
b) It aimed to promote Hindu–Muslim unity.
c) It was a campaign to abolish the caste system.
d) It sought to remove restrictions on Indian industries.

Question 27 :
Fill in the blank: The slogan "Swaraj in one year" was given by Mahatma Gandhi during the _______ Movement.
a) Non-Cooperation
b) Quit India
c) Swadeshi
d) Civil Disobedience

Question 28 :
Who among the following wrote the book Hind Swaraj?
a) Bal Gangadhar Tilak
b) Rabindranath Tagore
c) Mahatma Gandhi
d) Gopal Krishna Gokhale

Question 29 :
Fill in the blank: The Round Table Conferences were held in _______.
a) New Delhi
b) London
c) Paris
d) Geneva

question 30 :
What was the immediate impact of the Chauri Chaura incident?
a) British government imposed martial law.
b) Mahatma Gandhi called off the Non-Cooperation Movement.
c) The Simon Commission was appointed.
d) The Indian National Congress was banned.

Question 31 :
Fill in the blank: Mahatma Gandhi's first major public appearance in India was at the opening of _______ in 1916.
a) Aligarh Muslim University
b) Banaras Hindu University
c) Jamia Millia Islamia
d) Delhi University

Question 32 :
The Non-Cooperation Movement was withdrawn because of which incident?
a) Jallianwala Bagh massacre
b) Chauri Chaura incident
c) Arrest of Mahatma Gandhi
d) Simon Commission protests

Question 33 :
Fill in the blank: The Civil Disobedience Movement was formally launched with the _______ March in 1930.
a) Kheda
b) Dandi
c) Champaran
d) Bardoli

Question 34 :
Who among the following was NOT present at the Round Table Conferences?
a) Mahatma Gandhi
b) Jawaharlal Nehru
c) Dr. B.R. Ambedkar
d) Muhammad Ali Jinnah

Question 35 :
Fill in the blank: Mahatma Gandhi's political mentor was _______.
a) Bal Gangadhar Tilak
b) Lala Lajpat Rai
c) Gopal Krishna Gokhale
d) Subhas Chandra Bose

Question 36 :
Which act was introduced by the British to curb nationalist activities and allow imprisonment without trial?
a) Government of India Act, 1935
b) Rowlatt Act, 1919
c) Indian Councils Act, 1909
d) Morley-Minto Reforms

Question 37 :
Fill in the blank: Mahatma Gandhi's autobiography is titled The Story of My Experiments with _______.
a) Truth
b) Justice
c) Non-Violence
d) Satyagraha

Question 38 :
What was the primary demand of the Quit India Movement?
a) Formation of a Constituent Assembly
b) Complete withdrawal of British rule from India
c) Provincial autonomy
d) Protect
ion of Indian industries

Question 39 :
Fill in the blank: The Simon Commission was boycotted because it did not include any _______ member.
a) Congress
b) Indian
c) Muslim League
d) Britisher.

Question 40 :
Fill in the blank: The British officer responsible for the Jallianwala Bagh massacre in 1919 was _______.
a) Lord Irwin
b) General Dyer
c) Lord Linlithgow
d) Sir Stafford Cripps

Question 41 :
What was the primary objective of the Salt March led by Mahatma Gandhi?
a) To demand full independence from British rule
b) To protest against the heavy taxation on salt
c) To boycott foreign cloth and goods
d) To seek constitutional reforms from the British

Question 42 :
Fill in the blank: Mahatma Gandhi's philosophy of non-violence and Satyagraha was first experimented with in ______.
a) India
b) South Africa
c) England
d) Burma

Question 43 :
The Poona Pact of 1932 was an agreement between Mahatma Gandhi and ______.
a) B.R. Ambedkar
b) Sardar Patel
c) Jawaharlal Nehru
d) Muhammad Ali Jinnah

Question 44 :
Fill in the blank: The Civil Disobedience Movement led to the arrest of approximately ______ people in India.
a) 30,000
b) 60,000
c) 90,000
d) 1,20,000

Question 45 :
Who among the following called Mahatma Gandhi's Non-Cooperation Movement a "Himalayan blunder"?
a) Jawaharlal Nehru
b) Subhas Chandra Bose
c) Gopal Krishna Gokhale
d) Muhammad Ali Jinnah

Question 46 :
Which of the following social issues was NOT a major focus of Mahatma Gandhi's reforms?
a) Eradication of untouchability
b) Promotion of Hindu-Muslim unity
c) Women's rights and empowerment
d) Industrialization and large-scale mechanization

Question 47 :
Fill in the blank: Mahatma Gandhi was assassinated on ______.
a) 15 August 1947
b) 30 January 1948
c) 26 January 1950
d) 2 October 1948

Question 48 :
Assertion (A): Mahatma Gandhi called off the Non-Cooperation Movement in 1922.
Reason (R): The Chauri Chaura incident, where protesters burned a police station, led Gandhi to withdraw the movement to prevent further violence.
a) Both A and R are true, and R is the correct explanation of A.
b) Both A and R are true, but R is not the correct explanation of A.
c) A is true, but R is false.
d) A is false, but R is true.

Question 49 :
Assertion (A): Mahatma Gandhi supported the Khilafat Movement.
Reason (R): He believed that supporting the Khilafat Movement would strengthen Hindu-Muslim unity in India.
a) Both A and R are true, and R is the correct explanation of A.
b) Both A and R are true, but R is not the correct explanation of A.
c) A is true, but R is false.
d) A is false, but R is true.

Question 50 :
Who among the following led the Salt Satyagraha in Tamil Nadu?
a) Sardar Vallabhbhai Patel
b) C. Rajagopalachari
c) Jawaharlal Nehru
d) Subhas Chandra Bose

Question 51 :
Read the passage and answer the following questions:
Mahatma Gandhi's call for a Salt March in 1930 was a symbolic act of defiance against British rule. He and his followers marched over 240 miles to the coastal town of Dandi, where they broke the British monopoly on salt by making their own. The march sparked nationwide protests and strengthened the Civil Disobedience Movement.

1.What was the primary objective of the Salt March?
a) Demand for complete independence
b) Protest against the Rowlatt Act
c) Violation of British salt laws
d) Support for the Simon Commission

2.How did the British respond to the Salt March?
a) They ignored it completely
b) They arrested thousands of protesters, including Gandhi
c) They immediately abolished the salt tax
d) They passed the Government of India Act 1935

3. Fill in the blank: The Salt March began at ______.
a) Bombay
b) Sabarmati Ashram
c) Ahmedabad
d) Kheda

4. Which of the following best describes the impact of the Salt March?
a) It had minimal impact on Indian politics
b) It led to the immediate end of British rule
c) It mobilized people across the country and gained international attention
d) It was only supported by a small section of society

5.Which of the following statements about the Civil Disobedience Movement is correct?
a) It focused only on the urban middle class
b) It included mass participation from different sections of society
c) It had no effect on the British government
d) It was supported only by the Congress leaders

Chapter 14 : Understanding Partition

CONCISE KEY NOTES

Chapter Overview :
- "The joy of India's independence in 1947 was overshadowed by the horrors of Partition."
- "Partition led to the division of British India into two nations – India and Pakistan – accompanied by unprecedented violence."
- "Millions of people were displaced, and communal riots erupted across Punjab, Bengal, and Delhi."
- "This chapter examines the political developments leading to Partition and the human experiences associated with it."

Why And How Did Partition Happen :
Was Partition the Culmination of a Long History?
- "Some historians suggest that Partition was the inevitable outcome of long-standing Hindu-Muslim conflict."
- "However, this argument ignores the history of cultural exchange and co-existence between the communities."
- "Separate electorates for Muslims (introduced in 1909 and expanded in 1919) deepened communal identities."
- "Religious identities became tied to political competition, creating communal tensions."
- "Issues like cow protection, music-before-mosque, and religious conversions led to increased polarization in the 1920s and 1930s."

The Demand for Pakistan and the Muslim League's Role :
- "On 23 March 1940, the Muslim League passed the 'Pakistan Resolution' demanding autonomy for Muslim-majority regions."
- "The resolution did not initially mention Partition but was later interpreted as a demand for a separate nation."
- "Sikandar Hayat Khan opposed the idea of complete separation, advocating a loose confederation instead."

The Suddenness of Partition :
- "Partition happened within just seven years of the first demand for Pakistan in 1940."
- "Many people did not realize they would have to permanently leave their homes."
- "Violence escalated rapidly, and ordinary people were caught unprepared for the scale of displacement."

Cabinet Mission Plan (1946): A Failed Alternative to Partition
- "The British Cabinet Mission proposed a three-tier confederation keeping India united."
- "Muslim-majority provinces were to have autonomy, but a strong central government would be retained."
- "The Congress and Muslim League disagreed on the interpretation, leading to its rejection."

Violence And Massacres During Partition : Direct Action Day (16 August 1946)
- "The Muslim League declared Direct Action Day to press for Pakistan."
- "Riots erupted in Calcutta, leading to thousands of deaths."
- "Violence spread to Bengal, Bihar, Punjab, and the United Provinces."

Human Cost of Partition :
- "At least 15 million people were displaced, and 200,000 to 500,000 were killed."
- "Refugees fled with whatever they could carry, abandoning their homes and properties."
- "Women were abducted, raped, and sometimes killed by their own families to 'preserve honor'."

Gandhi's Efforts To Prevent Communal Violence : Gandhi's Role in Restoring Peace
- "Gandhi was the only leader who consistently opposed Partition."
- "He traveled to Noakhali, Bihar, Calcutta, and Delhi, trying to stop communal killings."
- "He fasted in January 1948 to end Hindu-Muslim riots in Delhi."
- Fig. 14.10 - Gandhi in Noakhali, trying to restore peace.

Assassination of Gandhi (30 January 1948) :
- "Gandhi was assassinated by Nathuram Godse, a Hindu extremist, who blamed him for appeasing Muslims."
- "His death marked the end of an era, but his message of non-violence and unity continues to inspire."

Memories Of Partition And Aftermath : Partition as a 'Holocaust'
- "The mass killings, rapes, and forced migrations led some historians to call Partition a 'holocaust'."
- "Survivors remember Partition as a time of chaos, trauma, and immense loss."
- Fig. 14.4 - Refugees carrying belongings in carts (1947).

Refugee Rehabilitation :
- "Both India and Pakistan struggled to provide housing, jobs, and food for millions of refugees."
- "New colonies were established in cities like Delhi, Lahore, and Karachi for displaced families."
- "The scars of Partition continued to affect Indo-Pak relations for decades."

Important Figures

Fig. 14.2
Photographs give us a glimpse of the violence of that time.

Fig. 14.3
Over 10 million people were uprooted from their homelands and forced to migrate.

Fig. 14.6
Mahatma Gandhi with Mohammad Ali Jinnah before a meeting with the Viceroy in November 1939

Fig. 14.7
Mahatma Gandhi in the NWFP, October 1938 with Khan Abdul Ghaffar Khan (who came to be known as Frontier Gandhi), Sushila Nayar and Amtus Salem

Fig. 14.10
Villagers of Noakhali hope for a glimpse of Mahatma Gandhi

Fig. 14.13
Faces of despair

Chapter 14 : Understanding Partition

QUESTIONS FROM ARCHIVES

Question 1 :

Assertion (A): Partition led to widespread violence, mass killings, and displacement of millions.

Reason (R): The communal divide had been deepened by policies like separate electorates introduced by the British.

(A) Both A and R are true, and R is the correct explanation of A.

(B) Both A and R are true, but R is not the correct explanation of A.

(C) A is true, but R is false.

(D) A is false, but R is true.

Question 2 :

Partition led to the uprooting of nearly _____ million people from their homelands.

(A) 5

(B) 10

(C) 15

(D) 20

Question 3 :

The term often used to describe the large-scale violence, killings, and forced migrations of Partition is _____.

(A) Genocide

(B) Exodus

(C) Holocaust

(D) Revolution

Question 4 :

The boundaries of India and Pakistan were drawn by the _____ Commission.

(A) Mountbatten

(B) Nehru

(C) Radcliffe

(D) Cripps

Question 5 :

Which of the following stereotypes were strengthened by the Partition?

(A) Hindus are invaders, and Muslims are the original inhabitants of India.

(B) Hindus are meat-eaters, while Muslims are vegetarians.

(C) Muslims are cruel and bigoted, while Hindus are kind and pure.

(D) Both (A) and (C)

Question 6 :

Which of the following was a major factor contributing to communal tensions in the early 20th century?

(A) Cow protection movements

(B) The policy of separate electorates

(C) Efforts by the Arya Samaj to reconvert Muslims

(D) All of the above

Question 7 :

What role did the colonial government play in deepening communal divisions before Partition?

(A) They promoted religious unity through policies like the Lucknow Pact.

(B) They introduced separate electorates, which encouraged sectarian politics.

(C) They actively prevented any communal riots from occurring.

(D) They abolished any policies that could divide communities.

Question 8 :

Which of the following best describes the impact of Partition?

(A) It was an orderly constitutional process that peacefully divided India and Pakistan.

(B) It was a sudden and violent event leading to mass displacement and atrocities.

(C) It was a state-led extermination similar to the Holocaust in Germany.

(D) It had no significant impact on inter-community relations in the long term.

Question 9 :

The partition of India and Pakistan in 1947 resulted in an estimated death toll ranging from:

(A) 50,000 to 100,000

(B) 100,000 to 200,000

(C) 200,000 to 500,000

(D) 500,000 to 1 million

Question 10 :

Which of the following methods was primarily used by historians to reconstruct the experiences of Partition survivors?

(A) Official government records

(B) Oral history and interviews

(C) British colonial reports

(D) Newspaper editorials

Question 11 :
Who played a crucial role in defining the boundaries between India and Pakistan?
(A) Lord Mountbatten
(B) Cyril Radcliffe
(C) Jawaharlal Nehru
(D) Mohammad Ali Jinnah

Question 12 :
The violence during Partition was mainly carried out by:
(A) The British army enforcing law and order
(B) State agencies under government control
(C) Self-styled representatives of religious communities
(D) United Nations peacekeeping forces

Question 13 :
The term "ethnic cleansing" in the context of Partition refers to:
(A) The legal migration process organized by the governments of India and Pakistan
(B) The forced removal and killing of people based on their religious identity
(C) The establishment of refugee camps for displaced people
(D) The peaceful resolution of communal tensions through diplomatic talks

Question 14 :
The Lucknow Pact of 1916 was an agreement between:
(A) The British government and the Indian National Congress
(B) The Indian National Congress and the Muslim League
(C) Hindu and Muslim religious leaders
(D) The British and the Muslim League

Question 15 :
The phrase used to describe the experience of Partition by contemporary observers and scholars is:
(A) "A peaceful transition"
(B) "A constitutional agreement"
(C) "A civil war"
(D) "A revolution"

Question 16 :
Fill in the blank: The process of forced removal of people based on religious identity during Partition is referred to as _____.
(A) Population transfer
(B) Ethnic cleansing
(C) Political reform
(D) Border regulation

Question 17 :
The boundaries between India and Pakistan were announced:
(A) On August 14, 1947
(B) On August 15, 1947
(C) Two days after formal independence
(D) One month before independence

Question 18 :
What role did oral history play in understanding Partition?
(A) It helped in documenting personal experiences of survivors
(B) It provided official government records of migration patterns
(C) It was the only reliable source of historical facts
(D) It replaced written historical evidence completely

Question 19 :
Which of the following best describes the impact of Partition on inter-community relations?
(A) It strengthened Hindu–Muslim unity
(B) It deepened religious stereotypes and divisions
(C) It had no effect on social structures
(D) It led to the complete abolition of communal conflicts

Question 20 :
Which of the following statements about Partition is NOT true?
(A) It was a peaceful and orderly transition
(B) It led to mass displacement and loss of life
(C) It created long-lasting tensions between India and Pakistan
(D) It resulted in one of the largest hum an migrations in history

Question 21 :
Who among the following played a significant role in advocating the Two-Nation Theory?
(A) Jawaharlal Nehru
(B) Mahatma Gandhi
(C) Mohammad Ali Jinnah
(D) Sardar Vallabhbhai Patel

Question 22 :
Fill in the blank: The Partition of India led to a major loss of _____, as people were forced to leave behind their homes, lands, and properties.
(A) Political representation
(B) Cultural heritage
(C) Military power
(D) Technological advancements

Question 23 :
What was the immediate effect of the announcement of the Partition plan in 1947?
(A) Economic growth in both India and Pakistan
(B) Peaceful migration of populations
(C) Outbreak of mass violence and killings
(D) Strengthening of Hindu-Muslim unity

Question 24 :
Fill in the blank: The Partition led to the formation of two countries, India and _____, which was divided into eastern and western regions.
(A) Bangladesh
(B) Afghanistan
(C) Pakistan
(D) Sri Lanka

Question 25 :
Which of the following regions witnessed some of the worst communal riots during Partition?
(A) Kerala and Tamil Nadu
(B) Punjab and Bengal
(C) Gujarat and Rajasthan
(D) Assam and Odisha

Question 26 :
Fill in the blank: Many survivors of Partition used terms like _____ to describe the chaotic and violent events of 1947.
(A) "Hullar" and "raula"
(B) "Prosperity" and "peace"
(C) "Revival" and "renaissance"
(D) "Constitutional agreement" and "diplomatic success"

Question 27 :
Which of the following was a significant challenge faced by refugees during Partition?
(A) Lack of proper transportation
(B) Shortage of food and shelter
(C) Outbreak of diseases in refugee camps
(D) All of the above

Question 28 :
Fill in the blank: The creation of Pakistan included two geographically separated regions known as West Pakistan and _____.
(A) Kashmir
(B) Punjab
(C) East Pakistan
(D) Sindh

Question 29 :
What was the primary reason for the delay in announcing the final borders of India and Pakistan?
(A) British officials were still negotiating with Indian leaders
(B) There was a lack of proper maps and data
(C) The British administration wanted to avoid immediate riots
(D) The Radcliffe Commission took time to finalize the demarcation

Question 30 :
Fill in the blank: The division of British India in 1947 was primarily based on _____.
(A) Economic status of the regions
(B) Administrative convenience
(C) Religious demographics
(D) Military presence in different areas

Chapter 15 : Framing The Constitution

CONCISE KEY NOTES

Chapter Overview :
- "The Indian Constitution, which came into effect on 26 January 1950, is the longest in the world."
- "It was framed between December 1946 and November 1949 through intense debates in the Constituent Assembly."
- "The Constitution aimed to unify the nation, ensure social justice, and uphold democracy."
- "It drew inspiration from various sources but was uniquely adapted to India's conditions."
- "This chapter explores the vision, debates, and challenges faced in framing the Constitution."

The Background Of Constitution-Making : A Tumultuous Time (1946-1949)
- "The years preceding the Constitution were marked by hope and disappointment."
- "India had won independence, but it was also divided."
- "Partition violence had left deep wounds, making national unity a priority."
- "There were also peasant uprisings, workers' protests, and Hindu-Muslim conflicts."

The Formation of the Constituent Assembly :
- "The Constituent Assembly was set up in December 1946, with members elected by provincial legislatures."
- "Congress dominated the Assembly, while the Muslim League boycotted it, demanding Pakistan."
- "There were 300 members, including leaders like Nehru, Patel, Rajendra Prasad, and Ambedkar."
- "The Assembly held 11 sessions over 165 days."

The Objectives Resolution : Nehru's Vision for the Constitution
- "On 13 December 1946, Nehru introduced the Objectives Resolution, outlining the ideals of independent India."
- "India would be an 'Independent Sovereign Republic', ensuring justice, equality, and freedom."
- "Minorities, backward communities, and tribals would have special safeguards."
- "Nehru declared that India would not simply copy Western models, but create a unique system suited to its people."

Debate on the Resolution :
- "Some members feared that community-based rights would lead to divided loyalties."
- "Govind Ballabh Pant argued: 'The citizen must count, not the community'."
- "Socialists like N.G. Ranga emphasized economic justice, calling poor peasants the real minorities."

Role Of B.R Ambedkar And Other Members : The Drafting Committee
- "B.R. Ambedkar was the Chairman of the Drafting Committee, guiding the Constitution through the Assembly."

- "He had earlier been a critic of Congress but was invited by Gandhi to join as Law Minister."
- "Other key members included K.M. Munshi and Alladi Krishnaswamy Aiyar."
- "B.N. Rau, the Constitutional Advisor, studied global constitutions to assist in drafting."

Conflicts and Compromises :

- "There were debates over language, secularism, and representation."
- On 27th August 1947, B. Pocker Bahadur from Madras demanded separate electorates for Muslims, but the demand was strongly opposed by R.V. Dhulekar, Sardar Patel, Govind Ballabh Pant.
- "Ambedkar opposed separate electorates but secured reservations for Scheduled Castes."
- "Muslim members like Begum Aizaas Rasul rejected separate electorates, calling them self-destructive."

Debates On Rights And Citizenship: Fundamental Rights And Equality

- "The Constitution granted equal rights to all citizens, irrespective of caste, religion, or gender."
- "Articles 14-17 ensured equality before the law and abolished untouchability."
- "Articles 25-28 guaranteed religious freedom and protection of minority cultures."
- "Reservations were provided for SCs and STs in legislatures and government jobs."

The Debate on Language :

- "Hindi was declared the official language, but English would continue for 15 years."
- "There were heated debates, with Tamil and Bengali members fearing Hindi domination."
- "Eventually, the three-language formula was adopted."

Secularism in the Constitution :

- "Unlike Western secularism, Indian secularism meant equal treatment of all religions, not their exclusion."
- "Religious instructions were banned in state schools, but communities could manage their institutions."

Finalization And Adoption Of The Constitution :

The Final Draft (November 1949) :

- "After three years of debate, the final draft was adopted on 26 November 1949."
- "Rajendra Prasad, as President of the Assembly, signed the Constitution."
- "It came into effect on 26 January 1950, celebrated as Republic Day."

Universal Adult Franchise

- "Unlike Western democracies, India granted voting rights to all adults from the start."
- "In other countries, voting rights were expanded gradually over decades."
- "This was a revolutionary step, ensuring full democracy from the beginning."

Important Committees of the Constituent Assembly & Presidents:

- Rules of Procedure Committee – Rajendra Prasad
- Union Powers Committee – Jawaharlal Nehru
- Union Constitution Committee – Jawaharlal Nehru
- Provincial Constitution Committee – Vallabhbhai Patel
- Steering Committee – Rajendra Prasad
- Drafting Committee – B.R. Ambedkar
- Flag Committee – J.B. Kripalani
- States Committee – Jawaharlal Nehru
- Advisory Committee – Vallabhbhai Patel
- Supreme Court Committee – S. Varadachariar
- Fundamental Rights Sub-Committee – J.B. Kripalani
- Minorities Sub-Committee – H.C. Mookerjee
- Constitution Review Commission – M.N. Venkatachaliah

Women Members of the Constituent Assembly:

- Ammu Swaminathan – Madras (General)
- Annie Mascarene – Travancore & Cochin Union
- Begum Aizaz Rasul – United Provinces (Muslim)
- Dakshayani Velayudan – Madras (General)
- G. Durgabai – Madras (General)
- Hansa Mehta – Bombay (General)
- Kamla Chaudhri – United Provinces (General)
- Leela Ray – West Bengal (General)
- Malati Chowdhury – Orissa (General)
- Purnima Banerji – United Provinces (General)
- Rajkumari Amrit Kaur – Central Provinces & Berar (General)
- Renuka Ray – West Bengal (General)
- Sarojini Naidu – Bihar (General)
- Sucheta Kripalani – United Provinces (General)
- Vijayalakshmi Pandit – United Provinces (General)

Important Events (1945-1949):

- 26 July 1945 – Labour Government comes to power in Britain
- Dec 1945 – Jan 1946 – General Elections in India
- 16 May 1946 – Cabinet Mission announces constitutional scheme
- 16 June 1946 – Muslim League accepts Cabinet Mission plan
- 16 June 1946 – Cabinet Mission proposes Interim Government
- 16 August 1946 – Muslim League announces Direct Action Day
- 2 September 1946 – Congress forms Interim Government (Nehru as Vice-President)
- 13 October 1946 – Muslim League joins Interim Government
- 9 December 1946 – Constituent Assembly begins sessions
- 29 January 1947 – Muslim League demands dissolution of Constituent Assembly
- 16 July 1947 – Last meeting of Interim Government
- 11 August 1947 – Jinnah elected President of Pakistan's Constituent Assembly
- 14 August 1947 – Pakistan gains independence (celebrations in Karachi)
- 14-15 August 1947 – India celebrates independence at midnight
- December 1949 – Constitution of India is signed

Important Figures

Fig. 12.2
Images of desolation and destruction continued to haunt members of the Constituent Assembly.

Fig. 12.3
Jawaharlal Nehru speaking in the Constituent Assembly at midnight on14 August 1947

Fig. 12.4
The Constituent Assembly in session

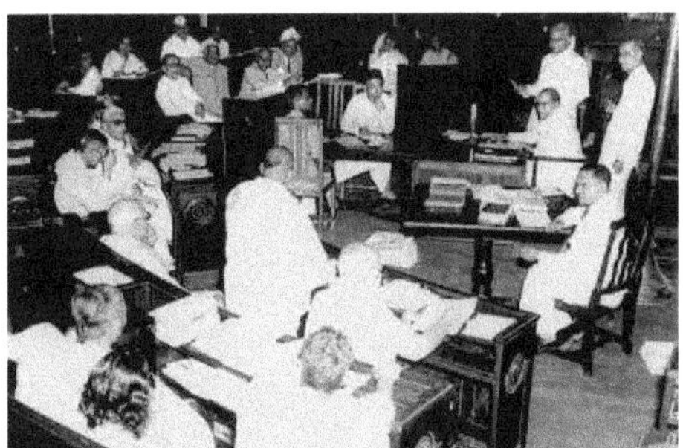

Fig. 12.5
B. R. Ambedkar presiding over a discussion of the Hindu Code Bill

Important Figures

Members of the Interim Government
Front row (left to right): Baldev Singh, John Mathai, C Rajagopalachari, Jawaharlal Nehru, Liaquat Ali Khan, Vallabhbhai Patel, I.I. Chundrigar, Asaf Ali, C.H. Bhabha.
Back row (left to right): Jagjivan Ram, Ghazanfar Ali Khan, Rajendra Prasad, Abdur Nishtar

Fig. 12.7
Edwin Montague (left) was the author of the Montague-Chelmsford Reforms of 1919 which allowed some form of representation in provincial legislative assemblies.

Fig. 12.8
In the winter of 1946 Indian leaders went to London for what turned out to be a fruitless round of talks with British Prime Minister Attlee. (Left to right: Liaquat Ali, Mohammad Ali Jinnah, Baldev Singh and Pethick-Lawrence)

Chapter 15 : Mapwork

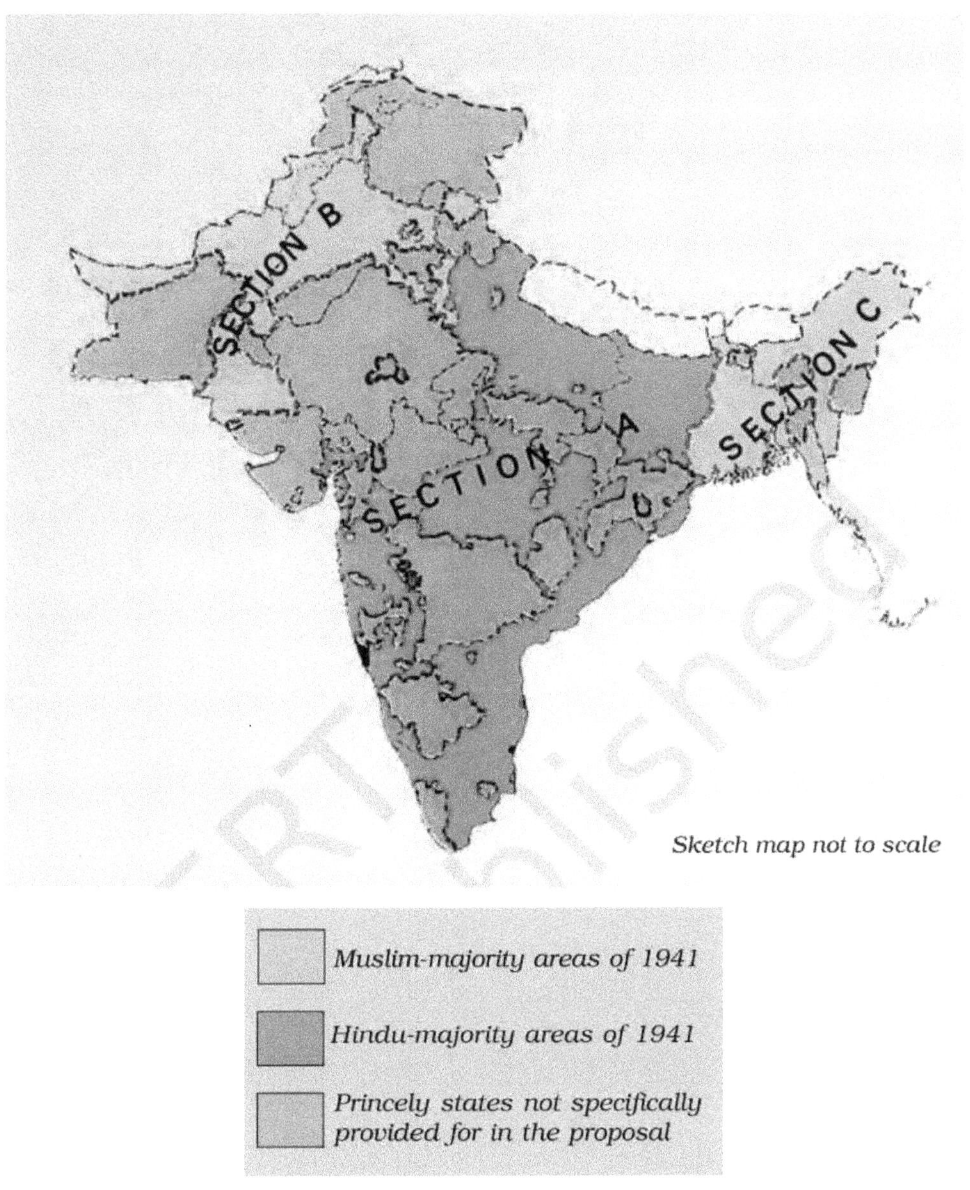

The Cabinet Mission proposal for an
Indian federation with three sections

Chapter 15 : Framing The Constitution

QUESTIONS FROM ARCHIVES

Question 1 :
Assertion (A): The Indian Constitution is the longest written constitution in the world.
Reason (R): India's size, diversity, and the need to integrate different communities required an elaborate constitutional framework.
A) Both A and R are true, and R is the correct explanation of A.
B) Both A and R are true, but R is not the correct explanation of A.
C) A is true, but R is false.
D) A is false, but R is true.

Question 2 :
Assertion (A): The Objectives Resolution provided a framework for the Indian Constitution.
Reason (R): It was inspired solely by the American and French Revolutions.
A) Both A and R are true, and R is the correct explanation of A.
B) Both A and R are true, but R is not the correct explanation of A.
C) A is true, but R is false.
D) A is false, but R is true.

Question 3 :
The Constituent Assembly was formed based on the provincial elections held in the year ___.
A) 1937
B) 1942
C) 1945–46
D) 1949

Question 4 :
The demand for separate electorates was opposed by nationalist leaders, particularly ___, who called it a "poison" that divided the nation.
A) Jawaharlal Nehru
B) B.R. Ambedkar
C) Sardar Vallabhbhai Patel
D) Rajendra Prasad

Question 5 :
The Fundamental Rights enshrined in the Indian Constitution include the right to ___, which prohibits discrimination based on religion, race, caste, sex, or place of birth.
A) Equality
B) Freedom
C) Property
D) Exploitation

Question 6 :
Which of the following was NOT a committee of the Constituent Assembly?
A) Drafting Committee
B) Union Power Committee
C) Language Committee
D) Election Commission Committee

Question 7 :
Who among the following was NOT a member of the Drafting Committee of the Indian Constitution?
A) B.R. Ambedkar
B) K.M. Munshi
C) Rajendra Prasad
D) Alladi Krishnaswamy Aiyar

Question 8 :
The Constitution of India was formally signed in ___.
A) January 1947
B) August 1948
C) December 1949
D) January 1950

Question 9 :
Who strongly advocated for the protection of tribal rights in the Constituent Assembly?
A) N.G. Ranga
B) Jaipal Singh
C) Govind Ballabh Pant
D) Sardar Patel

Question 10 :
Which language did Mahatma Gandhi propose as the national language of India?
A) Hindi
B) Urdu
C) Hindustani
D) Sanskrit

Question 11 :
The Constituent Assembly held a total of ___ sessions before finalizing the Constitution.
A) 5
B) 7
C) 11
D) 15

Question 12 :
Assertion (A): The Constituent Assembly was dominated by the Congress party.
Reason (R): The Muslim League and the Socialists initially refused to participate in the Constituent Assembly.
A) Both A and R are true, and R is the correct explanation of A.
B) Both A and R are true, but R is not the correct explanation of A.
C) A is true, but R is false.
D) A is false, but R is true.

Question 13 :
Assertion (A): Jawaharlal Nehru's "Objectives Resolution" was unanimously accepted in the Constituent Assembly.
Reason (R): The resolution ensured social justice, equality, and safeguards for minorities.
A) Both A and R are true, and R is the correct explanation of A.
B) Both A and R are true, but R is not the correct explanation of A.
C) A is true, but R is false.
D) A is false, but R is true.

Question 14 :
The Indian Constitution was drafted by the committee chaired by ___.
The Indian Constitution was drafted by the committee chaired by ___.
A) Sardar Vallabhbhai Patel
B) Rajendra Prasad
C) B.R. Ambedkar
D) Jawaharlal Nehru

Question 15 :
Nehru argued that the Indian Constitution should be based on democratic ideals but also include elements of ___.
A) Capitalism
B) Socialism
C) Feudalism
D) Colonialism

Question 16 :
Which of the following leaders strongly opposed separate electorates for minorities in the Constituent Assembly?
A) B. Pocker Bahadur
B) Sardar Vallabhbhai Patel
C) Jaipal Singh
D) N.G. Ranga

Question 17 :
Who among the following strongly advocated for the protection and upliftment of tribals in the Constituent Assembly?
A) Rajendra Prasad
B) Jaipal Singh
C) Govind Ballabh Pant
D) Somnath Lahiri

Question 18 :
The Constitution was finally adopted on ___, and came into effect on ___.
A) 15 August 1947; 26 January 1949
B) 26 November 1949; 26 January 1950
C) 14 August 1947; 15 August 1947
D) 26 January 1949; 15 August 1950

Question 19 :
Which of the following was NOT a key feature of the Indian Constitution as debated in the Assembly?
A) Secularism
B) Federalism
C) Absolute monarchy
D) Protection of minority rights

Question 20 :
Who insisted that democracy should be interpreted not just in political terms but also in economic terms to benefit the poor?
A) Sardar Patel
B) N.G. Ranga
C) Rajendra Prasad
D) G.D. Birla

Question 21 :
The Constitution of India was framed between December 1946 and ___.
A) August 1947
B) November 1949
C) January 1950
D) December 1950

Question 22 :
The Constituent Assembly sessions were spread over ___ days.
A) 100
B) 120
C) 165
D) 200

Question 23 :
Who moved the resolution proposing that the
National Flag of India be a tricolor with a navy
blue wheel at the center?
A) Rajendra Prasad
B) Jawaharlal Nehru
C) B.R. Ambedkar
D) Vallabhbhai Patel

Question 24 :
The Indian Constitution drew inspiration from
various sources but was adapted to fit ___.
A) European legal traditions
B) The Indian context
C) British constitutional monarchy
D) American presidential democracy

Question 25 :
Which leader strongly opposed the influence of
British imperialism on the Constituent Assembly
and urged complete independence?
A) Jaipal Singh
B) Somnath Lahiri
C) Govind Ballabh Pant
D) B.R. Ambedkar

Question 26 :
The demand for separate electorates for Muslims
was opposed mainly due to fears of ___.
A) Increased regional autonomy
B) Fragmentation of the nation
C) Hindu–Muslim unity
D) Economic instability

Question 27 :
The Constitution grants minorities cultural and
educational rights under ___.
A) Articles 10–12
B) Articles 14–18
C) Articles 25–28
D) Articles 29–30

Question 28 :
Who among the following argued that the real
minorities in India were the poor, landless, and
oppressed?
A) B.R. Ambedkar
B) Sardar Patel
C) N.G. Ranga
D) Jaipal Singh

Question 29 :
The official language of India, as per the
Constitution, was to be ___, with English
continuing for official purposes for 15 years.
A) Hindustani
B) Hindi in Devanagari script
C) Sanskrit
D) Urdu

Question 30 :
Who advocated for tribal rights in the
Constituent Assembly and highlighted the
historical neglect of Adivasis?
A) Rajendra Prasad
B) Jaipal Singh
C) Sardar Patel
D) Vallabhbhai Patel

Question 31 :
Assertion (A): The Indian Constitution sought
to integrate diverse communities and create a
unified nation.
 Reason (R): The Constitution was framed
entirely based on the Government of India
Act, 1935.
 A) Both A and R are true, and R is the
correct explanation of A.
 B) Both A and R are true, but R is not the
correct explanation of A.
 C) A is true, but R is false.
 D) A is false, but R is true.

Question 32 :
Assertion (A): The Constituent Assembly was
not elected by universal adult franchise.
 Reason (R): The members were chosen by
the provincial legislatures based on the 1945–
46 elections.
 A) Both A and R are true, and R is the
correct explanation of A.
 B) Both A and R are true, but R is not the
correct explanation of A.
 C) A is true, but R is false.
 D) A is false, but R is true.

Question 33 :
The Constituent Assembly was officially
formed in ___.
A) December 1946
B) August 1947
C) November 1949
D) January 1950

Question 34 :
The Indian Constitution was finalized and signed in ___.
A) August 1947
B) December 1949
C) January 1950
D) November 1950

Question 35 :
The Constituent Assembly of India was formed under the ___.
A) Cripps Mission Plan
B) Cabinet Mission Plan
C) Mountbatten Plan
D) Simon Commission Report

Question 36 :
Who was appointed as the Constitutional Advisor to the Constituent Assembly?
A) Dr. B.R. Ambedkar
B) Dr. Rajendra Prasad
C) Dr. B.N. Rau
D) Pandit Jawaharlal Nehru

Question 37 :
The 'Objectives Resolution' was moved in the Constituent Assembly on ___.
A) 15th August 1947
B) 26th January 1948
C) 13th December 1946
D) 9th December 1946

Question 38 :
Which of the following articles of the Indian Constitution deals with the Right to Freedom of Religion?
A) Articles 14-18
B) Articles 19-22
C) Articles 25-28
D) Articles 29-31

Question 39 :
The idea of 'Universal Adult Franchise' was adopted in the Indian Constitution to ensure ___.
A) Economic equality
B) Political representation
C) Social justice
D) Cultural integration

Question 40 :
Who among the following was NOT a member of the Constituent Assembly?
A) Mahatma Gandhi
B) Dr. B.R. Ambedkar
C) Dr. Rajendra Prasad
D) Jawaharlal Nehru

Question 41 :
The principle of 'Single Citizenship' in the Indian Constitution was adopted from the constitution of ___.
A) USA
B) UK
C) Canada
D) Australia

Question 42 :
The concept of 'Directive Principles of State Policy' was borrowed from the constitution of ___.
A) Ireland
B) France
C) Germany
D) South Africa

OFFICIAL NTA CUET-UG HISTORY QUESTION PAPERS (2023-24)

&

10 FULL-LENGTH REALISTIC MOCK TEST PAPERS

NTA CUET–UG HISTORY (314) 2023

Question 1:
In the British period of Indian history, Santhal and Paharia tribes lived in:
(1) Kedarkanta hills
(2) Uttarkashi hills
(3) Rajmahal hills
(4) Satpura hill

Question 2:
Match List – I with List – II:
List-I List II
(A) Delhi (I) Gonoo
(B) Kanpur (II) Kunwar Singh
(C) Arrah (III) Nana Sahib
(D) Chotanagpur (IV) Bahadur Shah
Choose the correct answer from the options given below:
(1) (A)–(1), (B)–(II), (C)–(III), (D)–(IV)
(2) (A)–(III), (B)–(1), (C)–(II), (D)–(IV)
(3) (A)–(IV), (B)–(III), (C)–(II), (D)–(1)
(4) (A)–(IV), (B)–(III), (C)–(1), (D)–(II)

Question 3:
The ______contained all kinds of information such as attendance at the court, grant of offices and titles, diplomatic missions, presents received, or the enquires made by the Mughal emperor about the health of an officer.
(1) Akhbarat (2) Waqia namis
(3) Madad–i maash (4) Sadr–us sudur

Question 4:
In which year was the Subsidiary Alliance introduced by Lord Wellesley in Awadh?
(1) 1800 (2) 1802
(3) 1803 (4) 1801

Question 5:
Match List-I with List – II:
List-I List-II
(A) Karaikkal Ammaiyar (I) Tamil Shalva hymns
(B) Nalayira Divyaprabandham
(II) Devotee of Shiva
(C) Andal (III) Tamil Veda
(D) Tevaram (IV) Women devotee of Vishnu
Choose the correct answer from the options given below:
(1) (A)–(I), (B)–(II), (C)–(III), (D)–(IV)
(2) (A)–(IV), (B)–(I), (C)–(III), (D)–(II)
(3) (A)–(III), (B)–(II), (C)–(I), (D)–(IV)
(4) (A)–(II), (B)–(III). (C)–(IV), (D)–(I)

Question 6:
Match List – I with List – II :
List –1 List – Ii
(A) Portuguese (I) Pondicherry
(B) Dutch (II) Panaji
(C) British (II) Masulipatnam
(D) French (IV) Madras

Choose the correct answer from the options given below :
(1) (A)–(IV), (B)–(III), (C)–(II), (D)–(I)
(2) (A)–(II), (B)–(III), (C)–(IV), (D)–(I)
(3) (A)–(III), (B)–(II), (C)–(I), (D)–(IV)
(4) (A)–(III), (B)–(II), (C)–(IV), (D)–(I)

Question 7:
Who wrote, "Gunijuriya is just sufficiently cultivated to show what glorious country this might be made, its beauty and riches might be made equal to almost any in the universe" ?
(1) Peter Mundy
(2) Jean-Baptiste Tavernier
(3) Francois Bernier
(4) Francis Buchanan

Question 8:
Aramaic and Greek scripts used by Asoka in which part of his Empire?
(1) Iran (2) Pakistan
(3) Afghanistan (4) Ceylon

Question 9:
26 January 1930, was observed as ___________, with the national flag being hoisted in different
(1) Boycott Day (2) Swadeshi Day
(3) Independence Day (4) Republic Day

Question 10:
Who among the following persuaded Gandhi to not restrict Dandi March protest with men alone ?
(1) Mahadev Desai
(2) Kasturba Gandhi
(3) Kamla Devi Chattopadhyay
(4) Jawaharlal Nehru

Question 11:
Kozhikode is the name of which medieval town/ city ?
(1) Calicut (2) Hampi
(3) Banaras (4) Koshambi

Question 12:
Arrange the following events in a chronological order.
(A) Santhal Rebellion
(B) Ryots Rebel in Deccan Villages
(C) Permanent Settlement of Bengal
(D) First Revenue Settlement in Bombay Deccan
Choose the correct answer from the options given below :
(1) (D), (C), (A), (B) (2) (A), (B), (C), (D)
(3) (C), (D), (A), (B) (4) (B), (A), (D), (C)

Question 13:
Many historians remain sceptical of oral history and dismiss it because of which reason?
(1) It broadens the boundaries of their discipline
(2) It enables historians to write vivid accounts of what happened.

(3) Uniqueness of personal experience makes
generalisation difficult.
(4) It has explored the experiences of those men
and women whose existence has been ignored.

Question 14:
Mahatma Gandhi was against separate electorates
for the Depressed Classes because:
(1) Depressed class people were against Mahatma
Gandhi.
(2) Gandhi called them Harijan.
(3) Gandhi and Ambedkar proposed two different
political ideologies.
(4) According to Gandhi, separate electorates
to the "Untouchables" would ensure their
bondage in perpetuity.

Question 15:
What was the most unique feature of the Harappan
civilisation ?
(1) Creation of railway track
(2) Evolution of parliamentary system
(3) Development of urban centres
(4) Matriarchal structure of the family

Question 16:
What is the meaning of the term 'Jins-I-Kamil" in
the Indo-Persian sources of Mughal period?
(1) Par excellence
(2) Cotton
(3) Perfect crops
(4) Sugar

Question 17:
Which of the following statements are TRUE about
the Permanent Settlement ?
(A) The Permanent Settlement came into operation
in 1773.
(B) The revenue demand was fixed in perpetuity.
(C) The zamindars were given proprietary rights
over the land.
(D) Failure in the timely payment of revenue led to
the confiscation and auction of the estate.
(E) Permanent Settlement was withdrawn within
20 years due to its unpopularity.
Choose the correct answer from the options given
below :
(1) (A), (B) and (C) only
(2) (B), (C) and (D) only
(3) (C), (D) and (E) only
(4) (B), (D) and (E) only

Question 18:
The 'Punch' which published the news related to
1857 was a:
(1) British Journal of Comedy
(2) British Journal of Tragedy
(3) British Journal of Comic Satire
(4) British Journal of Crime

Question 19:
Which one of the following is not related to the
Harappan religious belief system ?
(1) Proto Shiva
(2) Lingas
(3) Mother goddess
(4) Priest-Kings

Question 20:
The Great Bath was discovered at which of the
following Harappan sites ?
(1) Mohenjodaro
(2) Harappa
(3) Kalibanjan
(4) Dholavira

Question 21:
Match List – I with List – II
List – I List – II
(A) Kushanas (I) Copper coins
(B) Shakas (II) Names and images of greek
gods and goddesses
(C) Indo Greeks (III) Silver coins
(D) Yaudheyas (IV) Gold coins
Choose the correct answer from the options given
below :
(1) (A)–(IV), (B)–(II), (C)–(III), (D)–(1)
(2) (A)–(IV), (B)–(III), (C)–(II), (D)–(I)
(3) (A)–(IV), (B)–(III), (C)–(1), (D)–(II)
(4) (A)–(IV), (B)–(1), (C)–(II), (D)–(III)

Question 22:
Arrange the following Kingdoms in a chronological
order of their establishment.
(A) Bahamani Kingdom
(B) Vijayanagara Empire
(C) Delhi Sultanate
(D) Gajapati Kingdom
Choose the correct answer from the options given
below :
(1) (A), (C), (B), (D)
(2) (C), (B), (A), (D)
(3) (C), (D), (A), (B)
(4) (B), (A), (C), (D)

Question 23:
Who among the following was regarded as the
"establisher of the Yavana kingdom"
(1) Samudra Gupta
(2) Chandragupta Maurya
(3) Krishna Dev Raya
(4) Gautami Puto Sri Satkarmi

Question 24:
Which Governor General described the kingdom
of Awadh as 'a cherry that will drop into our
mouth one day" ?
(1) Lord Wellesley
(2) Lord Dalhousie
(3) Charles Cornwallis
(4) Lord Clive

Question 25:
Humayun, after being defeated by Sher Shah Suri
took refuge in the court of:
(1) Pashtun ruler of Kazakhastan
(2) Safavid ruler of Iran
(3) Turkish ruler of Egypt
(4) Moroccan ruler of Africa
Question 26:
Who took the first detailed photographs of
archaeological remains at Hampi in 1856 ?

(1) J.F. Fleet
(2) John Marshall
(3) Alexander Greenlaw
(4) Burton Stein

Question 27:
Who among the following was Gandhiji's political mentor ?
(1) Dadabhai Naoroji
(2) Gopal Krishna Gokhale
(3) Bal Gangadhar Tilak
(4) Rabindranath Tagore

Question 28:
On the basis of the accounts of the travellers, which statement regarding the status of women is not correct ?
(1) Prevalence of the practice of sati.
(2) They worked as agricultural and non agricultural workers.
(3) Women from merchant families participated in commercial activities.
(4) Women were confined to their homes.

Question 29:
Choose the correct statements.
(A) Naths, Jogis and Siddas were the religious cults that evolved outside the orthodox Brahmanical framework.
(B) Many of the leaders of these cults belonged to artisanal groups.
(C) The leaders of these cults accepted unquestioned authority of the Vedas.
(D) The language of their expression was literary Sanskrit, therefore, they could not influence ordinary masses.
Choose the correct answer from the options given below :
(1) (A) and (D) only
(2) (B) and (C) only
(3) (C) and (D) only
(4) (A) and (B) only

Question 30:
Arrange the following in a chronological order.
(A) Direct Action Day
(B) Salt March
(C) Gandhi returns to India from South Africa
(D) Gandhi's address at Banaras Hindu University
(E) Lahore session of the Indian National Congress
Choose the correct answer from the options given below :
(1) (D) (E), (C), (A), (B)
(2) (B), (C), (D), (E), (A)
(3) (C), (D), (E), (B), (A)
(4) (A) (C),(E), (D), (B)

Question 31:
Choose the correct statements about the Harappan script.
(A) It is deciphered.
(B) It has few signs.
(C) It has 20 signs.
(D) It was written from right to left.
(E) It has been found on seals, copper tools, tablets etc.

Choose the correct answer from the options given below :
(1) (D) and (E) only (2) (A) and (E) only
(3) (B) and (C) only (4) (C) and (D) only

Question 32:
Which of the following statements are correct ?
(A) Asoka" was mentioned in Brahmi and Kharosthi Scripts.
(B) Epigraphica Indica was first published in 1888.
(C) R.E.M. Wheeler publishes a set of Asokan inscriptions.
(D) James Prinsep deciphered Brahmi script of Asokan inscriptions.
(E) Asoka' was mentioned in Prakrit texts and inscriptions.
Choose the correct answer from the options given below :
(1) (B), (C) and (D) only
(2) (A), (C) and (E) only
(3) (C), (D) and (E) only
(4) (B), (D) and (E) only

Question 33:
Which one of the following rituals were not associated with the reign of Shah Jahan?
(1) Chahar (2) Taslim
(3 Sijda (4) Zaminbos

Question 34:
Who among the following was a Moroccan traveller ?
(1) Al-Biruni (2) Ibn Battuta
(3) Bernier (4) Marco Polo

Question 35:
Choose the correct statements about Shah Mal.
(A) He belonged to a village in Pargana Barout in U.P.
(B) He mobilised the headman and cultivators against the British.
(C) He got educated in Hyderabad and was known as Danka Shah.
(D) He was killed in a battle in July 1857.
(E) He fought the famous battle of Chinhat.
Choose the correct answer from the options given below :
(1) (A), (B) and (D) only
(2) (B), (C) and (D) only
(3) (C), (D) and (E) only
(4) (A), (B) and (E) only

Question 36:
Match List – I with List – II :
List – I List – II
(A) M.S. Vats (I) Excavation at Lothal
(B) S.R. Rao (II) Excavation at Kalibangan
(C) B.B. Lal (III) Excavation at Bahawalpur
(D) M.R. Mughal (IV) Excavation at Harappa
Choose the correct answer from the options given below :
(1) (A)–(IV), (B)–(I), (C)–(II), (D)–(III)
(2) (A)–(IV), (B)–(III), (C)–(I), (D)–(II)
(3) (A)–(II), (B)–(I), (C)–(IV), (D)–(III)
(4) (A)–(I), (B)–(III), (C)–(II), (D)–(IV)

Question 37:
What is the meaning of the word "Matriliny" ?
(1) Tracing the descent from father.
(2) Tracing the descent from grandfather.
(3) Tracing the descent from mother.
(4) Tracing the descent from outside gotra.

Question 38:
Daman-i-Koh, in the foothills of Rajmahal hills, was declared to be the land of which of the following tribes ?
(1) Gonds (2) Bhils
(3) Santhals (4) Paharia

Question 39:
Arrange the following dynasties which ruled over Vijayanagara Empire in a chronological order.
(A) Saluva dynasty (B) Tuluva dynasty
(C) Sangama dynasty (D) Aravidu dynasty
Choose the correct answer from the options given below :
(1) (C), (A), (B), (D) (2) (C), (B), (A), (D)
(3) (A), (C), (B), (D) (4) (B), (A), (C), (D)

Question 40:
Arrange the following religious teachers according to the timeline during which they lived in a chronological order.
(A) Tondaradippodi (B) Lal Ded
(C) Raidas (D) Ramanujacharya
Choose the correct answer from the options given below :
(1) (A), (D), (B), (C) (2) (D), (B), (A), (C)
(3) (D), (A), (C), (B) (4) (C), (A), (D), (B)

Question 41:
Read the passage and answer the question :
Who were these hill folks? Why were they so apprehensive of Buchanan's visit? Buchanan's journal gives us tantalising glimpses of these hill folks in the early nineteenth century. His journal was written as a diary of places he visited, people he encountered, and practices he saw. It raises questions in our mind, but does not always help us answer them. It tells us about a moment in time, but not about the longer history of people and places. For that, historians have to turn to other records.
Who were the 'hill folks" referred to in the passage above?
(1) Paharias (2) Jotedars
(3) Santhals (4) Dikus

Question 42:
Buchanan's survey gives glimpses of hill folks during which century ?
(1) Early nineteenth century
(2) Eighteenth century
(3) Sixteenth century
(4) Late nineteenth century

Question 43:
Which of the following is not true about Buchanana's account ?
(1) It gives a glimpse of hill folks.
(2) It raises questions in our minds.
(3) Hill folks were paying a heavy revenue to the East India Company.
(4) Its about people he encountered.

Question 44:
Which of the following is false ?
(1) Hill folks were not sure about Francis Buchanan's visit.
(2) Francis Buchanan was a Governor-General of India from 1794-1815.
(3) Francis Buchanan was a British surveyor who travelled through Rajmahal hills.
(4) Francis Buchanan wrote a journal.

Question 45:
Buchanan's survey provides us information about "hill folks" in the form of:
(1) Diary (2) Bohikhata
(3) Chronicle (4) Revenue Record

Question 46:
Why did Buddhist teachers travel to faraway places ?
(1) So that Buddhism does not spread from India.
(2) To circulate the teachings of the Buddha.
(3) To write texts in other countries.
(4) To bring the Chinese to India

Question 47:
From which country Buddhism spread to East Asia?
(1) Japan (2) China
(3) India (4) Tibet

Question 48:
Fa Xian and Xuan Zang came from which country to India ?
(1) Burma (2) China
(3) Japan (4) Srilanka

Question 49:
Modern translations of Buddhist manuscripts have been prepared from which of the following languages ?
(A) Pali and Sanskrit (B) Chinese and Tibetan
(C) Pali and Tamil (D) Tibetan and Hindu
Choose the correct answer from the options given below :
(1) (A), (B) only (2) (B), (C) only
(3) (A), (C) only (4) (C), (D) only

Question 50:
How were Buddhist texts popularised in China ?
(1) Children read them.
(2) The Buddhist texts were translated into Chinese.
(3) Buddhist texts were modernised.
(4) Buddhist texts were not translated.

Scan The QR Code To Get Answers With Detailed Explanations!

NTA CUET–UG HISTORY (314) 2024

Question 1:
Which of the following statements are correct ?
(A) Harappan seal was a most distinctive artifact of the Harappan Civilization.
(B) Harappan seal motifs conveyed a meaning to those unable to read it.
(C) Harappan seals had Sanskrit script on them.
(D) Harappan seals had Pali and Prakrit inscriptions on them.
(E) Some Harappan seals show wider spacing of script from right and cramping on the left.
Choose the correct answer from the options given below :
(1) (A) and (D) only
(2) (C), (D) and (E) only
(3) (A), (B) and (E) only
(4) (A), (C) and (D) only

Question 2:
Match List-I with List-II :
List-I List-II
(A) Kushanas (I) Piyadassi
(B) Ashoka (II) Devputra
(C) Samudragupta (III) Court-poet
(D) Harisena (IV) Prayaga Prashasti
Choose the correct answer from the options given below :
(1) (A) – (II), (B) – (I), (C) – (IV), (D) – (III)
(2) (A) – (I), (B) – (II), (C) – (III), (D) – (IV)
(3) (A) – (IV), (B) – (III), (C) – (II), (D) – (I)
(4) (A) – (III), (B) – (IV), (C) – (I), (D) – (II)

Question 3:
Name the first site from where the Indus Valley Civilization was discovered.
(1) Harappa
(2) Rakhigarhi
(3) Hulas
(4) Sinauli

Question 4:
Match List-I with List-II :
List-I List-II
(A) Alexander Greenlaw (I) Documenting the inscriptions on the temple walls
(B) John Marshall (II) Visits Vijayanagara in 1800
(C) J.F. Fleet (III) Conservation works of Vijyayanagara began under him
(D) Colin Mackenzie (IV) Detailed photography at Hampi
Choose the correct answer from the options :

given below :
(1) (A) – (III), (B) – (IV), (C) – (II), (D) – (I)
(2) (A) – (IV), (B) – (III), (C) – (I), (D) – (II)
(3) (A) – (IV), (B) – (I), (C) – (III), (D) – (II)
(4) (A) – (I), (B) – (IV), (C) – (III), (D) – (II)

Question 5:
Match List-I with List-II :
List-I List-II
(A) Duarte Barbosa (I) Morocco
(B) Marco Polo (II) Spain
(C) Ibn Battuta (III) Portugal
(D) Antonio Monserrate (IV) Italy
Choose the correct answer from the options given below :
(1) (A) – (I), (B) – (II), (C) – (IV), (D) – (III)
(2) (A) – (III), (B) – (IV), (C) – (I), (D) – (II)
(3) (A) – (I), (B) – (III), (C) – (IV), (D) – (II)
(4) (A) – (III), (B) – (IV), (C) – (II), (D) – (I)

Question 6:
Match List-I with List-II :
List-I List-II
(A) Pataliputra (I) Prakrit name of Rajgir, Bihar
(B) Rajgaha (II) Present day Coastal Odisha
(C) Kalinga (III) Present day Patna
(D) Arthasastra (IV) Kautilya
Choose the correct answer from the options given below :
(1) (A) – (III), (B) – (I), (C) – (II), (D) – (IV) (2) (A) – (I), (B) – (III), (C) – (II), (D) – (IV)
(3) (A) – (I), (B) – (II), (C) – (IV), (D) – (III) (4) (A) – (III), (B) – (IV), (C) – (I), (D) – (II)

Question 7:
Which of the following statements are correct ?
(A) Mahabharata has over 1,00,000 verses.
(B) Mahabharata was written by Valmiki.
(C) V.S. Sukthankar is associated with the critical edition of Mahabharata.
(D) The critical edition of Mahabharata took 47 years to complete.
(E) The critical edition of Mahabharata ran into over 13,000 pages.
Choose the correct answer from the options given below :
(1) (A) and (B) only (2) (B) and (E) only
(3) (A), (C), (D) and (E)only (4) (B) and (C) only

Question 8:
Match List-I with List-II :
List-I List-II
(A) Kula (I) Larger network of kinfolk
(B) Jati (II) Families
(C) Vamsha (III) People
(D) Jana (IV) Lineage
Choose the correct answer from the options given below :
(1) (A) – (I), (B) – (II), (C) – (III), (D) – (IV)
(2) (A) – (IV), (B) – (III), (C) – (II), (D) – (I)
(3) (A) – (II), (B) – (I), (C) – (IV), (D) – (III)
(4) (A) – (III), (B) – (IV), (C) – (II), (D) – (I)

Question 9:
Match List-I with List-II :
List-I List-II
(A) Meghe Dhaka Tara (I) Govind Nihalani
(B) Garam Hawa (II) Habib Tanvir
(C) Tamas (III) Ritvik Ghatak
(D) Jis Lahore Nahin Vekhya O Jamya-e-nai (IV) M.S. Sathyu
Choose the correct answer from the options given below :
(1) (A) – (IV), (B) – (III), (C) – (II), (D) – (I)
(2) (A) – (III), (B) – (IV), (C) – (I), (D) – (II)
(3) (A) – (I), (B) – (II), (C) – (III), (D) – (IV)
(4) (A) – (II), (B) – (I), (C) – (IV), (D) – (III)

Question 10:
Who was the first woman to be ordained as bhikkhuni ?
(1) Sigala (2) Karuni Pajapati
(3) Mahapajapati Gotami (4) Punna

Question 11:
Who amongst the following were the principal deities of the Vedic pantheon ?
(1) Brahma, Vishnu, Shiva (2) Vishnu, Shiva, Indra
(3) Agni, Indra, Soma (4) Agni, Varuna, Indra

Question 12:
Which of the following statements are not correct ?
(A) Vinay Pitaka does not describe the rules for monks.
(B) Buddhism grew only after the death of Buddha.
(C) Sutta Pitakaare the verses composed by bhikkunis.
(D) Punna was a rich land-lady.
(E) The word Chaitya may have been derived from the word chita.
Choose the correct answer from the options given below :
(1) (D) and (E) only (2) (A), (B) and (D) only
(3) (C) and (E) only (4) (B), (D) and (E) only

Question 13:
Madras, Bombay and Calcutta were the anglicised names of where the British first set up
trading posts.
(1) Cities (2) Villages (3) Towns (4) Capitals

Question 14:
Which of the following statements are correct ?
(A) Guru Arjan compiled Guru Nanak's hymns in the Adi Granth Sahib.
(B) Guru Tegh Bahadur laid the foundation of the Khalsa Panth.
(C) Guru Nanak composed the Guru Granth Sahib.
(D) Mirabai was a Maratha princess.
(E) Mirabai was a Rajput princess.
Choose the correct answer from the options given below :
(1) (A) and (D) only (2) (C) and (D) only
(3) (B) and(C) only (4) (A) and (E) only

Question 15:
Which Sufi teacher was also known as the 'Gharib Nawaz' ?
(1) Shaikh Nizamuddin Auliya (2) Khwaja Muinuddin
(3) Amir Khusrau (4) Shaikh Qutbuddin Bakhtiyar Kaki

Question 16:
Lord Jagannatha is a form of which God ?
(1) Surya (2) Vishnu (3) Shiva (4) Brahma

Question 17:
Which among the following travellers visited the city of Vijayanagara during the 15th century ?
(A) Domingo Paes
(B) Abdur Razzaq
(C) Afanasii Nikitin
(D) Fernao Nuniz
(E) Nicolo de Conti

Choose the correct answer from the options given below :
(1) (B), (C) and (E) only (2) (C), (D) and (E) only
(3) (A), (B) and (D) only (4) (B), (C) and (D) only

Question 18:
Match List-I with List-II :
List-I List-II
(A) Terracotta models of plough (I) Kalibangan
(B) Ploughed field (II) Shortughai
(C) Traces of canals (III) Dholavira
(D) Water reservoirs (IV) Cholistan
Choose the correct answer from the options given below :
(1) (A) – (IV), (B) – (I), (C) – (II), (D) – (III)
(2) (A) – (I), (B) – (II), (C) – (IV), (D) – (III)
(3) (A) – (I), (B) – (II), (C) – (III), (D) – (IV)
(4) (A) – (IV), (B) – (III), (C) – (II), (D) – (I)

Question 19:
Who, amongst the following, founded the Vijayanagara Empire ?
(1) Krishnadeva Raya (2) Harihara and Bukka
(3) Raja Raya (4) Rajendra II

Question 20:
Match List-I with List-II :
List-I List-II
(A) Shell (I) Shortughai
(B) Lapis-Lazuli (II) Nageshwar
(C) Carnelian (III) South Rajasthan
(D) Steatite (IV) Lothal
Choose the correct answer from the options given below :
(1) (A) – (III), (B) – (IV), (C) – (I), (D) – (II)
(2) (A) – (II), (B) – (I), (C) – (IV), (D) – (III)
(3) (A) – (I), (B) – (II), (C) – (III), (D) – (IV)
(4) (A) – (IV), (B) – (III), (C) – (II), (D) – (I)

Question 21:
Match List-I with List-II :
List-I List-II
(A) Mahals (I) Territorial unit
(B) Pahariyas and Santhals (II) Permanent Settlement
(C) 1793 (III) Rajmahal hills
(D) Taluq (IV) Estates
Choose the correct answer from the options given below :

(1) (A) – (I), (B) – (II), (C) – (III), (D) – (IV) (2) (A) – (IV), (B) – (III), (C) – (II), (D) – (I)
(3) (A) – (IV), (B) – (III), (C) – (I), (D) – (II) (4) (A) – (II), (B) – (I), (C) – (IV), (D) – (III)

Question 22:
Which of the following statements are correct ?
(A) Moneylenders were called 'dikus'.
(B) Zamindars hired the Santhals to reclaim land.
(C) Santhals were merchants.
(D) Land of the Santhals was demarcated as 'Damin-i-koh'.
(E) Santhals charged heavy land revenue from dikus moneylenders.
Choose the correct answer from the options given below :
(1) (A), (B) and (C) only (2) (C) and (E) only
(3) (A), (B) and (D) only (4) (C) and (D) only

Question 23:
Which of the following statements are true about the zamindars ?
(A) Milkiyat lands were cultivated for the general use of the people.
(B) Zamindars could sell, bequeath or mortgage the milkiyat lands.
(C) Zamindars collected revenue on behalf of themselves.
(D) Most Zamindars had fortresses as well as armed contingent.
(E) Control over military resources was another source of power for the Zamindars.
Choose the correct answer from the options given below :
(1) (A), (D) and (E) only (2) (C), (D) and (E) only
(3) (A), (B) and (C) only (4) (B), (D) and (E) only

Question 24:
Kauravas and Pandavas belonged to which ruling family ?
(1) Kuru (2) Panchal (3) Magadha (4) Vatsa

Question 25:
Which report reproduced zamindars' and ryots' petitions as appendices for consideration of the British Parliament ?
(1) The First Report (2) The Seventh Report
(3) The Sixth Report (4) The Fifth Report

Question 26:
The rebel leaders issued Proclamations and few _______ to propagate their ideas during the 1857 revolt.
Fill in the blank with the correct answer from the options given below :
(1) Cartridges (2) Ishtahars
(3) Sepoys (4) Taluqdars

Question 27:
In 1857 "the life has gone out of the body" was said in reference to which state ?
(1) Jhansi (2) Awadh
(3) Kanpur (4) Delhi

Question 28:
Which of the following statements are correct ?

(A) Bell of arms was a store room in which weapons were kept.
(B) The army of Awadh supported the British.
(C) Firangi is a term of Persian origin applied to the British by the rebels.
(D) The 7th Awadh Irregular Cavalry accepted the new cartridges in early May.
(E) Local leaders emerged, urging peasants, zamindars and tribals to revolt.
Choose the correct answer from the options given below :
(1) (A), (B) and (C) only
(2) (B) and (D) only
(3) (A), (C) and (E) only
(4) (D) and (E) only

Question 29:
Match List-I with List-II :
List-I List-II
(A) Nana Sahib (I) Awadh
(B) Rani Lakshmi Bai (II) Arrah
(C) Kunwar Singh (III) Kanpur
(D) Birjis Qadr (IV) Jhansi
Choose the correct answer from the options given below :
(1) (A) – (I), (B) – (II), (C) – (III), (D) – (IV)
(2) (A) – (I), (B) – (II), (C) – (IV), (D) – (III)
(3) (A) – (III), (B) – (IV), (C) – (II), (D) – (I)
(4) (A) – (II), (B) – (I), (C) – (III), (D) – (IV)

Question 30:
Who was the leader of the Santhal Revolt of 1855–56 ?
(1) Birsa Munda (2) Gonoo (3) Sidhu Manjhi (4) Shah Mal
Question 31:
Who fought in the famous Battle of Chinhat in which the British forces under Henry Lawrence were defeated ?
(1) Shah Mal (2) Maulvi Ahmadullah Shah
(3) Birjis Qadr (4) Kunwar Singh

Question 32:
Who was the Commissioner of Lucknow when the rebels besieged it during the Revolt of 1857 ?
(1) Colin Campbell (2) Henry Lawrence
(3) James Outram (4) Henry Havelock

Question 33:
The Sunset Law was associated with
(1) Zamindari System/Permanent Settlement (2) British Navy
(3) Imperial Court (4) Freedom Movement

Question 34:
During his 'Salt March' Gandhiji began walking towards the ocean from his ashram, located at

_______.
Fill in the blank with the correct answer from the options given below :
(1) Ahmedabad (2) Sabarmati (3) Wardha (4) Kochrab

Question 35:
5. Mahatma Gandhi's Salt March was notable as the first nationlist activity focused on _______.

(1) Women (2) Lord Irwin
(3) Subhas Chandra Bose (4) 15 March, 1930

Question 36:
"Purna Swaraj" as the goal of nationalism in India was aimed to achieve __________ .
(1) Partial freedom (2) Complete independence
(3) Indian identity (4) Partition

Question 37:
Which of the following statements of Gandhiji made at the opening of Banaras Hindu University are true ?
(A) Gandhiji charged the Indian elite with a lack of concern for the labouring poor.
(B) Gandhiji was not worried about the contrast between the "richly bedecked noblemen" and millions of poor Indians.
(C) Gandhiji said, "Our salvation can only come through lawyers, doctors and rich landlords."
(D) Gandhiji emphasised that farmers are going to secure the salvation of India.
(E) Gandhiji told the privileged invitees, "Strip yourself of this jewellery and hold it in trust for your countrymen."
Choose the correct answer from the options given below :
(1) (A), (B) and (C) only (2) (C), (D) and (E) only
(3) (B), (C), and (D) only (4) (A), (D) and (E) only

Question 38:
Match List–I with List–II :
List–I List–II
(A) Khilafat Movement (I) Mahatma Gandhi's biographer
(B) Jallianwala Bagh Massacre (II) Turkish ruler
(C) Kemal Ataturk (III) 1919
(D) Louis Fisher (IV) 1919–1920
Choose the correct answer from the options given below :
(1) (A) – (I), (B) – (II), (C) – (III), (D) – (IV)
(2) (A) – (I), (B) – (IV), (C) – (II), (D) – (III)
(3) (A) – (III), (B) – (I), (C) – (IV), (D) – (II)
(4) (A) – (IV), (B) – (III), (C) – (II), (D) – (I)

Question 39:
Who was the Judge who presided over Gandhiji's trial after the withdrawal of the Non–Cooperation Movement ?
(1) Justice C.N. Broomfield (2) Justice William Hodges
(3) Justice Joseph Noel (4) Justice Thomas Barker

Question 40:
When were separate electorates first created by the British Colonial Government ?
(1) 1919 (2) 1923 (3) 1909 (4) 1907
Read the passage and answer the five questions that follow:
Mughal chronicles, especially the Akbar Nama, written by Abu'l Fazl, have bequeathed a vision of empire in which agency rests almost solely with the emperor, while the rest of the kingdom has been portrayed as following his orders. Yet if we look more closely at the rich information, these histories provide information

about the apparatus of the Mughal State from which we may be able to understand the ways in which the imperial organization was dependent on several different institutions to be able to function effectively. One important pillar of the Mughal State was the nobility.

Question 41:
Mughal chronicles viewed the emperors as supreme sovereign because
(1) Nobility wanted him to be one.
(2) Vision of empire viewed the emperor as the sole ruler.
(3) Chronicles were a rich source of history.
(4) Imperial administration was weak.

Question 42:
Which section of the Mughal Court was viewed as very significant ?
(1) Imperial vision (2) The Empire
(3) Nobility (4) Mughal Chronicles

Question 43:
Which chronicle says that the entire kingdom has to follow the king's orders ?
(1) Urdu Akhbar (2) Badshah Nama
(3) Akbar Nama (4) Kitabkhana

Question 44:
The Mughal imperial administrative apparatus was effectively dependent on __________ .
(1) Travellers (2) Nobles (3) Masses (4) Mir Bakshi

Question 45:
Who is the author of Akbar Nama ?
(1) Chandrabhan Barahman (2) Muhammad Kazim
(3) Lahori (4) Abu'l Fazl

Read the passage and anwer the five questions that follow :
The Constituent Assembly deliberated upon the Indian Constitution, which came into effect on 26 January, 1950. It has the dubious distinction of being the longest in the world. But its length and complexity are perhaps understandable when one considers the country's size and diversity. At Independence, India was not merely large and diverse, but also deeply divided. A Constitution designed to keep the country together, and to take it forward, had necessarily to be an elaborate, carefully–worked–out, and painstakingly drafted document. For one thing, it sought to heal wounds of the past and the present, to make Indians of different classes, castes and communities come together in a shared political experiment. For another, it sought to nurture democratic institutions.

Question 46:
When did the Constitution of India come into force ?
(1) 26th January, 1950 (2) 15th August, 1947
(3) 31st January, 1929 (4) 6th November, 1949

Question 47:
Why is the Constitution of India described as the longest document in the world ?
(1) It is a painstakingly drafted document.
(2) It is carefully worked out.
(3) It imbibes culture of hierarchy.
(4) The country size and diversity impacted the Constitution length.

Question 48:
How can we say that the Constitution of India seeks to unify India ?
(1) It deals with the country's problems.
(2) The area of the subcontinent was under its control.
(3) It was designed to keep the country's divided classes, communities and castes together.
(4) It was to nurture democratic institutions.

Question 49:
In which body was the Constitution of India deliberated upon ?
(1) Parliament of India (2) Through Newspaper coverage
(3) Constituent Assembly (4) Princely States

Question 50:
The nature of the Constitution imbibed the right to
__________ .
(1) Cultural Rights (2) Educational Rights
(3) Equality (4) Religion

Scan The QR Code To
Get Answers With
Detailed Explanations!

CUET UG MOCK TEST – 1

1. Which of the following is NOT a characteristic of the Harappan Civilization?
(A) Urban planning with a grid pattern
(B) Advanced drainage system
(C) Large stone temples dedicated to deities
(D) Use of standardized weights and measures

2. Which Harappan site is known for evidence of a ploughed field?
(A) Dholavira
(B) Kalibangan
(C) Rakhigarhi
(D) Lothal

3. Which metal was not known to the Harappans?
(A) Copper
(B) Iron
(C) Bronze
(D) Tin

4. The term 'Janapada' refers to:
(A) A republic state
(B) A city
(C) A tribal assembly
(D) The settlement of a clan

5. Which Mahajanapada was associated with the first Buddhist Council?
(A) Magadha
(B) Kashi
(C) Kosala
(D) Vajji

6. Which ruler issued the famous 'Rummindei Pillar Inscription' marking Buddha's birthplace?
(A) Chandragupta Maurya
(B) Kanishka
(C) Ashoka
(D) Harshavardhana

7. Which Mauryan official was responsible for overseeing trade and commerce?
(A) Samaharta
(B) Sannidhata
(C) Panyadhyaksha
(D) Rajuka

8. The Gotra system was initially followed by:
(A) Brahmins
(B) Kshatriyas
(C) Vaishyas
(D) Shudras

9. Which of the following correctly describes Manusmriti?
(A) It was a Buddhist text on monastic discipline
(B) It provided legal codes on caste and gender relations
(C) It was written by Megasthenes
(D) It opposed the Gotra system

10. Which text is an important source for understanding the kinship structure of early India?
(A) Mahabharata
(B) Arthashastra
(C) Rigveda
(D) Sutta Pitaka

11. The Ajivikas, a sect contemporary to Buddhism and Jainism, were followers of:
(A) Makkhali Gosala
(B) Kapila
(C) Ajita Kesakambalin
(D) Patanjali

12. Which of the following is NOT a feature of early Buddhist architecture?
(A) Stupas
(B) Chaityas
(C) Viharas
(D) Nagara-style temples

13. Match the following important historical sites with their significance:

List–I (Site).	List–II (Significance)
(A) Sarnath.	I) First Buddhist sermon
(B) Bodh Gaya.	II) Buddha's enlightenment
C) Rajgir.	(III) First Buddhist Council
D) Kushinagar.	(IV) Buddha's Mahaparinirvana

(1) A–I, B–II, C–III, D–IV
(2) A–II, B–I, C–IV, D–III
(3) A–III, B–IV, C–I, D–II
(4) A–IV, B–III, C–II, D–I

14. Which of the following statements about Ashoka's Dhamma is correct?
(A) It was a religious policy advocating Buddhism alone
(B) It emphasized tolerance and welfare of all communities
(C) It was a military strategy to expand the Mauryan Empire
(D) It was restricted only to India and did not influence other regions

15. Which of the following travelers visited India during the reign of Akbar?
(A) Al-Biruni
(B) Ibn Battuta
(C) Francois Bernier
(D) Ralph Fitch

16. Which traveler compared Indian society to that of 17th-century France and criticized its land ownership system?
(A) Ibn Battuta
(B) FranÇois Bernier
(C) Marco Polo
(D) Duarte Barbosa

17. Which of the following is a major contribution of Al-Biruni's work 'Kitab-ul-Hind'?
(A) A detailed account of Mughal rule
(B) Translation of Sanskrit texts into Arabic
(C) A historical account of the Delhi Sultanate
(D) A study of European influences in India

18. Ibn Battuta's account of India is recorded in which text?
(A) Rihla
(B) Kitab-ul-Hind
(C) Ain-i-Akbari
(D) Tabaqat-i-Nasiri

19. Which Bhakti saint was a devotee of Krishna and composed the 'Sur Sagar'?
(A) Mirabai
(B) Kabir
(C) Surdas
(D) Tulsidas

20. Which Sufi saint is associated with the Chishti order and settled in Ajmer?
(A) Nizamuddin Auliya
(B) Baba Farid
(C) Muinuddin Chishti
(D) Shaikh Bahauddin Zakariya

21. What was the main aim of the Bhakti and Sufi movements?
(A) Establishing political rule
(B) Promoting social harmony and devotion
(C) Enforcing caste divisions
(D) Spreading Persian culture

22. Which of the following is NOT a feature of Bhakti poetry?
(A) It was written in Sanskrit only
(B) It expressed deep devotion to a personal god
(C) It was composed in regional languages
(D) It was often sung in temples

23. Which river flows near the Vijayanagara capital?
(A) Ganga
(B) Yamuna
(C) Krishna
(D) Tungabhadra

24. Which ruler of Vijayanagara was a great patron of Telugu and Sanskrit literature?
(A) Bukka Raya
(B) Devaraya I
(C) Krishnadevaraya
(D) Ramaraya

25. What was the major cause of the decline of the Vijayanagara Empire?
(A) Lack of trade
(B) Defeat in the Battle of Talikota
(C) Invasion by the British
(D) Weak administrative structure

26. Under the Mughal administration, who were the 'Raiyat'?
(A) Revenue officers
(B) Peasants
(C) Soldiers
(D) Nobles

27. What was the main purpose of the Jagirdari system under the Mughals?
(A) Land ownership for peasants
(B) Granting revenue rights to nobles
(C) Strengthening religious institutions
(D) Eliminating zamindars

28. Which Mughal emperor abolished the Jizya tax?
(A) Akbar
(B) Jahangir
(C) Shah Jahan
(D) Aurangzeb

29. Which historian wrote 'Tuzuk-i-Jahangiri'?
(A) Abu'l Fazl
(B) Jahangir
(C) Badauni
(D) Nizamuddin Ahmad

30. Match the following Mughal emperors with their policies:

Emperor	Policy
(A) Akbar.	(I) Din-i-Ilahi
(B) Jahangir.	(II) Policy of Justice
(C) Shah Jahan.	(III) Patronage of architecture
(D) Aurangzeb.	(IV) Reintroduction of Jizya

(1) A-I, B-II, C-III, D-IV
(2) A-II, B-I, C-IV, D-III
(3) A-III, B-IV, C-II, D-I
(4) A-IV, B-III, C-I, D-II

31. Assertion (A): The Mansabdari system was crucial in Mughal military administration.
Reason (R): It allowed efficient recruitment and payment of soldiers.
(1) Both A and R are true, and R correctly explains A
(2) Both A and R are true, but R does not explain A
(3) A is true, but R is false
(4) A is false, but R is true

32. Which of the following statements about Sufi saints is correct?
(A) They lived in monasteries and avoided contact with common people.
(B) They emphasized personal devotion and a direct connection with God.
(C) They rejected poetry and music.
(D) They were always opposed to Bhakti saints.

33. The Permanent Settlement of Bengal (1793) introduced by Lord Cornwallis aimed to:
(A) Improve the condition of peasants
(B) Make landlords (Zamindars) hereditary owners of land
(C) Increase the revenue of local rulers
(D) Reduce British control over revenue collection

34. Which of the following was a major reason for the indigo revolt of 1859-60?
(A) High taxes imposed on indigo cultivators
(B) Exploitative contracts forced upon farmers by planters
(C) The end of the British monopoly on indigo
(D) Government policies supporting Indian farmers

35. Which of the following was NOT a reason for the failure of the Revolt of 1857?
(A) Lack of unity among Indian rulers
(B) Absence of modern weapons and technology
(C) Direct military assistance from France to the British
(D) No centralized leadership among rebels

36. Who was the Mughal emperor during the Revolt of 1857?
(A) Akbar II
(B) Bahadur Shah Zafar
(C) Shah Alam II
(D) Jahangir

37. Which city was declared the capital of British India in 1911?
(A) Bombay
(B) Calcutta
(C) Madras
(D) Delhi

38. Which of the following was a major reason for the growth of colonial cities in the 19th century?
(A) Industrialization and trade expansion
(B) The abolition of Zamindari
(C) Government policies limiting urbanization
(D) Decline of European influence in India

39. The Non-Cooperation Movement was called off after:
(A) The Jallianwala Bagh massacre
(B) The Chauri Chaura incident
(C) The arrest of Mahatma Gandhi
(D) The signing of the Gandhi-Irwin Pact

40. Which of the following was NOT a part of Mahatma Gandhi's strategy in the Indian freedom struggle?
(A) Satyagraha
(B) Violent rebellion
(C) Boycott of British goods
(D) Civil disobedience

41. Which plan led to the partition of India?
(A) Mountbatten Plan
(B) Cripps Mission
(C) Simon Commission
(D) August Offer

42. Which of the following was a direct consequence of the Partition of India?
(A) Mass displacement of people across borders
(B) The formation of Bangladesh
(C) Gandhi becoming the first Prime Minister of India
(D) The end of the British presence in Africa

43. Who was the chairman of the Drafting Committee of the Indian Constitution?
(A) Jawaharlal Nehru
(B) Sardar Patel
(C) B.R. Ambedkar
(D) Rajendra Prasad

44. The Indian Constitution was adopted on:
(A) 15th August 1947
(B) 26th November 1949
(C) 26th January 1950
(D) 2nd October 1950

Read the passage below and answer the following questions :

The Civil Disobedience Movement began in 1930, with Mahatma Gandhi's symbolic Salt March to Dandi. This movement aimed at challenging British rule through non-violent resistance. It saw widespread participation across India, with women, students, and workers joining in large numbers. The movement led to many arrests, including that of Gandhi. It eventually resulted in the signing of the Gandhi-Irwin Pact in 1931."

45. Which event marked the beginning of the Civil Disobedience Movement?
(1) Quit India Movement
(2) Salt March
(3) Jallianwala Bagh Massacre
(4) Simon Commission protests

46. Which year did the Civil Disobedience Movement begin?
(1) 1920
(2) 1930
(3) 1942
(4) 1919

47. What was a major outcome of the Civil Disobedience Movement?
(1) India's independence
(2) The signing of the Gandhi-Irwin Pact
(3) Formation of the Indian National Army
(4) Establishment ofPakistan

48. Which section of society played an active role in the movement?
(1) Only landlords
(2) Women, students, and workers
(3) British officials
(4) Industrialists only

49. What method did Gandhi advocate for in the movement?
(1) Violent protests
(2) Non-violent resistance
(3) Military uprising
(4) Legal reforms within British rule

50. Identify which of the following had these carvings.

a) Carvings on Lotus Mahal
b) Carvings on Hazara Rama Temple
c) Carvings on Mahanavami Mandir
d) Carvings on Mahanavami Dibba

Scan The QR Code To Get Answers With Detailed Explanations!

CUET UG MOCK TEST – 2

1. Which of the following crops was NOT cultivated by the Harappans?
(A) Wheat
(B) Barley
(C) Rice
(D) Maize

2. Which Harappan site provides evidence of fire altars and ritual practices?
(A) Harappa
(B) Kalibangan
(C) Mohenjo-daro
(D) Rakhigarhi

3. Which of the following materials was commonly used for Harappan seals?
(A) Copper
(B) Bronze
(C) Steatite
(D) Gold

4. Which Mahajanapada had a republican form of government?
(A) Magadha
(B) Vajji
(C) Kashi
(D) Kosala

5. The Prayag-Prashasti (Allahabad Pillar Inscription) is associated with which ruler?
(A) Chandragupta Maurya
(B) Ashoka
(C) Samudragupta
(D) Harshavardhana

6. Which Mauryan ruler sent Buddhist missionaries to Sri Lanka and Southeast Asia?
(A) Chandragupta Maurya
(B) Ashoka
(C) Bindusara
(D) Brihadratha

7. Which Mauryan text provides the most detailed account of statecraft and governance?
(A) Arthashastra
(B) Indica
(C) Manusmriti
(D) Sutta Pitaka

8. The Satavahana dynasty followed which system of succession?
(A) Matrilineal
(B) Patrilineal
(C) Electoral
(D) None of the above

9. What does the term 'Dharmashastra' refer to?
(A) A Buddhist text on law
(B) A set of Hindu legal and ethical texts
(C) A manual on statecraft
(D) A Jain religious text

10. Which of the following correctly describes the varna system?
(A) It was based solely on occupation
(B) It was a flexible system with social mobility
(C) It became more rigid over time
(D) It was not mentioned in Vedic texts

11. Which of the following Buddhist sects is associated with the worship of Bodhisattvas?
(A) Theravada
(B) Hinayana
(C) Mahayana
(D) Vajrayana

12. The famous caves of Ajanta are primarily associated with which religion?
(A) Hinduism
(B) Buddhism
(C) Jainism
(D) Zoroastrianism

13. Match the following Buddhist symbols with their meanings:

List-I (Symbol)	List-II (Meaning)
(A) Bodhi Tree.	(I) Enlightenment
(B) Wheel (Dharma Chakra	(II) Teachings of Buddha
(C) Stupa.	(III) Burial mound for relics
(D) Footprints.	(IV) Presence of Buddha

(1) A-I, B-II, C-III, D-IV
(2) A-II, B-III, C-I, D-IV
(3) A-III, B-IV, C-II, D-I
(4) A-IV, B-III, C-II, D-I

14. Identify the following coin :

A) Aluminium coin depicting a Shaka Ruler
B) Silver coin depicting a Gupta Ruler
C) Silver coin depicting a Shaka Ruler
D) Alloy coin depicting a Gupta ruler

15. Which of the following statements about the Mahabharata is correct?
(A) It was originally composed in Sanskrit and later expanded over centuries
(B) It is only a religious text and has no historical significance
(C) It exclusively deals with the Kurukshetra war and does not discuss social structures
(D) It was composed by Kautilya during the Mauryan period

16. Which of the following travelers visited India during the reign of Akbar?
(A) Al-Biruni
(B) Ibn Battuta
(C) Francois Bernier
(D) Ralph Fitch

17. Which traveler compared Indian society to that of 17th-century France and criticized its landownership system?
(A) Ibn Battuta
(B) Francois Bernier
(C) Marco Polo
(D) Duarte Barbosa

18. Which of the following is a major contribution of Al-Biruni's work 'Kitab-ul-Hind'?
(A) A detailed account of Mughal rule
(B) Translation of Sanskrit texts into Arabic
(C) A historical account of the Delhi Sultanate
(D) A study of European influences in India

19. Ibn Battuta's account of India is recorded in which text?
(A) Rihla
(B) Kitab-ul-Hind
(C) Ain-i-Akbari
(D) Tabaqat-i-Nasiri

20. Which Bhakti saint was a devotee of Krishna and composed the 'Sur Sagar'?
(A) Mirabai
(B) Kabir
(C) Surdas
(D) Tulsidas

21. Which Sufi saint is associated with the Chishti order and settled in Ajmer?
(A) Nizamuddin Auliya
(B) Baba Farid
(C) Moinuddin Chishti
(D) Shaikh Bahauddin Zakariya

22. What was the main aim of the Bhakti and Sufi movements?
(A) Establishing political rule
(B) Promoting social harmony and devotion
(C) Enforcing caste divisions
(D) Spreading Persian culture

23. Which of the following is NOT a feature of Bhakti poetry?
(A) It was written in Sanskrit only
(B) It expressed deep devotion to a personal god
(C) It was composed in regional languages
(D) It was often sung in temples

24. Which river flows near the Vijayanagara capital?
(A) Ganga
(B) Yamuna
(C) Krishna
(D) Tungabhadra

25. Which ruler of Vijayanagara was a great patron of Telugu and Sanskrit literature?
(A) Bukka Raya
(B) Devaraya I
(C) Krishnadevaraya
(D) Ramaraya

26. What was the major cause of the decline of the Vijayanagara Empire?
(A) Lack of trade
(B) Defeat in the Battle of Talikota
(C) Invasion by the British
(D) Weak administrative structure

27. Under the Mughal administration, who were the 'Raiyat'?
(A) Revenue officers
(B) Peasants
(C) Soldiers
(D) Nobles

28. What was the main purpose of the Jagirdari system under the Mughals?
(A) Land ownership for peasants
(B) Granting revenue rights to nobles
(C) Strengthening religious institutions
(D) Eliminating zamindars

29. Which Mughal emperor abolished the Jizya tax?
(A) Akbar
(B) Jahangir
(C) Shah Jahan
(D) Aurangzeb

30. Which historian wrote 'Tuzuk-i-Jahangiri'?
(A) Abu'l Fazl
(B) Jahangir
(C) Badauni
(D) Nizamuddin Ahmad

31. Match the following Mughal emperors with their policies:

Emperor	Policy
(A) Akbar	(I) Din-i-Ilahi
(B) Jahangir	(II) Policy of Justice
(C) Shah Jahan	(III) Patronage of architecture
(D) Aurangzeb.	(IV) Reintroduction of Jizya

(1) A-I, B-II, C-III, D-IV
(2) A-IV, B-III, C-II, D-I
(3) A-II, B-IV, C-I, D-III
(4) A-III, B-I, C-IV, D-II

32. Assertion (A): The Mansabdari system was crucial in Mughal military administration.
Reason (R): It allowed efficient recruitment and payment of soldiers.
(1) Both A and R are true, and R correctly explains A
(2) Both A and R are true, but R does not explain A
(3) A is true, but R is false
(4) A is false, but R is true

33. Which of the following statements about Sufi saints is correct?
(A) They lived in monasteries and avoided contact with common people.
(B) They emphasized personal devotion and a direct connection with God.
(C) They rejected poetry and music.
(D) They were always opposed to Bhakti saints.

34. Which Vijayanagara ruler is known for his extensive military campaigns against the Bahmani Sultanate?
(A) Harihara I
(B) Bukka I
(C) Devaraya II
(D) Krishnadevaraya

35. Which of the following was NOT a major trade commodity in the Mughal period?
(A) Textiles
(B) Spices
(C) Silver
(D) Cotton

36. What was the primary aim of the Permanent Settlement of Bengal (1793)?
(A) To improve the conditions of peasants
(B) To ensure a fixed revenue for the British
(C) To eliminate the role of Zamindars
(D) To promote industrialization in rural areas

37. Which of the following best describes the impact of British land revenue policies in rural India?
(A) Strengthened the position of peasants
(B) Led to frequent peasant uprisings
(C) Increased self-sufficiency of villages
(D) Ensured equitable land distribution

38. Which of the following was NOT a major cause of the Revolt of 1857?
(A) The introduction of the Enfield rifle cartridges
(B) Heavy taxation on Indian landlords
(C) The Doctrine of Lapse
(D) The partition of Bengal

39. Which Indian ruler led the revolt in Kanpur during the 1857 uprising?
(A) Nana Saheb
(B) Rani Lakshmibai
(C) Tantia Tope
(D) Kunwar Singh

40. Which colonial city was planned to serve as the summer capital of British India?
(A) Bombay
(B) Madras
(C) Delhi
(D) Simla

41. Which of the following was a key reason for the British developing port cities in India?
(A) To promote Indian craftsmanship
(B) To facilitate export of Indian raw materials and British imports
(C) To spread Christianity in coastal regions
(D) To encourage Indian traders

42. Which movement was launched by Mahatma Gandhi in response to the failure of the Cripps Mission?
(A) Non-Cooperation Movement
(B) Civil Disobedience Movement
(C) Quit India Movement
(D) Khilafat Movement

43. What was the main objective of the Salt March (Dandi March)?
(A) To demand complete independence
(B) To protest against the British salt monopoly
(C) To gain support from Indian industrialists
(D) To oppose the partition of Bengal

Read the passage and Answer the following :
The Revolt of 1857 was a significant uprising against British rule. It began as a mutiny by Indian soldiers (sepoys) in the British army but soon spread to various parts of North India. The uprising was fueled by political, economic, and social grievances, including the Doctrine of Lapse, heavy taxation, and disrespect towards Indian traditions. While the rebellion saw strong resistance from leaders such as Rani Lakshmibai, Nana Saheb, and Bahadur Shah Zafar, it ultimately failed due to lack of coordination and superior British military strength. The revolt, however, marked the beginning of organized resistance against colonial rule.

44. Which of the following was an immediate cause of the Revolt of 1857?
(1) Introduction of the Enfield rifle cartridges
(2) The Rowlatt Act
(3) The passing of the Vernacular Press Act
(4) The formation of the Indian National Congress

45. Who was proclaimed the symbolic leader of the 1857 Revolt?
(1) Rani Lakshmibai
(2) Nana Saheb
(3) Bahadur Shah Zafar
(4) Kunwar Singh

46. What was one of the key reasons for the failure of the Revolt of 1857?
(1) Lack of unity among Indian leaders
(2) British support from France
(3) India's lack of natural resources
(4) Weakness of British forces

47. Which of the following leaders played a significant role in the Revolt of 1857?
(1) Subhas Chandra Bose
(2) Tantia Tope
(3) Jawaharlal Nehru
(4) Dadabhai Naoroji

48. Which of the following was a major consequence of the Revolt of 1857?
(1) The complete independence of India
(2) Direct rule of India by the British Crown
(3) The establishment of the Indian National Army
(4) The abolition of the caste system

49. Which of the following statements about the Indian National Movement is correct?
(A) It was a purely violent struggle against the British.
(B) The movement had diverse strategies, including non-violent resistance and revolutionary activities.
(C) Only men actively participated in the movement.
(D) The movement started only after World War II.
(1) A
(2) B
(3) C
(4) D

Assertion (A): The Quit India Movement of 1942 demanded an immediate end to British rule in India.
Reason (R): The British government, fearing international pressure, immediately granted independence.
(1) Both A and R are true, and R correctly explains A
(2) Both A and R are true, but R does not explain A
(3) A is true, but R is false
(4) A is false, but R is true

Scan The QR Code To Get Answers With Detailed Explanations!

CUET UG MOCK TEST – 3

1. Which of the following statements about the Harappan civilization is correct?
(A) The Harappan script has been fully deciphered.
(B) The Harappans did not have trade links with Mesopotamia.
(C) The Harappans built elaborate drainage systems.
(D) The Harappans primarily used iron tools.

2. Which Harappan city is known for a well-planned water conservation system with large reservoirs?
(A) Harappa
(B) Mohenjo-daro
(C) Lothal
(D) Dholavira

3. Which of the following is NOT a characteristic feature of the Harappan civilization?
(A) Use of burnt bricks
(B) Grid-pattern town planning
(C) Presence of large palaces and temples
(D) Standardized weights and measures

4. Which of the following was the most powerful Mahajanapada in the 6th century BCE?
(A) Vajji
(B) Magadha
(C) Kosala
(D) Avanti

5. The Mauryan Empire extended its rule over which of the following regions?
(A) Afghanistan
(B) Tamil Nadu
(C) Karnataka
(D) All of the above

6. Which foreign ambassador visited the Mauryan court and wrote an account of India?
(A) Herodotus
(B) Megasthenes
(C) Fa-Xian
(D) Hiuen Tsang

7. The term 'Dhamma' as used by Ashoka referred to:
(A) A rigid Buddhist doctrine
(B) A set of moral and ethical principles
(C) A religious law code
(D) Military strategies of the Mauryan empire

8. Which of the following texts primarily deals with social rules and duties in ancient India?
(A) Arthashastra
(B) Mahabharata
(C) Manusmriti
(D) Ramayana

9. Which of the following best describes the position of women in early Vedic society?
(A) They had equal rights in property inheritance
(B) They were allowed to participate in religious rituals
(C) They were completely secluded from public life
(D) They were permitted to become rulers

10. Which one of the following correctly defines the term 'Jati'?
(A) A major kingdom
(B) A ruling class
(C) A kinship-based social group
(D) A religious order

11. Which one of the following Buddhist councils led to the division of Buddhism into Hinayana and Mahayana?
(A) First Buddhist Council
(B) Second Buddhist Council
(C) Third Buddhist Council
(D) Fourth Buddhist Council

12. Which of the following is NOT a part of Buddhist architectural features?
(A) Stupa
(B) Chaitya
(C) Vihara
(D) Dravida-style temple

13. Match the following historical texts with their contents:

List–I (Text)	List–II (Description)
(A) Arthashastra.	(I) Political and economic treatise
(B) Manusmriti.	(II) Social and legal codes
(C) Mahabharata.	(III) Epic on war and kinship
(D) Jataka Tales.	(IV) Buddhist stories of past lives

1) A-I, B-II, C-III, D-IV
(2) A-II, B-III, C-I, D-IV
(3) A-III, B-IV, C-I, D-II
(4) A-IV, B-III, C-II, D-I

14. Assertion (A): The Mauryan rulers established a highly centralized administrative system.
Reason (R): The Mauryan Empire had a well-defined hierarchy of officials to regulate economic, social, and political life.
(1) Both A and R are true, and R correctly explains A
(2) Both A and R are true, but R does not explain A
(3) A is true, but R is false
(4) A is false, but R is true

15. Which of the following statements about Ashoka's administration is correct?
(A) Ashoka abandoned all warfare after the Kalinga War
(B) Ashoka sent Buddhist missionaries to Sri Lanka, Egypt, and Greece
(C) Ashoka's Dhamma was a religious doctrine promoting Buddhism alone
(D) Ashoka never issued inscriptions outside India

16. Which of the following travelers visited India during the reign of Muhammad bin Tughlaq and wrote about his rule?
(A) Al-Biruni
(B) Ibn Battuta
(C) Marco Polo
(D) Francois Bernier

17. Which of the following travelers gave a detailed account of Mughal society and administration?
(A) Al-Biruni
(B) Ibn Battuta
(C) Francois Bernier
(D) Marco Polo

18. Which traveler's account provides a comparison of the Mughal Empire with 17th-century France?
(A) Ibn Battuta
(B) Francois Bernier
(C) Marco Polo
(D) Duarte Barbosa

19. Al-Biruni's account of India is unique because he:
(A) Traveled widely across India and documented local traditions
(B) Criticized Indian social customs, especially the caste system
(C) Learned Sanskrit to understand Indian texts better
(D) All of the above

20. Which Bhakti saint is known for emphasizing unity between Hinduism and Islam?
(A) Mirabai
(B) Kabir
(C) Surdas
(D) Tulsidas

21. Which of the following Sufi saints was the founder of the Chishti order in India?
(A) Nizamuddin Auliya
(B) Muinuddin Chishti
(C) Shaikh Bahauddin Zakariya
(D) Baba Farid

22. Which language was primarily used in Bhakti poetry in North India?
(A) Sanskrit
(B) Persian
(C) Hindi and its dialects
(D) Telugu

23. Which of the following is a major feature of Sufi practice?
(A) Emphasis on ritual purity and caste system
(B) Seeking direct personal experience with God
(C) Strict adherence to Islamic law
(D) Complete rejection of poetry and music

24. Which of the following was the primary architectural feature of Vijayanagara temples?
(A) Tall gopurams (gateway towers)
(B) Domes and minarets
(C) Stupa-like structures
(D) Pyramid-shaped vimanas

25. The Battle of Talikota (1565) resulted in:
(A) The expansion of Vijayanagara rule
(B) The fall of Vijayanagara Empire
(C) Establishment of a Mughal base in South India
(D) Complete unification of Deccan Sultanates

26. Which traveler provided a firsthand account of Vijayanagara during Krishnadevaraya's rule?
(A) Ibn Battuta
(B) Domingo Paes
(C) Marco Polo
(D) Francois Bernier

27. The Mughal revenue system of 'Zabt' was introduced by:
(A) Babur
(B) Akbar
(C) Jahangir
(D) Aurangzeb

28. Which term refers to landowners who collected revenue on behalf of the Mughal state?
(A) Mansabdars
(B) Zamindars
(C) Raiyats
(D) Jagirdars

29. Which Mughal emperor is credited with commissioning the Persian translation of Mahabharata as 'Razmnama'?
(A) Akbar
(B) Jahangir
(C) Shah Jahan
(D) Aurangzeb

30. Who wrote 'Ain-i-Akbari', a detailed account of Akbar's administration?
(A) Badauni
(B) Abu'l Fazl
(C) Nizamuddin Ahmad
(D) Ibn Battuta

31. Match the following Bhakti saints with their major works:

Bhakti Saint.	Work
(A) Kabir.	(I) Bijak
(B) Tulsidas.	(II) Ramcharitmanas
C) Surdas.	(III) Sur Sagar
(D) Mirabai.	(IV) Padas and Bhajans

(1) A-I, B-II, C-III, D-IV
(2) A-II, B-I, C-IV, D-III
(3) A-III, B-IV, C-II, D-I
(4) A-IV, B-III, C-I, D-II

32. "Relief of Lucknow", painted by _______ in 1859.

A) Thomas Jones Barker
B) Thomas James Barker
C) George Frederic Watts
D) George Frederic Walker

33. Which of the following statements about Sufi orders is correct?
(A) The Chishti order rejected royal patronage.
(B) The Naqshbandi order emphasized music in worship.
(C) The Suhrawardi order was active in South India.
(D) The Qadiri order discouraged religious preaching.

34. Which of the following statements best describes the Mahalwari system?
(A) Revenue was fixed permanently and paid by Zamindars.
(B) Revenue was collected from individual farmers directly.
(C) Revenue was collected village-wise, and responsibility was given to headmen.
(D) It was a tax-free landholding system introduced in South India.

35. What was the primary reason for the Deccan Riots of 1875?
(A) High taxation imposed by the British government
(B) Exploitation of peasants by moneylenders
(C) Forced recruitment of peasants into the British army
(D) Religious discrimination against Indian farmers

36. Which British policy was directly responsible for the annexation of Indian princely states before 1857?
(A) Doctrine of Lapse
(B) Subsidiary Alliance
(C) Ryotwari System
(D) Zamindari Settlement

37. Which of the following cities was a major center of the Revolt of 1857?
(A) Amritsar
(B) Surat
(C) Lucknow
(D) Chennai

38. Which of the following colonial cities was known as the 'Second City of the Empire' after London?
(A) Madras
(B) Bombay
(C) Calcutta
(D) Delhi

39. Which of the following is true about the Town Planning policies of the British?
(A) They were aimed at improving sanitation in Indian cities.
(B) They segregated the Indian and British populations in different areas.
(C) They focused primarily on constructing fortifications for military use.
(D) They led to the complete demolition of Mughal-era structures.

40. Which of the following was a significant feature of the Civil Disobedience Movement?
(A) It was primarily led by industrialists and businessmen.
(B) It aimed to boycott British goods and institutions.
(C) It encouraged the use of violent tactics against British officials.
(D) It was limited only to rural India and ignored urban participation.

41. Which of the following acts was passed by the British in response to the Quit India Movement?
(A) Rowlatt Act
(B) Government of India Act 1935
(C) Defence of India Act 1942
(D) Indian Independence Act 1947

42. Read the passage below and answer the following questions:
The Indian National Congress, under Mahatma Gandhi's leadership, launched the Quit India Movement in 1942. The movement was a direct response to British refusal to grant India immediate independence during World War II. It was characterized by mass protests, strikes, and civil disobedience across the country. The British responded with severe repression, arresting thousands of leaders, including Gandhi, Nehru, and Patel. Despite its suppression, the movement marked a turning point in India's struggle for freedom.

43. In which year was the Quit India Movement launched?
(1) 1919
(2) 1930
(3) 1942
(4) 1947

44. What was the primary reason for launching the Quit India Movement?
(1) To support the British war effort
(2) To demand immediate independence from British rule
(3) To protest against the Simon Commission
(4) To oppose the Cripps Mission proposals

45. How did the British government respond to the Quit India Movement?
(1) By immediately granting independence
(2) By signing the Poona Pact
(3) By arresting major Congress leaders
(4) By negotiating with Subhas Chandra Bose

46. Which slogan became famous during the Quit India Movement?
(1) Inquilab Zindabad
(2) Swaraj is my birthright
(3) Do or Die
(4) Simon Go Back

47. What was a major impact of the Quit India Movement?
(1) It led to the establishment of Pakistan
(2) It forced the British to withdraw immediately
(3) It demonstrated India's strong resolve for independence
(4) It ended Mahatma Gandhi's role in the freedom struggle

48. Which of the following statements about the Partition of India is correct?
(A) It was entirely peaceful and did not lead to any violence.
(B) It resulted in the largest mass migration in human history.
(C) It was planned after World War I.
(D) The Partition was proposed by the Indian National Congress in 1947.
(1) A
(2) B
(3) C
(4) D

49. Assertion (A): The Simon Commission was boycotted by Indians.
Reason (R): The commission did not include any Indian members.
(1) Both A and R are true, and R correctly explains A
(2) Both A and R are true, but R does not explain A
(3) A is true, but R is false
(4) A is false, but R is true

50. Assertion (A): Akbar's court included scholars of various religions.
Reason (R): Akbar promoted a policy of religious tolerance and introduced Din-i-Ilahi.
(1) A is true, and R correctly explains A
(2) Both A and R are true, but R does not explain A
(3) A is true, but R is false
(4) A is false, but R is true

Scan The QR Code To Get Answers With Detailed Explanations!

CUET UG MOCK TEST – 4

1. Which of the following statements about the Harappan civilization is incorrect?
(A) Harappans used a standardized system of weights and measures.
(B) The Harappan civilization was primarily rural, with no major urban centers.
(C) Lothal is known for having a dockyard.
(D) Dholavira had an advanced water conservation system.

2. Which metal was the most commonly used in Harappan tools and weapons?
(A) Iron
(B) Copper
(C) Silver
(D) Lead

3. Which of the following features distinguishes the Harappan civilization from other contemporary civilizations?
(A) Extensive use of iron tools
(B) Highly developed urban planning and drainage system
(C) Construction of large pyramids
(D) Use of cuneiform script

4. Which of the following Mahajanapadas was known for its strong fortifications?
(A) Kashi
(B) Magadha
(C) Vajji
(D) Gandhara

5. Which Mauryan emperor is known for renouncing war after the Kalinga conquest?
(A) Chandragupta Maurya
(B) Bindusara
(C) Ashoka
(D) Brihadratha

6. Which of the following texts provides the most detailed description of the Mauryan administration?
(A) Indica
(B) Arthashastra
(C) Manusmriti
(D) Sangam literature

7. Which dynasty is credited with the establishment of the first large-scale empire in India?
(A) Maurya
(B) Gupta
(C) Kushana
(D) Satavahana

8. Which text is an important source for understanding social norms and family structures in ancient India?
(A) Panchatantra
(B) Arthashastra
(C) Jataka Tales
(D) Sangam literature

9. Which of the following terms refers to a broader kinship network in early Indian society?
(A) Vamsa
(B) Gotra
(C) Jnati
(D) Sabha

10. Which of the following statements about gender roles in early Indian society is correct?
(A) Women were completely excluded from education.
(B) Women had no rights over property.
(C) Some texts mention the presence of learned women participating in debates.
(D) Women could become rulers in early India.

11. Which one of the following Buddhist texts records the conversations between King Menander (Milinda) and the monk Nagasena?
(A) Jataka Tales
(B) Dipavamsa
(C) Milindapanha
(D) Sutta Pitaka

12. Which of the following is NOT a feature of early Buddhist architecture?
(A) Stupas
(B) Chaityas
(C) Viharas
(D) Shikhara-style temples

13. Match the following important Buddhist structures with their locations:

List-I (Structure)	List-II (Location)
(A) Sanchi Stupa.	(I) Madhya Pradesh
(B) Amaravati Stupa.	(II) Andhra Pradesh
(C) Dhamek Stupa.	(III) Sarnath
(D) Bharhut Stupa.	(IV) Madhya Pradesh

(1) A-I, B-II, C-III, D-IV
(2) A-II, B-I, C-III, D-IV
(3) A-III, B-I, C-II, D-IV
(4) A-I, B-III, C-II, D-IV

14. Assertion (A): Ashoka's Dhamma was influenced by Buddhist principles.
Reason (R): Ashoka converted to Buddhism and used Dhamma to promote social harmony.
(1) Both A and R are true, and R correctly explains A
(2) Both A and R are true, but R does not explain A
(3) A is true, but R is false
(4) A is false, but R is true

16. Identify the following sculpture.

A) Sand Sculpture of Kushana King
B) Sandstone Sculpture of Kushana King
C) Brickstone Sculpture of Kushana King
D) Mudstone Sculpture of Kushana King

16. Which traveler's account is an important source for understanding the administration of Muhammad bin Tughlaq?
(A) Ibn Battuta
(B) Al-Biruni
(C) Francois Bernier
(D) Niccolao Manucci

17. Which of the following is a major theme in Francois Bernier's account of India?
(A) Mughal military conquests
(B) The prevalence of economic and social inequalities
(C) The expansion of the Vijayanagara Empire
(D) The impact of the Bhakti movement

18. Which of the following foreign travelers visited the Vijayanagara Empire and documented its prosperity?
(A) Ibn Battuta
(B) Domingo Paes
(C) Al-Biruni
(D) Francois Bernier

19. Why did Al-Biruni refer to the caste system as 'contrary to the laws of nature'?
(A) He believed it was beneficial for Indian society
(B) He thought it was discriminatory and rigid
(C) He supported its role in social organization
(D) He saw similarities between it and the European feudal system

20. Who among the following is considered the founder of the Bhakti movement in North India?

(A) Ramanuja
(B) Kabir
(C) Mirabai
(D) Guru Nanak

21. Which of the following statements about the Sufi movement is correct?
(A) Sufis completely rejected interaction with Hindus
(B) Sufi saints emphasized love and devotion to God
(C) Sufism originated in India
(D) Sufi saints focused only on rituals and legal aspects of Islam

22. Which of the following Bhakti saints composed the devotional poetry collection 'Bijak'?
(A) Tulsidas
(B) Kabir
(C) Surdas
(D) Guru Nanak

23. The Chishti order of Sufism is best known for:
(A) Encouraging royal patronage
(B) Promoting mystical music and devotional songs (Qawwali)
(C) Rigidly following Islamic legal traditions
(D) Supporting political leaders in warfare

24. Which river was crucial for the prosperity of the Vijayanagara Empire?
(A) Ganga
(B) Yamuna
(C) Tungabhadra
(D) Krishna

25. Which architectural feature is commonly found in Vijayanagara temples?
(A) Tall, elaborate gopurams
(B) Large domes and minarets
(C) Indo-Greek sculptures
(D) Buddhist stupas

26. The Battle of Talikota (1565) resulted in:
(A) The fall of Vijayanagara
(B) Expansion of the Vijayanagara Empire
(C) The establishment of Mughal rule in the Deccan
(D) A treaty between Vijayanagara and the Deccan Sultanates

27. The term 'Raiyat' in Mughal India referred to:
(A) Tax collectors
(B) Peasants
(C) Military officers
(D) Traders

28. Which of the following systems was introduced by Akbar to assess agricultural taxation?
(A) Jagirdari system
(B) Zabt system
(C) Zamindari system
(D) Mansabdari system

29. Which Mughal emperor is credited with abolishing the Jizya tax?
(A) Babur
(B) Akbar
(C) Jahangir
(D) Aurangzeb

30. Who wrote the Mughal chronicle 'Badshahnama'?
(A) Abu'l Fazl
(B) Abdul Hamid Lahori
(C) Badauni
(D) Ibn Battuta

31. Match the following travelers with the Indian rulers they wrote about:

Traveler.   Indian Ruler
(A) Ibn Battuta.   (I) Muhammad bin Tughlaq
(B) Francois Bernier.   (II) Aurangzeb
(C) Niccolao Manucci. (III) Shah Jahan
(D) Domingo Paes.   (IV) Krishnadevaraya

(1) A-I, B-II, C-III, D-IV
(2) A-II, B-I, C-IV, D-III
(3) A-III, B-IV, C-II, D-I
(4) A-IV, B-III, C-I, D-II

32. Assertion (A): The Mughal administration was highly centralized.
Reason (R): The Mansabdari system ensured efficient governance and military control.
(1) Both A and R are true, and R correctly explains A
(2) Both A and R are true, but R does not explain A
(3) A is true, but R is false
(4) A is false, but R is true

33. Which of the following statements about the Sufi movement is correct?
(A) It rejected rigid religious formalism
(B) It discouraged music and poetry
(C) It supported caste hierarchy
(D) It only accepted Muslim followers

34. Which of the following was a direct consequence of the Permanent Settlement of Bengal (1793)?
(A) Peasants became landowners
(B) Zamindars were made hereditary owners of land
(C) Land revenue was collected directly from peasants
(D) It led to the decline of British control over agriculture

35. The Indigo Rebellion (1859–60) was caused primarily by:
(A) High land revenue demands
(B) British forcing peasants to grow indigo under exploitative conditions
(C) Famines caused by excessive indigo farming
(D) Zamindars refusing to allow indigo cultivation

36. Which of the following social groups did NOT participate actively in the Revolt of 1857?
(A) Sepoys
(B) Peasants
(C) Industrial workers
(D) Zamindars

37. Which of the following was a significant impact of the Revolt of 1857?
(A) The British Crown took direct control of India
(B) The Mughal Empire expanded its territory
(C) The British East India Company was given more powers
(D) The Indian National Congress was formed immediately

38. Which of the following was a major colonial city known for its textile industry?
(A) Calcutta
(B) Madras
(C) Bombay
(D) Simla

39. The 'Black Town' in colonial cities was an area where:
(A) British officials lived
(B) Indian elites resided
(C) Poor Indian workers and traders lived
(D) European merchants established their businesses

40. Which agreement led to the suspension of the Civil Disobedience Movement in 1931?
(A) Lucknow Pact
(B) Gandhi–Irwin Pact
(C) Poona Pact
(D) Cripps Mission Agreement

41. What was the main reason behind the launching of the Non–Cooperation Movement?
(A) To demand complete independence
(B) To protest against the Jallianwala Bagh massacre and Rowlatt Act
(C) To support the British government during World War I
(D) To promote industrialization in India

Read the passage below and answer the following questions:
The Partition of India in 1947 was one of the most traumatic events in South Asian history. It resulted in the division of British India into two independent nations, India and Pakistan. The partition led to massive communal violence, with large-scale migrations of Hindus, Muslims, and Sikhs. Millions were displaced, and numerous lives were lost. The Mountbatten Plan of June 1947 finalized the partition, and British rule in India officially ended on August 15, 1947.

42. Which year did the Partition of India take place?
(1) 1942
(2) 1945
(3) 1947
(4) 1950

43. Which British plan led to the finalization of Partition?
(1) Cripps Mission
(2) Simon Commission
(3) Mountbatten Plan
(4) Cabinet Mission Plan

44. Which community suffered large-scale migration due to Partition?
(1) Only Hindus
(2) Only Muslims
(3) Hindus, Muslims, and Sikhs
(4) Only Parsis

45. What was one of the major consequences of the Partition?
(1) Increase in British investment in India
(2) Mass displacement and communal violence
(3) Strengthening of Indian–British relations
(4) Creation of three separate nations

46. Which of the following was an important leader involved in Partition negotiations?
(1) Sardar Patel
(2) Bal Gangadhar Tilak
(3) Lala Lajpat Rai
(4) Raja Rammohan Roy

47. Assertion (A): The Rowlatt Act (1919) was strongly opposed by Indian leaders.
Reason (R): The Act allowed the British government to imprison people without trial.
(1) Both A and R are true, and R correctly explains A
(2) Both A and R are true, but R does not explain A
(3) A is true, but R is false
(4) A is false, but R is true

48. Which of the following statements about the Indian National Congress (INC) is correct?
(A) It was founded in 1920 as a revolutionary organization.
(B) It was initially a moderate organization but later adopted more radical nationalist strategies.
(C) It never participated in any negotiations with the British government.
(D) It supported the Partition of India from the beginning.
(1) A
(2) B
(3) C
(4) D

49. Which of the following statements about the Mughal emperor Jahangir is correct?
(A) He introduced the Mansabdari system
(B) He allowed the English East India Company to establish a factory in Surat
(C) He abolished the Jizya tax
(D) He translated the Mahabharata into Persian

50. What was the significance of 'Sulh-i-Kul' in Mughal administration?
(A) It was a revenue collection system
(B) It was a policy of universal religious tolerance under Akbar
(C) It was a diplomatic treaty with the Deccan Sultanates
(D) It was a system for organizing Mughal chronicles

Scan The QR Code To Get Answers With Detailed Explanations!

CUET UG MOCK TEST – 5

1. Which of the following is NOT an important characteristic of Harappan cities?
(A) Well-planned streets and drainage systems
(B) Widespread use of iron tools
(C) Granaries and warehouses
(D) Use of standardized weights and measures

2. Which Harappan site is located in present-day Haryana and is one of the largest sites?
(A) Lothal
(B) Kalibangan
(C) Dholavira
(D) Rakhigarhi

3. What was the primary purpose of the Great Bath at Mohenjo-daro?
(A) Water storage for agriculture
(B) A public bathing and ritual site
(C) A place for royal gatherings
(D) A reservoir for trade ships

4. Which of the following Mahajanapadas emerged as the most powerful and led to the formation of the first empire in India?
(A) Kashi
(B) Magadha
(C) Kosala
(D) Gandhara

5. Which of the following was the capital of the Mauryan Empire under Chandragupta Maurya?
(A) Ujjain
(B) Pataliputra
(C) Taxila
(D) Mathura

6. Who among the following was NOT a part of the Mauryan administration?
(A) Rajuka
(B) Panyadhyaksha
(C) Amatya
(D) Senapati

7. Which of the following sources provides an account of Chandragupta Maurya's court and administration?
(A) Arthashastra
(B) Indica
(C) Manusmriti
(D) Sangam literature

8. Which of the following texts is considered a significant source for understanding the caste system in ancient India?
(A) Mahabharata
(B) Manusmriti
(C) Sutta Pitaka
(D) Indica

9. Which of the following was a key feature of the Gotra system in early Indian society?
(A) It was a kinship-based lineage system.
(B) Women retained their original Gotra after marriage.
(C) It was followed only by the Kshatriya varna.
(D) It was introduced during the Mughal period.

10. What does the term 'Kula' refer to in early Indian texts?
(A) A large urban settlement
(B) A kinship-based family unit
(C) A form of taxation
(D) A type of temple architecture

11. Which of the following was an important feature of Mahayana Buddhism?
(A) Rejection of idol worship
(B) Emphasis on individual enlightenment only
(C) Worship of Bodhisattvas
(D) Strict adherence to Pali scriptures

12. Which of the following statements is true about Ashokan inscriptions?
(A) They were written only in Prakrit and Brahmi.
(B) They were mainly found in South India.
(C) They were used to spread the ideas of Dhamma.
(D) They were issued only after the Kalinga War.

13. Match the following Buddhist symbols with their meanings:

List-I (Symbol).   List-II (Meaning)
(A) Lotus.   (I) Spiritual awakening
(B) Dharma Chakra.   (II) Teachings of Buddha
(C) Stupa.   (III) Relics of Buddha
(D) Bodhi Tree.   (IV) Enlightenment

(1) A-I, B-II, C-III, D-IV
(2) A-II, B-I, C-III, D-IV
(3) A-III, B-IV, C-I, D-II
(4) A-IV, B-III, C-II, D-I

14. Identify the following :

A) A inscribed panel from Mathura depicting travellers
B) A sculpted panel from Dwaraka depicting travellers
C) A inscribed panel from Dwaraka depicting travellers
D) A sculpted panel from Mathura depicting travellers

15. Which of the following statements about the spread of Buddhism is correct?

(A) Buddhism declined completely after the Gupta period.
(B) Ashoka sent Buddhist missionaries to Sri Lanka and Central Asia.
(C) Buddhist teachings were never written down.
(D) Buddhism remained confined to India.

16. Which traveler wrote about the Indian caste system and compared it to Persian social divisions?
(A) Ibn Battuta
(B) Francois Bernier
(C) Marco Polo
(D) Al-Biruni

17. Ibn Battuta traveled extensively in India during the reign of which Delhi Sultan?
(A) Balban
(B) Alauddin Khalji
(C) Muhammad bin Tughlaq
(D) Firoz Shah Tughlaq

18. Which of the following is true about Al-Biruni's Kitab-ul-Hind?
(A) It was written in Arabic and focused on Indian culture and traditions
(B) It was a Persian translation of Indian scriptures
(C) It was based on Ibn Battuta's travel experiences
(D) It was written to promote European influence in India

19. Who among the following Bhakti saints was a devotee of Lord Krishna and composed the 'Sur Sagar'?
(A) Mirabai
(B) Surdas
(C) Kabir
(D) Tulsidas

20. Which Sufi order in India was known for its emphasis on simple living and rejection of royal patronage?
(A) Suhrawardi
(B) Naqshbandi
(C) Chishti
(D) Qadiri

21. What was the key feature of Bhakti traditions in medieval India?
(A) Use of vernacular languages in religious compositions
(B) Strict adherence to caste-based hierarchy
(C) Patronage exclusively from Muslim rulers
(D) Promotion of complex rituals for salvation

22. Which river was crucial for the prosperity of the Vijayanagara Empire?
(A) Krishna
(B) Godavari
(C) Kaveri
(D) Tungabhadra

23. Which European traveler visited Vijayanagara and described it as a prosperous and well-planned city?
(A) Marco Polo
(B) FranÇois Bernier
(C) Domingo Paes
(D) Al-Biruni

24. Which architectural feature was prominent in Vijayanagara temples?
(A) Large domes and minarets
(B) Tall gopurams (gateway towers)
(C) Stupa-like structures
(D) Gothic-style windows

25. Who were the 'Raiyat' in Mughal agrarian society?
(A) Tax collectors
(B) Peasants
(C) Soldiers
(D) Traders

26. Which Mughal emperor introduced the Zabt system for revenue collection?
(A) Akbar
(B) Babur
(C) Aurangzeb
(D) Jahangir

27. The 'Zamindars' in Mughal India were primarily responsible for:
(A) Judicial administration
(B) Collecting land revenue
(C) Military recruitment
(D) Religious affairs

28. Which Mughal emperor commissioned the Persian translation of Mahabharata as 'Razmnama'?
(A) Akbar
(B) Jahangir
(C) Shah Jahan
(D) Aurangzeb

29. Who wrote the Mughal chronicle 'Ain-i-Akbari'?
(A) Badauni
(B) Abu'l Fazl
(C) Nizamuddin Ahmad
(D) Ibn Battuta

30. Match the following Mughal court historians with their works:

Historian	Work
(A) Abu'l Fazl.	(I) Akbarnama
(B) Badauni.	(II) Muntakhab-ut-Tawarikh
(C) Nizamuddin Ahmad.	(III) Tabaqat-i-Akbari
(D) FranÇois Bernier.	(IV) Travels in Mughal India

(1) A-I, B-II, C-III, D-IV
(2) A-II, B-I, C-IV, D-III
(3) A-III, B-IV, C-II, D-I
(4) A-IV, B-III, C-I, D-II

31. Assertion (A): The Mughal administration was highly centralized.
Reason (R): The Mansabdari system ensured efficient governance and military control.
(1) Both A and R are true, and R correctly explains A
(2) Both A and R are true, but R does not explain A
(3) A is true, but R is false
(4) A is false, but R is true

32. Which of the following statements about the Bhakti movement is correct?
(1) It rejected caste-based discrimination
(2) It promoted idol worship exclusively
(3) It was confined to North India
(4) It originated during the British period

33. Which of the following factors contributed most to the expansion of the Mughal Empire under Akbar?
(A) His policy of religious tolerance and alliance with Rajputs
(B) The decline of European powers in India
(C) The construction of the Taj Mahal
(D) The influence of Sufi saints in his court

34. The Jagirdari system under the Mughals was primarily related to:
(A) Land grants to military officers and nobles
(B) Revenue collection from urban merchants
(C) Trade policies of the Mughals with foreign countries
(D) Appointment of provincial governors in South India

35. What was one of the primary objectives of Akbar's Din-i-Ilahi?
(A) To establish a new political party
(B) To merge the best elements of various religions and promote unity
(C) To replace the existing Mughal administration
(D) To enforce Islamic law more strictly

36. Which of the following was a major cause of the Indigo Rebellion (1859-60)?
(A) High land revenue imposed by the British government
(B) The oppressive conditions forced by European planters on Indian farmers
(C) Peasants' demand for factory-made cloth instead of indigo
(D) Lack of rainfall leading to indigo crop failure

37. Which land revenue system was introduced in South and West India by the British?
(A) Permanent Settlement
(B) Ryotwari System
(C) Mahalwari System
(D) Zamindari System

38. Which of the following was NOT a reason for the failure of the Revolt of 1857?
(A) Lack of unity among Indian rulers
(B) Advanced military technology of the British
(C) Active participation of peasants in leadership roles
(D) Absence of strong centralized command

39. What was the immediate trigger for the Revolt of 1857?
(A) The Partition of Bengal
(B) The introduction of the Enfield rifle cartridges greased with animal fat
(C) The British arrest of Mahatma Gandhi
(D) The abolition of the Zamindari system

40. Which of the following was a reason for British emphasis on urban planning in colonial India?
(A) To accommodate the growing population of Indian merchants
(B) To create separate living spaces for British and Indians
(C) To preserve the Mughal-style architecture in cities
(D) To allow free access to all communities in government buildings

41. Which colonial city was known as the 'Second City of the Empire' after London?
(A) Bombay
(B) Madras
(C) Calcutta
(D) Delhi

42. Which of the following was the main objective of the Civil Disobedience Movement?
(A) To demand complete independence from British rule
(B) To support British war efforts in World War II
(C) To gain representation for Indians in the British Parliament
(D) To increase British investment in Indian industries

43. Which of the following was a direct outcome of the Quit India Movement (1942)?
(A) British agreed to immediate Indian independence
(B) Large-scale arrests of Indian leaders
(C) Creation of separate electorates for Muslims
(D) British recognition of Indian autonomy

Read the passage and answer the following:
The Partition of India in 1947 was one of the most significant and traumatic events in South Asian history. The division of British India into two independent nations, India and Pakistan, led to large-scale migrations, communal riots, and political instability. Millions of people were displaced, and thousands lost their lives in the ensuing violence. The Mountbatten Plan of June 1947 finalized the partition, bringing an end to British colonial rule in the subcontinent.

44. Which year did the Partition of India take place?
(1) 1942
(2) 1945
(3) 1947
(4) 1950

45. Which British plan led to the finalization of Partition?
(1) Simon Commission
(2) Mountbatten Plan
(3) Cripps Mission
(4) Cabinet Mission Plan

46. Which of the following was a major cause of Partition?
(1) Growing demand for industrialization in India
(2) Rising communal tensions between Hindus and Muslims
(3) Economic depression in British colonies
(4) Disputes between Congress and the British over taxation policies

47. Which leader played a key role in negotiating the terms of Partition?
(1) B.R. Ambedkar
(2) Sardar Patel
(3) Bhagat Singh
(4) Dadabhai Naoroji

48. What was one of the most immediate effects of Partition?
(1) Strengthening of India's economy
(2) Mass migration and violent communal riots
(3) Peaceful integration of princely states
(4) The British withdrawal from all Asian colonies

49. Assertion (A): The Indian Constitution guarantees fundamental rights to all citizens.
Reason (R): The Constitution of India is based on the British legal system and maintains monarchy.
(1) Both A and R are true, and R correctly explains A
(2) Both A and R are true, but R does not explain A
(3) A is true, but R is false
(4) A is false, but R is true

50. Which of the following statements about the Indian Independence Movement is correct?
(A) It was completely based on non-violent methods.
(B) It included both non-violent resistance and armed struggles.
(C) It was led only by Mahatma Gandhi.
(D) The movement began only after 1945.
(1) A
(2) B
(3) C
(4) D

Scan The QR Code To Get Answers With Detailed Explanations!

CUET UG MOCK TEST – 6

1. Assertion (A): The Harappans did not build temples.

   Reason (R): Harappan society did not have a state religion.

   a) Both A and R are true and R is the correct explanation of A

   b) Both A and R are true but R is not the correct explanation of A

   c) A is true but R is false

   d) A is false but R is true

2. The Harappan site of Dholavira is located in present-day:

   a) Punjab

   b) Rajasthan

   c) Gujarat

   d) Haryana

3. Harappan settlements were often located near:

   a) Dense forests

   b) Mountain passes

   c) River systems

   d) Deserts

4. The earliest coins in India were known as:

   a) Gold dinars

   b) Punch-marked coins

   c) Copper tokens

   d) Silver bars

5. Sanchi, Sarnath, and Amaravati are sites of:

   a) Jain temples

   b) Buddhist stupas

   c) Harappan granaries

   d) Mauryan palaces

6. Fill in the blank: The Rigveda is composed in _________.

   a) Prakrit

   b) Pali

   c) Sanskrit

   d) Tamil

7. Assertion (A): Many Harappan settlements were abandoned around 1900 BCE.

   Reason (R): Climatic changes and river shifts might have led to their decline.

   a) Both A and R are true and R is the correct explanation of A

   b) Both A and R are true but R is not the correct explanation of A

   c) A is true but R is false

   d) A is false but R is true

8. The Mahajanapada that became most powerful in the 6th century BCE was:

   a) Kosala

   b) Kuru

   c) Magadha

   d) Gandhara

9. Fill in the blank: The earliest evidence of writing in India comes from _________.

   a) Vedic texts

   b) Harappan seals

   c) Ashokan inscriptions

   d) Jain manuscripts

10. Match the following:

   A. Harappan Civilization – 1. Citadel

   B. Ashoka – 2. Dhamma

   C. Mahavira – 3. Jainism

   D. Viharas – 4. Buddhist Monks' residence

   a) A-1, B-2, C-3, D-4

   b) A-2, B-1, C-4, D-3

   c) A-3, B-4, C-2, D-1

   d) A-4, B-3, C-1, D-2

11. Megasthenes was the ambassador of:

   a) Seleucus Nikator

   b) Alexander the Great

   c) Cyrus the Great

   d) Augustus Caesar

12. Fill in the blank: According to the Dharmasutras, women were expected to be under the control of their _________.

   a) Priests

   b) Teachers

   c) Male relatives

   d) Servants

13. The Harappan script is:

   a) Alphabetic

   b) Pictographic and undeciphered

   c) Fully translated

   d) Based on Brahmi

14. In the later Vedic period, the term 'Brahmana' referred to:

   a) Landowners

   b) Warrior chiefs

   c) Priestly class

   d) Merchants

15. Assertion (A): Buddha believed in an eternal soul.

   Reason (R): The concept of atman was central to Buddhist doctrine.

   a) Both A and R are true and R is the correct explanation of A

   b) Both A and R are true but R is not the correct explanation of A

   c) A is true but R is false

   d) A is false but R is true

16. Fill in the blank: The famous terracotta figure of a woman found in Mohenjo-daro is often referred to as ________.
a) Mother Earth
b) Dancing girl
c) Queen of Indus
d) Harappan bride

17. Prakrit was the language used in:
a) Vedic sacrifices
b) Buddhist and Jain texts
c) Harappan inscriptions
d) Persian edicts

18. The term 'Shudra' in the Varna system referred to:
a) Priests
b) Kings
c) Servile class
d) Merchants

19. Fill in the blank: Stupas were generally built over the ________ of the Buddha or Buddhist monks.
a) Clothes
b) Tools
c) Relics
d) Books

20. Assertion (A): Early Buddhist texts were transmitted orally.
Reason (R): Writing was not prevalent during the Buddha's lifetime.
a) Both A and R are true and R is the correct explanation of A
b) Both A and R are true but R is not the correct explanation of A
c) A is true but R is false
d) A is false but R is true

21. Ibn Battuta visited India during the reign of:
a) Akbar
b) Muhammad bin Tughlaq
c) Sher Shah Suri
d) Firoz Shah Tughlaq

22. The Bhakti poet-saint Kabir composed his verses in the language ________.
a) Persian
b) Sanskrit
c) Avadhi
d) A mix of Hindi, Persian and regional dialects

23. Assertion (A): Francois Bernier described Mughal India as a land dominated by the crown and the nobles.
Reason (R): He believed that there was no concept of private property in Mughal India.
a) Both A and R are true and R is the correct explanation of A
b) Both A and R are true but R is not the correct explanation of A
c) A is true but R is false
d) A is false but R is true

24. Krishnadeva Raya was associated with which empire?
a) Chola
b) Maratha
c) Vijayanagara
d) Mughal

25. The main source of revenue for the Mughal Empire was:
a) Custom duties
b) Land revenue
c) Trade tax
d) Religious donations

26. The Silsila of Chishti Sufis was established in India by ________.
a) Nizamuddin Auliya
b) Shaikh Muinuddin Chishti
c) Baba Farid
d) Nasiruddin Chiragh

27. Assertion (A): Mughal chronicles such as the Akbarnama were written by court historians.
Reason (R): These chronicles were meant to glorify the emperor and his reign.
a) Both A and R are true and R is the correct explanation of A
b) Both A and R are true but R is not the correct explanation of A
c) A is true but R is false
d) A is false but R is true

28. Who among the following travellers visited the court of Shah Jahan?
a) Duarte Barbosa
b) Niccolao Manucci
c) Abdur Razzaq
d) Francois Bernier

29. The Amara-nayaka system was prevalent in:
a) Mughal India
b) Vijayanagara Empire
c) Maratha Empire
d) Sultanate of Delhi

30. Match the following:
A. Kabir - 1. Nirguna Bhakti saint
B. Francois Bernier - 2. French traveler
C. Abul Fazl - 3. Author of Akbarnama
D. Hazrat Nizamuddin - 4. Chishti Sufi saint
a) A-1, B-2, C-3, D-4
b) A-2, B-3, C-4, D-1
c) A-3, B-4, C-2, D-1
d) A-1, B-3, C-2, D-4

31. Ain-i Akbari is a part of the chronicle ________.
a) Baburnama
b) Shahjahannama
c) Akbarnama
d) Tuzuk-i-Jahangiri

32. The main architectural feature of Hampi was:
a) Stone temples with intricate carvings
b) Dome structures
c) Iron pillars
d) Marble mosques

33. Who composed the Tuzuk-i-Baburi?
a) Abul Fazl
b) Babur
c) Badauni
d) Al-Biruni

34. Assertion (A): Sufis believed in spiritual closeness with God through love and devotion.
Reason (R): They completely rejected rituals and lived in isolation.
a) Both A and R are true and R is the correct explanation of A
b) Both A and R are true but R is not the correct explanation of A
c) A is true but R is false
d) A is false but R is true

35. Zamindars were considered ________ of the land under the Mughal revenue system.
a) Renters
b) Owners
c) Intermediaries
d) Traders

36. The Permanent Settlement was introduced in:
a) 1773
b) 1793
c) 1805
d) 1820

37. Assertion (A): The 1857 Revolt was a major armed resistance to British rule.
Reason (R): It was sparked mainly due to the annexation of Hyderabad.
a) Both A and R are true and R is the correct explanation of A
b) Both A and R are true but R is not the correct explanation of A
c) A is true but R is false
d) A is false but R is true

38. The city known as the "White Town" and "Black Town" during colonial times was:
a) Bombay
b) Delhi
c) Calcutta
d) Madras

39. The Champaran Satyagraha was associated with:
a) Indigo planters
b) Land revenue
c) Salt tax
d) Forest laws

40. The Cabinet Mission Plan came to India in:
a) 1942
b) 1945
c) 1946
d) 1947

41. One major outcome of the 1857 Revolt was:
a) Reinforcement of company rule
b) Transfer of power to the British Crown
c) Complete withdrawal of British troops
d) Rise of Communist movement

42. The Constitution of India was adopted on:
a) 15th August 1947
b) 26th January 1950
c) 26th November 1949
d) 30th January 1948

43. Who led the protest against the Simon Commission in Lahore?
a) Subhas Chandra Bose
b) Jawaharlal Nehru
c) Lala Lajpat Rai
d) Sardar Vallabhbhai Patel

44. Assertion (A): Colonial urban planning led to segregation between the British and Indians.
Reason (R): British officials wanted to maintain sanitation and order.
a) Both A and R are true and R is the correct explanation of A
b) Both A and R are true but R is not the correct explanation of A
c) A is true but R is false
d) A is false but R is true

45. The INA trials were held at:
a) Allahabad
b) Delhi Red Fort
c) Calcutta
d) Bombay

46. The Moplah Rebellion occurred in:
a) Gujarat
b) Tamil Nadu
c) Kerala
d) Punjab

47. Gandhi's idea of Satyagraha emphasized:
a) Violent resistance
b) Non-cooperation with hatred
c) Passive resistance
d) Truth and non-violent protest

48. Match the following:
List I.   List II
A. Permanent Settlement.   Indigo Satyagraha
B. Champaran.   Purna Swaraj Resolution
C. Lahore Session of 1929.   Zamindari System
D. Mountbatten Plan.   Partition and Independence plan

a) A-3, B-1, C-2, D-4
b) A-1, B-3, C-4, D-2
c) A-2, B-4, C-1, D-3
d) A-4, B-2, C-3, D-1

49. The famous journal 'Harijan' was started by:
a) Ambedkar
b) Tilak
c) Nehru
d) Gandhi

50. Assertion (A): The Constituent Assembly had representatives from different regions, religions, and communities.
Reason (R): It was formed through direct elections.
a) Both A and R are true and R is the correct explanation of A
b) Both A and R are true but R is not the correct explanation of A
c) A is true but R is false
d) A is false but R is true

 Scan The QR Code To Get Answers With Detailed Explanations!

CUET UG MOCK TEST – 7

1. Which of the following animals was not commonly depicted in Harappan seals?
a) Unicorn
b) Bull
c) Elephant
d) Horse

2. Fill in the blank: The town associated with the discovery of the Great Bath is _________.
a) Harappa
b) Mohenjodaro
c) Lothal
d) Kalibangan

3. The earliest inscriptions were composed in which language?
a) Sanskrit
b) Prakrit
c) Tamil
d) Pali

4. Assertion (A): Early Vedic texts were memorized and orally transmitted.
Reason (R): Writing was considered inauspicious in Vedic culture.
a) Both A and R are true and R is the correct explanation of A
b) Both A and R are true but R is not the correct explanation of A
c) A is true but R is false
d) A is false but R is true

5. The site where evidence of rice cultivation in the Harappan period has been found is:
a) Ropar
b) Dholavira
c) Lothal
d) Mehrgarh

6. According to the Dharmasutras, the ideal occupation of a Brahmana was:
a) Trade
b) Agriculture
c) Teaching and performing sacrifices
d) Iron smelting

7. Fill in the blank: In the Ashokan edicts, Dhamma refers to a code of conduct promoting _________.
a) Ritual sacrifice
b) Economic welfare
c) Moral and social responsibility
d) Religious orthodoxy

8. Who among the following rulers is associated with the construction of cave dwellings at Barabar Hills?
a) Harsha vardhana
b) Ashoka
c) Kanishka
d) Chandragupta

9. The Satavahana rulers issued coins predominantly made of:
a) Silver
b) Copper
c) Lead
d) Iron

10. Assertion (A): The Buddhist texts were preserved in monasteries.
Reason (R): These monasteries served as centres of learning and religious activities.
a) Both A and R are true and R is the correct explanation of A
b) Both A and R are true but R is not the correct explanation of A
c) A is true but R is false
d) A is false but R is true

11. The Jaina concept of Ahimsa means:
a) Ritual cleanliness
b) Non-injury to living beings
c) Meditation
d) Truthfulness

12. Fill in the blank: The Sanskrit term Gotra literally means _________.
a) Lineage
b) Caste
c) Occupation
d) Birthplace

13. Which one of the following was a center of both Buddhist learning and trading?
a) Sarnath
b) Bharhut
c) Taxila
d) Ujjayini

14. The idea that "kingship is divine and based on the power of Dhamma" is most associated with:
a) Gupta rulers
b) Mauryan Empire under Ashoka
c) Harappan cities
d) Rig Vedic kings

15. Which one of the following is not true about Harappan writing?
a) It is yet to be fully deciphered
b) It was written on baked seals
c) It was alphabetic in nature
d) It was pictographic

16. Match the following:
A. Harappan Site – 1. Sanchi
B. Buddhist Monument – 2. Lothal
C. Mauryan Pillar Edict – 3. Lauriya Nandangarh
D. Ashokan Stupa – 4. Amaravati

a) A-2, B-4, C-3, D-1
b) A-4, B-2, C-1, D-3
c) A-1, B-2, C-4, D-3
d) A-2, B-1, C-3, D-4

17. The Harappan civilization covered present-day:
a) India, Pakistan, and Afghanistan
b) Only Pakistan
c) Only northwest India
d) India and Sri Lanka

18. Fill in the blank: The Mahabharata was compiled over a period of about _________ years.
 a) 100
 b) 500
 c) 1000
 d) 2000

19. The "Ashokan lion capital" was found at:
 a) Sarnath
 b) Sanchi
 c) Lumbini
 d) Ujjain

20. Assertion (A): Jainism was more inclusive towards women than many Brahmanical traditions.
 Reason (R): Women were allowed to join the Jain Sangha.
 a) Both A and R are true and R is the correct explanation of A
 b) Both A and R are true but R is not the correct explanation of A
 c) A is true but R is false
 d) A is false but R is true

21. Ibn Battuta's account, Rihla, provides valuable information about life under which ruler?
 a) Alauddin Khalji
 b) Muhammad bin Tughlaq
 c) Akbar
 d) Aurangzeb

22. Krishnadeva Raya's reign is remembered as the golden period of the _________ empire.
 a) Mughal
 b) Chola
 c) Vijayanagara
 d) Maratha

23. Assertion (A): The Chishti Sufis believed in renunciation of the world.
 Reason (R): They lived in khanqahs and preached devotion to God.
 a) Both A and R are true and R is the correct explanation of A
 b) Both A and R are true but R is not the correct explanation of A
 c) A is true but R is false
 d) A is false but R is true

24. Francois Bernier compared Mughal India to which European political structure?
 a) City-states of Italy
 b) Feudal system in Europe
 c) Absolute monarchy in France
 d) Theocratic states

25. The Bhakti saint who believed in the formless God and used simple Hindi in his compositions was:
 a) Mirabai
 b) Tulsidas
 c) Kabir
 d) Surdas

26. The chief architect of Fatehpur Sikri was influenced by which regional style?
 a) Dravidian
 b) Indo-Islamic
 c) Buddhist
 d) Romanesque

27. Assertion (A): Abul Fazl was one of the Navaratnas in Akbar's court.
 Reason (R): He was the author of Akbarnama and Ain-i Akbari.
 a) Both A and R are true and R is the correct explanation of A
 b) Both A and R are true but R is not the correct explanation of A
 c) A is true but R is false
 d) A is false but R is true

28. The sacred place associated with Virupaksha, a form of Shiva, was located at:
 a) Delhi
 b) Madurai
 c) Hampi
 d) Ujjain

29. Abdur Razzaq was a traveler from _________ who visited Vijayanagara.
 a) Arabia
 b) Turkey
 c) Persia
 d) Afghanistan

30. The term 'zamindar' during the Mughal period referred to:
 a) Soldiers
 b) Traders
 c) Revenue collectors
 d) Artisans

31. Kabir's poems are compiled in which of the following texts?
 a) Bijak
 b) Adi Granth
 c) Ramcharitmanas
 d) Tulsidas Ramayana

32. The Mughal court historian who translated Mahabharata into Persian was:
 a) Abul Fazl
 b) Abdul Hamid Lahori
 c) Faizi
 d) Badauni

33. The architectural style of Vijayanagara included which of the following?
 a) Domes and minarets
 b) Tall gopurams and mandapas
 c) Marble inlay work
 d) Arched gateways

34. Assertion (A): Travellers like Duarte Barbosa noted the prosperity of Indian ports.
 Reason (R): Indian ocean trade was significant during the 15th-17th centuries.
 a) Both A and R are true and R is the correct explanation of A
 b) Both A and R are true but R is not the correct explanation of A
 c) A is true but R is false
 d) A is false but R is true

35. The Ain-i Akbari is primarily a document about:
a) Akbar's wars
b) Akbar's personal life
c) Administration and regulations of the Mughal Empire
d) Religious discourses of Akbar

36. The Indigo Revolt of 1859-60 was led primarily by:
a) Peasants
b) Zamindars
c) British officials
d) Factory workers

37. The partition of Bengal in 1905 was reversed in:
a) 1909
b) 1911
c) 1915
d) 1917

38. Assertion (A): Gandhi launched the Non-Cooperation Movement in 1920.
Reason (R): It was a reaction to the Rowlatt Act and the Jallianwala Bagh massacre.
a) Both A and R are true and R is the correct explanation of A
b) Both A and R are true but R is not the correct explanation of A
c) A is true but R is false
d) A is false but R is true

39. The term "Drain of Wealth" was popularized by:
a) Dadabhai Naoroji
b) B.R. Ambedkar
c) Mahatma Gandhi
d) Gopal Krishna Gokhale

40. The revolt of 1857 began in:
a) Meerut
b) Delhi
c) Lucknow
d) Kanpur

41. The Simon Commission was boycotted because:
a) It demanded partition
b) It did not include any Indian members
c) It favored princely states
d) It rejected the Congress

42. Who among the following was not associated with the drafting of the Indian Constitution?
a) Dr. B.R. Ambedkar
b) Dr. Rajendra Prasad
c) Bal Gangadhar Tilak
d) Jawaharlal Nehru

43. Fill in the blank: The Act of Union of 1858 transferred power from the East India Company to the __________.
a) Indian National Congress
b) Crown
c) Provincial Governments
d) Queen's Council

44. Who coined the term "Swaraj is my birthright and I shall have it"?
a) Bal Gangadhar Tilak
b) Lala Lajpat Rai
c) Bipin Chandra Pal
d) Dadabhai Naoroji

45. Assertion (A): British urban planning often favored European sections of cities.
Reason (R): The British promoted Indian craftsmanship and architecture.
a) Both A and R are true and R is the correct explanation of A
b) Both A and R are true but R is not the correct explanation of A
c) A is true but R is false
d) A is false but R is true

46. The All India Muslim League demanded Pakistan in the year:
a) 1940
b) 1942
c) 1946
d) 1947

47. The Indian National Army was formed by:
a) Jawaharlal Nehru
b) Mahatma Gandhi
c) Subhas Chandra Bose
d) Bhagat Singh

48. Match the following:

List I	List II
A. 1857 Revolt.	1932
B. Gandhi-Irwin Pact.	1946
C. Cabinet Mission.	1857
D. Poona Pact.	1931

a) A-3, B-4, C-2, D-1
b) A-1, B-2, C-3, D-4
c) A-2, B-1, C-4, D-3
d) A-4, B-3, C-1, D-2

49. Fill in the blank: Mahatma Gandhi's autobiography is titled ________.
a) India Wins Freedom
b) My Experiments with Truth
c) Hind Swaraj
d) Discovery of India

50. Assertion (A): The Constituent Assembly was based on the Cabinet Mission Plan.
Reason (R): Members were elected directly by the people.
a) Both A and R are true and R is the correct explanation of A
b) Both A and R are true but R is not the correct explanation of A
c) A is true but R is false
d) A is false but R is true

Scan The QR Code To Get Answers With Detailed Explanations!

CUET UG MOCK TEST – 8

1. The city of Lothal is known for its:
a) Fortified granaries
b) Dockyard
c) Temple architecture
d) Iron tools

2. Fill in the blank: Harappan houses often had doors opening towards _________.
a) The main road
b) Courtyards
c) Drainage channels
d) Open fields

3. Which one of the following was not a Mahajanapada?
a) Vajji
b) Gandhara
c) Avanti
d) Ayodhya

4. Assertion (A): The Ashokan inscriptions were written in multiple scripts and languages.
Reason (R): Ashoka wanted his message to reach people across vast linguistic and regional boundaries.
a) Both A and R are true and R is the correct explanation of A
b) Both A and R are true but R is not the correct explanation of A
c) A is true but R is false
d) A is false but R is true

5. Fill in the blank: The priest-kings found in Harappan sculptures wore a robe with _________ motifs.
a) Bull
b) Fish
c) Trefoil
d) Sun

6. According to the Manusmriti, women were:
a) To be given education
b) Allowed to choose husbands
c) Under male authority throughout life
d) Allowed to become rulers

7. The famous stupa at Sanchi was originally commissioned by:
a) Chandragupta
b) Ashoka
c) Harshavardhana
d) Kanishka

8. Who among the following translated Buddhist texts into Chinese?
a) I-Tsing
b) Fa-Xian
c) Xuan Zang
d) None of these

9. Fill in the blank: The Harappan civilization belonged to the _________ Age.
a) Iron
b) Bronze
c) Copper
d) Stone

10. In the Buddhist tradition, a Bodhisattva is:
a) A lay follower
b) One who is yet to achieve enlightenment
c) A teacher of Upanishads
d) A ruler who followed Dhamma

11. The term 'Jatakas' refers to:
a) Rules of monastic discipline
b) Stories of Buddha's previous births
c) Hindu epics
d) Ancient trade routes

12. Assertion (A): Harappan cities had elaborate drainage systems.
Reason (R): They lacked knowledge of sanitation.
a) Both A and R are true and R is the correct explanation of A
b) Both A and R are true but R is not the correct explanation of A
c) A is true but R is false
d) A is false but R is true

13. Who composed the text Mahabharata as we know it today?
a) Valmiki
b) Panini
c) Vyasa
d) Kalidasa

14. Fill in the blank: The Ashvamedha was a _________ ritual.
a) Harvest
b) Horse sacrifice
c) Rain-invoking
d) Temple consecration

15. Who among the following issued the Prayaga Prashasti?
a) Ashoka
b) Kanishka
c) Samudragupta
d) Harshavardhana

16. The Buddhist Sangha was open to:
a) Only Brahmanas
b) Men and women from all social strata
c) Only Kshatriyas
d) Foreigners

17. Which one of the following is correctly matched?
a) Brahmi - Harappan script
b) Sanchi - Buddhist Stupa
c) Vatsyayana - Arthashastra
d) Patanjali - Vedas

18. Fill in the blank: In early India, inscriptions were often engraved on _________.
a) Wood
b) Paper
c) Palm leaves
d) Stone and metal

19. Which of the following best describes 'Ganas' and 'Sanghas'?
a) Royal dynasties
b) Republics or oligarchies
c) Sacred groves
d) Military units

20 . Assertion (A): The Buddha rejected the caste system.
Reason (R): He believed in universal compassion and the equality of all beings.
a) Both A and R are true and R is the correct explanation of A
b) Both A and R are true but R is not the correct explanation of A
c) A is true but R is false
d) A is false but R is true

21. Francois Bernier criticized the Mughal system of land ownership as being detrimental to:
a) Agriculture
b) Trade
c) Craft production
d) Private property rights

22. The Bhakti-Sufi traditions emphasized:
a) Idol worship
b) Rituals and ceremonies
c) Personal devotion to God
d) The caste system

23. Assertion (A): The Mughal emperors maintained elaborate court rituals.
Reason (R): These rituals were meant to establish the divine status of the emperor.
a) Both A and R are true and R is the correct explanation of A
b) Both A and R are true but R is not the correct explanation of A
c) A is true but R is false
d) A is false but R is true

24. Which of the following was a major export item from Mughal India noted by European travellers?
a) Spices
b) Silk textiles
c) Wheat
d) Horses

25. The Bhakti saint who composed verses in Marathi and promoted devotion to Vithoba was:
a) Tukaram
b) Tulsidas
c) Surdas
d) Kabir

26. Hampi, the capital of Vijayanagara, was located near which river?
a) Krishna
b) Tungabhadra
c) Godavari
d) Kaveri

27. Assertion (A): Many Sufi saints adopted local languages for preaching.
Reason (R): They believed that using Persian exclusively would spread their message better.
a) Both A and R are true and R is the correct explanation of A
b) Both A and R are true but R is not the correct explanation of A
c) A is true but R is false
d) A is false but R is true

28. Niccolao Manucci's travel account is titled:
a) Rihla
b) Storia do Mogor
c) Ain-i Akbari
d) Tarikh-i-Firozshahi

29. In Mughal agrarian society, the term 'jagir' referred to:
a) A tax
b) A grant of land
c) A trading right
d) A noble's title

30. The Bhakti poet Mirabai was devoted to:
a) Lord Shiva
b) Lord Krishna
c) Lord Rama
d) Lord Vishnu

31. Which Mughal emperor is associated with the maximum number of official histories written during his reign?
a) Babur
b) Akbar
c) Shah Jahan
d) Aurangzeb

32. Which form of architecture is prominently seen in Vijayanagara temples?
a) Indo-Islamic
b) Dravidian
c) Nagara
d) Buddhist

33. Assertion (A): The Mughal emperors believed in Sulh-i-Kul or universal tolerance.
Reason (R): This policy promoted respect for all religions in the empire.
a) Both A and R are true and R is the correct explanation of A
b) Both A and R are true but R is not the correct explanation of A
c) A is true but R is false
d) A is false but R is true

34. Kabir rejected both ________ and ________ as paths to salvation.
a) Wealth and fame
b) Ritualism and caste
c) Devotion and poetry
d) Music and meditation

35. Which traveller compared the Mughal empire to the decline of Roman Empire due to overcentralization?
a) Ibn Battuta
b) Duarte Barbosa
c) Francois Bernier
d) Abdur Razzaq

36. The Permanent Settlement of Bengal was introduced in:
a) 1765
b) 1793
c) 1813
d) 1858

37. Mahatma Gandhi first used the method of Satyagraha in India during the:
a) Non-Cooperation Movement
b) Champaran movement
c) Salt March
d) Quit India Movement

38. The 1857 Revolt was described as the "First War of Independence" by:
a) R.C. Majumdar
b) Jawaharlal Nehru
c) Vinayak Damodar Savarkar
d) S.N. Sen

39. The main source of revenue for the colonial government after the Permanent Settlement was:
a) Salt tax
b) Land revenue
c) Customs duties
d) Income tax

40. The capital of British India was shifted from Calcutta to Delhi in:
a) 1905
b) 1911
c) 1919
d) 1935

41. Fill in the blank: The _________ Commission was set up to look into the conditions of the agrarian sector in Bengal.
a) Hunter
b) Simon
c) Floud
d) Butler

42. Assertion (A): The Revolt of 1857 spread quickly across North India.
Reason (R): Discontentment against British policies had been brewing among all sections of society.
a) Both A and R are true and R is the correct explanation of A
b) Both A and R are true but R is not the correct explanation of A
c) A is true but R is false
d) A is false but R is true

43. Who among the following played a crucial role in drafting the Objectives Resolution in the Constituent Assembly?
a) B.R. Ambedkar
b) Rajendra Prasad
c) Jawaharlal Nehru
d) Sardar Patel

44. The Quit India Movement was launched in the year:
a) 1930
b) 1935
c) 1942
d) 1947

45. The Urdu term 'Zamindar' refers to:
a) A local merchant
b) A peasant cultivator
c) A revenue collector
d) A British officer

46. Who said "The British rule is a bleeding wound"?
a) Lala Lajpat Rai
b) Mahatma Gandhi
c) Bal Gangadhar Tilak
d) Swami Vivekananda

47. The term 'Communal Award' is associated with:
a) Mountbatten Plan
b) Cripps Mission
c) Macdonald Award
d) Nehru Report

48. Match the following:

List I.	List II
A. Champaran Satyagraha.	1905
B. Dandi March.	1930
C. Partition of Bengal.	1917
D. INA Trials.	1945

a) A-3, B-2, C-1, D-4
b) A-2, B-1, C-3, D-4
c) A-1, B-3, C-4, D-2
d) A-4, B-3, C-2, D-1

49. Fill in the blank: The Satyagraha in Kheda was primarily related to _________.
a) Salt production
b) Textile mills
c) Tax waiver due to crop failure
d) Indigo plantation

50. Assertion (A): The partition of India led to large-scale violence and mass migration.
Reason (R): The boundaries were drawn hastily and without adequate understanding of ground realities.
a) Both A and R are true and R is the correct explanation of A
b) Both A and R are true but R is not the correct explanation of A
c) A is true but R is false
d) A is false butb R is true

Scan The QR Code To Get Answers With Detailed Explanations!

CUET UG MOCK TEST – 9

1. Who among the following was the author of the Arthashastra?
a) Patanjali
b) Kautilya
c) Kalidasa
d) Panini

The most distinctive feature of Harappan cities was the presence of:
a) Monumental temples
b) Planned drainage system
c) Palaces
d) Rock-cut caves

Fill in the blank: The ruler who adopted the title Devanampiya Piyadassi was _________.
a) Chandragupta Maurya
b) Harshavardhana
c) Ashoka
d) Bindusara

Assertion (A): Buddhist monasteries became centres of learning.
Reason (R): They were located in urban trading centres.
a) Both A and R are true and R is the correct explanation of A
b) Both A and R are true but R is not the correct explanation of A
c) A is true but R is false
d) A is false but R is true

What was the primary purpose of the Great Bath at Mohenjodaro believed to be?
a) Storage of grain
b) Religious ritual
c) Public performance
d) Royal entertainment

The Prashastis were written by:
a) Merchants
b) Poets in praise of kings
c) Farmers
d) Monks

Fill in the blank: Sutta Pitaka is a part of the sacred texts of _________.
a) Jainism
b) Shaivism
c) Buddhism
d) Vaishnavism

Which one of these is a Harappan site located in present-day Gujarat?
a) Kalibangan
b) Rakhigarhi
c) Dholavira
d) Banawali

9. The Satavahanas ruled primarily over:
a) Northern India
b) North-East India
c) Deccan region
d) Kashmir Valley

10. Assertion (A): Women were not allowed to study the Vedas in early Vedic society.
Reason (R): Patriarchal norms dominated the Brahmanical system.
a) Both A and R are true and R is the correct explanation of A
b) Both A and R are true but R is not the correct explanation of A
c) A is true but R is false
d) A is false but R is true

11. he Harappan script was mostly inscribed on:
a) Palm leaves
b) Copper plates
c) Seals and terracotta tablets
d) Rock surfaces

12. Fill in the blank: Ashoka's inscriptions were written in _________ in most regions.
a) Sanskrit
b) Prakrit
c) Tamil
d) Pali

13. The Gahapati in early historical India referred to a:
a) King
b) Slave
c) Householder or master of a household
d) Merchant guild head

14. Who among the following was not associated with Buddhist philosophical debates?
a) Nagarjuna
b) Vasubandhu
c) Charvaka
d) Ashvaghosha

15. The Mahajanapadas emerged during which period?
a) Harappan age
b) Vedic age
c) 6th century BCE
d) Gupta period

16.Match the following:
A. Sanchi – 1. Buddhist Stupa
B. Lothal – 2. Dockyard
C. Kausambi – 3. Urban centre with punch-marked coins
D. Brahmi – 4. Script used in Ashokan edicts

a) A-1, B-2, C-3, D-4
b) A-2, B-1, C-4, D-3
c) A-1, B-3, C-2, D-4
d) A-3, B-2, C-4, D-1

17. Fill in the blank: The Rigveda is composed in _________.
a) Prakrit
b) Sanskrit
c) Tamil
d) Pali

18. The term 'Jatakas' refers to:
a) Jain law books
b) Stories about the previous births of Buddha
c) Vedic hymns
d) Puranic genealogies

19. Assertion (A): Brahmanical texts often emphasized patriliny.
Reason (R): Inheritance was generally passed through the female line.
a) Both A and R are true and R is the correct explanation of A
b) Both A and R are true but R is not the correct explanation of A
c) A is true but R is false
d) A is false but R is true

20. According to Buddhist tradition, after enlightenment, Buddha delivered his first sermon at:
a) Bodh Gaya
b) Lumbini
c) Sarnath
d) Kushinagar

21. The Sufi practice of visiting the dargah of a saint is known as:
a) Ziyarat
b) Namaz
c) Hajj
d) Fatiha

22. The sacred tank at Hampi was located near the temple of:
a) Virupaksha
b) Ranganatha
c) Vitthala
d) Meenakshi

23. Assertion (A): Mughal paintings were an important part of court culture.
Reason (R): Paintings were used to depict imperial ideologies and glorify the emperor.
a) Both A and R are true and R is the correct explanation of A
b) Both A and R are true but R is not the correct explanation of A
c) A is true but R is false
d) A is false but R is true

24. The Bhakti poet known for composing Ramcharitmanas was:
a) Surdas
b) Kabir
c) Tulsidas
d) Tukaram

25. The Mughal emperor who commissioned the Shah Jahan Nama was:
a) Akbar
b) Jahangir
c) Shah Jahan
d) Aurangzeb

26. Which of the following cities was developed as the imperial capital by Krishnadeva Raya?
a) Vijayanagara
b) Delhi
c) Madurai
d) Bijapur

27. Assertion (A): Abul Fazl played a major role in crafting Akbar's image as an ideal ruler.
Reason (R): He was a military general and led campaigns in the Deccan.
a) Both A and R are true and R is the correct explanation of A
b) Both A and R are true but R is not the correct explanation of A
c) A is true but R is false
d) A is false but R is true

28. Francois Bernier viewed Indian society as lacking:
a) Trade networks
b) Scientific temper
c) Social mobility
d) Military strength

29. Kabir's poems reflect a synthesis of:
a) Islamic and Jain philosophies
b) Sufi and Bhakti ideas
c) Vedic and Tantric traditions
d) Christian and Hindu beliefs

30. The Mughal source that systematically recorded administrative and statistical details of the empire was:
a) Baburnama
b) Shah Jahan Nama
c) Akbarnama
d) Ain-i Akbari

31. The term 'mandapa' in temple architecture refers to:
a) Temple tower
b) Sanctum sanctorum
c) Pillared hall
d) Water tank

32. The Portuguese traveler Duarte Barbosa mainly wrote about:
a) North Indian temples
b) Coastal trade and markets
c) Mughal military campaigns
d) Hindu rituals

33. Assertion (A): The Bhakti-Sufi movements helped in spreading regional languages.
Reason (R): They preached in Sanskrit and Persian to reach the masses.
a) Both A and R are true and R is the correct explanation of A
b) Both A and R are true but R is not the correct explanation of A
c) A is true but R is false
d) A is false but R is true

34. The Mughal emperor most associated with court chroniclers and painters was:
a) Aurangzeb
b) Babur
c) Jahangir
d) Humayun

35. Match the following:
I. Kabir — A. Bijak
II. Abul Fazl — B. Ain-i Akbari
III. Francois Bernier — C. Travels in the Mughal Empire
IV. Krishnadeva Raya — D. Amuktamalyada

a) I-A, II-B, III-C, IV-D
b) I-C, II-D, III-A, IV-B
c) I-D, II-A, III-B, IV-C
d) I-B, II-C, III-D, IV-A

36. The Indigo Revolt of 1859-60 was primarily led by:
a) Zamindars
b) British planters
c) Peasants
d) Factory workers

37. The Revolt of 1857 began in which of the following places?
a) Lucknow
b) Jhansi
c) Delhi
d) Meerut

38. The capital city of colonial India that showcased British architectural influence was:
a) Calcutta
b) Madras
c) Bombay
d) New Delhi

39. The idea of 'Swaraj' by Gandhi implied:
a) Complete British withdrawal
b) Self-rule by Indians
c) Installation of a monarchy
d) Rule by zamindars

40. The Constituent Assembly adopted the Constitution of India on:
a) 15 August 1947
b) 26 January 1948
c) 26 November 1949
d) 30 January 1950

41. Fill in the blank: The __________ movement was Gandhi's first mass civil disobedience movement in India.
a) Civil Disobedience
b) Khilafat
c) Non-Cooperation
d) Quit India

42. Assertion (A): Urbanisation under British rule led to the growth of new cities.
Reason (R): The British promoted urban planning to ensure health and sanitation for Indian populations.
a) Both A and R are true and R is the correct explanation of A
b) Both A and R are true but R is not the correct explanation of A
c) A is true but R is false
d) A is false but R is true

43. The 'Drain of Wealth' theory was proposed by:
a) Dadabhai Naoroji
b) M.G. Ranade
c) R.C. Dutt
d) B.R. Ambedkar

44. The Constituent Assembly was formed in the year:
a) 1946
b) 1947
c) 1948
d) 1949

45. Which city was referred to as the "Second Capital of the British Empire"?
a) Madras
b) Delhi
c) Calcutta
d) Shimla

46. The Rowlatt Act of 1919 was opposed because it:
a) Imposed high taxes on peasants
b) Curtailed civil liberties
c) Allowed communal representation
d) Encouraged Indian industries

47. Fill in the blank: The __________ was the first major peasant uprising against British indigo planters.
a) Kheda Movement
b) Champaran Movement
c) Bardoli Satyagraha
d) Tebhaga Movement

48. Match the following:

List I.	List II
A. Jallianwala Bagh Massacre.	1947
B. Gandhi-Irwin Pact.	1946
C. Cabinet Mission Plan.	1931
D. Mountbatten Plan.	1919

a) A-4, B-3, C-2, D-1
b) A-3, B-4, C-1, D-2
c) A-1, B-2, C-3, D-4
d) A-2, B-1, C-4, D-3

49. Who among the following was NOT a member of the Constituent Assembly?
a) Dr. Rajendra Prasad
b) Jawaharlal Nehru
c) Muhammad Ali Jinnah
d) B.R. Ambedkar

50. Assertion (A): Gandhi's leadership marked a shift in Indian nationalism.
Reason (R): Gandhi involved industrialists and zamindars as the core of nationalist support.
a) Both A and R are true and R is the correct explanation of A
b) Both A and R are true but R is not the correct explanation of A
c) A is true but R is false
d) A is false but R is true

Scan The QR Code To Get Answers With Detailed Explanations!

CUET UG MOCK TEST – 10

1. Which of the following was a raw material used by Harappans for making beads?
   a) Lapis lazuli
   b) Bronze
   c) Iron
   d) Silver

2. Fill in the blank: The capital of the Mauryan Empire was _________.
   a) Ujjain
   b) Taxila
   c) Pataliputra
   d) Kausambi

3. Assertion (A): Harappan settlements were often located near sources of water.
   Reason (R): Water was essential for agriculture, trade, and daily use.
   a) Both A and R are true and R is the correct explanation of A
   b) Both A and R are true but R is not the correct explanation of A
   c) A is true but R is false
   d) A is false but R is true

4. Who among the following rulers issued inscriptions in Kharosthi script?
   a) Samudragupta
   b) Ashoka
   c) Kanishka
   d) Harshavardhana

5. Fill in the blank: The term 'grihapati' in early societies referred to the _________.
   a) Royal treasurer
   b) Vedic scholar
   c) Master of a household
   d) Head of a guild

6. The Buddhist Chaityas were primarily meant for:
   a) Residence
   b) Meditation and worship
   c) Debate
   d) Storage

7. What was found in large quantities in Harappa that suggests long-distance trade?
   a) Iron tools
   b) Seals
   c) Oil lamps
   d) Painted pottery

8. Assertion (A): Gotami-puta referred to herself as a bhikkhuni.
   Reason (R): Women were not allowed to enter the Sangha.
   a) Both A and R are true and R is the correct explanation of A
   b) Both A and R are true but R is not the correct explanation of A
   c) A is true but R is false
   d) A is false but R is true

9. The earliest coins in India were:
   a) Gold coins of Kushanas
   b) Gupta silver coins
   c) Indo-Greek coins
   d) Punch-marked coins

10. Fill in the blank: The Harappan site known for its water management and reservoir system is _________.
    a) Harappa
    b) Mohenjodaro
    c) Dholavira
    d) Lothal

11. Who was the famous Indo-Greek ruler who adopted Buddhism?
    a) Menander
    b) Antiochus
    c) Alexander
    d) Seleucus

12. Which ancient Indian text contains rules about kinship and caste?
    a) Manusmriti
    b) Rigveda
    c) Ramayana
    d) Jataka

13. The elaborate Buddhist stupa at Sanchi was built during the reign of:
    a) Ashoka
    b) Chandragupta I
    c) Harshavardhana
    d) Kanishka

14. Fill in the blank: Upanishads are primarily known for their focus on _________.
    a) Rituals and sacrifices
    b) Mythological stories
    c) Philosophical concepts
    d) Laws of the king

15. Assertion (A): Mahajanapadas were 16 large states during the 6th century BCE.
    Reason (R): The growth of iron tools and agriculture led to their emergence.
    a) Both A and R are true and R is the correct explanation of A
    b) Both A and R are true but R is not the correct explanation of A
    c) A is true but R is false
    d) A is false but R is true

16. Match the following:
    A. Brahmi - 1. Ancient script used in Ashokan edicts
    B. Harappa - 2. First Indus Valley site discovered
    C. Prakrit - 3. Language used in inscriptions of Ashoka
    D. Sangha - 4. Buddhist monastic community

    a) A-1, B-2, C-3, D-4
    b) A-2, B-1, C-4, D-3
    c) A-3, B-2, C-1, D-4
    d) A-1, B-3, C-2, D-4

17. Fill in the blank: According to Buddhist tradition, Tripitaka was compiled in the language _________.
    a) Sanskrit
    b) Pali
    c) Tamil
    d) Prakrit

18. Which one of these women was a prominent Buddhist lay follower and donor?
    a) Amrapali
    b) Maitreyi
    c) Gargi
    d) Sulabha

19. The term 'dhamma' as used by Ashoka referred to:
a) Buddhist doctrine
b) Moral law for harmonious living
c) Vedic sacrifice
d) Royal taxes

20. The name of the priest-king sculpture was given to a figure found at:
a) Kalibangan
b) Harappa
c) Mohenjodaro
d) Lothal

21. Kabir believed in a formless God and rejected:
a) Vedas and Upanishads
b) Temple worship and caste distinctions
c) Agricultural rituals
d) Warfare and weapons

22. The principal deity worshipped in the Virupaksha temple at Hampi is:
a) Krishna
b) Vishnu
c) Shiva
d) Brahma

23. Assertion (A): Travellers like Ibn Battuta and Bernier provided important insights into Indian society.
   Reason (R): They were official chroniclers of the Mughal Empire.
a) Both A and R are true and R is the correct explanation of A
b) Both A and R are true but R is not the correct explanation of A
c) A is true but R is false
d) A is false but R is true

24. The term sulh-i kul means:
a) Victory in battle
b) Agricultural tax
c) Peace with all
d) Religious conversion

25. The Mughal emperor who imposed jizya tax on non-Muslims in 1679 was:
a) Babur
b) Akbar
c) Jahangir
d) Aurangzeb

26. One of the key architectural features of Vijayanagara temples is the:
a) Pyramid dome
b) Gopuram
c) Stupa
d) Minaret

27. Assertion (A): Sufis believed in renouncing materialism.
   Reason (R): They thought spiritual closeness to God could be attained through poverty and devotion.
a) Both A and R are true and R is the correct explanation of A
b) Both A and R are true but R is not the correct explanation of A
c) A is true but R is false
d) A is false but R is true

28. Ain-i Akbari was compiled by:
a) Akbar
b) Badauni
c) Abul Fazl
d) Bernier

29. The saint who composed Amuktamalyada in Telugu was:
a) Tulsidas
b) Krishnadeva Raya
c) Alvars
d) Kabir

30. Which of the following was not a part of the Mughal court culture?
a) Court paintings
b) Persian chronicles
c) Republican decision-making
d) Ceremonial gatherings

31. Ibn Battuta was a traveller from:
a) Turkey
b) France
c) Morocco
d) Portugal

32. Kabir's verses are compiled in which of the following texts?
a) Akbarnama
b) Bijak
c) Baburnama
d) Ain-i Akbari

33. Assertion (A): Hampi flourished as a centre of trade and culture.
   Reason (R): Its strategic location helped control inland and coastal trade routes.
a) Both A and R are true and R is the correct explanation of A
b) Both A and R are true but R is not the correct explanation of A
c) A is true but R is false
d) A is false but R is true

34. The Bhakti saint who emphasized Nirguna bhakti (devotion without attributes) was:
a) Mirabai
b) Tulsidas
c) Kabir
d) Surdas

35. Francois Bernier's writings suggested that Mughal India lacked:
a) Gold reserves
b) Scientific thinking
c) Private property rights
d) Urban centres

36. The Champaran Satyagraha was related to the problems faced by:
a) Salt workers
b) Indigo cultivators
c) Factory workers
d) Cotton farmers

37. The idea of Separate Electorates for Muslims was first introduced by:
a) Simon Commission
b) Government of India Act, 1935
c) Morley-Minto Reforms
d) Cripps Mission

38. The Partition of Bengal took place in the year:
a) 1905
b) 1947
c) 1919
d) 1935

39. The Constituent Assembly debates were published as:
a) The People's Constitution
b) The Draft Constitution
c) Constituent Assembly Debates
d) The Final Constitution

40. Fill in the blank: The colonial state often used __________ as a tool of control and surveillance in rural areas.
a) Railways
b) Archives
c) Zamindars
d) Police Stations

41. Assertion (A): British officials created detailed land records in rural India.
Reason (R): This helped them extract higher land revenues and control agrarian relations.
a) Both A and R are true and R is the correct explanation of A
b) Both A and R are true but R is not the correct explanation of A
c) A is true but R is false
d) A is false but R is true

42. The Revolt of 1857 was referred to by the British as:
a) Civil War
b) Indian Freedom Movement
c) Sepoy Mutiny
d) Peasant Uprising

43. Who among the following wrote "The Discovery of India"?
a) M.K. Gandhi
b) B.R. Ambedkar
c) Jawaharlal Nehru
d) Rajendra Prasad

44. The British built New Delhi primarily as:
a) A center for Indian commerce
b) A strategic military location
c) A symbol of imperial power
d) A site of pilgrimage

45. Fill in the blank: Mahatma Gandhi first applied satyagraha in India at ________.
a) Champaran
b) Ahmedabad
c) Kheda
d) Bardoli

46. Which of the following was a major feature of colonial urban planning?
a) Displacement of Indian population
b) Promotion of cottage industries
c) Agricultural zoning
d) Inclusion of Indian heritage sites

47. The INA (Indian National Army) was led by:
a) Bhagat Singh
b) Mangal Pandey
c) Subhas Chandra Bose
d) Lala Lajpat Rai

48. Match the following:

List I.	List II
A. 1857 Revolt.	1885
B. Formation of Indian National Congress.	1915
C. Partition of India.	1857
D. Gandhi's return to India.	1947

a) A-3, B-1, C-4, D-2
b) A-4, B-3, C-1, D-2
c) A-2, B-4, C-1, D-3
d) A-1, B-2, C-3, D-4

49. The term "Divide and Rule" was associated with British:
a) Revenue policies
b) Political strategy
c) Military tactics
d) Economic planning

50. Assertion (A): Gandhi called for the Quit India Movement in 1942.
Reason (R): The Cripps Mission had failed and World War II was intensifying.
a) Both A and R are true and R is the correct explanation of A
b) Both A and R are true but R is not the correct explanation of A
c) A is true but R is false
d) A is false but R is true

Scan The QR Code To Get Answers With Detailed Explanations!

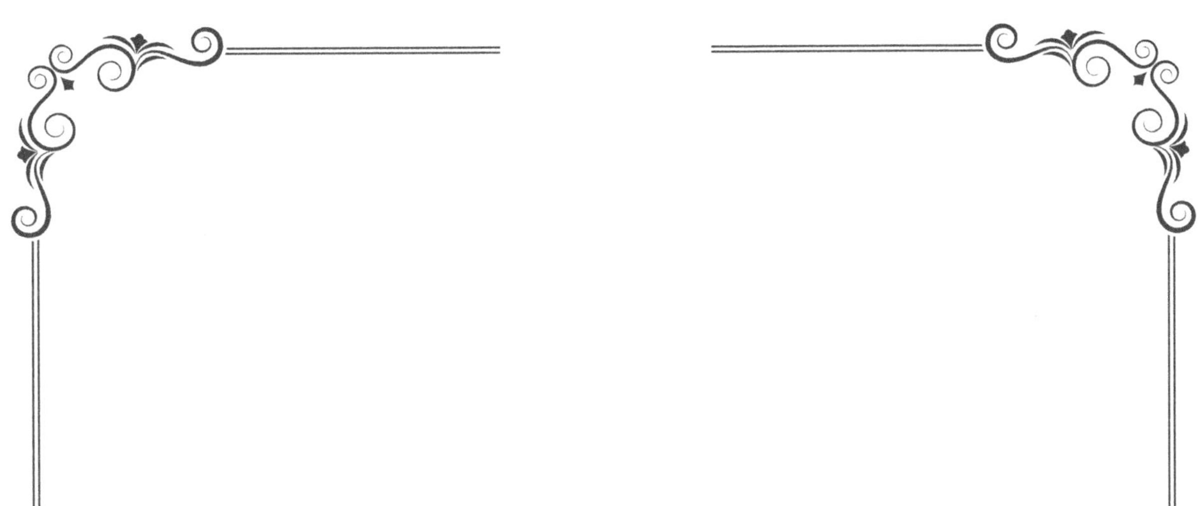

CHAPTERWISE ANSWER KEY
WITH DETAILED EXPLANATIONS

Chapter 1 : Bricks Beads And Bones

Question 1 : (b) is correct
Explanation : Harappan civilisation is also known as the Indus Valley Civilisation because it developed along the Indus River and its tributaries.

Question 2 : (c) is correct
Explanation : The most distinctive artefact of the Harappan civilisation is the seal, often made of steatite and engraved with animals and script.

Question 3 : (d) is correct
Explanation : Harappan seals were typically made of steatite, a soft stone that was easy to carve and then hardened by heating.

Question 4 : (a) is correct
Explanation : The mature phase of the Harappan civilisation is dated from approximately 2600 BCE to 1900 BCE.

Question 5 : (d) is correct
Explanation : Harappan culture is known for its use of seals, beads, weights, and baked bricks—showing advanced craftsmanship and planning.

Question 6 : (b) is correct
Explanation : There are a total of 65 known Harappan sites in the Sind region of present-day Pakistan.

Question 7 : (a) is correct
Explanation : Specialists who study ancient plant remains are called archaeo-botanists, helping reconstruct past agricultural practices.

Question 8 : (a) is correct
Explanation : Millets have been found at several Harappan sites in Gujarat, indicating early knowledge of dryland farming.

Question 9 : (d) is correct
Explanation : A variety of grains like wheat, barley, and chickpeas have been discovered at Harappan archaeological sites.

Question 10 : (d) is correct
Explanation : Both archaeo-zoologists and zoo-archaeologists specialize in studying ancient animal remains to understand past environments and diets.

Question 11 : (c) is correct
Explanation : Statements (i), (ii), and (iv) are correct. Harappans consumed a wide range of plant and animal products, archaeologists studied dietary practices through charred remains, and domesticated animals' bones were found. Statement (iii) is incorrect as archaeo-zoologists study animal remains, not plant remains.

Question 12 : (c) is correct
Explanation : Terracotta models of ploughs have been found at both Cholistan and Banawali, providing insights into Harappan agricultural practices.

Question 13 : (d) is correct
Explanation : Evidence of a ploughed field has been found at Kalibangan, showing an advanced understanding of agriculture.

Question 14 : (a) is correct
Explanation : Both the assertion and the reason are true, and the reason correctly explains that the two sets of furrows at right angles suggest two crops were grown together.

Question 15 : (c) is correct
Explanation : Traces of canals used for irrigation have been found at Shortughai, a Harappan site in present-day Afghanistan.

Question 16 : (d) is correct
Explanation : Shortughai is a Harappan outpost located in present-day Afghanistan, indicating the civilisation's wide trade network.

Question 17 : (d) is correct
Explanation : Dholavira, in Gujarat, is known for its sophisticated water reservoir system, a unique feature among Harappan sites.

Question 18 : (b) is correct
Explanation : Most Harappan sites are located in semi-arid lands, which influenced their water conservation and irrigation strategies.

Question 19 : (a) is correct
Explanation : The most unique feature of the Harappan civilisation was it's development of urban centres .

Question 20 : (c) is correct
Explanation : Mohenjodaro is the most well-known site of the Harappan Civilisation, famous for its urban layout, Great Bath, and advanced infrastructure.

Question 21 : (d) is correct
Explanation : Alexander Cunningham is known as the father of Indian Archaeology due to his pioneering work in documenting and excavating ancient Indian sites.

Question 22 : (b) is correct
Explanation : The carefully planned drainage system was the most distinctive feature of Harappan cities, showing their advanced urban planning.

Question 23 : (b) is correct
Explanation : The Lower Town at Mohenjodaro was the residential area where common people lived, in contrast to the Citadel.

Question 24 : (a) is correct
Explanation : Scholars estimate that there were about 700 wells in Mohenjodaro.

Question 25 : (c) is correct
Explanation : The Great Bath, a significant public structure, was discovered at Mohenjodaro and is considered one of the most remarkable features of the site.

Question 26 : (b) is correct
Explanation : John Marshall, as the Director-General of the ASI, officially announced the discovery of the Indus Valley Civilisation in the 1920s.

Question 27 : (a) is correct
Explanation : Both the assertion and reason are true, and the reason correctly explains that the Citadel (higher part) was built on a raised platform.

Question 28 : (a) is correct
Explanation : Mohenjodaro is often referred to as the "Mound of the Dead" due to its name's meaning and archaeological findings.

Question 29 : (a) is correct
Explanation : Both the assertion and reason are true, and the presence of grave goods like ornaments and pottery suggests a belief in an afterlife.

Question 30 : (a) is correct
Explanation : Archaeologists use burial practices and artefact analysis to determine social and economic differences, making the reason a valid explanation.

Question 31: (d) is correct
Explanation: All the statements about the Great Bath are accurate. It was located in the Citadel, had a rectangular tank with steps on both ends, was surrounded by corridors, and likely used for ritual bathing.

Question 32: (c) is correct
Explanation: The assertion is true — artefacts are divided into utilitarian and luxury types. But the reason is false — utilitarian artefacts were made from everyday materials, not costly or non-local ones.

Question 33: (a) is correct
Explanation: Chanhudaro was a small Harappan site devoted entirely to craft production including bead-making, shell cutting, metalwork, and more.

Question 34: (d) is correct
Explanation: All the statements are correct about beads — their material, variety, and shape show the artistic and cultural richness of the Harappan civilization.

Question 35: (c) is correct
Explanation: Pots of faience were made from a glazed, non-local material and were considered luxury objects. Sickle and quern were utilitarian.

Question 36: (c) is correct
Explanation: Shortughai is the only site listed that lies outside present-day India: it's in northern Afghanistan.

Question 37: (a) is correct
Explanation: Nageshwar and Balakot were coastal Harappan settlements, known for shell-working and marine trade.

Question 38: (d) is correct
Explanation: Lapis lazuli was sourced mainly from Shortughai in Afghanistan, an important trade partner of the Harappans.

Question 39:
I) Nageshwar and Balakot → b) shells

II) Khetri region of Rajasthan → d) Copper

III) South India → a) Gold

IV) Bharuch in Gujarat → c) Carnelian

Question 40: (d) is correct
Explanation: Steatite is a very soft stone used widely in Harappan seals and beads due to its ease of carving.

Question 41: (b) Khetri
Explanation: Khetri in Rajasthan is associated with the Ganeshwar-Jodhpura culture, known for its early copper artefacts and links to Harappan civilization.

Question 42: (a) Waterways
Explanation: Harappans used waterways (rivers and sea routes) for long-distance and inter-country trade, including with Mesopotamia and Oman.

Question 43: (b) Oman
Explanation: Mesopotamian texts refer to Magan as a source of copper, which most scholars identify with modern-day Oman.

Question 44: (b) Bahrain
Explanation: The region of Dilmun mentioned in Mesopotamian texts is widely believed to be Bahrain, which was a trading hub.

Question 45: (b) Harappan Region
Explanation: The Mesopotamian name Meluhha refers to the Harappan region, high
lighting their trade relationship.

Question 46: (a) Seafarers
Explanation: Meluhha was described as a land of seafarers, indicating that Harappans engaged in overseas maritime trade.

Question 47: (a) Chert
Explanation: Harappan weights were made from chert, a type of hard stone, and followed a binary system for precise trade regulat
ion.

Question 48: (a) Priest King

Question 49 : (d) All of the above are correct
Explanation:
Seals were used for communication (i)
They often included names/titles (ii)
The script was right to left (iii)
It had 375-400 signs (iv)

Question 50 : (b) Deadman Lane
Explanation: A narrow alley between 3 to 6 feet wide is often referred to as a Deadman Lane in archaeological and historical contexts.

Question 51 : (d) R.E.M. Wheeler
Explanation: "My Archaeological Mission to India and Pakistan" was written by Sir Mortimer Wheeler (R.E.M. Wheeler), who conducted extensive excavations post-Independence.

Question 52 : (c) Bull
Explanation: The image (not shown here) likely refers to the "Unicorn Bull" seal, one of the most iconic Harappan seals.

Question 53 : (c) Stratigraphy
Explanation: The study of layers in archaeological sites is called stratigraphy, which helps date artefacts based on depth and sequence.

Question 54 : (c) S.N. Roy
Explanation: S.N. Roy authored "The Story of Indian Archaeology", providing a detailed account of its development and key discoveries.

Question 55 : (a) R.E.M. Wheeler
Explanation: In 1944, R.E.M. Wheeler, an ex-army brigadier, became Director-General of ASI and introduced systematic excavation techniques.

Question 56 : (d) Mother Goddess
Explanation: Based on the likely image, the answer is Mother Goddess, a terracotta figurine found in Harappan sites symbolizing fertility.

Question 57 : (c) 1970
Explanation: R.E.M. Wheeler wrote "My Archaeological Mission to India and Pakistan" in 1970.

Question 58 : (c) Rudra
Explanation: Rudra is the name of Shiva used in Vedic and early Puranic traditions.

Question 59 : (a) Proto-Shiva
Explanation: The image likely refers to the "Pashupati Seal" found at Mohenjodaro, interpreted by some as Proto-Shiva seated in yogic posture

Question 60 : (c) Unicorn
Explanation : the one-horned animal, often called the "unicorn" – depicted on seals seem to be mythical, composite creatures

Question 61 : (c) shamans
Explanation : Shamans are men and women who claim magical and healing powers, as well as an ability to communicate with the other world.

Chapter 2 : Kings, Farmers and Towns

Question 1 : (a) is correct
Explanation: Epigraphy is the study of inscriptions engraved on materials like stone or metal.

Question 2 : (c) is correct
Explanation: James Prinsep was the officer of the East India Company who deciphered the Brahmi and Kharosthi scripts.

Question 3 : (c) is correct
Explanation: The two earliest scripts used in inscriptions and coins were Brahmi and Kharosthi.

Question 4 : (a) is correct
Explanation: Piyadassi means "pleasant to behold" and was used as a title by Emperor Ashoka.

Question 5 : (b) is correct
Explanation: The earliest inscriptions were written in Prakrit, a common language in ancient India.

Question 6 : (c) is correct
Explanation: Inscriptions refer to writings engraved on hard surfaces such as stone, metal, or pottery.

Question 7 : (d) is correct
Explanation: Megaliths are large stones placed over graves, especially in central and south India, used in burial practices.

Question 8 : (d) is correct
Explanation: Palaeography is the study of ancient styles of writing.

Question 9 : (c) is correct
Explanation: Oligarchy refers to a form of government where power is held by a small group of men.

Question 10 : (d) is correct
Explanation: Magadh was the most powerful Mahajanapada from the 6th to 4th century BCE due to its strong military and administration.

Question 11 : (c) is correct
Explanation: Both statements are correct. The sixth century BCE marks a significant historical turning point with the emergence of states, cities, iron use, coinage, and new philosophies like Buddhism and Jainism.

Question 12 : (a) is correct
Explanation: There were 16 Mahajanapadas as mentioned in ancient Buddhist and Jain texts.

Question 13 : (d) is correct
Explanation: Awadh was not a Mahajanapada: the others like Avanti, Panchala, and Kosala were among the 16 Mahajanapadas.

Question 14 : (c) is correct
Explanation: Dharmasutras were ancient Sanskrit texts composed by Brahmanas to codify social and moral rules.

Question 15 : (c) is correct
Explanation: Ashoka, the Mauryan emperor, won the Battle of Kalinga and later embraced Buddhism due to the immense bloodshed.

Question 16 : (a) is correct
Explanation: The original capital of Magadha was Rajagaha (modern-day Rajgir in Bihar).

Question 17 : (d) is correct
Explanation: Later, the capital of Magadha was shifted to Pataliputra (modern-day Patna) for better administration and strategic advantage.

Question 18 : (c) is correct
Explanation: This statement is incorrect. Magadha was not near the sea: it was inland. Hence, it wasn't a sea-trade hub. The other reasons contributed to its growth.

Question 19 : (d) is correct
Explanation: Chandragupta Maurya was the founder of the Mauryan Empire with help from Chanakya/Kautilya.

Question 20 : (b) is correct
Explanation: Megasthenes was the Greek ambassador in Chandragupta Maurya's court and author of Indica.

Question 21 : (c) is correct
Explanation: Kautilya (also known as Chanakya) is the author of Arthashastra, an ancient Indian treatise on statecraft, economic policy, and military strategy.

Question 22 : (a) is correct
Explanation: The special officers appointed by Ashoka to spread the message of Dhamma were called Dhamma Mahamatta.

Question 23 : (c) is correct
Explanation: The Ashokan inscriptions were written in Prakrit, Aramaic, and Greek to reach a wider audience across his empire.

Question 24 : (b) is correct
Explanation: Indica is the book written by the Greek ambassador Megasthenes during his stay at the court of Chandragupta Maurya.

Question 25 : (c) is correct
Explanation: All statements are correct. There were five major political centers in the Mauryan Empire, Megasthenes wrote Indica, and mentions a committee for military activities. Ashoka propagated dhamma to maintain unity.

Question 26 : (d) is correct
Explanation: Shakas, a people of Central Asian origin, established kingdoms in the north-western and western parts of the Indian subcontinent

Question 27 : (a) is correct
Explanation: Silappadikaram is a Tamil epic written in the classical Tamil language, considered one of the five great epics of Tamil literature.

Question 28 : (c) is correct
Explanation: The Cholas, Cheras, and Pandyas were the major Tamil kingdoms, covering regions of present-day Andhra Pradesh, Kerala, and Tamil Nadu.

Question 29 : (b) is correct
Explanation: Kushana rulers adopted the title Devaputra, meaning "son of the god," as part of their royal titulary.

Question 30 : (b) is correct
Explanation: Prayaga Prashasti is also known as the Allahabad Pillar inscription, which is a significant source of historical information about the Gupta period.

Question 31 : (a) is correct
Explanation: The Prayaga Prashasti (also known as the Allahabad Pillar Inscription) was composed in Sanskrit.

Question 32 : (a) is correct
Explanation: Harishena, the court poet, composed the Prayaga Prashasti in Sanskrit under the patronage of King Samudragupta.

Question 33 : (b) is correct
Explanation: According to the rock inscription of Sudarshan Lake, an artificial reservoir was repaired by King Rudradaman.

Question 34 : (a) is correct
Explanation: The Jatakas were written in Pali, and they are a collection of stories about the previous lives of the Buddha.

Question 35 : (b) is correct
Explanation: The Gandatindu Jataka describes the plight of the subjects under a wicked king, including elderly women, men, cultivators, herders, village boys, and even animals.

Question 36 : (d) is correct
Explanation: All the statements (I, II, III, IV) are correct. They highlight various strategies for increasing agricultural production, such as the use of iron-tipped ploughshares, transplantation, irrigation, and royal support recorded in inscriptions.

Question 37 : (c) is correct
Explanation: Gahapati refers to the head of a household, not an official of the king. They were typically landowners or wealthy individuals who owned resources like land and animals.

Question 38 : (b) is correct
Explanation: In Tamil Sangam literature, slaves were referred to as Adimai.

Question 39 : (d) is correct
Explanation: In Tamil Sangam literature, large landowners were referred to as Vellalar.

Question 40 : (c) is correct
Explanation: Harshacharita is the biography of Harshavardhana, written by his court poet Banabhatta.

Question 41 : (c) is correct
Explanation: Harshacharita was composed by Banabhatta, a court poet of King Harshavardhana.

Question 42 : (a) is correct
Explanation: Harshavardhana was the ruler of Kanauj.

Question 43 : (b) is correct
Explanation: Prabhavati Gupta was the daughter of Chandragupta II.

Question 44 : (c) is correct
Explanation: Ashoka was the first ruler to inscribe his messages on stone surfaces, including natural rocks and polished pillars.

Question 45 : (d) is correct
Explanation: Gahapati was the owner, master, or head of a household.

Question 46 : (a) is correct
Explanation: An Agrahara was a land granted to a Brahmin, usually exempted from paying land revenue and other dues to the king.

Question 47 : (a) is correct
Explanation: The Chinese pilgrim Xuanzang visited Pat aliputra in the 7th century.

Question 48 : (b) is correct
Explanation: Suvarnagiri literally means Golden Mountain, and it was important for tapping the gold mines of Karnataka.

Question 49 : (b) is correct
Explanation: The correct match is:
i) Pataliputra – b) riverine routes
ii) Ujjayini – d) near coast sea routes
iii) Puhar – c) bustling centres
iv) Mathura – a) land routes

Question 50 : (a) is correct
Explanation: The guilds of the merchants and craftsmen were called Shrenis.

Question 51: (d) is correct
Explanation: Periplus in Greek means sailing around. It refers to a maritime voyage or journey around coastal regions.

Question 52: (a) is correct
Explanation: Erythraean was the Greek name for the Red Sea.

Question 53: (c) is correct
Explanation: The first gold coin was issued in the first century CE by the Kushanas.

Question 54: (a) is correct
 Explanation: The spectacular gold coins, which facilitated long–distance transactions, were issued by the Kushanas.

Question 55: (c) is correct
Explanation: The study of coins is known as Numismatics.

Question 56: (d) is correct
Explanation: The Yaudheyas belonged to both Haryana and Punjab.

Question 57: (b) is correct
Explanation: James Princep was able to decipher Ashokan Brahmi in 1828.

Question 58: (d) is correct
Explanation: Both inscriptions and coins are used as archaeological sources to reconstruct ancient Indian history.

Question 59: (b) is correct
 Explanation: Ashoka is mentioned by the titles Devanampiya and Piyadassi in his inscriptions.

Question 60: (d) is correct
 Explanation: Archaeologists faced all of the above problems while deciphering inscriptions, including faint letters, damaged letters, and the exact meaning of words.

Question 61: The correct answer is (c) ii & iii
 Explanation: A chief's position is usually hereditary (statement ii).
Generally, chiefdoms did not have regular armies and officials (statement iii), which makes this statement incorrect.

Question 62 : (a) Sandstone sculpture of Kushana King

Question 63 : (b) Mathura
Explanation : The gift of an image This is part of an image from Mathura. On the pedestal is a
Prakrit inscription, mentioning That a woman named Nagapiya, the wife of a goldsmith (sovanika) named Dharmaka, installed this image in a shrine.

Chapter 3 : Kinship, Caste and Class

Question 1: (d) is correct

Explanation: The Rigveda provides the earliest and most comprehensive insights into the social categories and kinship structures in early Indian society.

Question 2: (c) is correct

Explanation: V.S. Sukthankar led the project to prepare the Critical Edition of the Mahabharata in 1919.

Question 3: (c) is correct

Explanation: According to the Dharmashastras, Shudras were assigned the occupation of servitude.

Question 4: (c) is correct

Explanation: Patriliny refers to the lineage traced through the father.

Question 5: (b) is correct

Explanation: The Manusmriti prescribes eight forms of marriage, with the first four considered "good."

Question 6: (a) is correct

Explanation: Both assertions are true, and the reason explains the assertion that Satavahana rulers identified themselves through matronymics, as regional variations to Brahmanical patriliny existed.

Question 7: (a) is correct

Explanation: Both assertions are true, and the reason explains that the didactic sections were likely added later to emphasize social norms in the Mahabharata.

Question 8: (c) is correct

Explanation: The term Kula was used in Sanskrit texts to refer to the larger network of kinfolk.

Question 9: (b) is correct

Explanation: In the Majjhima Nikaya, King Avantiputta and Kachchana discuss social distinctions based on birth.

Question 10: (c) is correct

Explanation: B.B. Lal excavated Hastinapura in 1951-52, believed to be the capital of the Kuru kingdom.

Question 11: (b) is correct

Explanation: The Manusmriti is considered the most important Dharmashastra, compiled between c. 200 BCE and 200 CE.

Question 12: (c) is correct

Explanation: The Mahabharata describes the feud over land and power between the Kauravas and Pandavas.

Question 13: (c) is correct

Explanation: The Purusha Sukta of the Rigveda claims that the varna system originated from different parts of the cosmic being Purusha.

Question 14: (a) is correct

Explanation: Siri-Satakani, a Satavahana ruler, is known for claiming the title "Eka Bamhana" (Unique Brahmana).

Question 15: (a) is correct

Explanation: Both assertions are true, and the reason explains that the Mahabharata evolved through oral traditions before being written down by Brahmanas.

Question 16: (a) is correct

Explanation: Both assertions are true, and the reason explains that the practice of kanyadana reinforced patriarchal control over marriage alliances.

Question 17: (b) is correct

Explanation: The Mahabharata describes a marriage system called Polyandry, where one woman marries multiple husbands.

Question 18: (b) is correct

Explanation: The excavation at Hastinapura by B.B. Lal found evidence of houses made of mud and mud-bricks in the second phase (c. 12th-7th century BCE).

Question 19: (b) is correct

Explanation: Kula was the term used in Sanskrit texts to designate families.

Question 20: (c) is correct

Explanation: The Mahabharata was considered an itihasa, which means a historical account.

Question 21: (c) is correct

Explanation: The Satavahanas were known for having women retain their father's gotra name instead of adopting their husband's gotra.

Question 22: (c) is correct

Explanation: Drona refused to teach archery to Ekalavya because he had already promised Arjuna that he would be the best archer.

Question 23: (a) is correct

Explanation: The Mahabharata was initially composed by charioteer-bards (sutas), and later taken over by Brahmanas and written down systematically.

Question 24: (b) is correct

Explanation: B.B. Lal's excavations at Hastinapura revealed houses with walls made of mud and mud-bricks during the second phase of settlement.

Question 25: (c) is correct

Explanation: In the Mahabharata, Yudhishthira is depicted as the eldest of the Pandava brothers.

Question 26: (c) is correct

Explanation: The term gotra was primarily associated with Brahmanas in early Indian texts.

Question 27: (b) is correct

Explanation: Brahmanical texts discouraged exogamy to maintain the purity of the varna system.

Question 28: (a) is correct
Explanation: The Mahabharata is classified under the genre of Itihasa, which is a historical narrative.

Question 29: (c) is correct
Explanation: The Satavahana rulers often used matronymics in their names, but this did not indicate a matrilineal system prevalent in their society.

Question 30: (b) is correct
Explanation: In the context of early Indian society, exogamy refers to the practice of marrying outside one's own gotra.

Question 31: (b) is correct
Explanation: The Mahabharata was traditionally attributed to the sage Vyasa, also known as Vedavyasa.

Question 32: (c) is correct
Explanation: Rudradaman is known to have rebuilt the Sudarshana Lake, as mentioned in inscriptions.

Question 33: (c) is correct
Explanation: The Critical Edition of the Mahabharata was led by V.S. Sukthankar and took 47 years to complete.

Question 34: (b) is correct
Explanation: According to the Manusmriti, Brahmanas were responsible for performing sacrifices and receiving gifts.

Question 35: (b) is correct
Explanation: The term Shreni refers to occupational guilds in early Indian society.

Question 36: (b) is correct
Explanation: The Mahabharata was composed over 1,000 years and had multiple contributors.

.Question 37: (c) is correct
Explanation: Kanyadana, where the bride is given as a gift to a groom, was considered the ideal form of marriage in Brahmanical texts.

Question 38: (d) is correct
Explanation: The unequal distribution of wealth, extension of agriculture into forested areas, and the emergence of craft specialists as distinct social groups all contributed to social differences in early Indian societies.

Question 39: (a) is correct
Explanation: The Mahabharata contained multiple versions and regional variations because it was orally transmitted for centuries before being written down

Question 40: (b) is correct
Explanation: Gandharva marriage involved a woman choosing her partner voluntarily, often without the involvement of family elders

Question 41: (a) is correct
Explanation: The Mahabharata was composed over a long period, reflecting multiple social ideas. The text contains both narrative and didactic sections, and these sections were added over centuries, making the reasoning correct as well.

Question 42: (a) is correct
Explanation: The Dharmashastras described Shudras as being restricted to servitude, but early Buddhist texts provide evidence that some Shudras accumulated wealth and gained social status, making the reasoning an accurate explanation of the assertion.

Question 43: (b) is correct
Explanation: The Manusmriti prescribed that chandalas should live in isolated settlements outside villages and cities, reinforcing their marginalization in society.

Question 44: (b) is correct
Explanation: According to the Mahabharata, Ekalavya was a Nishada by birth but mastered archery despite being denied formal training.

Question 45 : (d) 1,2 and 3
Explanation : The Manusmriti laid down the "duties" of the chandalas. They had to live outside the village, use discarded utensils, and wear clothes of the dead and ornaments of iron. They could not walk about in villages and cities at night. They had to dispose of the bodies of those who had no relatives and serve as executioners.

Question 46 : (c) Satvahana Ruler and his wife
Explanation : A Satavahana ruler and his wife This is one of the rare sculptural depictions of a ruler from the wall of a cave donated to Buddhist monks. This sculpture dates to c. second century BCE.

Question 47 : (b) Fa Xian
Explanation : Fa Xian (c. fifth century CE) wrote that "untouchables" had to sound a clapper in the streets so that people could avoid seeing them.

Question 48 : (c) As a generous man who helps bards despite not being very rich
Explanation: In the Purananuru, a classical Tamil poetic work, many poems describe patrons who are generous and kind-hearted, even if they are not extremely wealthy. The excerpt typically highlights the value of generosity over riches.

Chapter 4 : Thinkers, Beliefs and Buildings

Question 1: (b) Bhopal
Explanation: Sanchi is located near Bhopal in Madhya Pradesh, India, and is famous for its ancient Buddhist stupas and monuments.

Question 2: (d) Shahjehan Begum
Explanation: "Taj-ul-Iqbal Tarikh Bhopal" (A History of Bhopal) was translated by Shahjehan Begum, the Begum of Bhopal.

Question 3: (b) i-c, ii-d, iii-b, iv-a
Explanation: Zarathustra is associated with Iran, Plato and Aristotle with Greece, Kong zi (Confucius) with China, and Gautama Buddha with India.

Question 4: (a) Kutagrashala
Explanation: A hut with a pointed roof is known as Kutagrashala, commonly referred to in ancient Indian texts.

Question 5: (c) Vinaya Pitaka
Explanation: The Vinaya Pitaka includes the rules and regulations for those who joined the sangha or monastic order.

Question 6: (b) Sutta Pitaka
Explanation: The Sutta Pitaka contains Buddha's teachings, focusing on his discourses and teachings to his followers.

Question 7: (d) Iran
Explanation: Zarathustra (or Zoroaster) is a prophet from ancient Iran, and his teachings form the basis of Zoroastrianism.

Question 8: (d) Abhidhamma Pitaka
Explanation: The Abhidhamma Pitaka deals with philosophical matters, elaborating on the teachings of the Sutta Pitaka.

Question 9: (a) Vardhaman
Explanation: Mahavira, the 24th Tirthankara of Jainism, was born as Vardhaman

Question 10: (a) Agni, Indra, Soma
Explanation: The Rigveda consists of hymns in praise of various deities, including Agni, Indra, and Soma.

Question 11: (d) Fire
Explanation: Agni is the Vedic god of fire.

Question 12: (c) i, ii, iii are correct
Explanation: Jainism emphasizes that the world is animated, asceticism and penance are necessary for liberation, and non-injury (Ahimsa) to all living beings is central. Though Ahimsa is important in both Jainism and Buddhism, it is more deeply emphasized in Jainism.

Question 13: (a) Both A and R are true and R is the correct explanation of A
Explanation: Jaina monks and nuns took five vows, which include non-violence, truth, non-stealing, celibacy, and non-possession. The Reason correctly explains the Assertion.

Question 14: (d) A biography of saints and spiritual leaders
Explanation: Hagiography refers to writings or biographies about saints or religious/spiritual figures.
Question 15:

Question 15 : (a) Sakya
Explanation: Gautama Buddha's father, Śuddhodana, was the chief of the Sakya clan.

Question 16: (a) Lumbini
Explanation: Buddha was born in Lumbini, which is in present-day Nepal.

Question 17: (d) Mahapajapati Gotami
Explanation: She was the Buddha's foster mother and the first woman to be ordained as a Bhikkhuni (nun).

Question 18: (b) Buddha
Explanation: This quote is attributed to Buddha, encouraging self-reliance on the path to enlightenment.

Question 19: (d) Sarnath
Explanation: Buddha gave his first sermon at Sarnath, also known as the Dharmachakra Pravartana.

Question 20: (b) Bodh Gaya
Explanation: Buddha attained enlightenment under the Bodhi tree in Bodh Gaya.

Question 21: (b) China
Explanation : pilgrims such as Fa Xian and Xuan Zang travelled all the way from China to India in search of texts. These they
took back to their own country, where they were translated by scholars.

Question 22 :(b) Stupa
Explanation: Stupas were burial mounds that housed relics of the Buddha or items used by him.

Question 23 :(c) Buddhist
Explanation: Ashokavandana is a Sanskrit text associated with the Buddhist tradition, particularly related to Emperor Ashoka.

Question 24 : (b) Peshawar
Explanation: Shah-ji-ki-Dheri is an archaeological site near Peshawar, Pakistan, known for Buddhist remains.

Question 25 : (a) Harmika
Explanation: Harmika is a square railing-like structure atop a stupa that represents the abode of gods.

Question 26 : (c) Amaravati
Explanation: The Elliot Marbles are sculptures from Amaravati, now housed partly in the British Museum.

Question 27 : (b) H.H. Cole
Explanation: H.H. Cole criticized the removal of original ancient artworks from their sites, calling it "a suicidal and indefensible policy."

Question 28 : (c) Walter Elliot
Explanation: Walter Elliot was appointed Commissioner of Guntur in 1854 and contributed to documenting Amaravati's findings.

Question 29 : (b) Both A and R are true but R is not the correct explanation of A
Explanation: Both statements are true—Amaravati was indeed discovered early and not well preserved, and Sanchi remained largely intact—but the reason given does not directly explain the assertion.

Question 30 : (b) 1818
Explanation: Sanchi was discovered in 1818 by a British officer.

Question 31 : (b) Auspicious Symbol
Explanation: The Shailabhanjika motif (a woman and tree symbol) is generally considered an auspicious symbol linked to fertility and prosperity in Indian art.

Question 32 : (a) Charanachitras
Explanation: Charanachitras were wandering storytellers who used scrolls with pictures (painted on cloth or paper) to narrate stories.

Question 33 : (d) India
Explanation: Buddhism originated in India and later spread to East Asia via missionaries, trade routes, and cultural exchanges.

Chapter 5 : Through The Eyes Of Travellers

Question 1 : (d) is correct
Explanation: Al-Biruni was born in Khwarazm, which is in present-day Uzbekistan.

Question 2 : (d) is correct
Explanation: Ibn Battuta was a Moroccan traveler who visited India during the reign of Muhammad bin Tughlaq.

Question 3 : (b) is correct
Explanation: Al-Biruni studied Euclid's works as part of his interest in Greek mathematics and science.

Question 4 : (a) is correct
Explanation: Metrology is the science of measurement, including units and their standards.

Question 5 : (d) is correct
Explanation: Al-Biruni belonged to Khwarazm in present-day Uzbekistan.

Question 6 : (d) is correct
Explanation: Abdur Razzaq Samarqandi came from Herat, a city in present-day Afghanistan.

Question 7 : (a) is correct
Explanation: Sultan Mahmud of Ghazni took Al-Biruni along during his invasions and brought him to Ghazni.

Question 8 : (c) is correct
Explanation: 'Kitab-ul-Hind' was written by Al-Biruni based on his observations and studies of Indian society and culture.

Question 9 : (d) is correct
Explanation: Al-Biruni developed his interest in India while living in Ghazni, after coming with Mahmud of Ghazni.

Question 10 : (c) is correct
Explanation: Abdur Razzaq, an ambassador from Herat, gave a significant account of the Vijayanagara Empire in the 15th century.

Question 11 : (b) is correct
Explanation: Al-Biruni translated several Sanskrit works, including Patanjali's grammar, into Arabic.

Question 12 : (b) is correct
Explanation: The statement "It's a voluminous text divided into 100 chapters" is incorrect. Kitab-ul-Hind is actually divided into 80 ch
apters

Question 13 : (c) is correct
Explanation: Al-Biruni was born in Khwarizm, which is in present-day Uzbekistan.

Question 14 : (b) is correct
Explanation: Kitab-ul-Hind is divided into 80 chapters.

Question 15 : (c) is correct
Explanation: Ibn Battuta's book of travels is called Rihla, meaning "The Journey".

Question 16 : (a) is correct
Explanation: Ibn Battuta was a Moroccan traveler who visited India during the 14th century.

Question 17 : (b) is correct
Explanation: Ibn Battuta was born in Tangier, Morocco.

Question 18 : (b) is correct
Explanation: Sharia is the Islamic religious law derived from the Quran and Hadith.

Question 19 : (a) is correct
Explanation: Ibn Battuta set off for India in the year 1332-1333 CE.

Question 20 : (c) is correct
Explanation: Ibn Battuta returned home after traveling for 30 years.

Question 21 : (d) is correct
Explanation: When Ibn Battuta reached Sindh in 1333, Muhammad Bin Tughlaq was the Sultan of Delhi.

Question 22 : (i) is correct
Explanation: Ibn Battuta was appointed as Qazi (judge) by Muhammad Bin Tughlaq. The other statements are incorrect—Travels in the Mughal Empire was not written by him, he didn't translate Patanjali's work, and he wasn't known as a doctor or philosopher.

Question 23 : (d) is correct
Explanation: Ibn Battuta's travel accounts are often compared to those of Marco Polo due to their wide scope and historical importance.
Question 25 : (d) is correct

Question 24 : (a) is correct
Explanation: According to Ibn Battuta, it took him about 40 days to travelfrom Sindh to Delhi.

Question 25 : (d) is correct
Explanation: Duarte Barbosa wrote a detailed account of trade and society in South India.

Question 26 : (b) is correct
Explanation: Jean Baptiste Tavernier was a renowned French jeweller and traveler in India.

Question 27 : (a) is correct
Explanation: Dara Shukoh was the eldest son of Emperor Shah Jahan.

Question 28 : (d) is correct
Explanation: Francois Bernier belonged to France.

Question 29 : (a) is correct

Explanation: Francois Bernier dedicated his major writings to King Louis XIV of France.

Question 30 : (c) is correct

Explanation: Slavery was not mentioned by Al-Biruni as a barrier to understanding Indian society. He focused on language, religious differences, and cultural insularity.

Question 31 : (b) is correct

Explanation: Ibn Battuta described the paan and the coconut in detail in his travel writings about India.

Question 32 : (d) is correct

Explanation: Tarababad was known as a marketplace for both male and female singers.

Question 33 : (a) is correct

Explanation: Both the assertion and the reason are correct, and the reason explains why Ibn Battuta found the Indian subcontinent exciting — due to its bustling cities and colorful markets.

Question 34 : (c) is correct

Explanation: Ibn Battuta mentioned that Daulatabad rivalled Delhi in size.

Question 35 : (a) is correct

Explanation: Abdur Razzaq's travelogue was written in the 1440s.

Question 36 : (c) is correct

Explanation: Ibn Battuta's account provides information about the efficient postal system in the Delhi Sultanate.

Question 37 : (a) is correct

Explanation: The horse post system was known as Uluq.

Question 38 : (d) is correct

Explanation: Francois Bernier wrote the book Travels in the Mughal Empire.

Question 39 : (b) is correct

Explanation: According to Bernier, crown ownership of land led to no private land ownership, poor productivity, and inability to pass land to descendants.

Question 40 : (a) is correct

Explanation: The concept of the Asiatic mode of production was developed by Karl Marx in the 19th century.

Question 41 : (d) is correct

Explanation: Francois Bernier described Mughal cities as "camp towns" because they were often temporary and developed around military and administrative activities.

Question 42 : (a) is correct

Explanation: The nagarsheth was the head of the merchant community in a town or city during medieval times.

Question 43 : (d) is correct

Explanation: Abdur Razzaq referred to the bustling port of Calicut as being inhabited by a "strange nation," highlighting its cosmopolitan and diverse nature.

Question 44 : (a) is correct

Explanation: Al-Biruni gave a detailed description of the practice of sati in his work Kitab-ul-Hind.

Question 45 : (b) is correct

Explanation: Ibn Battuta described the presence and roles of female slaves in India during his travels.

Question 46 : (c) is correct

Explanation: Kozhikode is the medieval name for the city of Calicut, a major trading port in Kerala.

Chapter 6 : Bhakti-Sufi Traditions

Question 1 : (c) is correct
Explanation: The terms Great and Little Traditions were coined by sociologist Robert Redfield to describe the interaction between elite (Great) and folk (Little) cultural elements in a society.

Question 2 : (d) is correct
Explanation: The principal deities of the Vedic pantheon were Agni, Indra, and Soma, as frequently mentioned in the Rigveda.

Question 3 : (c) is correct
Explanation: The Alvars were Tamil poet-saints who were devotees of Vishnu and played a major role in promoting the bhakti movement.

Question 4 : (c) is correct
Explanation: Tantric practices were influenced by Shaivism and Buddhism and were often esoteric in nature. They were open to women and lower castes, so (b) is incorrect, making (c) the best choice.

Question 5 : (b) is correct
Explanation: The Nayanars were a group of Tamil Shaiva bhakti saints, devoted to Lord Shiva.

Question 6 : (c) is correct
Explanation: The Nalayira Divyaprabandham, meaning "Four Thousand Sacred Compositions," is a major anthology of the Alvars' hymns and is referred to as the Tamil Veda

Question 7 : (i) is correct
Explanation: Only statement (i) is correct. Nirguna bhakti refers to the worship of a formless God, and Saguna bhakti focuses on specific deities like Shiva, Vishnu, Devi, etc., so statements (ii) and (iii) are reversed and incorrect

Question 8 : (a) is correct
Explanation: Andal is the only female Alvar known for expressing her devotional love for Vishnu through her verses.

Question 9 : (b) is correct
Explanation: The Tevaram is a collection of devotional poems composed by Appar, Sambandar, and Sundarar, all of whom were Shaiva saints.

Question 10 : (b) is correct
Explanation:
Andal → (ii) Devotee of Vishnu
Tondaradippodi → (iii) Alvar Brahmana
Appar → (iv) Nayanar Saint
Karaikkal Ammaiyar → (i)Devotee of Shiva

Question 11 : (a) is correct
Explanation: In Thanjavur, Tamil Nadu, the deity that resides as Marperu is Shiva, particularly in the Shiva temples constructed by the Cholas.

Question 12 : (d) is correct
Explanation: The magnificent Shiva temples built by the Chola rulers include Chidambaram, Thanjavur, and Gangaikondacholapuram, making option (d) the correct choice.

Question 13 : (c) is correct
Explanation: The Chola ruler who consecrated metal images of Appar, Sambandar, and Sundarar in a Shiva temple was Parantaka II.

Question 14 : (d) is correct
Explanation: Lingayats believe that after death, the devotee will be united with Shiva and will not return to this world, focusing on the worship of Shiva.

Question 15 : (d) is correct
Explanation: The personality who rejected sacrifices, ritual baths, image worship, and authorities, advocated Nirguna Bhakti, organized his followers into a community, and proposed connecting with the Divine through "shabad" was Guru Nanak.

Question 16 : (b) is correct
Explanation: The religious literature of Lingayats is known as Vachana, which consists of devotional poems written in Kannada by the followers of Basavanna.

Question 17 : (d) is correct
Explanation: Basavanna was the minister in the court of the Kalachuri ruler, and he was an important figure in the Virashaiva movement.

Question 18 : (c) is correct
Explanation: Jangama refers to a wandering monk in the Lingayat tradition, who travels from place to place to spread the teachings.

Question 19 : (d) is correct
Explanation: The 12th century witnessed the emergence of a new movement in Karnataka, which was led by the Brahmana Basavanna, who played a pivotal role in the Virashaiva movement.

Question 20 : (d) is correct
Explanation: All the statements are correct about the Lingayats:
They encouraged practices disapproved in the Dharmasutras, like post-marriage and remarriage of widows.
The Virashaiva tradition is derived from Vachanas composed by men and women who joined the movement, making option (d) the correct choice.

Question 21 : (b) Nirguna
Explanation: The worship of an abstract form of God is known as Nirguna worship, where God is worshipped without form or attributes.

Question 22:
1. (a) Lord of the world
  Explanation: The literal meaning of Jagannatha is "Lord of the World."

2. (a) Vishnu
  Explanation: Lord Jagannatha is considered a form of Vishnu, specifically worshipped in Puri.

3. (b) Orissa
  Explanation: Lord Jagannatha is the principal deity of Orissa (now Odisha), where the famous Jagannath Temple is located.

4. (b) Centre
  Explanation: In the traditional iconography, Lord Jagannatha is usually depicted in the center of the image, with Balrama on the left and Subhadra on the right.

5. (d) Integration of cults
  Explanation: The depiction of Jagannatha, Balrama, and Subhadra reflects an example of the integration of cults, as it symbolizes the merging of various religious beliefs and practices.

Question 23 : (b) Law governing Muslim community
  Explanation: Sharia refers to the Islamic law that governs the behavior and practices of the Muslim community.

Question 24 : (b) Muhammad Qasim
  Explanation: In 711, the Arab general Muhammad Qasim conquered Sindh, making it part of the Caliph's domain.

Question 25 : (a) scholars of Islamic studies
  Explanation: Ulama refers to the Islamic scholars who are trained in religious knowledge and serve as interpreters of Islamic law and teachings.

Question 26 : (d) Jizya
  Explanation: Jizya is the tax that non-Muslims had to pay to the government in exchange for protection and exemption from military service during the medieval Islamic period.

Question 27 : (c) Offering prayers four times a day
  Explanation: The incorrect statement is "Offering prayers four times a day", because Muslims are required to pray five times a day (Fajr, Dhuhr, Asr, Maghrib, and Isha).

Question 28 : (b) Shah Hamadan Mosque
Explanation: The Shah Hamadan mosque in Srinagar, on the banks of the Jhelum, is often regarded as the "jewel in the crown" of all the existing mosques of Kashmir. Built in 1395, it is one of the best examples of Kashmiri wooden architecture. Notice the spire and the beautifully carved eaves. It is decorated with papier mache.

Question 29 : (c) Karaikkal Ammaiyar
  Explanation: The picture shows Karaikkal Ammaiyar, one of the Nayanmar saints and an important figure in the Tamil Bhakti movement.

Question 30 : (c) Silsila
  Explanation: Silsila means a chain that signifies a continuous link between master and disciple, commonly used in Sufi traditions.
Question 31 : (a) Matrilocal residence
  Explanation: Matrilocal residence is a practice where women, after marriage, remain in their natal home with their children, and the husbands may come to stay with them.

Question 32 : (c) Malik Muhammad Jayasi
  Explanation: Malik Muhammad Jayasi composed the Prem-akhyan Padmavat, which is a famous epic in the Sufi tradition.

Question 33 : (c) Jama'at khana
  Explanation: Shaikh Nizamuddin's hospice comprised several small rooms and a large hall called Jama'at Khana, where gatherings and spiritual discussions took place.

Question 34 : (b) Ajmer
  Explanation: Shaikh Muinuddin Chishti's shrine (Dargah) is located in Ajmer, Rajasthan.

Question 35 : (a) Guru Tegh Bahadur
  Explanation: The ninth Guru of the Sikhs, whose compositions were compiled in the Guru Granth Sahib, was Guru Tegh Bahadur.

Question 36 : (a) Prayer Hall
  Explanation: Naam Ghar refers to a prayer hall used for religious gatherings, especially in the Vaishnavite tradition of Assam.

Question 37 : (a) Shankaradeva
  Explanation: Shankaradeva, a great saint and social reformer from Assam, composed the Kirtana-ghosha, which is a significant religious text in the Vaishnavite tradition.

Question 38 : (c) Uttar Pradesh
  Explanation: Tulsidas, a prominent leader of the Bhakti Movement and the composer of Ramcharitmanas, belonged to Uttar Pradesh

Question 39 : (b) Amir Khusrau
  Explanation: Amir Khusrau wrote the biography of Shaikh Muinuddin Chishti, titled As Munis al Arwah.

Question 40 : (c) (ii) & (iii)
  Explanation:(ii) Mirabai was a Rajput princess from Merta in Marwar who was married to a prince of the Sisodia clan of Mewar in Rajasthan, contrary to her wishes.
(iii) Mirabai's preceptor was Raidas, a leather worker, according to some traditions.
Thus, the incorrect options are (ii) & (iii) because both statements are historically correct.

Question 41: (b) He was born a Hindu but raised by a Muslim family of weavers.

Explanation: According to many Vaishnava hagiographies, Kabir Das was born a Hindu but was raised by a Muslim family of weavers, reflecting the syncretic nature of his teachings and the blending of Hindu and Muslim cultural elements in his life.

Question 42: (c) Guru Ramananda

Explanation: Guru Ramananda is often suggested as the one who initiated Kabir Das into the practice of bhakti, as per some accounts of Kabir's life and teachings.

Question 43:
Which historical place is this?
(C) Atiya Mosque
Explanation: The picture refers to the Atiya Mosque

Which material has been used to build it?
(D) Brick
Explanation: Atiya mosque built with brick

Present-day it is located in which country?
(D) Bangladesh
Explanation: Atiya mosque, Mymensingh district, Bangladesh, built with brick, 1609

Question 44: (b) Gharib Nawaz

Explanation: Khwaja Muinuddin Chishti is popularly known as Gharib Nawaz, which means "Benefactor of the Poor". His shrine in Ajmer is one of the most revered in the Sufi tradition.

Question 45: Match Column A with Column B
A) Shri Chaitanya → I) Bengal
B) Muktabai → III) Maharashtra
C) Ramananda → IV) Uttar Pradesh
D) Meera bai → II) Rajasthan
E) Ramanujacharya → V) Tamil Nadu
Correct Option: (A)

Explanation:

Shri Chaitanya is associated with Bengal.
Muktabai is associated with Maharashtra.
Ramananda is associated with Uttar Pradesh
Meera Bai is associated with Rajasthan.
Ramanujacharya is associated with Tamil Nadu.

Chapter 7 : An Imperial Capital Vijayanagara

Question 1: (d) Colin Mackenzie
 Explanation: The ruins at Hampi were brought to light by Colin Mackenzie, an engineer and antiquarian, in 1800.

Question 2: (a) 1336
 Explanation: The Vijayanagara Empire was founded in 1336 by Harihara I and Bukka Raya I.

Question 3: (c) Karnataka Samrajyamu
 Explanation: While historians use the term Vijayanagara Empire, contemporaries referred to it as Karnataka Samrajyamu, meaning the Kingdom of Karnataka.

Question 4: (b) Thanjavur
 Explanation: The Brihadishvara Temple is located in Thanjavur, Tamil Nadu.

Question 5: (a) Belur
 Explanation: The Chennakeshava Temple is located in Belur, Karnataka.

Question 6: (d) Kudirai Chettis
 Explanation: The local communities of merchants, particularly those involved in horse trade, were known as Kudirai Chettis.

Question 7: (a) C, A, B, D
 Explanation: The chronological order of the dynasties of the Vijayanagara Empire is:
Tuluva Dynasty (C)
Saluva Dynasty (A)
Sangama Dynasty (B)
Aravidu Dynasty (D)

Question 8: (d) Sangam Dynasty
 Explanation: The first dynasty to rule the Vijayanagara Empire was the Sangama Dynasty.

Question 9: (d) Rayas
 Explanation: The Deccan Sultans were termed as Rayas in the Vijayanagara kingdom.

Question 10: (a) Vijayanagara
 Explanation: The Kamalapuram Tank is located in Vijayanagara.

Question 11: (d) Krishnadeva Raya
 Explanation: Amuktamalyada was composed by Krishnadeva Raya, the famous ruler of the Vijayanagara Empire.

Question 12: (c) Bijapur, Ahmednagar, Golconda
 Explanation: The combined armies of Bijapur, Ahmednagar, and Golconda routed the army of Rama Raya in the Battle of Talikota in 1565.

Question 13: (b) Krishnadeva Raya
 Explanation: Krishnadeva Raya found the suburban township of Nagalapuram near Vijayanagara after the death of his mother.

Question 14: (a) Yavana
 Explanation: The word Yavana was used to refer to the Greeks and other people who entered the subcontinent from the northwest.

Question 15: (d) Rama Raya
 Explanation: Rama Raya is regarded as the "establisher of the Yavana kingdom".

Question 16: (c) Tuluva
 Explanation: Krishnadeva Raya belonged to the Tuluva Dynasty.

Question 17: (a) Telugu
 Explanation: Amuktamalyada was composed in Telugu.

Question 18: (b) Nayakas
 Explanation: The military chiefs were called Nayakas in the Vijayanagara Empire.

Question 19: (b) Sixteenth century
 Explanation: The Kamalapuram tank was built in the sixteenth century.

Question 20: (d) Pampadevi
 Explanation: The local goddess of Vijayanagara was Pampadevi.

Question 21: (c) Samara

Question 22 : (d) The Amara-nayakas were military commanders who were given territories to govern by the raya
 Explanation: The Amara-nayaka system was a military and administrative system in the Vijayanagara Empire where the Amara-nayakas (military commanders) were given territories to govern by the raya (king).

Question 23: (c) 1986
 Explanation: Hampi was declared a World Heritage Site by UNESCO in 1986.

Question 24: (d) All of the above
 Explanation: The quote is attributed to John M. Fritz, George Michell, and M.S. Nagaraja Rao, who collectively discussed the architectural elements of the Vijayanagara monuments.

Question 25: (a) 1976
 Explanation: Hampi was recognized as a site of national importance in 1976.

Question 26: (b) Lord Vishnu
 Explanation: The Vitthala temple is dedicated to Lord Vishnu.

Question 27: (a) Shiva
 Explanation: Virupaksha is recognized as a form of Lord Shiva.

Question 28: (c) The king and his family
 Explanation: The Hazara Rama temple was used by the king and his family, particularly for religious and ceremonial purposes

Question 28: (c) The king and his family
Explanation: The Hazara Rama temple was used by the king and his family, particularly for religious and ceremonial purposes.

Question 29: (b) A place where king met his advisors

Question 30: (b) Collin Mackenzie
Explanation: Collin Mackenzie captured the first detailed photograph of archaeological remains at Hampi.

Question 31: (a) Abdur Razzaq
Explanation: Abdur Razzaq was the Persian ambassador sent to Calicut during the reign of Vijayanagara Empire.

Question 32: (b) Krishna, Tungabhadra
Explanation: The two main rivers that served as the source of water for the Vijayanagara Kingdom were the Krishna and Tungabhadra rivers.

Question 33: (c) Tuluva
Explanation: The Hiriya Canal was built by the kings of the Tuluva Dynasty during the reign of Krishnadeva Raya.

Question 34: (a) Domingo Paes
Explanation: Domingo Paes, a Portuguese traveler, referred to the Mahanavami Dibba as the "house of victory" during his visit to Vijayanagara.

Chapter 8 : Peasants , Zamindars and the State

Question 1: (d) 85 percent
 Explanation: During the sixteenth and seventeenth centuries, approximately 85 percent of India's population lived in its villages.

Question 2: (a) Village
 Explanation: The village was the basic unit of agricultural society in India.

Question 3: (c) Abul Fazal
 Explanation: Abul Fazal wrote the Ain-i-Akbari, which provides a detailed account of the administration, culture, and society during the reign of Akbar.

Question 4: (a) Akbar
 Explanation: Abul Fazal was the court historian of the Mughal emperor Akbar.

Question 5: (b) Raiyat
 Explanation: The term most frequently used to denote a peasant in Indo-Persian sources during the Mughal period was Raiyat.

Question 6: (a) Khud Kashta
 Explanation: Khud Kashta refers to peasants who ploughed fields, demarcated them with borders of earth, brick, or thorn for identification.

Question 7: (d) Maize
 Explanation: Maize (corn) was one of the new crops introduced to India via Africa and Spain during the 17th century.

Question 8: (c) Jins-i-Kamil
 Explanation: The term Jins-i-Kamil was used for the perfect or ideal crop in Mughal agriculture.

Question 9: (b) All of these
 Explanation: Sugarcane, Maize, and Wheat were all important Jins-i-Kamil crops in Central India.

Question 10: (d) Jahangir
 Explanation: Jahangir was so
concerned about its addiction
that he banned it.

Question 11: (a) New World
 Explanation: Chillies and tomatoes were introduced to India from the New World (the Americas) after the Columbian Exchange.

Question 12: (b) Deccan
 Explanation: This plant, which arrived first
in the Deccan

Question 13 : (a) 5
Explanation : The Ain is made up of five books (daftars)

Question 14: (b) 4th book of Ain
 Explanation: Akbar's "auspicious sayings" were included in the 4th book of the Ain-i-Akbari.

Question 15: (d) All of the above
 Explanation: All the statements about Ain-i-Akbari are correct:
Mulk-Abadi gives information about the fiscal aspect of the state.
Manzil-Abadi relates to the royal household.
Sipah-Abadi is related to civil and military administration.

Question 16: (c) Halalkhoran
 Explanation: The Halalkhoran community was considered a menial (low-status) community.

Question 17: (c) Mukundaram Chankrabarti
 Explanation: Mukundaram Chankrabarti composed the poem Chandimangala, which is a notable work in Bengali literature.

Question 18: (a) Makka : Maize
 Explanation: The pairing Makka : Maize is not correct because Makka refers to wheat in some regions, and maize is a different crop.

Question 19: (b) Ahirs
 Explanation: The Ahirs, who were traditionally pastoralists, cultivated land around Vrindavan, which is in Uttar Pradesh.

Question 20: (d) Sadgops, Kaivartas
 Explanation: In the eastern region of India, communities like Sadgops and Kaivartas, which were traditionally pastoralists and fishermen, acquired the status of peasants.

Question 21: (c) Both a and b
 Explanation: The Panchayat was headed by a headman known as either a Mandal or a Muqaddam in different regions.

Question 22: (d) Assam
 Explanation: The Ahom kings belonged to Assam, where they ruled for several centuries.

Question 23: (b) Perfect crops
 Explanation: Jins-i-Kamil refers to the perfect crops or ideal crops that were highly valued during the Mughal Empire.

Question 24: (c) Both are correct
 Explanation:
Statement 1: The Panchayat had an important role in maintaining caste boundaries within the village.
Statement 2: The Panchayat also had the authority to levy fines and impose punishments, including expulsion from the community.

Question 25: (c) Both
 Explanation: Early British rule village surveys and documents in both Marathi and Bengali revealed the existence of substantial numbers of artisans in villages, sometimes as high as 25 percent of total households.

Question 26: (a) Both assertion and Reason are true and Reason is the correct explanation of assertion
 Explanation:
Assertion: Zamindars in Bengal remunerated blacksmiths, carpenters, and goldsmiths by paying them a daily allowance and diet money.
Reason: This system later came to be described as the Jajmani system, where local artisans were supported by the landholders.

Question 27: (c) Statement i, ii, iv are correct
Explanation:
Statement i: Women and men worked together in the fields, with men tilling and ploughing while women sowed, weeded, threshed, and winnowed.

Statement ii: In certain regions, menstruating women were not allowed to touch the plough or enter specific areas like betel-leaf groves.

Statement iv: Women were considered a valuable resource because of their labor and role in childbearing in agrarian society.

Note: Statement iii is incorrect because women worked both in the fields and in other areas like home-based craft production.

Question 28: (a) Jangli
Explanation: Forest dwellers were referred to as jangli in contemporary texts.

Question 29: (a) Pargana
Explanation: An administrative subdivision of a Mughal province was called a Pargana.

Question 30: (c) Peasants who were resident of the village
Explanation: Khud-Kashta refers to peasants who were the residents of the village and worked the land there.

Question 31: (d) Bengal
Explanation: According to the Ain-i-Akbari, Bengal produced 50 varieties of rice alone, highlighting the region's agricultural diversity and prominence.

Question 32: (b) Rice
Explanation: During the Mughal period, Bengal was famous for its rice production, making it an essential crop in the region's economy.

Question 33: (b) By the village elders
Explanation: The mandal or muqaddam (headman) was chosen through the consensus of village elders, ensuring local involvement and governance.

Question 34: (b) Peshkash
Explanation: The Peshkash was a form of tribute collected by the Mughal state, often in the form of gifts or cash presented to the emperor.

Question 35: (b) Jati panchayat
Explanation: In the panchayat system, each caste had its own Jati panchayat, which was responsible for resolving disputes and maintaining order within the caste.

Question 36: (a) Bengal
Explanation: In the 18th century, women zamindars were notable in Bengal, where they played an important role in land management and administration.

Question 37: (b) Punjab
Explanation: tribes, like the Lohanis in the Punjab, were engaged in overland trade, between India and Afghanistan, and in the town-country trade in the Punjab itself.

Question 38: (b) A small piece of land of Zamindar
Explanation: Milkiyat refers to the small piece of land that belonged to a Zamindar and was typically cultivated or used for various purposes.

Question 39: (a) 2 to 3 years
Explanation: Chachar refers to land that has been left fallow for 2 to 3 years, during which the soil rejuvenates for future cultivation.

Question 40: (c) Both are correct
Explanation:
Statement 1: The Mughal Empire was indeed one of the large territorial empires in Asia during the 18th and 17th centuries, consolidating power and resources effectively.

Statement 2: The Mughal Empire existed alongside other prominent empires like the Ming (China), Safavid (Iran), and Ottoman (Turkey), which were contemporaneous global powers.

Question 41: (c) Jean Baptiste Tavernier
Explanation: Jean Baptiste Tavernier, a French jeweler and traveler, provides a graphic account of the way silver traveled across the globe, including its arrival in India during the Mughal period.

Question 42: (d) Silver
Explanation: Silver coins were more prevalent during the Mughal empire, used extensively in trade and transactions, including the famous Rupee.

Question 43: (a) Manzil Abadi
Explanation: The first book of the Ain-i-Akbari is called Manzil-Abadi, concerns the imperial household and its maintenance.

Question 44: (d) Ahmad Shah Abdali
Explanation: In the Third Battle of Panipat (1761), the Marathas were defeated by Ahmad Shah Abdali, the ruler of Afghanistan.

Question 45: (c) All of the above
Explanation: All statements are correct:
The Ain-i-Akbari has been translated by several scholars.
Henry Blochmann was indeed associated with the Asiatic Society of Bengal and provided the standard translation of the first volume.
H.S. Jarrett translated the other two volumes of the Ain-i-Akbari.

Question 46: (c) Sipah Abadi
Explanation: The second book, sipah-abadi, covers the military and civil administration and the establishment of servants.

Question 47: (b) mulk Abadi
Explanation: The third book, mulk-abadi, is the one which deals with the fiscal side of the empire

Question 48: (d) All of the above
Explanation: All the given statements about the Ain-i-Akbari are correct:
Sipah-Abadi deals with military and civil administration.
Mulk-Abadi concerns the fiscal side of the empire.
Manzil-Abadi addresses the imperial household and its maintenance.

Question 49: (a) Kalaketu

 Explanation: sixteenth-century Bengali poem,
Chandimangala, composed by Mukundaram Chakrabarti.
The hero of the poem, Kalaketu, set up a kingdom by
clearing forests.

Question 50: (b) Aurangzeb

 Explanation: The coin in question was issued by
Aurangzeb, the sixth Mughal emperor, known for his long
reign and significant contributions to the Mughal currency
system.

Chapter 9 : Kings And Chronicles

Question 1: B. Timurids
Explanation: The Mughal rulers traced their lineage to Timur and preferred to call themselves "Timurids" to emphasize their noble and prestigious Central Asian ancestry rather than identifying as Mughals or Mongols, which had different connotations.

Question 2: C. Akbar
Explanation: Akbar promoted Persian as the language of administration and high culture in the Mughal court. This policy played a key role in establishing Persian as the lingua franca of the elite in the subcontinent.

Question 3: C. A is true, but R is false.
Explanation: The Mughal court indeed followed strict protocols for diplomatic envoys, including specific ceremonies and etiquettes. However, ambassadors were *not* allowed to freely move around: they had to adhere to strict customs, making the reason false.

Question 4: B. Abu'l Fazl
Explanation: Abu'l Fazl, a court historian and close confidant of Akbar, wrote the *Akbar Nama*, which includes a detailed account of Akbar's reign and his administration.

Question 5: B. Akbar
Explanation: Akbar introduced the policy of *sulh-i kul* or "universal peace," which promoted tolerance and respect for all religions and was a central principle of his governance.

Question 6: C. Jahangir
Explanation: Jahangir shifted the Mughal capital to Lahore and ruled from there for about 13 years, largely due to his fondness for the city and its strategic importance.

Question 7: B. Abdul Hamid Lahori
Explanation: Abdul Hamid Lahori was commissioned by Shah Jahan to write the *Badshah Nama*, an official chronicle of his reign.

Question 8: A. Akbar Nama
Explanation: The *Ain-i Akbari* is the third volume of the *Akbar Nama*, written by Abu'l Fazl. It provides detailed information about Akbar's administration, court, and empire.

Question 9: A. Complete prostration before the emperor
Explanation: *Sijda* was a court ritual in which courtiers and visitors performed complete prostration before the emperor to show absolute submission and loyalty.

Question 10: C. Jahangir
Explanation: Jahangir was fascinated by the Sufi philosophy of divine light (*nur*), which he incorporated into his idea of kingship, often portraying himself with a radiant halo in paintings.

Question 11: B. Kitabkhana
Explanation: The *Kitabkhana* was the imperial library where manuscripts were written, illustrated, and preserved. It was an important center of knowledge and art in the Mughal court.

Question 12: A. Both A and R are true, and R is the correct explanation of A.
Explanation: The Mughal nobility indeed consisted of a mix of ethnic and religious groups such as Persians, Central Asians, Rajputs, and Indian Muslims. The emperors deliberately structured their administration to ensure no group gained overwhelming power, fostering balance and stability.

Question 13: C. Qandahar
Explanation: The Safavid rulers of Iran and the Mughal emperors frequently clashed over Qandahar due to its strategic and symbolic importance. Control over this city changed hands multiple times between the two empires.

Question 14: C. Axis mundi
Explanation: *Axis mundi* is a cosmological concept used to describe the Mughal emperor as the center or axis of the universe. This symbolic status emphasized the emperor's supreme authority and divine right to rule.

Question 15: C. Aurangzeb
Explanation: Aurangzeb re-imposed the jizya tax on non-Muslims in 1679, reversing Akbar's earlier policy of religious tolerance and causing widespread discontent among his non-Muslim subjects.

Question 16: A. Both A and R are true, and R is the correct explanation of A.
Explanation: The Mughal emperors adopted European artistic elements like shading, perspective, and realism in their miniature paintings, largely influenced by the European artworks brought by Jesuit missionaries.

Question 17: C. Shah Jahan
Explanation: Shah Jahan established *Shahjahanabad* (now known as Old Delhi) as his new capital. It featured grand architectural structures, including the Red Fort and Jama Masjid, reflecting the zenith of Mughal architecture.

Question 18: A. Umara
Explanation: The *Umara* were the elite class of nobles and high-ranking officers in the Mughal court. They held significant power, received jagirs, and occupied important positions in administration and military.

Question 19: B. Diwan-i Ala
Explanation: The *Diwan-i Ala* was the Mughal finance minister responsible for revenue collection, budgeting, and financial administration across the empire.

Question 20: A. Akhbarat
Explanation: The *Akhbarat* were official court bulletins or newsletters that documented daily activities, orders, and events in the Mughal court. They served as administrative records.

Question 21: A. Both A and R are true, and R is the correct explanation of A.
Explanation: The Mughal Empire was religiously diverse, and Akbar's policy of *sulh-i kul* (universal peace) promoted religious tolerance, which helped in maintaining peace and stability among different communities.

Question 22: A. Both A and R are true, and R is the correct explanation of A.
Explanation: The motif of a lion and lamb sitting peacefully symbolized the emperor's ability to provide justice and protection to all—both strong and weak—under his rule. It reflected the ideal of a just and moral ruler.

Question 23: B. Akbar
Explanation: Akbar abolished the jizya and pilgrimage tax as part of his inclusive policies, encouraging religious harmony and reducing discrimination against non-Muslim subjects.

Question 24: D. Aurangzeb
Explanation: Aurangzeb assumed the title *'Alamgir'* which means "Conqueror of the World," reflecting his imperial ambitions and expansionist policies during his long reign.

Question 25: A. Madad-i Maash
Explanation: *Madad-i Maash* was the Persian term used for land grants given to religious scholars and institutions by the Mughals. These were tax-free and served as a reward for service in the religious and educational fields.

Question 26: B. Akbar
Explanation: Akbar transferred his court to Lahore for strategic reasons, primarily to strengthen Mughal control over the northwest frontier and to counter threats from Central Asia and the Safavids.

Question 27: B. Mansabdari system
Explanation: The *Mansabdari system* ranked Mughal officials based on two criteria: *zat* (personal rank) and *sawar* (number of cavalrymen to be maintained). It was introduced by Akbar to organize the military and bureaucracy.

Question 28: C. Shah Jahan
Explanation: The *Badshah Nama* was a chronicle commissioned by Emperor Shah Jahan to document his reign. It was written by Abdul Hamid Lahori and is one of the most important sources of Mughal history during his rule.

Question 29: C. The halo
Explanation: In Mughal paintings, a *halo* behind the emperor's head symbolized his divine authority and semi-divine status, indicating a connection to the divine order.

Question 30: C. Tajwiz
Explanation: A *tajwiz* was a formal petition or recommendation presented by a nobleman to the emperor, often related to appointments or favors for candidates seeking imperial service.

Question 31: B. Akbar
Explanation: Akbar abolished the practice of *sijda* (complete prostration) at court, replacing it with more respectful yet non-religious gestures, reflecting his policy of religious moderation and dignity.

Question 32: B. Nauroz
Explanation: *Nauroz* was the Persian New Year, celebrated with grandeur at the Mughal court. It symbolized prosperity and new beginnings, and reflected Persian cultural influence.

Question 33: C. Akbar
Explanation: *Jharoka Darshan* was introduced by Akbar to allow the public to have daily audience with the emperor, reinforcing his presence and fostering a sense of divine kingship.

Question 34: B. Religious tolerance
Explanation: *Sulh-i Kul* means "peace with all" and was a core principle of Akbar's rule. It promoted religious tolerance and unity in the diverse Mughal Empire.

Question 35: C. Diwan-i Ala
Explanation: The *Diwan-i Ala* was the finance minister in the Mughal administration, responsible for overseeing revenue collection, taxation, and financial management.

Question 36: B. Abu'l Fazl
Explanation: Abu'l Fazl was a scholar, court historian, and close advisor of Akbar. He wrote the *Akbarnama* and *Ain-i Akbari*, and also served in Humayun's time before rising to prominence under Akbar.

Question 37: C. Fatehpur Sikri
Explanation: *Fatehpur Sikri* was built by Akbar as his capital city near Agra. It was later abandoned due to severe water shortages, despite its grand architecture and planning.

Question 38: B. Humayun
Explanation: Humayun was defeated by Sher Shah Suri and forced into exile. After Sher Shah's death, Humayun returned and reclaimed the Mughal throne with Persian support.

Question 39: C. Persian
Explanation: Both the *Akbar Nama* (by Abu'l Fazl) and the *Badshah Nama* (by Abdul Hamid Lahori) were written in Persian, the official language of the Mughal court.

Question 40: B. Kitabkhana
Explanation: The *Kitabkhana* was the royal library and manuscript production workshop of the Mughals. It played a central role in creating illustrated manuscripts and preserving texts.

Question 41: B. Nastaliq
Explanation: *Nastaliq* was a highly aesthetic Persian calligraphic style favored in Akbar's court, especially for copying royal manuscripts and religious texts.

Question 42: B. Akbar
Explanation: Akbar initiated a translation project where Sanskrit texts, including the *Mahabharata* and *Ramayana*, were translated into Persian to promote cultural synthesis and understanding.

Question 43: C. Razmnama
Explanation: The Persian translation of the *Mahabharata* commissioned by Akbar was called *Razmnama*, meaning "Book of War." It was richly illustrated and culturally significant.

Question 44: B. Akbar
Explanation: The art of *miniature painting* flourished under Akbar, who established a large imperial atelier. He invited artists from Persia and India to collaborate, blending styles.

Question 45: C. Raising the right hand to the forehead in salute
Explanation: *Kornish* was a gesture of deep respect where nobles raised their right hand to their forehead while bowing slightly before the emperor, symbolizing loyalty and submission.

Question 46: A. Mir Sayyid Ali
Explanation: *Mir Sayyid Ali* was a famous Safavid painter who was invited by Humayun to the Mughal court. He later worked under Akbar and contributed to the development of Mughal miniature art.

Question 47: C. Painting
Explanation: In Mughal chronicles, *taswir* refers to paintings, particularly those that illustrated texts or depicted courtly life, battles, and historical scenes.

Question 48: C. Orthodox Muslim scholars (ulama)
Explanation: The production of human and animal images in Mughal manuscripts caused tension with *ulama* (Orthodox Islamic scholars), who viewed such depictions as un-Islamic according to certain interpretations of religious law.

Question 49: C. Shah Jahan
Explanation: *Shah Jahan* built both the *Red Fort* and the *Jama Masjid* in Delhi. His reign is known for grand Mughal architecture, including the Taj Mahal in Agra.

Question 50: B. The Persian concept of Divine Light in kingship
Explanation: *Farr-i Izadi* means "Divine Glory" and refers to the idea that a king's authority is divinely sanctioned, giving him an almost god-like aura and legitimacy in Persian and Mughal political thought.

Question 51: C. Jahangir
Explanation: *Jahangir* is often depicted in paintings with a *halo*, symbolizing divine approval and royal sanctity, especially in court portraits to reinforce his image as a just and enlightened ruler.

Question 52: B. King of the Kings
Explanation: *Shahenshah* is a Persian term meaning *"King of Kings"*. It was a regal title used by the Mughal emperors to emphasize their supreme authority over other rulers.

Question 53: B. Gujarat
Explanation: The *Buland Darwaza* at Fatehpur Sikri was built by Akbar in 1601 to commemorate his victory over *Gujarat*. It stands as a massive gateway symbolizing Mughal grandeur and triumph.

Chapter 10 : Colonialism And the Countryside

Question 1:
(a) Both A and R are true, and R is the correct explanation of A.
Explanation: The Permanent Settlement of 1793 was introduced by the British in Bengal to ensure fixed revenue demands for zamindars, as they were seen as a loyal class who would maintain political and economic stability for the British.

Question 2:
(a) Both A and R are true, and R is the correct explanation of A.
Explanation: The Santhals initially accepted British rule and settled in the Damin-i-Koh region, where they were assured of permanent land ownership and protection from exploitation by the British, which led to their initial acceptance.

Question 3:
(a) Both A and R are true, and R is the correct explanation of A.
Explanation: The Paharias resisted British efforts to bring them under settled agriculture because the British associated forests with wildness and wanted to "civilize" forest dwellers, such as the Paharias, by encouraging settled farming.

Question 4:
(a) Benami
Explanation: The Raja of Burdwan avoided losing his zamindari by using Benami purchases at auctions, where land was purchased in the name of others to keep it away from the control of the British.

Question 5:
(c) Moneylenders'
Explanation: The Deccan Riots of 1875 were primarily caused by the exploitation of peasants by moneylenders, who charged exorbitant interest rates on loans, leading to the unrest.

Question 6:
(a) Fifth Report
Explanation: The Fifth Report submitted to the British Parliament in 1813 highlighted the mismanagement of the East India Company, exposing the issues in the governance and exploitation of India.

Question 7:
(b) Permanently fixed, irrespective of production
Explanation: Under the Permanent Settlement, zamindars were expected to pay a fixed revenue, irrespective of production, which created issues as it didn't account for fluctuating agricultural yields.

Question 8:
(c) Santhal Pargana
Explanation: The Santhal Revolt (1855-56) led to the creation of the Santhal Pargana, a separate administrative region, to govern and address the needs of the Santhal people.

Question 9:
(a) The British overestimated the financial capabilities of zamindars
Explanation: The main reason for the failure of the Permanent Settlement in Bengal was that the British overestimated the financial capabilities of zamindars, who were unable to pay the fixed revenue, leading to instability.

Question 10:
(c) Restrict the accumulation of interest on moneylenders' loans
Explanation: The Limitation Law of 1859 was passed to restrict the accumulation of interest on loans made by moneylenders, which helped in protecting peasants from exploitation.

Question 11: (a) Both A and R are true, and R is the correct explanation of A.
Explanation: The jotedars in Bengal were indeed more powerful than the zamindars in rural areas because they lived in villages, controlled the land, and resisted the zamindars' attempts to increase rents.

Question 12: (c) A is true, but R is false.
Explanation: The Paharias of Rajmahal hills were known for their resistance to settled agriculture, but the British policy of pacification (providing allowances to Paharia chiefs) did not lead to their complete acceptance of British rule, as they continued their resistance.

Question 13: (a) Both A and R are true, and R is the correct explanation of A.
Explanation: The Santhals were initially encouraged by the British to settle in the Damin-i-Koh region, as the British wanted to transform the Santhals into settled agriculturists to generate more land revenue.

Question 14: (c) A is false, but R is true.
Explanation: The Deccan Riots of 1875 were not primarily directed against the British administration, but rather against the oppressive practices of moneylenders (sahukars). The British had introduced harsh land revenue policies, which indirectly led to the riots, but they were not the direct target of the riots.

Question 15: (b) Limitation Law
Explanation: The Limitation Law of 1859 was passed to limit the validity of loan bonds to three years, protecting peasants from long-term indebtedness.

Question 16: (b) Moneylenders (sahukars)
Explanation: The Deccan Riots of 1875 were primarily caused by the oppressive practices of moneylenders (sahukars) who exploited peasants by charging exorbitant interest rates on loans, leading to widespread unrest.

Question 17: (c) Deccan Riots Commission Report
Explanation: The Deccan Riots Commission Report was presented in 1878 to investigate the causes of the Deccan Riots, focusing on the exploitation by moneylenders and the impact of British revenue policies.

Question 18: (c) Cotton
Explanation: The expansion of cotton cultivation in the Bombay Deccan during the American Civil War led to increased indebtedness of peasants as demand for cotton surged and peasants became dependent on loans from moneylenders to finance their cultivation.

Question 19: (a) Zamindars were inefficient in collecting revenue
Explanation: The British introduced the Ryotwari Settlement in the Bombay Deccan because they believed that zamindars were inefficient in collecting revenue, and directly settling revenue with ryots would help maintain more control over the land.

Question 20: (a) Exploitation by zamindars, moneylenders, and British officials
Explanation: The Santhal Rebellion (1855-56) was caused by the exploitation of the Santhals by zamindars, moneylenders, and British officials, leading to their resistance and rebellion.

Question 21: (c) Permanent Settlement
Explanation: The Permanent Settlement was introduced in Bengal in 1793 to ensure a fixed revenue demand from zamindars, providing the British with a steady income while making the zamindars responsible for paying the land tax.

Question 22: (b) In a permanently fixed amount regardless of production
Explanation: Under the Permanent Settlement, zamindars were required to pay a fixed revenue amount, irrespective of agricultural production, which caused problems during poor harvests.

Question 23: (c) Jotedars
Explanation: The Jotedars were a class of rich peasants in Bengal who controlled local trade, lent money to poorer peasants, and resisted zamindari demands, making them more powerful than zamindars in many areas.

Question 24:(b) Sunset Law
Explanation: The Sunset Law was introduced by the British, stating that if revenue was not paid by sunset of the due date, the zamindari would be auctioned off, ensuring timely payments from zamindars.

Question 25: (b) Damin-i-Koh
Explanation: The Santhals were given land to settle in the Damin-i-Koh region by the British in the early 19th century to transform them into settled agriculturists.

Question 26: (b) Failed to pay the fixed revenue
Explanation: In 1797, an auction was held in Burdwan where the estates of the Raja were sold because he had failed to pay the fixed revenue, leading to the British seizing his property.

Question 27: (b) The problems of permanent settlement in Bengal
Explanation: The Fifth Report (1813) primarily discussed the problems of the Permanent Settlement in Bengal, especially focusing on the exploitation of peasants and the challenges faced by zamindars in paying revenue.

Question 28: (b) Expand settled agriculture
Explanation: The Santhals were brought to the Rajmahal Hills by the British to expand settled agriculture and bring these regions under cultivation, boosting agricultural productivity.

Question 29:
(c) Raiding settled villages and attacking outsiders
Explanation: The Paharias primarily resisted British rule by raiding settled villages and attacking outsiders to defend their land and resist colonial control.

Question 30:
(b) Aimed to increase land revenue from agriculture
Explanation: The British encouraged the clearing of forests in India because they aimed to increase land revenue from agriculture, as cleared land could be used for cultivation and taxed.

Question 31:
(a) High revenue demands and debt traps of moneylenders
Explanation: The Deccan Riots of 1875 were mainly caused by high revenue demands and the debt traps of moneylenders, which caused peasants to revolt against exploitation.

Question 32: (a) Buying property in the name of a fictitious person
Explanation: The term "benami purchase" refers to buying property in the name of a fictitious person to hide the true owner, typically used to avoid taxes or other legal constraints.

Question 33: (c) The Bombay Deccan
Explanation: The Ryotwari system was introduced in the Bombay Deccan as an alternative to the zamindari system, where revenue was directly settled with individual ryots (peasants).

Question 34: (a) The revenue demand was set too high
Explanation: A key reason for the failure of many zamindars to pay revenue under the Permanent Settlement was that the revenue demand was set too high, and it was fixed, regardless of agricultural c
onditions.

Question 35: (b) Control the excessive charging of interest by moneylenders
Explanation: The Limitation Law of 1859 was introduced to control the excessive charging of interest by moneylenders, which had caused significant distress to peasants and ryots.

Question 36: (c) Santhal Rebellion
Explanation: The Santhal Rebellion (1855-56) was led by the Santhals against the exploitation by moneylenders, zamindars, and British officials, marking a major tribal uprising.

Question 37: (b) Ryotwari
Explanation: The Ryotwari system in the Bombay Deccan directly settled revenue with individual ryots (peasants) rather than with zamindars, making peasants re
sponsible for paying the revenue.

Question 38:(d) Sidhu Manjhi
Explanation: Sidhu Manjhi - leader of the Santhal rebellion.

Question 39: (c) Cotton
Explanation: During the American Civil War (1861-65), the demand for cotton from India increased, leading to a short-term economic boom in the Deccan, as cotton became a crucial raw material for the textile industry.

Question 40: (b) Fifth Report
Explanation: The Fifth Report (1813) was presented to the British Parliament and highlighted the mismanagement and corruption within the East India Company, particularly in relation to its

Question 41: (b) Lord Cornwallis
Explanation: The Permanent Settlement was introduced by Lord Cornwallis in 1793 in Bengal, aiming to fix the revenue demand and make zamindars responsible for collecting taxes.

Question 42: (c) Ryots (peasants)
Explanation: Under the Ryotwari system, revenue was collected directly from the ryots (peasants) rather than through intermediaries like zamindars.

Question 43: (c) 1875

Explanation: The Deccan Riots Commission was established in 1875 to investigate the causes of the Deccan Riots and the exploitation faced by peasants.

Question 44: (a) High initial revenue demands

Explanation: The main reason why zamindars defaulted on revenue payments under the Permanent Settlement was the high initial revenue demands that were fixed by the British, making it difficult for them to meet the payments.

Question 45: (b) Santhal Rebellion

Explanation: The Santhal Pargana was created after the Santhal Rebellion (1855-56), as a way of pacifying the region and organizing it under colonial control.

Question 46: (c) Offering allowances to their chiefs

Explanation: The British pacification policy towards the Paharias included offering allowances to their chiefs in exchange for cooperation, while also attempting to reduce their resistance through other means.

Question 47: (b) Controlling local trade and land

Explanation: The jotedars in Bengal were wealthy peasants who controlled local trade and land, and they were influential figures in the rural economy, often acting as intermediaries between peasants and zamindars.

Question 48: (c) Moneylenders (sahukars)

Explanation: The moneylenders (or sahukars) were primarily responsible for providing loans to peasants in colonial India, often trapping them in debt due to high-interest rates and exploitative practices.

Question 49: (a) The American Civil War

Explanation: The cotton boom in the Deccan was triggered by the American Civil War (1861-65), which disrupted cotton supplies from the United States. This led to an increased demand for cotton from India, particularly from the Deccan region.

Question 50 : (b) Fifth Report

Explanation: The Fifth Report (1813) was a significant source of information about the impact of British rule on rural Bengal in the 18th century. It highlighted the issues with the permanent settlement, the exploitation of peasants, and the failure of the zamindari system.

Question 51: (b) Expand settled agriculture and increase land revenue

Explanation: The British encouraged the settlement of Santhals in Damin-i-Koh primarily to expand settled agriculture and increase land revenue. This was part of their strategy to promote agricultural productivity in the region.

Question 52:(a) Shifting his zamindari to his mother's name

Explanation: The Raja of Burdwan attempted to avoid revenue payment by shifting his zamindari to his mother's name in an attempt to evade the taxes that he owed to the British government.

Question 53: (b) His estate was auctioned to recover the arrears

Explanation: Under the Permanent Settlement, if a zamindar failed to pay the revenue on time, his estate was auctioned by the British to recover the arrears, often resulting in the loss of his lands.

Question 54: (a) The intrusion of Santhal settlers into their lands

Explanation: The Paharias withdrew deeper into the Rajmahal Hills primarily due to the intrusion of Santhal settlers into their lands, which was part of British efforts to bring more land under cultivation by encouraging Santhal settlement.

Question 55. (a) A-1, B-2, C-3, D-4

Explanation:

A. Paharias - 1. Rajmahal Hills
B. Santhals - 2. Damin-i-Koh
C. Ryots - 3. Bengal and Deccan
D. Jotedars - 4. North Bengal

Question 56 : (b) Moneylenders who exploited peasants

Explanation: The Deccan Riots of 1875 were mainly targeted at moneylenders who exploited peasants through usurious lending practices, forcing many to fall into debt.

Question 57 :(c) Control the accumulation of interest on debts

Explanation: The British passed the Limitation Law in 1859 to control the accumulation of interest on debts, which was a significant issue for peasants who were often exploited by moneylenders charging exorbitant interest rates.

Question 58 :(c) Shifting cultivation and forest produce gathering

Explanation: Before British intervention, the Paharias primarily practiced shifting cultivation and gathered forest produce. Their lifestyle was closely connected to the forest and its resources, which was disrupted by British policies.

Question 59 : (a) The British wanted to justify their control over rural Bengal

Explanation: The Fifth Report exaggerated the collapse of zamindari power because the British wanted to justify their control over rural Bengal. By emphasizing the failure of zamindars, they aimed to promote their own system of revenue collection and administration.

Question 60 : (a) A-1, B-2, C-3, D-4

Explanation:

A. Lord Cornwallis - 1. Introduced Permanent Settlement
B. Augustus Cleveland - 2. Policy of pacification for the Paharias
C. Francis Buchanan - 3. Conducted surveys on rural economy
D. Charles Cornwallis - 4. Governor-General during American War of Independence

Question 61 : 1 - (b) Heavy taxes, high-interest loans, and zamindari control

Explanation: The Santhals lost their cultivated land due to the heavy taxes imposed by the state, high-interest loans from moneylenders, and the control asserted by zamindars over the land.

2. (c) Moneylenders and exploiters
 Explanation: The term "dikus" refers to the moneylenders
and other exploiters who charged high-interest rates and
took over the land when debts remained unpaid.

3. (b) To overthrow the zamindars and moneylenders
 Explanation: The Santhals rebelled against the
exploitation by zamindars, moneylenders, and the British
colonial state to create an ideal world for themselves.

4. (b) They created the Santhal Pargana region
 Explanation: After the revolt, the British created the
Santhal Pargana region, which was carved out from the
districts of Bhagalpur and Birbhum to settle the Santhals.

5. (a) The British promised them land ownership and
protection
 Explanation: The Santhals agreed to settle in Damin-i-
Koh because the British promised them land ownership
and protection from local zamindars.

Question 62 : (a) A-3, B-1, C-2, D-4
 Explanation:
A. Permanent Settlement – 3. Revenue fixed permanently
B. Ryotwari Settlement – 1. Revenue collected directly from
ryots
C. Mahalwari Settlement – 2. Revenue collected through
zamindars
D. Sunset Law – 4. Zamindars lost land if revenue was
unpaid by sunset

Question 63 : (a) A-1, B-2, C-3, D-4
 Explanation:
A. Santhal Revolt (1855-56) – 1. Creation of the Santhal
Parganas
B. Deccan Riots (1875) – 2. Establishment of a commission
to investigate moneylender practices
C. American Civil War – 3. Increased demand for Indian
cotton
D. Fifth Report (1813) – 4. Criticism of East India
Company's land policies

Chapter 11 : Rebels and the Raj

Question 1: (b) is correct
Explanation: The Subsidiary Alliance system was introduced by Lord Wellesley, which aimed at controlling Indian rulers by requiring them to maintain a British force in their territory.

Question 2: (a) is correct
Explanation: Nana Sahib was one of the prominent leaders of the rebellion in Kanpur during the uprising of 1857.

Question 3: (c) is correct
Explanation: Bahadur Shah ,led revolt in Delhi 1857.

Question 4: (a) is correct
Explanation: Rani Lakshmi Bai led the revolt in Jhansi and is one of the most iconic figures in the 1857 rebellion.

Question 5: (c) is correct
Explanation: The soldiers at Meerut cantonment rebelled on May 10, 1857, marking the beginning of the revolt of 1857.

Question 6: (d) is correct
Explanation: Lord William Bentinck, the Governor-General, aimed to reform Indian society through policies such as the abolition of Sati and the introduction of Western education.

Question 7: (c) is correct
Explanation: The immediate cause of the 1857 rebellion was the introduction of greased cartridges, which offended the religious sentiments of both Hindu and Muslim soldiers.

Question 8: (c) is correct
Explanation: The British referred to the kingdom of Awadh as "a cherry that will one day fall into their lap" due to its strategic importance.

Question 9: (b) is correct
Explanation: The revolt of 1857 first began at Meerut, where soldiers rebelled against the British authorities on May 10, 1857.

Question 10: (c) is correct
Explanation: Maulvi Ahmadullah was known by the title "Danka Shah" during the revolt of 1857, as he was a prominent figure in the rebellion, especially in the regions of Lucknow and Faizabad.

Question 11: (a) is correct
Explanation: The annexation of Awadh in 1857 by the British was not due to Wajid Ali Shah's unpopularity. The reasons included the British desire for control and economic exploitation rather than any specific unpopularity of the Nawab.

Question 12: (b) is correct
Explanation: The practice of Sati was abolished in India in 1829 by Lord William Bentinck through the Bengal Sati Regulation, which made it illegal.

Question 13: (a) is correct
Explanation: The uprising of 1857 was initiated by the sepoys (Indian soldiers in the British army), who mutinied against their British officers, marking the beginning of the revolt.

Question 14: (b) is correct
Explanation: Nana Sahib led the rebellion in Kanpur. He was a key leader in the revolt of 1857 and played a crucial role in the events in Kanpur

Question 15: (b) is correct
Explanation: The correct match of leaders with places where they led the revolt is:
(i) Delhi – Bahadur Shah
(ii) Kanpur – Nana Sahib
(iii) Arrah – Kunwar Singh
(iv) Lucknow – Birjis Qadr

Question 16: (c) is correct
Explanation: Lord Dalhousie compared the kingdom of Awadh to a cherry, which he believed would eventually fall into the British lap.

Question 17: (a) is correct
Explanation: Awadh was officially annexed into the British Empire in 1856, marking a significant event leading to the revolt of 1857.

Question 18: (c) is correct
Explanation: All the statements (i), (ii), (iii), and (iv) regarding the 1857 revolt are accurate. The sepoys in Meerut mutinied, were supported by local people, looted weapons, attacked Europeans, and reached the Red Fort gates.

Question 19: (a) is correct
Explanation: The term "Bell of Arms" refers to a storeroom for storing weapons. It was used metaphorically to signify the importance of arms and ammunition in the context of
military readiness.

Question 20 :(d) is correct
Explanation: "Bell of Arms" refers to a place where arms or weapons are stored, not food. Hence, the term is mismatched in its meaning

Question 21: (a) is correct
Explanation: Nawab Wajid Ali Shah was exiled to Calcutta for alleged misgovernance, but he was not an unpopular ruler, and many followed him to Kanpur, mourning his departure. The incorrect statements are (ii) and (iv).

Question 22: (a) is correct
Explanation: Bahadur Shah Zafar led the revolt in Delhi during the 1857 uprising. He was a symbolic leader of the rebellion, though his actual influence was limited.

Question 23 : (d) is correct
Explanation: The rumor that the British aimed to abolish the caste system was not a 19th-century rumor during the British colonial period. The other three rumors were widely believed at the time.

Question 24 : (a) is correct
Explanation: Birjis Qadr was the younger son of Nawab Wajid Ali Shah, the ruler of Awadh, and he played an important role in the revolt of 1857, particularly in Lucknow.

Question 25 : (c) is correct

Explanation: Awadh and Satara were annexed under the Doctrine of Lapse, a policy implemented by Lord Dalhousie, which allowed the British to annex princely states without a male heir.

Question 26: (a) is correct

Explanation: Nana Sahib joined the 1857 revolt after the British refused to give him the pension of his adopted father, Peshwa Baji Rao II, which was a significant reason for his participation in the uprising.

Question 27 : (b) is correct

Explanation: Kunwar Singh was a prominent leader from Bihar during the 1857 revolt. He led a resistance in Bihar and was a key figure in the rebellion in the eastern part of India.

Question 28 : (d) is correct

Explanation: Annie Besant started the Home Rule Movement in India. She played a key role in promoting self-rule for Indians under British colonial rule.

Question 29 : (d) is correct

Explanation: Shah Mal was not the leader of the revolt in Awadh. Instead, he led the revolt in a different region. Therefore, this pair of revolt centers and their leaders is incorrect.

Question 30 :(b) is correct

Explanation: "Relief of Lucknow" was painted by Thomas Jones Barker, commemorating the British heroes during the rebellion of 1857.

Question 31 : (c) is correct

Explanation: "In Memoriam," dedicated to the courage of British women during the Revolt of 1857, was created by
Joseph Noel Paton.

Question 32 : (a) is correct

Explanation: Miss Wheeler was the Englishwoman who bravely resisted Indian rebels in Kanpur during the uprising of 1857.

Question 33 : (a) is correct

Explanation: All the statements about the 1857 revolt are correct: Rumors played a significant role, Nana Saheb was adopted by Peshwa Baji Rao II, the British struggled to control the rebels in May and June 1857, and Awadh was indeed a key center of the revolt.

Question 34 : (a) Foreigner

Explanation: The term 'Firangi' was used in India to refer to foreigners, particularly Europeans.

Question 35 : (b) September

Explanation: The British recaptured Delhi in September 1857 after months of intense fighting.

Question 36 :(c) 1856

Explanation: Awadh was annexed by the British East India Company in 1856, just before the revolt.

Question 37 : (d) Chaurasee Des

Explanation: Shah Mal organized a resistance against the British by gathering village headmen and farmers in Chaurasee Des

Question 38 : Answer: (c) 1858

Explanation: She died fighting the British forces in Gwalior in June 1858 during the Revolt of 1857.

39 : Question 1: Who led the rebellion in Kanpur during the Revolt of 1857?
 Answer: (b) Nana Saheb

Question 2: Which British general led the forces to lay siege to Kanpur?
 Answer: (a) General Havelock

Question 3: What was the significance of the siege and relief of Kanpur in the Revolt of 1857?
 Answer: (b) It was a pivotal moment with intense battles and heavy losses on both sides.

Question 4: Which statement is incorrect regarding Kanpur during the Revolt of 1857?
 Answer: (c) The British lost control of Kanpur after the siege.
 Explanation: This is false. The British regained control after the siege, not lost it.

Question 5: What was the outcome of the British siege of Kanpur?
 Answer: (b) The British forces regained control of Kanpur after intense
 fighting.

Chapter 12 : Colonial Cities

Question 1 : (c) Indian settlements often near bazaars and temples
Explanation: In colonial cities, the term "Black Town" referred to areas where Indians lived, typically near markets, temples, and traditional quarters. These were contrasted with "White Towns," where Europeans resided.

Question 2 : (b) Fort St George
Explanation: Madras (now Chennai) developed around Fort St George, which was built by the British East India Company in 1644 as a strategic trading and administrative center.

Question 3 : (b) Sirajudaula
Explanation: Calcutta's Fort William was rebuilt by the British after the Battle of Plassey in 1757, where they defeated Sirajudaula, the Nawab of Bengal.

Question 4 : (c) Hindu and Muslim architectural elements with European forms
Explanation: The Indo-Saracenic style was a blend of Indian (Hindu and Muslim) architectural traditions with Gothic, neoclassical, and Victorian European styles, commonly used in colonial public buildings.

Question 5 : (c) Seven islands
Explanation: The city of Bombay (now Mumbai) was formed by reclaiming land and joining seven islands, which were originally part of a Portuguese dowry gifted to the British in 1661.

Question 6 : (c) Lottery Committee
Explanation: The Lottery Committee, established in 1817 in Calcutta, was responsible for urban improvements like roads, drainage, and lighting. It raised funds through public lotteries.

Question 7 : (a) Both A and R are true, and R is the correct explanation of A
Explanation: Town planning in colonial India indeed prioritised European quarters. The British perceived Indian areas as chaotic, unhygienic, and prone to disease, justifying their neglect in urban development.

Question 8 : (b) Cotton
Explanation: During the American Civil War (1861-1865), cotton supplies from the US to Britain were disrupted. Bombay emerged as a key exporter of Indian cotton, leading to an economic boom.

Question 9 : (c) 1881
Explanation: The first synchronous all-India census was conducted in 1881, under British administration, laying the foundation for decennial censuses thereafter.

Question 10 : (b) Sutanati, Kolkata, Govindapur
Explanation: The city of Calcutta (now Kolkata) originally developed from three villages: Sutanati, Govindapur, and Kalikata (not "Kolkata" as modern spelling). These were granted to the British by the Mughal emperor and later grew into a major colonial city.

.Question 11 : (a) Both A and R are true, and R is the correct explanation of A
Explanation: Railway stations in colonial India did indeed become major urban hubs. They functioned as key points for collecting raw materials (like cotton and coal) from hinterlands and distributing British manufactured goods—making the Reason a correct explanation.

Question 12 : (c) Premchand Roychand
Explanation: The Rajabai Clock Tower in Bombay was financed by the wealthy stockbroker Premchand Roychand, who named it after his mother, Raja bai.

Question 13 : (c) Neo-Gothic
Explanation: The Victoria Terminus (now Chhatrapati Shivaji Maharaj Terminus) in Bombay was built in the Neo-Gothic style, incorporating pointed arches, ribbed vaults, and stained glass windows—typical of European Gothic architecture.

Question 14 : (d) Simla
Explanation: Simla (now Shimla) was the first hill station where the British Viceroy moved his council during the summer to escape the heat of the plains. It became the summer capital of British India.

Question 15 : (b) Ganga Dhar Nehru
Explanation: Ganga Dhar Nehru, the grandfather of Jawaharlal Nehru, worked as the kotwal (chief police officer) of Delhi before the Revolt of 1857.

Question 16 : (d) A is false, and R is false
Explanation: British census data often suffered from inaccuracies due to language barriers, classification biases, and limited understanding of local social structures. The process was far from objective, especially in categorizing caste and religion.

Question 17 : (a) 1767
Explanation: The Survey of India was established in 1767 to carry out detailed geographical surveys and mapping of Indian territory, playing a vital role in colonial administration and control.

Question 18: (a) Indo-Saracenic
Explanation:The Indo-Saracenic style blended medieval Indian architecture (like domes and arches) with European elements such as Gothic spires. The Gateway of India in Mumbai is a prime example.

Question 19 : (d) Chintadripet
Explanation: Chintadripet in Madras was originally established as a weavers' settlement by the British East India Company to boost textile production and trade.

Question 20 : (c) Municipal Corporation
Explanation: Municipal Corporations were established by the British to administer cities and collect taxes annually for urban services like lighting, sanitation, and roads.

Question 21: (a) Ooty
Explanation: Ooty (Udhagamandalam) in the Nilgiris was the first colonial hill station, developed during and after the Gurkha War (1814-16), as a retreat for British officials

Question 22 :(a) Calcutta
Explanation: The Imperial Gazetteer described Calcutta as having a semi-rural feel with rice fields surrounding parts of the city even during colonial rule.

Question 23 : (c) Local languages
Explanation: "Dubash" (literally "two languages") referred to Indians fluent in English and local Indian languages who served as translators and intermediaries between British officials and local people.

Question 24 : (c) Sanitize Indian towns due to fear of disease spreading
Explanation: The British introduced piped water and drainage systems in the 1860s-70s primarily out of fear of epidemics like cholera and plague, especially near European quarters and port cities.

Question 25 : (a) Both A and R are true, and R is the correct explanation of A
Explanation: Chawls in Bombay were overcrowded tenements, but the shared spaces helped build a sense of community among working-class residents.

Question 26 : (c) Unobstructed military defence
Explanation: Fort William in Calcutta was surrounded by a cleared space (the Maidan) for security reasons, providing a clear field of fire and no hiding spots for attackers.

Question 27 : (c) Gateway of India
Explanation: The Gateway of India in Bombay was built in Indo-Saracenic style with Gujarati influence to commemorate the 1911 visit of King George V and Queen Mary.

Question 28 : (b) Binodini Dasi
Explanation: Binodini Dasi was a pioneering Indian actress and writer in the 19th century who authored Amar Katha, one of the earliest autobiographies by an Indian woman in theatre.

Question 29 : (b) Civil Lines
Explanation: Civil Lines were spacious, well-planned areas where British officials lived—seen as orderly, in contrast to densely populated Indian settlements.

Question 30 : (b) Binodini Dasi
Explanation: Binodini Dasi, a pioneering actress, founded Star Theatre in Calcutta and later wrote her autobiography Amar Katha.

Question 31 : (a) Both A and R are true, and R is the correct explanation of A
Explanation: Indians started adopting European architectural styles like Gothic and Classical as these were perceived as symbols of progress and status.

Question 32 : (b) Neo-Gothic
Explanation: Neo-Gothic architecture, with pointed arches and intricate detailing, was used in colonial buildings like Bombay University and the High Court.

Question 33 :(b) Royapuram
Explanation: Royapuram was a Christian fishing village and home to boatmen who worked for the East India Company in Madras.

Question 34 :(c) Premchand Roychand
Explanation: The Rajabai Tower in Bombay was funded by Premchand Roychand, a prosperous businessman, in memory of his mother .

Question 35 : (c) To maintain a clear line of fire around Fort St George
Explanation: The Black Town near Fort St George in Madras was demolished to ensure a clear field of fire for the fort's defense.

Question 36 : (c) Qasbah
Explanation: A qasbah was a small town in rural India, typically a seat of a zamindar or notable person and a centre for local trade and culture.

Question 37 : (c) Lottery
Explanation: The Lottery Committee, formed in 1817, was instrumental in planning and developing Calcutta by raising funds through public lotteries.

Question 38 : (b) A residential block for Company servants
Explanation: The Writers' Building was initially constructed to house junior servants or "writers" of the East India Company.

Question 39 : (c) Broad streets, bungalows, and European clubs
Explanation: "White Towns" were well-planned European quarters with open spaces, large bungalows, and exclusive social institutions.

Question 40 : (a) Maidan
Explanation: The Maidan was an open area around Fort William in Calcutta, left intentionally vacant for defensive military purposes.

Question 41 : (c) Bombay
Explanation: Bombay was termed Urbs Prima in Indis, meaning "the first city of India," due to its importance as a commercial and administrative hub.

Question 42 : (b) Chenapattanam
Explanation: Before becoming Madras, the area was known locally as Chenapattanam, believed to be named after a fishing village or a local chieftain.

Question 43 : (c) Shift in trade to British-controlled port cities
Explanation: With the rise of port cities like Calcutta, Bombay, and Madras under British control, older inland trade centres like Surat and Dhaka declined.

Question 44 : (a) Bungalow
Explanation: The bungalow was a typical colonial house with sloping roofs, wide verandas, and outbuildings like servant quarters.

Question 45 : (b) Urban policing
Explanation: Municipal corporations were mainly responsible for civic services like water supply, health, and taxation. Policing was generally handled by separate colonial police forces , not municipal bodies.

Chapter 13 : Mahatma Gandhi and the Nationalist Movement

Question 1 : (a) Lord Irwin
Explanation : - Lord Irwin was the Viceroy of India when the Civil Disobedience Movement began in 1930.

Question 2 : (d) Salt Laws
Explanation : - The Civil Disobedience Movement was initiated in response to the British monopoly over salt, symbolized by the Salt Laws.

Question 3 : (c) Violation of the Salt Laws
Explanation : - The Dandi March, led by Mahatma Gandhi in 1930, involved the symbolic breaking of the Salt Laws.

Question 4 : (b) 1931
Explanation : - The Second Round Table Conference took place in London in 1931.

Question 5 : (b) Subhas Chandra Bose
Explanation : - Subhas Chandra Bose was not involved in the Quit India Movement as he had already left India and formed the Indian National Army.

Question 6 : (c) Quit India
Explanation : - The slogan "Do or Die" was given by Mahatma Gandhi during the Quit India Movement in 1942.

Question 7 : (b) To end the Civil Disobedience Movement
Explanation : - The Gandhi-Irwin Pact was an agreement to suspend the Civil Disobedience Movement in return for certain concessions.

Question 8 : (b) Mahatma Gandhi
Explanation : - Mahatma Gandhi opposed the idea of separate electorates for the Depressed Classes, which led to the Poona Pact with Dr. Ambedkar.

Question 9 : (b) 1920
Explanation : - The Non-Cooperation Movement was launched by Mahatma Gandhi in 1920.

Question 10 : (c) Increased participation of women in the freedom struggle
Explanation : - One of the significant impacts of the Civil Disobedience Movement was the rise in active participation of women.

Question 11 : (d) Lord Irwin
Explanation : - Lord Irwin was the Viceroy, not a leader of the Non-Cooperation Movement, and hence not associated as a participant.

Question 12 : (b) 1931
Explanation : - The Gandhi-Irwin Pact was signed in 1931.

Question 13 : (c) Chauri Chaura Incident
Explanation : - Mahatma Gandhi called off the Non-Cooperation Movement after the violent incident at Chauri Chaura in 1922, where a mob killed 22 policemen.

Question 14 : (b) 1919
Explanation : - The Rowlatt Act was passed by the British government in 1919, giving powers for the arrest of individuals without trial.

Question 15 : (b) Failure of the Cripps Mission
Explanation : - The Quit India Movement was launched in 1942 after the failure of the Cripps Mission to secure Indian support during World War II.

Question 16 : (b) Khilafat Movement
Explanation : - The Khilafat Movement aimed at uniting Hindus and Muslims to protest against the dismemberment of the Ottoman Empire and the abolition of the Caliphate.

Question 17 : (b) Gopal Krishna Gokhale
Explanation : - Gopal Krishna Gokhale was Mahatma Gandhi's political mentor, and his ideas greatly influenced Gandhi's views on social reforms and self-rule.

Question 18 : (b) 1919
Explanation : - The Jallianwala Bagh Massacre took place in Amritsar in 1919, where British troops, under General Dyer, killed hundreds of unarmed civilians.

Question 19 : (a) He considered it a social evil that must be eradicated.
Explanation : - Mahatma Gandhi strongly opposed untouchability, viewing it as a social evil, and worked to eradicate it throughout his life.

Question 20 : (b) Simon
Explanation : - The British government sent the Simon Commission in 1928 to review the political situation in India, though it was met with widespread protests for not including Indian members.

Question 21 : (a) Jawaharlal Nehru
Explanation : - Jawaharlal Nehru was the first to officially refer to Mahatma Gandhi as the "Father of the Nation" in a speech in 1947.

Question 22 : (b) Sabarmati Ashram
Explanation : - The Dandi March, led by Mahatma Gandhi, started from Sabarmati Ashram in Ahmedabad on March 12, 1930.

Question 23 : (b) General Dyer
Explanation : - General Reginald Dyer was responsible for ordering the Jallianwala Bagh massacre in 1919.

Question 24 : (c) To support the Turkish Caliphate and oppose British policies
Explanation : - The main objective of the Khilafat Movement (1919-1924) was to protect the Ottoman Caliphate and resist British policies in the Middle East.

Question 25 : (b) 6
Explanation : - Mahatma Gandhi was arrested in March 1922 and sentenced to 6 years of imprisonment for his role in the Non-Cooperation Movement.

Question 26 : (a) It was a protest against British taxation policies.
Explanation : - The Salt March (Dandi March) in 1930 was a non-violent protest against the British monopoly on salt and the tax imposed on it.

Question 27 : (a) Non-Cooperation
Explanation : - The slogan "Swaraj in one year" was given by Mahatma Gandhi during the Non-Cooperation Movement, aiming for self-rule within one year.

Question 28 : (c) Mahatma Gandhi
Explanation : - Mahatma Gandhi wrote the book Hind Swaraj in 1909, where he expressed his views on self-rule and criticism of Western civilization.

Question 29 : (b) London
Explanation : - The Round Table Conferences were held in London between 1930 and 1932 to discuss constitutional reforms in India.

Question 30 : (b) Mahatma Gandhi called off the Non-Cooperation Movement.
Explanation : - After the Chauri Chaura incident in 1922, where a mob killed 22 policemen, Mahatma Gandhi called off the Non-Cooperation Movement to prevent further violence.

Question 31 : (b) Banaras Hindu University
Explanation : - Mahatma Gandhi made his first major public appearance in India at the opening of the Banaras Hindu University in 1916.

Question 32 : (b) Chauri Chaura incident
Explanation : - The Non-Cooperation Movement was withdrawn by Mahatma Gandhi following the Chauri Chaura incident, where violence broke out.

Question 33 : (b) Dandi
Explanation : - The Civil Disobedience Movement was formally launched with the Dandi March in 1930, where Mahatma Gandhi broke the salt law.

Question 34 : (a) Mahatma Gandhi
Explanation : - Mahatma Gandhi was not present at the Round Table Conferences. He was in jail during the first two conferences and refused to attend the third.

Question 35 : (c) Gopal Krishna Gokhale
Explanation : - Mahatma Gandhi's political mentor was Gopal Krishna Gokhale, who deeply influenced Gandhi's views on social issues and self-rule.

Question 36 : (b) Rowlatt Act, 1919
Explanation : - The British introduced the Rowlatt Act in 1919 to curb nationalist activities and allow imprisonment of individuals without trial.

Question 37 : (a) Truth
Explanation : - Mahatma Gandhi's autobiography is titled The Story of My Experiments with Truth, where he shares his personal and political journey based on his principles of truth and non-violence.

Question 38 : (b) Complete withdrawal of British rule from India
Explanation : - The primary demand of the Quit India Movement, launched in 1942, was the immediate and complete withdrawal of British rule from India.

Question 39 : (b) Indian
Explanation : - The Simon Commission was boycotted by Indians because it did not include any Indian members, leading to widespread protests.

Question 40 : (b) General Dyer
Explanation : - General Reginald Dyer was the British officer responsible for ordering the massacre of hundreds of unarmed civilians at Jallianwala Bagh in 1919

Question 41 : (b) To protest against the heavy taxation on salt
Explanation : - The primary objective of the Salt March (Dandi March) was to protest against the British monopoly on salt and the heavy tax levied on it.

Question 42 : (b) South Africa
Explanation : - Mahatma Gandhi first experimented with his philosophy of non-violence (Ahimsa) and Satyagraha during his time in South Africa, especially in the struggle for the rights of the Indian community there.

Question 43 : (a) B.R. Ambedkar
Explanation : - The Poona Pact of 1932 was an agreement between Mahatma Gandhi and Dr. B.R. Ambedkar to resolve the issue of separate electorates for the Depressed Classes.

Question 44 : (b) 80,000
Explanation : - The Civil Disobedience Movement led to the arrest of approximately 80,000 people, reflecting the widespread participation in the struggle against British rule.

Question 45 : (d) Muhammad Ali Jinnah
Explanation : - Muhammad Ali Jinnah called Mahatma Gandhi's Non-Cooperation Movement a "Himalayan blunder," expressing his disagreement with the approach.

Question 46 : (d) Industrialization and large-scale mechanization
Explanation : - Mahatma Gandhi was critical of large-scale mechanization and industrialization, believing they led to exploitation and the destruction of self-sufficiency. His reforms focused more on social issues like untouchability, Hindu-Muslim unity, and women's rights.

Question 47 : (b) 30 January 1948
Explanation : - Mahatma Gandhi was assassinated on 30 January 1948 by Nathuram Godse, shortly after India gained independence.

Question 48 : (a) Both A and R are true, and R is the correct explanation of A.
Explanation : - Mahatma Gandhi called off the Non-Cooperation Movement in 1922 after the Chauri Chaura incident, where violent clashes led to the deaths of police officers. Gandhi withdrew the movement to prevent further violence.

Question 49 : (a) Both A and R are true, and R is the correct explanation of A.
Explanation : - Mahatma Gandhi supported the Khilafat Movement because he believed that supporting it would promote Hindu-Muslim unity, which was a crucial element of his vision for India's freedom struggle.

Question 50 : (b) C. Rajagopalachari
Explanation : - C. Rajagopalachari led the Salt Satyagraha in Tamil Nadu, making a significant contribution to the national movement in the region.

51 - Question 1 : (c) Violation of British salt laws
Explanation : - The primary objective of the Salt March was to break the British monopoly on salt by violating the salt laws, which were a symbol of colonial oppression.

Question 2 : (b) They arrested thousands of protesters, including Gandhi
Explanation : - In response to the Salt March, the British government arrested thousands of participants, including Mahatma Gandhi, and used force to suppress the movemeint.

Question 3 : (b) Sabarmati Ashram
Explanation : - The Salt March began at Sabarmati Ashram, located in Ahmedabad, where Mahatma Gandhi initiated the march towards the coastal town of Dandi

Question 4 : (c) It mobilized people across the country and gained international attention
Explanation : - The Salt March had a profound impact on Indian politics. It mobilized large sections of the population, garnered international attention, and became a major symbol of non-violent resistance.

Question 5 : (b) It included mass participation from different sections of society
Explanation : - The Civil Disobedience Movement included mass participation from various sections of Indian society, from urban middle classes to rural populations, as they engaged in the struggle against British rule.

Chapter 14 : Understanding Partition

Question 1: (A) is correct
Explanation: Both statements are true and connected: British policies like separate electorates fostered communal divisions, contributing to the violence and displacement during Partition.

Question 2 : (C) is correct
Explanation: Around 15 million people were displaced during the Partition—the largest mass migration in human history.

Question 3 : (C) is correct
Explanation: The term "Holocaust" is often used metaphorically to describe the scale of brutality and forced migration during Partition.

Question 4 :(C) is correct
Explanation: The Radcliffe Commission, headed by Cyril Radcliffe, was responsible for drawing the boundaries between India and Pakistan.

Question 5 : (D) is correct
Explanation: Stereotypes like "Muslims are cruel and Hindus are pure" and "Hindus are invaders" were reinforced by communal narratives around Partition.

Question 6 : (D) is correct
Explanation: All these factors—cow protection movements, separate electorates, and reconversion efforts—fueled communal tension in pre-Partition India.

Question 7 : (B) is correct
Explanation: The British colonial government introduced separate electorates, which encouraged sectarian political identities and deepened communal divides.

Question 8 : (B) is correct
Explanation: Partition was abrupt and accompanied by brutal violence, dislocation, and trauma for millions, not a peaceful constitutional process.

Question 9 : (D) is correct
Explanation: Estimates suggest that between 500,000 and 1 million people died as a result of Partition-related violence and displacement.

Question 10 : (B) is correct
Explanation: Oral history and survivor interviews have been the primary tools for understanding the lived experiences of Partition, as many official records were limited or sanitized.

Question 11 : (B) Cyril Radcliffe
Explanation: Cyril Radcliffe chaired the boundary commission and drew the borders between India and Pakistan in 1947.

Question 12 : (C) Self-styled representatives of religious communities
Explanation: Much of the Partition violence was carried out by mobs and individuals acting in the name of religious communities, not official agencies.

Question 13 : (B) The forced removal and killing of people based on their religious identity
Explanation: "Ethnic cleansing" during Partition refers to mass killings and forced displacement of people due to their religious identity.

Question 14 : (B) The Indian National Congress and the Muslim League
Explanation: The Lucknow Pact of 1916 was an agreement between these two political parties to present a united front to the British.

Question 15 : (C) "A civil war"
Explanation: Many scholars and observers describe Partition as a civil war due to the scale and nature of the communal violence

Question 16 :(B) Ethnic cleansing
Explanation: This term refers to the forced removal and killing of people based on their religion during Partition.

Question 17 : (C) Two days after formal independence
Explanation: The Radcliffe Line was officially revealed on August 17, 1947, two days after independence.

Question 18 : (A) It helped in documenting personal experiences of survivors
Explanation: Oral history captures the lived experiences of ordinary people affected by Partition.

Question 19 : (B) It deepened religious stereotypes and divisions
Explanation: Partition intensified mistrust and divisions between religious communities.

Question 20 : (A) It was a peaceful and orderly transition
Explanation: This is not true — Partition involved mass violence, chaos, and suffering

Question 21 : (C) Mohammad Ali Jinnah
Explanation: Jinnah strongly advocated the Two-Nation Theory, which argued for a separate nation for Muslims.

Question 22 : (B) Cultural heritage
Explanation: Millions lost their homes, traditions, and centuries-old community ties during forced migration.

Question 23 : (C) Outbreak of mass violence and killings
Explanation: The announcement triggered panic, riots, and massacres across the subcontinent.

Question 24 : (C) Pakistan
Explanation: Partition created India and Pakistan, with Pakistan consisting of East and West regions (East Pakistan later became Bangladesh.

Question 25 : (B) Punjab and Bengal
Explanation: These border regions witnessed some of the most horrific riots and killings during Partition.

Question 26 : (A) "Hullar" and "raula"
Explanation: These regional terms, especially in Punjabi, were often used by survivors to describe the chaos and noise of violence during Partition.

Question 27 : (D) All of the above
Explanation: Refugees faced severe challenges, including transportation shortages, lack of shelter and food, and diseases in camps.

Question 28 : (C) East Pakistan
Explanation: Pakistan was created with two parts—West Pakistan (now Pakistan) and East Pakistan (now Bangladesh).

Question 29 : (D) The Radcliffe Commission took time to finalize the demarcation
 Explanation: The commission had just five weeks to draw the borders, leading to delayed announcements and confusion.

Question 30 : (C) Religious demographics
Explaination - The division of British India in 1947, resulting in the creation of India and Pakistan, was primarily based on religious lines—with Pakistan formed as a Muslim-majority nation and India as a secular state with a Hindu majority.

Chapter 15 : Framing the Constitution

Question 1: a) Both A and R are true, and R is the correct explanation of A
 Explanation: The Indian Constitution is the longest in the world because of India's diversity, complexity, and the need to integrate multiple communities—hence, R correctly explains A.

Question 2: c) A is true, but R is false
 Explanation: The Objectives Resolution did provide a framework, but it was not inspired solely by the American and French Revolutions. It reflected Indian political values and realities.

Question 3: c) 1946-46
 Explanation: The Constituent Assembly was formed as a result of the elections held in 1946-46 under the Cabinet Mission Plan.

Question 4: a) Jawaharlal Nehru
 Explanation: Nehru strongly opposed the idea of separate electorates, calling it a "poison" that would divide the nation on communal lines.

Question 5: a) Equality
 Explanation: The Right to Equality includes the prohibition of discrimination on grounds of religion, race, caste, sex, or place of birth (Article 16).

Question 6: d) Election Commission Committee
 Explanation: This was not a committee of the Constituent Assembly. Other mentioned ones like the Drafting and Language Committees were indeed present.

Question 7: c) Rajendra Prasad
 Explanation: Dr. Rajendra Prasad was the President of the Constituent Assembly, but he was not a member of the Drafting Committee.

Question 8: c) December 1949
 Explanation: The Constitution was signed on 24th December 1949, after being adopted on 26th November 1949, and came into effect on 26th January 1950.

Question 9: b) Jaipal Singh
 Explanation: Jaipal Singh Munda advocated strongly for the rights and protection of tribal communities in the Constituent Assembly.

Question 10: c) Hindustani
 Explanation: Gandhi favored Hindustani—a blend of Hindi and Urdu—as a national language to unify people across linguistic boundaries.

Question 11: c) 11
 Explanation: The Constituent Assembly held 11 sessions between 1946 and 1949 to debate and frame the Constitution.

Question 12: a) Both A and R are true, and R is the correct explanation of A
 Explanation: The Congress dominated the Constituent Assembly largely because the Muslim League and Socialists initially refused to participate, making R the correct explanation for A.

Question 13: a) Both A and R are true, and R is the correct explanation of A
 Explanation: Nehru's "Objectives Resolution" was indeed accepted unanimously, and it focused on justice, equality, and minority safeguards, which justifies the assertion.

Question 14: c) B.R. Ambedkar
 Explanation: Dr. B.R. Ambedkar was the Chairman of the Drafting Committee of the Indian Constitution.

Question 15: b) Socialism
 Explanation: Nehru emphasized democratic ideals infused with socialism to ensure equity and justice for all citizens.

Question 16: b) Sardar Vallabhbhai Patel
 Explanation: Sardar Patel was a strong opponent of separate electorates, believing it would further divide the country.

Question 17: b) Jaipal Singh
 Explanation: Jaipal Singh Munda vocally advocated for the rights, protection, and development of tribal communities in the Assembly.

Question 18: b) 26 November 1949; 26 January 1950
 Explanation: The Constitution was adopted on 26 November 1949 and enforced on 26 January 1950 to commemorate the declaration of Purna Swaraj in 1930.

Question 19: c) Absolute monarchy
 Explanation: India chose democracy over monarchy. Features like secularism, federalism, and minority rights were key principles of the Constitution.

Question 20: b) N.G. Ranga
 Explanation: N.G. Ranga emphasized that democracy should be meaningful to the poor and include economic justice.

Question 21: b) November 1949
 Explanation: The Constitution was framed from December 1946 to November 1949, completing a nearly 3-year drafting process.

Question 22: c) 166
 Explanation: The Constituent Assembly held sessions over 166 days, carefully debating and discussing every article.

Question 23: b) Jawaharlal Nehru
 Explanation: Nehru moved the resolution for adopting the Indian National Flag as a tricolor with the Ashoka Chakra.

Question 24: b) The Indian context
 Explanation: Though it borrowed elements from other constitutions, the Indian Constitution was tailored to suit India's unique social, cultural, and historical context.

Question 25: b) Somnath Lahiri
 Explanation: Somnath Lahiri strongly criticized British imperialism's lingering influence and was the only member to oppose the Objectives Resolution, demanding full independence
.

Question 26: b) Fragmentation of the nation
 Explanation: Separate electorates were seen as a threat to national unity, potentially dividing the country along religious lines.

Question 27: d) Articles 29-30
 Explanation: Articles 29 and 30 provide cultural and educational rights to minorities, ensuring the protection of their heritage and institutions.

Question 28: c) N.G. Ranga
 Explanation: N.G. Ranga emphasized that the real minorities were not just religious groups but the poor, landless, and oppressed classes.

Question 29: b) Hindi in Devanagari script
Explanation: Hindi in the Devanagari script was adopted as the official language, while English was allowed for official use for 15 years.

Question 30: b) Jaipal Singh
Explanation: Jaipal Singh passionately spoke for Adivasi rights, highlighting their historical neglect and the need for special protections.

Question 31: c) A is true, but R is false
Explanation: While the Constitution aimed to unify India, it was not entirely based on the Government of India Act, 1935—only parts of it were used as a reference.

Question 32: a) Both A and R are true, and R is the correct explanation of A
Explanation: The Constituent Assembly wasn't elected by universal adult franchise; its members were chosen by provincial legislatures from the 1946-46 elections.

Question 33: a) December 1946
Explanation: The Constituent Assembly of India held its first meeting on 9 December 1946.

Question 34: b) December 1949
Explanation: The Constitution was finalized and signed on 26 November 1949, but the process concluded formally in December 1949.

Question 35: b) Cabinet Mission Plan
Explanation: The Cabinet Mission Plan of 1946 led to the formation of the Constituent Assembly of India.

Question 36: c) Dr. B.N. Rau
Explanation: Dr. B.N. Rau was appointed as the Constitutional Advisor to the Constituent Assembly and prepared the initial draft.
Question 37: c) 13th December 1946
Explanation: - The Objectives Resolution was moved by Jawaharlal Nehru in the Constituent Assembly on 13th December 1946, laying the foundational philosophy of the Constitution.

Question 38: c) Articles 25-28
Explanation: - These articles ensure the Right to Freedom of Religion, allowing individuals to profess, practice, and propagate any religion.

Question 39: b) Political representation
Explanation: - Universal Adult Franchise was adopted to ensure that every adult citizen, regardless of caste, gender, or class, had the right to vote and be represented.

Question 40: a) Mahatma Gandhi
Explanation: - Mahatma Gandhi was not a member of the Constituent Assembly, although his ideas greatly influenced its members.

Question 41: b) UK
Explanation: - The concept of Single Citizenship was adopted from the British Constitution, ensuring that all Indians are citizens of India only, not of individual states.

Question 42: a) Ireland
Explanation: - The Directive Principles of State Policy were borrowed from the Irish Constitution, aiming to create a welfare state by guiding government policy.

LAST-DAY PREPARATION GUIDE & REVISION STRATEGIES

Your entire preparation comes down to this, the last day, the final shot. This is the moment where your months of dedication, late-night studies, early-morning revisions, and endless mock tests all come together. This is the day you cement your victory.

"Medals are won in training: tournaments are where you pick them up."

You have already built the foundation. You have grinded through every chapter, revised keynotes, solved 1200+ questions, and conquered 10 full-length mock tests. But now? Now is the final test before the real battle.

This is the last lap. The final charge. Your focus today will determine your score tomorrow.

So let's attack this last day like a warrior preparing for war. No hesitation, no self-doubt, just pure execution.

STEP 1: START WITH THE CONCISE KEYNOTES - THE FASTEST WAY TO RECALL IT ALL

Forget deep reading. Forget over-analysis. This is about speed and sharpness.

- Begin your day by flipping through the Concise Keynotes. This is your instant-access revision material, every major event, every crucial date, every must-know fact is there.

- Focus on visual memory: Read, visualize, and lock it in. If you can't picture it, you haven't memorized it yet.

- Key trick: Try to recall each topic before looking at the explanation. Active recall is 10X more powerful than passive reading.

- If you have handwritten notes, mnemonics, or mind maps, go through them now. Your brain retains what your hands have written.

STEP 2: THE FINAL TEST BEFORE THE REAL TEST - SIMULATE THE EXAM

- This is the single most important part of your last-day preparation.
- Take one full-length mock test in the morning (9 AM - 11 AM). Treat it like the real exam. No distractions. No second attempts.
- Time yourself strictly. If you can't do it in the given time today, you won't be able to do it tomorrow.

STEP 3: SECOND MOCK TEST - CONFIRM YOUR READINESS

- Take another full-length mock test in the evening (6 PM - 8 PM).
- Follow the same strict timing, disciplined approach, and error analysis as in the morning test.
- By now, you should see a clear trend in your strengths and weak areas.
- Scan through your underlined textbook pages this will give you a mental boost, knowing that you have revised everything comprehensively.

STEP 4: LOCK YOUR PERFORMANCE - KNOW WHERE YOU STAND

- Take your past 10 realistic mock test scores.
- Calculate the average score.
- LOCK IT.
- This average score is your most accurate predictor for tomorrow. If you have been consistently scoring above 185+, then you're already set to conquer the exam.

Now, NO MORE NEW TOPICS.
- Forget FOMO. If you haven't read it yet, don't touch it now.
- Remember, you can leave 10 questions unanswered. It's not about attempting everything,it's about maximizing correct answers.
- The only way to improve now? Go deeper into what you already know. Strengthen, don't stretch.

STEP 5: FINAL HOUR REVISION - EXECUTE WITH PRECISION

Your last few hours before the exam should be strategic, not chaotic.
No blind reading. No panic-scrolling through the book. No "one more topic" syndrome.

First 30 minutes:
- Quick scan of time capsules. Read like a checklist. Mark the ones that don't instantly click, and revise those again.

Next 20 minutes:
- Review your morning & evening mock test mistakes. Correct them. Absorb them. Never repeat them.

Last 10 minutes:
- Close the book. Mentally recall everything you just revised. If something feels unclear, open the book ONLY for that one thing.

DO NOT start a new topic. If you don't know it by now, learning it last-minute will only confuse you.
DO NOT panic. If you've followed your plan, you are already ahead of most aspirants.

STEP 6: EXAM HALL STRATEGY - THE SMART PLAY TO MAXIMIZE SCORE

- First pass: Answer all the EASY ones without overthinking. This builds confidence and saves time.
- Second pass: Tackle the moderate questions. Use elimination, logical reasoning, and past question patterns.
- Third pass: Attempt the tricky ones ONLY IF you are at least 50-60% sure.
- 40/45 Rule:
    - Aim for 40 sure-shot corrects and 5 calculated risks.
    - You are not here to attempt everything. You are here to score the MAXIMUM MARKS POSSIBLE.

Dear Aspirants,
If you are reading this, you are not just another candidate but you are someone determined to make history, quite literally. And so, I have written down what I call the "Secret Path to 200/200", not just a dream, but a strategy carved from experience, insight, and relentless execution.

Here is the essentials:
- Concise Time Capsules = Non-Negotiable
- PYQs = The Blueprint of CUET-UG History
- Mock Tests (Morning + Evening) = Your Real Performance Check
- Average Score = Your Locked Prediction
- 40/45 Rule = The Smartest Way to Play

And one more thing : Tomorrow is not the day to doubt. Tomorrow is the day to execute. Tomorrow is the day to own the paper.

Go in like a warrior. Stay sharp like a scholar. Walk out knowing you made history 200/200 isn't a fantasy. It's a plan. Now, go make it yours.

Yours sincerely,
Anuradha

WHY THIS BOOK IS THE COMPASS FOR YOUR HISTORY SUCCESS?

- ANCIENT
- MEDIEVAL
- MODERN

FEELING TRAPPED IN TIMELINES?

The only compass you need for your success!

- Simplify dense topics into easily understandable and memorable nuggets.
- Revise Like a Scholar with Curated summaries for focused, efficient learning.
- Conquer the Exam Narrative and Tackle diverse question types and scenarios with ease.
- Boost Confidence, Build Mastery with Mock tests and explanations prepare you to face any challenge.
- Analyze & Strategize with Leverage PYQs to identify trends and focus on high-priority areas.
- Ace Board Examinations & CUET-UG with one smart resource aligned to patterns, MCQs, and critical thinking.